STOLEN LIVES

Published by Dene House Publishing
Dene House, Walton, Warwick, CV35 9HX
www.meetatdawnunarmed.co.uk

Designed by Ruth Smith, Damson Creative Ltd.
www.damsoncreative.co.uk

Printed and bound in Slovenia on behalf of Latitude Press Ltd.
www.latitudepress.co.uk

ISBN 978-0-9561820-2-9

Opposite page: A soldier tending a comrade's grave near Ypres on 1 October 1917, possibly of Sapper L.J. Knowles of the Royal Engineers who died on 7 June 1917 and was buried at Chester Farm Cemetery   IWM Q006037

STOLEN LIVES

Individual Tragedies of the Great War

by
Andrew Hamilton
and
Alan Reed

Additional photography by **James Kerr**
Maps and two biographies by **George Sayell**

CONTENTS

Opposite page: Tyne Cot Cemetery   *J Kerr*

THE SOMME: DAY 5 ITINERARY: OPTIONAL

V   ABBREVIATIONS and GLOSSARY

VI ACKNOWLEDGEMENTS and BIBLIOGRAPHY

VII INDEX

THE AUTHORS

The authors at the 'Aristocrats' Plot' in Zillebeke Churchyard, Belgium   *J Kerr*

Andrew Hamilton (on right): retired in 1989 from teaching History at schools in Hereford and Worcester. He was responsible for the restoration of a watermill to full working order in Warwickshire and managed it as a popular tourist attraction. Since 2008 he has been writing and lecturing on the Great War and started Dene House Publishing in 2009 with the publication of the well-received ***Meet at Dawn, Unarmed***, a commentary on his grandfather Robert Hamilton's diary of his experiences with the Royal Warwicks in 1914 and his part in the Christmas Truce at St. Yvon in Belgium.

Alan Reed (on left): retired from full-time teaching in Cheshire in 1996 to concentrate on guiding school and adult groups on the Western Front. He gives numerous talks on various aspects of the Great War. His interest was inspired by his father who worked for the Commonwealth War Graves Commission in northern France. A fluent French speaker, his vast knowledge of the battlefield sites of France and Belgium has been invaluable in the research and planning for ***Meet at Dawn, Unarmed*** and ***Stolen Lives***.

Reactions to ***Meet at Dawn, Unarmed***:

Professor Richard Holmes: 'Very many thanks for sending me a copy of your book. It is quite magnificent, all the more so because of the many illustrations synthesised into the text. It is more than usually interesting for a variety of reasons, amongst them the occasional appearances of both B.L. Montgomery and Bruce Bairnsfather, and, of course for another view of the Christmas Truce. .. It is a really stupendous effort.'

Major Tonie and Valmai Holt: 'An exceptional book that adds so much to our knowledge of the early days of WW1.'

Chris Baker in *The Long, Long Trail* website: 'It is the treatment of the Christmas Truce that makes this book stand out.'

Dominiek Dendooven, In Flanders Fields Museum, Ypres: 'It's very different to the other Christmas Truce books... it's a must for the museum shop.'

Mark Warby, Editor of *The Old Bill Newsletter* about Bruce Bairnsfather: 'I think the book is excellent and I'm very pleased to have been involved in a small way.'

I

STOLEN LIVES - INTRODUCTION
'The Great War that darkens the whole world'

A mother who lost a son, killed on the Somme in December 1915, wrote that the Great War 'darkens the whole world.' For the four years between 1914 and 1918, the grim spectre of death haunted families throughout not only Britain but her Empire and the other combatant countries. The initial euphoria and war fever of August 1914 soon gave way to a belief that the War would not, as had been widely expected, be 'over by Christmas.' Few predicted, however, the sheer scale of the senseless human tragedy that would unfold until, after millions of lives had been lost or blighted by wounds, the Armistice was signed on 11 November 1918, thus bringing an end to 'The World's Illness', as it was described by an American actress who lost her British 'leading man' in 1916.

Sons (and some daughters) from every stratum of society were destined never to return home. They were buried or commemorated near the scene of their deaths in Belgium and northern France. Annie Souls raised six sons in a four-roomed cottage in Gloucestershire and lost the five who were old enough to volunteer for their King and Country. At the other end of the social spectrum Royalty was touched by the War: one of the early casualties in November 1914 was Queen Victoria's fortieth grandchild Prince Maurice of Battenberg. The Prime Minister H.H. Asquith suffered the loss of Raymond his academically brilliant son and prospective Liberal M.P. The popular writer and supporter of Empire, the author of the *Just So* stories, Rudyard Kipling, scarcely recovered from the guilt of pressurising his son John into joining up despite having been rejected by the recruiting authorities for his extreme myopia.

The majority of those buried or commemorated were ordinary working men from families that provided the economic backbone of their rural or industrial communities. The Sayell family committed 21 men to the Western Front, seven of whom fell- a farm manager, two farm labourers, a saw miller, railway porter, invoice clerk and a decorator. The five Souls brothers worked on local farms, and in towns and cities across Britain and her Empire, groups of all kinds bonded together and enlisted en masse. 'The Mobbs Own' was a 'battalion' 400 strong raised by the former rugby international Edgar Mobbs who volunteered in August 1914 but much to his annoyance, was turned down for being too old at the age of 32. Pals battalions were formed nationwide consisting of men from all walks of life; on the fateful first day of the Battle of the Somme at Serre on 1st July 1916, the Sheffield Pals lost 18 officers and 495 other ranks. Many of those to fall were cut down in the prime of their lives with much still to offer, like the miner and poet Will Streets and the Eisteddfod winner Ellis Evans. The Warwickshire cricketer, Percy Jeeves, was on the verge of selection for the England cricket team but would be denied the opportunity to walk through the pavilion gate at Lord's to represent his country.

The lives of pre-War 'celebrities' whose enlistment was so crucial for encouraging recruitment, were extinguished by undiscerning shells and bullets. Crowds at Kent's County Cricket ground in Canterbury would never again savour the wizardry of spin bowler Colin Blythe. Ronnie Poulton Palmer's jinking, body-swerving runs at Twickenham would merely be memories to treasure for rugby enthusiasts; four times winner of Wimbledon, the athletic and blond New Zealander, Tony Wilding, would be robbed of the chance to tilt for his fifth Men's Singles title. The boards of London's West End theatres would no longer be trodden by the king of revue and star of the moment, Basil Hallam, famous for his stage character 'Gilbert the Filbert'. The music-making of George Butterworth, Cecil Coles and F.S. Kelly would be silenced for ever.

Subjects of this book from the rank of major to private, from aristocrat to farm labourer, shared many of the same experiences: the initial flag-waving patriotic fervour and excitement, the pressures to join up, the numbing tedium of weeks and months of training followed by the horrors and discomforts of trench warfare, the wanton destruction, deaths of friends and comrades, homesickness, the assault on nerves of the thunderous noise of the new industrial weaponry, the calming effect of nature and the humour of those aware that their witty story or joke could be their last.

They all suffered horrific deaths on the Western Front. Their parents and loved ones were left to find ways of coping with their loss. Professor of Physics, Sir Oliver Lodge, sought solace in spiritualism as a way to communicate with his son Raymond; Marie Leighton wrote *Boy of My Heart* in 1916, a few months after her son Roland's death, as a commemoration of his life. Roland Leighton's fiancée, Vera Brittain, would dedicate to him much of her powerful condemnation of the Great War in *Testament of Youth* written in 1933. Rudyard Kipling embarked on a desperate quest to find the body of his 'Boy Jack' and after the War devoted himself to the inspirational work of the Imperial War Graves Commission.

We chronicle the lives and deaths of a cross-section of those who fell, including one woman, a staff nurse from Wakefield. Most were British but the stories are also told of two Australians, an Indian Sikh, a New Zealander, a West Indian, an Irish M.P., an American Francophile poet, French and German air aces and a Canadian who, it was alleged, was 'crucified' by the Germans. There are sportsmen, musicians, poets and the sons of the famous, but well represented are those from less privileged and protected backgrounds. Cavalrymen and pilots feature but most were infantrymen.

It is important not to underestimate the importance of the role played by Britain's Empire in the Great War. Over 1,000,000 Indians fought on all fronts, 160,000 of them on the Western Front. Their contribution was recognised by *The Times*: 'The Indian Empire has overwhelmed the British nation by the completeness and unanimity of its enthusiastic aid.' Australia sent 322,000 troops on overseas service, Canada 420,000, New Zealand 100,000, South Africa 150,000 plus 85,000 from the black population and the British West Indies 15,000. Many of the thousands who had enlisted with wholehearted devotion had been born in Britain or were first generation: ties with the 'mother country' were still strong. In the region of 650,000 were killed or wounded. There can be little doubt that without the support of her Empire, Britain would have struggled to play a decisive part in the conflict.

There is a range of ages, from the 16 year old British under-age volunteers, Horace Iles and Albert French and a 14 year old German Paul Mauk, to the oldest- the Surrey stockbroker 'Harry' Webber who insisted on 'doing his bit' but was killed at the tender age of 67. Some were professional or regular soldiers who had seen service in the Boer War and were the mainstay of the British Expeditionary Force in the desperate first few weeks of the campaign in August and September 1914. Territorials provided replacements from October 1914 but the majority of our subjects volunteered before conscription was introduced in March 1916, a necessity due to the massive losses of men.

The main reason for joining up in the heady summer atmosphere of 1914 was a desire to defend King and Country but men did not necessarily enlist because of any great sense of duty. There were other factors- the young poet Ellis Evans, chose to volunteer in the place of his brother Bob, whom he felt was too young to fight. Many privates like the Belfast shipyard apprentice James Crozier, were not imbued with lofty ideals; the onset of war offered prospects of adventure and excitement and of course there was a financial inducement: 'The King's Shilling'. The poet and painter, Isaac Rosenberg, signed up due to a shortage of money. As an Irish Nationalist M.P., Willie Redmond passionately believed that his participation at the Front would encourage Catholics and Protestants to unite and work together for an Ireland with devolved powers or 'Home Rule'. The novelist Hector H. Munro ('Saki') spent many years in Russia and France as a news correspondent and believed in the strategy of maintaining a 'balance of power' in Europe; hence his decision to enlist and play his part in curbing German aggrandisement.

The concept of 'duty' was a key concept for the officer class gazetted to commissions after war broke out. 'Duty' was an ideal that required sacrifice, to honour the 1839 promise to defend Belgium against aggressors and to save 'England's green and pleasant land'. Roland Leighton was due to take up a place at university in the autumn of 1914 and felt that to do so 'would seem a somewhat cowardly shirking of my obvious duty. I feel that I am meant to take an active part in the war.' The professional footballer and teacher Donald Bell who would be awarded a V.C. in 1916, asked the Directors of Bradford City to release him from his contract as 'I am duty bound to join the ranks.' However much soldiers hated the War, it was their 'duty' to see it through and Violet Asquith wrote of her brother Arthur ('Oc') that 'he never, even when he joined up, "romanticised" the war… he just considered the whole thing a "beastly duty."' The patriotism of all men over the age of 18 at the outbreak of hostilities was severely put to the test; they were subjected to relentless pressure to enlist. When the socialite daughter of the Duke of Rutland, Diana Manners, complained to John Simon, the Liberal Attorney-General and future Home Secretary in Asquith's 1915 Coalition Government about how 'awful' it was that Raymond Asquith was going to the Front, she was firmly rebuked: 'No, I think it is quite right. The time has come now when one can only feel sorry for those who are unable to go.'

The contribution of women during the Great War cannot be underestimated. Smashed windows in Downing Street and a fatality at the Epsom Derby in 1913, had violently brought the issue of women's suffrage to the fore and was an example of the social unrest faced by H.H. Asquith's Liberal government on the eve of war. The Suffragette movement's militant campaign, however, was put on hold in 1914. Women mostly from middle and upper-class families were keen to 'do their bit' as nurses and drivers at the Front, exposing themselves to great danger. Vera Brittain, daughter of a paper mill owner and Nellie Spindler, whose father was a police inspector in Wakefield, worked tirelessly in France and Belgium. Willie Redmond M.P. respected their contribution: 'Who can estimate how much has been done by the women who have crossed the seas and come to nurse the soldiers?... Hats off to the brave nurses in the War and God bless them.' Two motorcycle enthusiasts, Elsie Knocker (Baroness de T'Serclaes) and Mairi Chisholm, set up their own dressing station close

to the Belgian trenches and, against official British regulations, went to the front line to rescue the wounded. The Duchess of Sutherland joined the ranks of V.A.D. nurses and two American actresses who lost loved ones at the Front, threw themselves into the war effort- Maxine Elliott dispensed aid to Belgian refugees and wounded soldiers from a specially converted barge and Elsie Janis entertained Tommies stationed near the front line. The death of Nellie Spindler in August 1917 was no less significant than Emily Wilding Davison's when hit by the King's horse Anmer at the Derby, in hastening the introduction of 'Votes for Women' after the War.

Volunteers were desperate to get to the Front. Months of training drove many to distraction. Notice how young the boys are on the left in this training session at Branksome near Bournemouth IWM Q053581

A common complaint expressed by many featured in this book was the nature of the training they had to undergo before they were sent to the Front- particularly the endless route marches and drills. The musician George Butterworth of the 13/ Durham Light Infantry railed against the 'irritating, futile, endless parades' and Raymond Asquith protested to his wife Katharine that 'my prospects of really serious and strangling boredom have never been higher.'

While Lord Kitchener's vast new Army of volunteers was undergoing its training, the regulars in the British Expeditionary Force were desperately holding back the German offensive. At first it was a 'war of movement' but the warfare soon became static and attritional, with both sides by late autumn 1914 digging themselves into defensive trenches sometimes as little as 70 yards apart. For four or five days at a time, the front line trenches were the uncomfortable and dangerous home for officers and men. In the words of Willie Redmond the trench in winter was 'dark, damp, forbidding and gloomy.'

The grim reality of the warfare and the increasing numbers of deaths at the Front had been common knowledge from early in the conflict. By 1915 no one was in any doubt that the War would be fought to the bitter end. The Rev. Charles Doudney, chaplain for the 18th Brigade of the 6th Division, left the readers of the parish magazine for St. Luke's Church in South Lyncombe near Bath well aware of the horrors being experienced on the front line. It was all a far cry from the tranquillity of life in rural Somerset: 'It is just simply hell on earth...'

'Hell' was a word often and justifiably used to describe conditions- Captain Robert Hamilton of the 1/ Royal Warwicks recorded in his diary that the fighting on 19 September 1914 was 'the hell. I look 50 and I feel 70.' Private William Tapp of the same regiment, referring to the fighting in November 1914, noted that 'once or twice I had a glimpse of hell'. The 7/ Northants were subjected to a fearful barrage in February 1916 in the trenches at Railway Wood near Ypres. Major Edgar Mobbs described

it as 'a very hot time, we have lost 30 men in the last two days, "hell" could not be worse than what we have been through the last 24 hours, they have shelled us nearly all the time.' Brigadier General Frank Crozier described six months of front line life in winter as 'Rain, rain, rain! Rain and rum and mud and slush and shells. Four days "in" and four days "out"… Hell.'

The reality of front line warfare on the Ypres Salient   Sanctuary Wood (Hill 62) Museum

Life in the trenches was appalling enough without the added discomforts of lice and trench foot. The ear-splitting noise of gunfire and bombardments preyed on the nerves. Lieutenant George Butterworth observed: 'It is extraordinary how soon one gets accustomed to all this rattle.' Captain Geoffrey Donaldson informed his mother that he was 'rapidly becoming accustomed to the noises' and unlike others, he considered he was coping well with the constant assaults on his nerves. Others, however, were not so fortunate. Captain Charles Bentley of the 1/ Royal Warwicks was one of the first officers of the B.E.F. to suffer from shell shock or what would nowadays be described as severe combat stress. To alleviate his nervous tension and depression, he found consolation in alcohol, too much so for fellow officers Captain Hamilton and

the future Field Marshal of World War II, Bernard Law Montgomery who was a lieutenant at this early stage of the War.

Trenches were attractive locations for rats. George Butterworth claimed that 'there are enough rats in trench breastwork to eat up the whole British army' and Raymond Asquith conceded that 'this is no place for those who mind rats, as the little rascals are very numerous, well-nourished and daring. They gnaw the corpses- then gallop over one's face when one lies down.'

Death: it is not surprising many survivors were reluctant to share their experiences after the War- entrance to a German dugout near Zonnebeke north east of Ypres on 23 September 1917   IWM Q003116

Mud was the scourge of all at the Front. Roland Leighton summed up the situation in a letter to his fiancée Vera Brittain on 9 December 1915: 'The whole of one's world, at least one's visible and palpable world, is mud in various stages of solidity or sickliness… One consolation is that the German trenches seem to be, if anything, worse than ours… everyone is walking around in what the Ordnance Stores describe as "boots, gum, high". I am wearing some now, and came into the dug-out looking like a peripatetic ball of mud…' Captain Noel Chavasse, a surgeon with the R.A.M.C. and double V.C. did not mince his words: 'I am sick of seeing men sent to die in the mud.'

Chavasse was not in a minority of those horrified by the catalogue of deaths- death was an all-consuming, everyday fact of life at the Front. Friends and colleagues could be lost at any time. Bodies had to be located and recovered often in dangerous locations, paperwork dealt with, wooden crosses made and if possible a dignified burial performed. Nowadays, the calm and beauty of many cemeteries obscure the appalling reality of what happened to those who died. How often does one hear that a grandfather or great uncle 'could not talk about his experiences'?

To modern eyes, some deaths were unspeakably callous. Privates James Crozier and the West Indian Herbert Morris were Shot at Dawn for alleged cowardice- in all probability they had been suffering from shell shock. In general a hard line was taken: at least some officers before 1916 were aware of the need to treat soldiers whose nerve had gone with sensitivity as did Geoffrey Donaldson who understood the effects of battle fatigue on the men under his command. Rather than take punitive action, he sent men suffering from shell shock behind the lines to take on lighter duties. In his opinion there were no exceptions for officers like Captain Bentley: 'An officer is a different thing, because on him depend the nerves of the men.'

An important role for chaplains was keeping track of wounded soldiers, here during the Battle of the Somme 1916 IWM Q004056

It was not only soldiers who lost their nerve. The horrors and brutality of the War deeply affected the auxiliary 'army' of chaplains, medical officers and nurses, all of whom had vital roles to play but were faced with a 'hell' that they had never encountered before. It must have been unimaginably tough for chaplains of all denominations like one described by Donaldson who returned home, his nerves in tatters, finding 'the work in the rear, waiting for news, burying and so on, too much for his nerves. He couldn't stand it.' And who could blame him? The horrors he witnessed must have troubled his Christian principles. It was a completely different world that 'padres' had stepped into. Raymond Asquith told of 'a parson… a Cambridge don, who wanted to hold a service today in our battalion mess room, but the walls have been so thickly papered with French pictures of naked women that he had to confess the site was inappropriate for any holy purpose'!

Noel Chavasse was acerbically critical of Anglican chaplains in his diaries. The son of the Anglican Bishop of Liverpool, he was complimentary about the conduct of a Roman Catholic Mass and the Holy Communion which was 'very simple, yet very impressive… It seemed to me a perfect picture of prayer before battle, and I knew that every man was commending his soul to God.' Contrast that positive view with his send off to the Liverpool Scottish Battalion's Anglican chaplain whom he referred to as 'our fat useless old lump…'! He was equally critical of doctors but many of those he grumbled about were neither as resilient nor as determined as himself. He was after all, the only double V.C. winner of the Great War.

As was his wont, the Roman Catholic Willie Redmond was more upbeat. Padres of all denominations, he opined, were the 'prop and comfort' of the Army at the Front. It is doubtful that their paths crossed but the Rev. Charles Doudney would have been in the category so admired by Chavasse, of the chaplain who rolled up his sleeves and was at hand in or near the trenches to minister to the suffering and dying: 'Who can measure the consolation they bring' he asked 'or who can describe the comfort and happiness of the soldier whose eyes before they close for ever, rest upon the face of the priest of his own faith?'

It is difficult to assess the extent to which Christianity suffered at the hands of such carnage and inhumanity. For some, their beliefs still held firm. Donald Bell V.C. implored his wife not to worry

A cross being made for a burial   IWM Q004023

about him as 'I believe that God is watching over me and it rests with him whether I pull through or not.' He was killed at Contalmaison in the Somme on 10 July 1916. The Rev. Bloomfield Slight must have reflected the views of many clergymen at home in their parishes. He admitted in a letter of condolence to Edgar Mobbs's father Oliver that 'these events are so full of mystery. They are beyond all human comprehension.'

Amidst the horrors, an officer's first duty of care was to the well-being and safety of the men under his command and he was expected to act as a role model and to keep cool under pressure. The poet W.N. Hodgson had obviously earned the respect of his men and his batman in particular, Private Ogden, who was prepared to take a major risk on behalf of his officer. Captain Robert Hamilton had forged an excellent relationship with his batman, Private Sperry, who wrote a letter from Aberdeen hospital where he was being treated for his wounds to Hamilton's wife Renie, wishing her husband a 'Happy Christmas' in 1914, for 'if there was a man who deserved a welcome home, it is dear old Captain Hamilton. He is loved by every man in the regiment he tries to make every man happy like himself.'

An increasingly negative mood of those at the Front was in great part caused by the scenes of destruction that surrounded them. Noel Chavasse's description of Sanctuary Wood, just south of Hooge on the Ypres Salient, evokes the pervasively grim atmosphere: 'A smell of death hung on the damp air. Bullets snapped among the splintered and blasted trees, and every now and then a shell fell and bust somewhere... It is indeed the Valley of the Shadow of Death. Bunyan alone could describe its weird horror. It fairly grips the heart.'

The ruins of the Cloth Hall on the left and the Cathedral in Ypres 1919.   *Antony of Ypres*

Soldiers marching through towns and villages became inured to the devastation and the flattening of houses, shops, churches and town halls. Nowhere suffered more than the small Belgian city of Ypres, to such an extent that, when the Rev. Charles Doudney entered its shattered remains, the sight was one he would never forget: 'As far as one could see there was not a house that was intact. All the buildings were deserted and it was literally the city of the dead. The sun had set and there was a weird twilight in which things looked ghastly and unreal.' For 2nd Lieutenant Raymond Lodge of 2/ South Lancs who witnessed the city on fire, it was an 'unpleasant place to pass now.'

A sizeable proportion of the 750,000 men who had volunteered for Kitchener's Army by the end of September 1914, were not cut out to be soldiers in a bloody war- enthusiastic and dutiful but true soldiers they were not. Elsie Janis, the American actress, who co-starred in *The Passing Show* with Basil Hallam, was adamant that he was 'peace personified'. Roland Leighton considered it would be 'just part of the irony of life if I don't come back, because I am such a lover of peace.' However, some volunteers like George Butterworth enjoyed the challenges they faced and life on the front line.

Two composers, Cecil Coles and F.S. Kelly, had furthered their musical knowledge and skills in Germany. The composer Gustav Holst, who was a great admirer of Coles's talents, underlines how incongruous it was that Coles was fighting his former German hosts: 'He never joined in the ordinary hatred of Germany; he was utterly incapable of hatred under any provocation whatsoever.' The poet Ellis Evans, according to his local Methodist Minister, 'wasn't a soldier by nature'; Frederick Septimus Kelly, concert pianist, composer and Olympic gold medallist was, in Arthur 'Oc' Asquith's view, 'not and never would have made an enthusiastic soldier', as he spent most of his leisure hours composing music and reading.

However suitable or unsuitable as soldiers they may have been, they accepted that they could be just another name on the lengthening casualty lists and at any time. Much has been made of privates and N.C.O.s being the 'cannon fodder' of trench warfare but statistically, the chances of an officer being killed were much higher. The officers of the rank of major, captain, lieutenant and 2nd lieutenant were, after the whistle had been blown, the first to lead the charge 'over the top'- 37,500 British officers died on the Western Front. Edgar Mobbs refers on several occasions to the loss of officers- on 28 January 1916 he wrote that the 7/ Northants were 'getting short of officers again, having lost three in the last two days.' Confined to trench warfare and liable to have to lead their men into No Man's Land, most officers knew their chances of survival were limited and that their card could be marked at any time.

The mood of men in the trenches was understandably melancholic but in adversity, humour was a great release for men of all ranks. Noel Chavasse reported that he had just heard 'one poor digger remark that by now the whole of Belgium must have been put into sandbags.' There was much hilarity amongst officers of the Worcestershire Regiment, when in May 1915, the Prime Minister H.H. Asquith was visiting the Front. Roland Leighton and two other subalterns in mischievous mood, decided to have a bath at the same time and timed it so successfully that 'we all three welcomed Asquith dressed only in an identity disc!'

Captain Robert Hamilton recalled the humorous comment of one of the Tommies under his command in a diary entry for 11 December 1914: 'It rained all night and the whole of today. When I went round the sentries I found them quite resigned to another flood. They were amused. One Private Carter said, "It will lay the dust, sir, won't it?" at which I laughed heartily and so did they.'

Hamilton was a friend from pre-war Warwickshire days of Bruce Bairnsfather who joined the 1/ Royal Warwicks at Armentières on 20 November 1914 as a machine-gun officer. He proceeded to entertain men of all ranks with his cartoons or 'sketches' as he preferred to call them, based on conversations amongst officers behind the lines in *cafés* and *estaminets*. Tommies like Lance Corporal 'Pat' Rafferty of Handsworth in Birmingham presented him with material for his cartoon figures- 'Berts', 'Alfs' and his lasting creation, the much loved 'Old Bill, Leo Maritimus, full of plum and apple and determination.'

Bairnsfather had produced a portfolio of 'sketches' by New Year's Day 1915- enough to fill *Fragments from France,* the first of several volumes of cartoons published by *The Bystander* magazine. Bairnsfather returned to 'Blighty' after suffering from shell shock during the Second Battle of Ypres in late April 1915. At least he was alive and pleased that in his absence his sketches were being widely pored over at the Front; just three months after publication it was estimated that by March 1916, 200,000 copies of *Fragments* had been sold. Brigadier General Frank Crozier who was responsible for ordering the execution of the young 'deserter' James Crozier and who thought 'nothing of "throwing away" a thousand men in half an hour providing a position is gained or held' nonetheless maintained that 'humour pulls us through the war.' He was a devotee of Bairnsfather's work: 'In each British mouth is a big cigar held at an angle in his teeth, while in order to effect a balance, as it were on the heads- at an opposite angle, rest the tin hats. Bairnsfather at his best I say.'

FIRST DISCOVERED IN THE ALLUVIAL DEPOSITS OF SOUTHERN FLANDERS.
FEEDS ALMOST EXCLUSIVELY ON JAM AND WATER BISCUITS.
HOBBY: FILLING SANDBAGS, ON DARK AND RAINY NIGHTS

Bruce Bairnsfather's 'Old Bill'   *Barbara Bruce Bairnsfather*

Officers and men were great fans of Bairnsfather's work- the Establishment was not so enamoured, which may explain the lack of recognition accorded officially to the cartoonist in the hundred years since the War's end. If Bairnsfather had heard about George V falling off his horse and injuring his pelvis during one of his 'morale boosting' inspections of troops on 28 October 1915, he might well have been tempted to sketch a cartoon of the event! Bairnsfather was massively successful in his portrayal of life at the Front but by 1917, after the horrors of the Somme and those being endured at Passchendaele, his popularity began to wane. There was by now nothing remotely amusing about the War.

A few like Willie Redmond M.P. were more positive. He congratulated the authorities on the creation of the 'New Army', necessitated by the huge numbers of casualties and enabled by the introduction of conscription in 1916. Writing in February 1917 he lauded volunteers and conscripted men who formerly had been protected from cold and rough conditions who 'hold the line this bitter winter' and he considered it 'a marvellous and wonderful achievement when one realises it all and remember that the Army is a new army almost from top to bottom', a perception confirmed by the promotion in just 18 months of Frank Crozier from private to brigadier general. Unbelievable and contrary to army regulations was the promotion by 1918 of Walter Tull from private to 2nd lieutenant- remarkable in that he was one of the British Army's first black officers.

Men at the Front craved any crumb of comfort to alleviate their mental and physical suffering. It was understandable that they should turn their gaze homewards- British soldiers received millions of letters and eagerly awaited parcels full of cigarettes, cigars, warm socks and underwear to help them overcome hellish times in the trenches and homesickness. Ronnie Poulton Palmer emphasised in a letter to his mother written on 25 April 1915 that 'it is THE great thing to get the mail in the evening in the trenches.' Robert and Renie Hamilton, wrote over 200 letters to each other during Robert's five months at the Front between 24 August 1914 and 12 January 1915- a potential mine of information... such a shame, therefore, that their daughter unwittingly threw them out after their deaths.

Animals and pets provided a link with life at home. It is extraordinary how many photographs of dogs can be found in the Imperial War Museum's collection! A dog, cat and horse were above war and man's inhumanity; they could offer friendship and company. Noel Chavasse was befriended by a cat which lived on bully beef and milk and a year later by a 'jolly nice little fox terrier' he hoped would 'settle the rat question in the trenches.' Willie Redmond penned a delightful short story about Jack, a fox terrier that 'joined' the 6/ Royal Irish but was sadly lost, presumed dead in No Man's Land in the Somme. (see p.284)

One of the best ways for soldiers to escape their harsh existence was to enjoy and to commune with Nature which despite Man's best efforts to destroy it, managed to survive and offer comfort to the combatants. Roland Leighton wrote lyrically of the sun looking like 'a shield of burnished gold in a sea of turquoise; the bees are in the clover that overhangs the trench…' It was, he mused, 'a pity to kill people on a day like this.' Willie Redmond observed that, while human beings slaughtered each other day and night, 'Nature marches her course unruffled' - in summer, blood red poppies and blue cornflowers added a dash of colour to earth charred by warfare. He and his men were inspired by a skylark that sang 'a wonderful song', unperturbed by the deafening din of shell fire.

Man's best friend- particularly in times of adversity   IWM Q006477

For Noel Chavasse it was 'wonderful to see how quietly and how graciously Nature tries to hide the hideous scars made by men in the countryside.' There was a downside, of course. Thousands of horses were killed on or near the battlefields. Even a carp, lying on the surface of the lake at Château Elverdinghe had been killed, Roland Leighton speculated, by shell shock. Chavasse was unable to assess 'how very much the singing of birds affects me out here. It is quite uplifting, in the rather mournful surroundings, it gives a feeling of hope.' His description of a nightingale singing during hostilities does justice to how 'uplifting' it must have been: 'It was about 11 p.m. and in the copse a nightingale sang most sweetly; this was remarkable because bullets were splattering through the trees all the time and frequently shells burst quite near so that its song was drowned… But it did not mind and continued singing all the time. It sings every night and I love to hear it.' The melodies of skylarks can still be heard high above the battlefield sites and cemeteries of the Somme and there is still annual evidence of the once ubiquitous poppy.

There were sporadic outbreaks of humanity during the ceaseless carnage, the most famous of which was the Christmas Truce of 1914 when many temporary armistices and fraternisations took place along the 450 mile Western Front. The truce at St. Yvon in Belgium between the 1/ Royal Warwicks and the 134th Saxons is one of the most renowned, documented in detail by the authors in *Meet at Dawn, Unarmed.* Batman William Tapp's account of it is to be found on p.74. The authorities swiftly clamped down on such un-warlike activities- General Smith-Dorrien was hopping mad when news came

Photograph of the Christmas fraternisation at St. Yvon between the Royal Warwicks and 134th Saxons taken by 2nd Lieutenant Drummond of the Royal Field Artillery on Boxing Day 1914   IWM HU 35801

through of Christmas armistices and as early as Boxing Day, was seeking details of officers and units who had taken part 'with a view to disciplinary action.' Few took place thereafter, although Noel Chavasse described what was, in effect, a tacitly agreed cessation of hostilities at Christmas time in 1915: 'No one seemed to have the heart to try to kill or maim one another on that day, but as far as

The scale of the slaughter- Tyne Cot Cemetery is the largest British cemetery with nearly 12,000 graves, over 70% of which are of unidentified soldiers   J Kerr

I know, there was no fraternising.' They did not dare. He considered it a great tribute to the 'very firm though hidden hold which Christianity has on every heart that war had to cease on Christmas Day.'

Back home in 'Blighty' families dreaded receipt of the impersonal telegram or letter informing them of the loss of their loved one. Later they would suffer the humiliation of taking delivery of the deceased's belongings. Marie Leighton wrote in *Boy of My Heart* that 'a Mrs. Orme learnt on Christmas Day of the loss of her son. I went and heard the whole story and was shown the still more pitiful clothes with the bullet holes in them, and the identity disc and wrist watch and the cigarette case and the periscope and all the other things the War Office kindly sends back to homes of fallen officers.' Marie Leighton would suffer the same humiliating experience herself, described by Vera Brittain, Roland's fiancée, in a most powerful and depressing piece about the Leightons' unpacking of their son's damp and blood-stained uniform. All deaths in the Great War were a tragedy regardless of the dead soldier's standing, so Vera Brittain's reaction to news of Rudyard Kipling's loss of his young son 'Jack' is surprising: 'I always feel sorrier when they are sons of intellectual and brilliant people. I don't know why I should be but somehow I always feel that they must mean even more to their parents than those of the more ordinary ones do theirs…' Mrs. Annie Souls may not have been an intellectual but the tragedy of her losses was no different to those of Bishop Chavasse and Rudyard Kipling.

An understandable method of consoling grieving families was the composition of favourable obituaries that were, in a way, a 'surfeit of the truth'. Every effort was made to ease the pain of family loss often by overstating the bravery of the deceased or playing down the nature of the wounds. Captain Charles Bentley was praised for being at the head of 20 men who survived gunfire during an attack on German positions in October 1914. When he fell, it was reported that he was 'sniped in three places' but 'never seemed to think of his wounds and just went on cheering the men'. The truth of his death was rather different. He was hit by a shell while being arrested for drunkenness. Captain Basil Hallam Radford fell 3,000 feet from his observation balloon to a horrific death-virtually every bone in his body was broken but his girlfriend Elsie Janis was assured by a witness that 'his face was untouched and he was almost smiling.' Harbingers of dreadful news emphasised the lack of suffering before death and the peaceful smiles with which it was accepted …

In the ensuing pages of **Stolen Lives** we examine the lives of over 50 who were killed: their upbringing, education, occupations, reasons for joining the war effort, their performance at the Front, how they met their death and where they were buried or commemorated. Some were famous, some were not. They came from widely differing backgrounds. Their stories, their diaries, their letters leave us, one hundred years later, in awe of their spirit and humour in the face of the sheer hell they experienced.

The majority of those who volunteered led lives with no connection to military life. The War for non-regulars was a novel and extraordinary experience, by turns stimulating and frightening. But they were denied a future- their aspirations and hopes were buried in the mud on the Ypres Salient and in the Somme. It is unbelievable that the skills and talents of a generation should have been destroyed in a four year long act of such futility.

Stolen Lives is about the people involved at the sharp end of the Great War. It is not an analysis of tactics and strategy, nor of the rights or wrongs of decision-making by the politicians and generals. It is not an appraisal of Britain's contribution to the defeat of Germany, nor a glorification of it. It offers an insight into the lives of a selected few of the hundreds of thousands who died fighting, whether they liked it or not, for their King and Country. It provides a snap-shot of life and society in Britain before the onset of war. Strands from the shared experiences of each life from 1914 to 1918 weave a detailed picture of what the conflict was like for those fighting on the Western Front and how the War affected them and their families. Wherever possible we have incorporated their descriptions, feelings and views of life at the Front without changing their modes of expression and have quoted them verbatim.

We hope that readers may be prompted during the centenary years of the Great War to visit the battlefields of the Western Front. As there are over 1,000 cemeteries and memorials it is difficult to know which to visit- the suggested itineraries, based on the personalities in the book, should provide a focus for a trip. Rather than being overwhelmed and overawed by the anonymity of the endless rows of names inscribed on the great British Memorials or on the serried ranks of cemetery gravestones, the pen portraits, we hope, may help to bring to life a name inscribed on a grave in a cemetery or on a memorial panel.

In the words of Marie Leighton, the Great War did indeed 'darken the whole world' and one cannot disagree with Elsie Janis's description of it as 'The World's Illness'. It was an appalling self-inflicted human tragedy. The pages that follow highlight the futility of it all- the waste of talent, skill and potential and the shattering of high-minded and deeply held beliefs in duty and patriotism.

The cemeteries and memorials of France and Belgium are evocative tributes to those whose lives were so cruelly foreshortened. They are unquestionably well worth a visit.

One of the smaller cemeteries, Hyde Park Corner (Royal Berks), contains 87 graves including those of rugby international Ronald Poulton Palmer and 16 year old Albert French   *J Kerr*   **11**

II

CEMETERIES AND MEMORIALS

'This massed multitude of silent witnesses to the desolation of war'

The graves and commemorations of those we cover in this book take us on a journey to most of the great British Memorials and to a selection of the thousand or so cemeteries of differing sizes and locations scattered throughout the towns, villages and remote rural spots of Belgium and northern France.

To have buried and commemorated in excess of one million soldiers with such methodical efficiency and sensitivity was a tribute to the prime movers of the Imperial War Graves Commission which was later renamed the Commonwealth War Graves Commission in 1960.

Rare example of original I.W.G.C. signs on the Lille Gate, Ypres   *A Reed*

The driving force behind the Commission's formation in 1917 by Royal Charter and its organisation until a year before his death in 1949, was Sir Fabian Ware. He was a visionary with a social conscience whose tenacity in the face of many hurdles and political skills ensured a dignified final resting place or commemoration for the British and Imperial soldiers who died fighting for their King and Country.

Sir Frederic Kenyon, Director of the British Museum, was appointed as the Commission's first architectural adviser. He oversaw the designs of the four principal architects, Edwin Lutyens, Reginald Blomfield, Herbert Baker (all three were knighted for their work) and Charles Holden. Much of their work was carried out by assistants like the younger Harold Chalton Bradshaw who experienced the horrors of the War, serving as a captain in the Royal Engineers in France and Belgium where he was gassed and wounded, and finally Italy, where he was awarded the Italian Croce de Guerra.

The celebrated author and chronicler of the British Empire, Rudyard Kipling, offered his literary expertise to the Commission, inspired by the loss of his only son John who died at the Battle of Loos in 1915, aged only 18. He chose the memorable wording for cemeteries' Stones of Remembrance: THEIR NAME LIVETH FOR EVERMORE taken from the Old Testament's Book of Ecclesiastes Chapter 44, Verse 14; for graves of the unidentified: A SOLDIER OF THE GREAT WAR KNOWN UNTO GOD, and for the Thiepval Memorial: THE MISSING OF THE SOMME. Kipling's contribution was acknowledged by Ware who wrote that he

Stone of Remembrance at Tyne Cot Cemetery- design by Sir Edwin Lutyens, words by Rudyard Kipling   *A Hamilton*

offered his genius 'freely and wholeheartedly in the service of the commemoration of the dead.'

The philosophy of the Imperial War Graves Commission was underpinned by a number of principles which have been zealously adhered to ever since. Equality of treatment, regardless of rank, was the overriding aim of the Commission: 'In death, all from General to Private of whatever race or creed, should receive equal honour.' Hence Brigadier General James Foster Riddell, killed by a sniper during the Second Battle of Ypres at St. Julien, was buried in Tyne Cot Cemetery amongst 'other ranks'.   **13**

One of 185,254 graves of unidentified soldiers of the British Army　　*A Hamilton*

Linked to the belief in equality of treatment was the view that bodies should not be repatriated- if families of a higher social standing, wealthy enough to fund the process, had insisted on bringing the bodies of their loved ones home, the cemeteries on the Western Front would have been an odd preserve of 'other ranks' and N.C.O.s. The repatriation of a lieutenant of the highest social rank, His Highness Prince Maurice of Battenberg, was proposed by Lord Kitchener in 1914, but there was little opposition to his mother's strongly held belief that, as an officer, he should be laid to rest alongside the men of his company in 1/ King's Royal Rifle Corps with whom he had fought.

Brigadier General James Foster Riddell's grave at Tyne Cot Cemetery is amongst those of 'other ranks'　*A Hamilton*

By an Act of Parliament, passed in 1920, the principle of 'No Repatriation' was confirmed in law, before which about only 60 bodies had been repatriated.

In some British cemeteries visitors will see a tablet in stone which states that 'this land is the free gift of the French Nation'. In 1915 a law was passed by the French Assembly which offered a 'perpetual resting place of those who are laid there,' a stance also taken by the Belgian Government. In contrast the Germans who had been unwelcome invaders of the two countries were not gifted the land for their cemeteries.

Private Albert Ingham's grave at Bailleulmont Cemetery in the Somme
A Hamilton

British cemeteries were standardised by the I.W.G.C. Wooden crosses had originally marked where bodies had been buried and, to provide longer-lasting markers, it was agreed to adopt Sir Edwin Lutyens's design of headstones that were to be of a uniform height, 2 feet and 8 inches (81 cm) and shaped with a curved top and straight sides. White Portland stone from near Weymouth in Dorset was used in preference to red Corsehill or Lochariggs stone which, as can be seen in the photograph of graves (see p.270) in the experimental cemetery of Martinsart in the Somme, was somewhat unappealing in comparison, especially after a shower of rain.

Inscriptions by MacDonald Gill were designed in a Roman style; a serviceman's regimental badge would be engraved at the top of the stone, under which there could be an appropriate religious symbol.

Families were allowed to choose an inscription and for the most part, the Commission acceded to families' wishes. As it was not a military institution, the Commission allowed itself some leeway in allowing wording that would have been unacceptable to the Army. **PRIVATE ALBERT INGHAM** of the 18/ Manchester Regiment was Shot at Dawn on 1 December 1916, aged 24, for desertion, having been caught absconding with his friend, 21 year old **PRIVATE ALBERT LONGSHAW**, aboard a Swedish ship in Dieppe. Their claim to be Americans did not wash with the Intelligence Corps who, it can be assumed, were unconvinced by their American accents. Initial reports were that Ingham had died of 'gunshot wounds', which was, of course, a severe economy of the truth. He was buried in

Bailleulmont Communal Cemetery in the Pas-de-Calais. When the true nature of his son's death came to light, George Ingham was furious at the deceit and insisted his son be properly remembered. His request was granted and Albert Ingham was accepted to have been:

SHOT AT DAWN
ONE OF THE FIRST TO ENLIST
A WORTHY SON
OF HIS FATHER

It was a surprisingly even-handed gesture to allow Mr. Ingham to make his point with such damning simplicity. The Bailleulmont Communal Cemetery contains only 34 graves and unusually includes graves of three soldiers Shot at Dawn- Ingham and Longshaw were both executed on 1 December 1916 and buried next to each other. 20 year old **PRIVATE WILLIAM HUNT** of the same battalion was also shot for desertion a fortnight earlier on 14 November. Another interesting inscription agreed by the Commission was that of 2nd **LIEUTENANT ARTHUR YOUNG** which can be found in Tyne Cot Cemetery:

SACRIFICED TO THE FALLACY
THAT WAR CAN END WAR

Inscriptions were designed by MacDonald Gill, here, on the Memorial at Loos 　　　　*A Hamilton*

Private monuments were discouraged. The bell 'Alexis' was installed in Zillebeke church by Baroness Henriette de Gunzburg in memory of her son Baron Alexis. As it was in the church, it was not under the jurisdiction of the Imperial War Graves Commission and his grand grave in the churchyard was one of a few exceptions to a principle that was applied from 1915 onwards.

It was established that wherever possible, a marked grave would be provided for every soldier whose body could not be identified. In total 580, 346 graves were identified and 185, 254 were not. In Tyne Cot Cemetery near Ypres, the largest Commonwealth war cemetery, there are 11,956 burials of which 8,369 are of unidentified soldiers- a staggering 70%.

One of Fabian Ware's greatest achievements was to reach an agreement over the standardisation of cemeteries. For those with more than 400 burials, a cemetery would incorporate Lutyens's non-religious Stone of Remembrance. Ware bowed to pressure from Anglican lobbyists who campaigned for the installation of a Cross of Sacrifice, the eye-catching design of Reginald Blomfield- a dark crusader-type sword set into a white stone cross.

The understated simplicity of the cemeteries' layout is a tribute to Ware's team and provided havens of peace and tranquillity. The aim was to create in the cemeteries, a little corner of England in 'foreign fields'. Great thought went into doing so in the image of an English garden, ablaze in summer with colour. Red roses, a myriad of flowers, manicured lawns, hedges and trees have, for nearly a century, been lovingly nurtured by Commonwealth War Graves Commission gardeners. Fabian Ware sought

Sir Reginald Blomfield's 'Cross of Sacrifice' 　　*J Kerr*

15

Cemeteries in the image of an English garden from top to bottom:
1. *Lijssenthoek*   J Kerr
2. *Couin New British* A Hamilton
3. *Le Trou Aid Post*   J Kerr

the advice of the garden designer Gertrude Jekyll whose expertise was harnessed for several of Lutyens's initial cemetery designs like Louvencourt in the Somme.

Early in the planning process it was proposed to build 12 memorials in France and Belgium. The French Government took umbrage at the prospect of such a large number of British memorials on their territory so plans were scaled down. The two great commemorations to those with no known grave are the Menin Gate in Ypres, designed by Reginald Blomfield, and Edwin Lutyens's Thiepval Memorial in the Somme. The other major memorials were

The 'sneering' lion at the Ploegsteert memorial sculpted by Gilbert Ledward   J Kerr

constructed in France at Arras (Lutyens), Cambrai (Bradshaw), La Ferté-sous-Jouarre (G. Goldsmith) and Neuve Chapelle (Herbert Baker, for Indians with no known grave). Tyne Cot (Baker) and Ploegsteert (Bradshaw) are located in Belgium. Memorials dedicated to missing Imperial troops are the National Canadian Memorial at Vimy (built and funded by the Canadian government and designed by Walter Seymour Allward), the Longueval Memorial for New Zealanders (Baker), the South African Memorial at Delville Wood (Baker) and Villers-Bretonneux for fallen Australians (Lutyens).

The site of the Menin Gate Memorial was chosen because hundreds of thousands of British and Imperial soldiers had marched through it on their way to and from the battlefields of the Ypres Salient. Works started in 1923 and its inauguration followed in 1927. Names of over 54,400 officers and men, including Edgar Mobbs, William Tapp and the Canadian Harry Band, were engraved on the panels of the Menin Gate, men who fell in the three Battles of Ypres- in the autumn of 1914, April 1915 and the infamous Battle of Passchendaele up to mid-August 1917.

The Menin Gate is a commanding edifice that dominates the cathedral city of Ypres which was razed to the ground during the War. Contemporary critics complained about its size- however, the need to accommodate so many names determined this. Siegfried Sassoon, the poet who survived the War, damned it as 'this sepulchre of crime' but arguably it does not appear triumphalist in tone; it is an impressive tribute to those who fought and lost their lives rather than a monument dedicated to a glorious victory. From the outset the locals took the Menin Gate to their hearts- since 1929, apart from during the 2nd World War, hardly a day has passed without a commemoration to the fallen, marked by the Last Post

The Menin Gate Memorial designed by Sir Reginald Blomfield   J Kerr

Ceremony which is held every evening at 8.00 p.m. and definitely worth attending.

Lutyens's Thiepval Memorial to 'The Missing of the Somme' is even more dominating than the Menin Gate, due mainly to the need to find space for nearly 18,000 more names. It stands on the German front line which proved so impenetrable during the first stages of the Somme offensive in 1916. The original intention was for a memorial to straddle the Albert to Bapaume road which was unacceptable to the French Government. Its eventual site at Thiepval overlooking some of the killing fields below in the Ancre Valley where, on 1st July 1916, 19,000 British and Newfoundland troops were killed and about 39,000 wounded, was agreed with the French Government and was a testament to Sir Fabian Ware's diplomatic skills. The structure was dedicated 'Aux Armées Française et Britannique l'Empire Britannique reconnaissant' (To the French and British Armies, from the grateful British Empire). Behind the memorial, a cemetery for French and British soldiers emphasises that the Somme offensive was a combined operation.

The Thiepval Memorial designed by Sir Edwin Lutyens
J Kerr

The Thiepval Memorial was completed in 1932 and inaugurated on 1 August by the Prince of Wales, the future Edward VIII. Like the Menin Gate, the Thiepval Memorial does not glorify victory over the Germans; it has a timeless quality that impressively rises above the senseless brutality of the battlefield on which it stands. From whichever direction one approaches it, the memorial makes a statement- its size alone, accommodating 73,000 names of men whose bodies could not be found, condemns those that failed to end the mind-blowing slaughter. The Thiepval Memorial is a shocking indictment of those who were unable to call a halt to it.

When one peruses the panels of the Menin Gate and Thiepval, it is impossible to comprehend the enormity of how men's lives and achievements were reduced to a mere inscription. Row upon row of gravestones in cemeteries are at least more tangible illustrations of the outrages that took place. In his capacity as Chairman of the Imperial War Graves Commission, George V visited the British war cemeteries in May 1922 and his reaction has struck a chord with passing generations: 'In the course of my pilgrimage, I have many times asked myself whether there can be more potent advocates of peace upon earth, through the years to come than this massed multitude of silent witnesses to the desolation of war.'

However appalling the effects of the Great War were, at least Sir Fabian Ware, Rudyard Kipling and the architects of the cemeteries and memorials, created remarkable tributes to those whose lives were sacrificed. George V expressed the hope that 'the existence of these visible memorials, will eventually serve to draw all peoples together in sanity and self-control.'

Sir Fabian Ware's C.W.G.C. grave at Amberley, Gloucestershire   *A Hamilton*

It was tragic that the sight of all the cemeteries and memorials in Belgium and northern France- British, Belgian, French and German, failed to prevent further human folly two decades later in 1939.

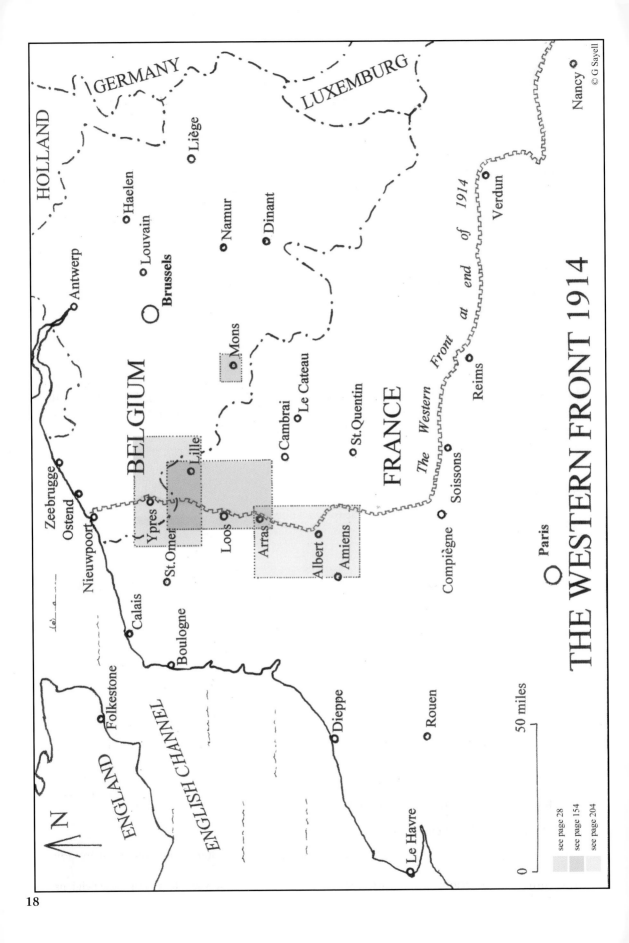

THE WESTERN FRONT 1914

© G Sayell

N

ENGLAND
ENGLISH CHANNEL
HOLLAND
GERMANY
LUXEMBURG
BELGIUM
FRANCE

The Western Front at end of 1914

Folkestone
Le Havre
Dieppe
Rouen
Boulogne
Calais
Nieuwpoort
Ostend
Zeebrugge
Antwerp
Haelen
Louvain
Brussels
Liège
Namur
Dinant
Mons
St.Omer
Ypres
Lille
Loos
Arras
Albert
Amiens
Cambrai
Le Cateau
St.Quentin
Soissons
Compiègne
Reims
Verdun
Nancy
Paris

see page 28
see page 154
see page 204

0   50 miles

III

THE BRITISH ARMY ON THE WESTERN FRONT
1914 to 1918 - an Overview

1914

By the summer of 1914 Europe was engulfed by a febrile atmosphere of antagonistic patriotism. France and Germany were looking for any excuse to go to war. It would not take much to light the touch paper and the spark that set Europe alight was the murder of Archduke Franz Ferdinand in Sarajevo on 28 June. It set off a chain reaction and within weeks Germany and Austria-Hungary were at war with France and Russia. The British Foreign Secretary Sir Edward Grey famously declared on 3 August, with chilling accuracy, that 'The lights are going out all over Europe'. There was little chance of Britain remaining on the side lines. On the following day the British Government issued Germany with an ultimatum: if the German Army invaded Belgium, Britain would be forced, by the terms of the 1839 Anglo-Belgian Treaty of London, to take up arms in her defence. When Kaiser Wilhelm II refused to rescind the order to invade Belgium and once the 11 p.m. deadline had passed, Britain declared war on Germany.

The confidently held mantra in Britain was that the War would be 'Over by Christmas'. It was not long before reality took hold- it increasingly became a question of 'which Christmas?' The generals of all sides were unable to conjure up a strategy or a weapon that would break the deadlock of what would prove to be a gruesome war of attrition. The first industrial war would produce an alarming death toll. The numbers of casualties detailed below defy belief and from a 21st century perspective are hard to understand and justify morally.

A British Expeditionary Force composed of professionals, many of whom had served in the Boer War at the turn of the century, landed in France on 16 August under the command of Sir John French. Compared to the German and French Armies, the B.E.F. was a small force only 70,000 strong, consisting of four infantry divisions and one cavalry division. It was disdainfully dismissed by the Kaiser as 'Sir John French's contemptible little army'.

Soldiers of the Royal Warwickshire Regiment about to embark for France in August 1914
David Vaux

The B.E.F.'s first action was to protect the left flank of the French Army and on 23 August it was for the first time confronted by the far superior First Army commanded by Alexander von Kluck on the outskirts of the Belgian mining town of Mons. The highly trained regulars inflicted heavy casualties on the Germans due, in the main, to their expert use of the .303 Lee Enfield rifle. However, the B.E.F. was overwhelmed and forced to retreat south into France. On 26 August General Horace Smith-Dorrien organised a successful holding operation at Le Cateau. The Germans' objective was Paris which was now in grave danger. The German Armies were only 25 miles away.

🦆 *John Parr was killed on 21 August*

The B.E.F. supported the French in checking the German advance south of the river Marne in early September. By the middle of the month, it counter-attacked and pushed back the enemy north of the river Aisne. Early in October the newly formed Royal Naval Division was sent to reinforce the Belgians in their defence of the port of Antwerp- the idea of the First Lord of the Admiralty Winston Churchill.

Although Antwerp fell, the time it took to capture it had caused another irritating delay for the Germans. By mid-October despite increasing losses, the B.E.F. was sent into northern France and Flanders to halt the Germans who were now aiming to capture the Channel ports in a phase known as the 'Race to the Sea'. The next encounters were the battles of La Bassée, Armentières and the First Battle of Ypres.

🌺 *Charles Bentley* . . . .*23 October*

🌺 *Prince Maurice of Battenberg* . .*27 October*

The situation had become desperate for the Allies. So confident were the Germans that, in early November, Kaiser Wilhelm arrived at the Front to witness and enjoy the capture of Ypres. However, the 'contemptible little army' held its lines in spite of suffering heavy losses. It was at this stage that the nature of the warfare changed dramatically. The armies were no longer on the move but began to 'dig in', facing each other in trenches with only a few hundred yards separating them. The static trench warfare of attrition had begun. The Germans occupied the high ground in a semi-circle round the city, establishing a 'bulge' in the front line known as the Ypres Salient which the British successfully defended at great cost in manpower for the rest of the War. The first five months had proved costly for the B.E.F. with casualties of 3,600 officers and 86,200 other ranks.

🌺 *Baron Alexis de Gunzburg* . . *6 November*

🌺 *Avenel St. George* . . . .*15 November*

Territorial units of trained volunteer reserves were sent to increase numbers and more than a remarkable 1,100,000 enlisted throughout the country as a result of Lord Kitchener's recruitment campaign. Training such huge numbers was to prove a massive military and bureaucratic undertaking. The casualty figures were mounting ominously. The French had sustained 341,000 casualties and the Germans 371,000. After five months of brutal warfare, the year ended with an extraordinary episode when over Christmas, along some sectors of the front line, soldiers laid down their arms and agreed a cessation of hostilities: the iconic Christmas Truce.

1915

As numbers of reinforcements increased, the British Army started to take over from the over-stretched French more of the front line to the south. The year was marked by a series of battles which defined the increasingly horrific and futile nature of the fighting: little territorial gain and mounting casualties. In mid-March four British divisions, including Indian troops, captured the French village of Neuve Chapelle but failure of communication and a shortage of shells helped the Germans to foil the attack. The British suffered 13,000 casualties, the Germans 12,000.

🌺 *Manta Singh* . . . .*10 March*

The Second Battle of Ypres began on 22 April and was notable for the Germans' use of chlorine gas north of Ypres against the French first and Canadian troops two days later. It continued until 25 May. The German attacks were successful enough to reduce the Ypres Salient to a third of its size. Allied casualties amounted to 70,000, the Germans' 38,000. Anti-German antagonism was fuelled on 7 May when a German submarine sunk the Cunard liner *Lusitania*; over 1,000 lives were lost including 128 U.S. citizens. The British launched their next attack two days later from Neuve Chapelle towards the Aubers Ridge. It was repulsed at a cost of 11,000 casualties for the British and 3,000 for the Germans. It was followed by a further attack at Festubert south of Neuve Chapelle, when there were over 16,000 British casualties for a gain of 1,300 yards.

🌺 *Harry Band* . . . .*24 April*   🌺 *Ronald Poulton Palmer*. . . . *5 May*

🌺 *Gilchrist Maclagan* . . . .*25 April*   🌺 *Anthony Wilding* . . . . *9 May*

🌺 *William Tapp* . . . .*25 April*

The major British action of the year focused on the French mining town of Loos. Six divisions were deployed on 25 September and though the first use of gas by the British was disrupted by a change of wind direction, initial success was nonetheless achieved with the capture of Loos but a lack of supplies and reserves allowed the Germans to counter-attack. The British renewed their offensive in October to no avail at a total cost of more than 50,000 men. Anti-German feelings were heightened when a British nurse, Edith Cavell, having been court-martialled by the Germans for helping British soldiers to escape, was executed in Brussels on 12 May. The year ended with Sir John French's replacement by Sir Douglas Haig. French was blamed for the lack of progress during the year and his poor performance at Loos. Soon after his appointment, Haig agreed with the Commander-in-Chief of the French Army, General Joseph Joffre, to launch a joint offensive the following summer.

British troops in Ypres in 1916   *Antony of Ypres*

Approximately 2,400,000 men had enlisted in the British Army by the year's end.

Raymond Lodge . . . .*14 September*   **Rev. Charles Doudney** . . . . . *16 October*

John Kipling . . . .*27 September*   **Roland Leighton** . . . . *23 December*

1916

The year began with the introduction of conscription on 27 January, a forced reaction to dwindling numbers of volunteers and mounting losses. The British and French were preparing for 'The Big Push' at a point where their front lines met in the Somme. Their planning was pre-empted in February when the Germans launched a massive attack against the French at the symbolic fortress city of Verdun in eastern France. General Erich von Falkenhayn aimed 'to bleed the French Army white'.

James Crozier . . . .*27 February*

The Battle of Verdun would prove to be the longest of any war in history and ended in stalemate by mid-December at a combined cost of 700,000 casualties. As a result the British had to assume a leading role in the Somme and, pressed by the French, launched the offensive earlier than planned. British High Command was confident that a one-week preliminary bombardment would destroy the German defences and morale. The assault would be a 'walk-over'. General Henry Rawlinson's Fourth Army, the majority of whom were Kitchener's volunteers, organised into Pals battalions, were sent 'over

Thiepval Memorial in the Somme   *J Kerr*

the top' at 7.30 a.m. on a beautiful summer's morning. The 1st July was a momentous day in the history of the British Army. Of the 58,000 casualties, 19,000 men were killed.

🌺 *William Noel Hodgson* . . . .*1st July*   🌺 *Horace Iles* . . . . *1st July*

🌺 *Charles Bertie Prowse* . . . . .*1st July*   🌺 *Will Streets.* . . . . *1st July*

The Germans had emerged from their deep and well-constructed dugouts and along most of their line had halted the British advance in No Man's Land. The Battle of the Somme continued relentlessly throughout the summer.

🌺 *Alan Seeger* . . . . *4 July*   🌺 *Percy Jeeves.* . . . . *22 July*

🌺 *Donald Bell V.C.* . . . .*10 July*   🌺 *George Butterworth* . . . . . *5 August*

🌺 *Geoffrey Donaldson* . . . . . .*19 July*   🌺 *Basil Hallam Radford* . . . *20 August*

🌺 *Harry Webber* . . . .*21 July*

Tanks were introduced for the first time in September- championed by Winston Churchill. The onset of winter and muddy conditions brought an end to the fighting in mid-November by which time there had been 420,000 British casualties for a maximum gain of a meagre eight miles. In addition the French suffered 200,000 casualties and the Germans approximately 500,000. Professor Richard Holmes calculated the grim statistic that there were three British lives lost for every 12 inches of ground gained. The War had truly become a 'numbers game' to such an extent that a German general confided in his diary that 'if we continue to lose men at this rate, we shall lose the war'. The British Army would never be the same again. The spirit of 1914 when men volunteered with innocent enthusiasm had been shattered, destroyed by the harsh reality of the remorseless nature of the conflict. The newly-conscripted troops had no illusions as to what awaited them. It was ironic that General Haig survived the failure to break through on the Somme but at home Prime Minister Herbert Asquith, head of the Coalition Government, was manoeuvred out of power by David Lloyd George.

🌺 *Jack the Pet Dog* . . . . *9 September*   🌺 *Frederick S. Kelly* . . . . . . *13 November*

🌺 *Raymond Asquith* . . . .*15 September*   🌺 *Hector Munro (Saki)* . . . . *14 November*

🌺 *James Richardson V.C.* . . . . *9 October*

The Spanbroekmolen Crater known as the 'Pool of Peace' was caused by one of the 19 Messines mines. The photo was taken in November 1998 when the water was covered with an appropriately red-coloured algae
A Reed

1917

In the course of the year the British Army at last claimed some victories but there would be another 'Somme', this time in Belgium. Gradual changes in fighting methods and tactics allowed the British Army and Imperial forces to achieve their first real success of the War when the Canadian Corps led by General Julian Byng captured Vimy Ridge over Easter at a cost of 11,000 casualties. This action was part of a general offensive known as the Battle of Arras which lasted until late May and involved more attritional fighting east of the French city with at most a gain of five miles.

Casualties amounted to 159,000 British and 100,000 Germans. The daily casualty rate during the Battle of Arras was the highest for the British Army in the entire war, averaging over 4,000 per day even more, therefore, than on the Somme. The aim had been to divert attention from the French offensive by General Robert Nivelle at the Chemin des Dames, north of the Aisne, a disaster with 271,000 French casualties in 10 days. Large sections of the French Army mutinied and, as a result, the British had to bear the burden of responsibility for major future offensives on the Western Front.

Haig and his generals planned a major attack in Flanders in two phases: the first to secure the Messines Ridge south of Ypres and the second to achieve a breakthrough by driving the Germans away from the Passchendaele Ridge. General Sir Herbert Plumer's Second Army successfully captured the Ridge on 7 June after 19 mines, a total weight of one million pounds of explosives, created gaps in the German line. Such was its force that, allegedly, it shook the drinks cabinet in 10 Downing Street!

🌺 *Albert Ball V.C.* . . . . *7 May*   🌺 *William Redmond* . . . . . . *7 June*

In mid-July the Germans introduced a new form of chemical attack near Ypres- the use of mustard gas known as 'Yperite'.

After a delay for mainly organisational reasons, the Fifth Army commanded by General Hubert Gough initiated the second phase on 31 July.

🌺 *Ellis Evans* . . . . *31 July*   🌺 *Edgar Mobbs* . . . . *31 July*

A week-long bombardment of three million shells preceded Zero Hour. Initial progress was hampered by torrential rain and German resistance at various strongholds like the cluster of bunkers at Tyne Cot. High Command prolonged the offensive despite the fact that the fighting around Passchendaele in particular had become a slogging match conducted in a morass of mud, so deep that soldiers were known to have drowned. It only ended when the ruined village of Passchendaele was taken on 10 November. The ground gained during this, the Third Battle of Ypres, was about six miles at a combined cost of 500,000 casualties for both sides.

🌺 *Noel Chavasse V.C. & Bar* . . *4 August*   🌺 *Werner Voss* . . . . *23 September*

🌺 *Samuel Sayell* . . . .*17 August*   🌺 *Frederick Millins* . . . . *9 October*

🌺 *Nellie Spindler* . . . .*21 August*   🌺 *Clarence Jeffries V.C.* . . . . *12 October*

🌺 *Georges Guynemer* . . . .*11 September*   🌺 *Colin Blythe* . . . . *8 November*

🌺 *Herbert Morris* . . . .*20 September*

Troops around a brazier at the Menin Gate, Ypres in 1917   IWM Q008356

The British commenced yet another offensive in France, the Battle of Cambrai south east of Arras on 20 November. It was a mass attack involving for the first time as many as 476 tanks. The element of surprise allowed Byng's Third Army to break through in most sections of the Germans' line of trenches. A determined German counter-attack and problems with a shortage of reserves meant that most of the ground gained was lost. When the fighting died down in early December there had been 40,000 casualties on each side.

It had been a mixed year for the British: technical and tactical lessons had been learnt but mounting casualties were becoming unsustainable. Haig requested more reinforcements. For their part the Germans were satisfied to have checked attacks against their line. Their morale was boosted by the potential 30% increase of troops released from the Eastern Front following the end of hostilities with the Russians after the October Revolution.

A defining moment in the War was the entry of the U.S.A. when they declared war against Germany on 6 April but it would take another year, however, for American troops to make a significant impact.

1918

At the start of the year the Allies expected a major German offensive. The previous November a Supreme War Council was formed at Versailles with the hope of improved co-ordination. Before the Americans had time to build up their numbers, General Erich Ludendorff planned a series of attacks with the prime aim of defeating the British in Flanders. Operation Michael opened on 21 March near Arras; it was followed in April by Operation Georgette along the river Lys and the following month Operation Blücher north of the Aisne in order to divert French troops from the British sector. A final effort was initiated in the Marne during mid-June. At first the Germans made sweeping gains. In the Somme the British were forced to retreat for 40 miles which in Great War terms was a significant distance. Paris was shelled. It was a bleak outlook for the Allies as a decisive breakthrough by the Germans appeared likely. Haig issued his famous 'with our backs to the wall' order on 11 April. The Royal Navy raided the German submarine base at Zeebrugge on St. George's Day and although it did not achieve its aims, the raid was, nonetheless, a morale booster back home. Ultimately the German attacks petered out because their army was exhausted and demoralised, their lines overstretched and the soldiers were guilty of looting captured British supply dumps.

Walter Tull . . . . .25 March		Alfred Souls . . . . 20 April	
Isaac Rosenberg . . . . 1 April		Cecil Coles . . . . 26 April	

One of nearly 1,000,000 soldiers in the British Army who lost their lives, this one during the German offensive in Picardy 3 April 1918. The wooden cross is already prepared

IWM Q011578

Numbers of casualties had reached such a level that it was clear hostilities could not continue for much longer. By the end of Operation Michael, for example, the British casualties were 178,000, the French 77,000 and the Germans' 250,000. By the beginning of May the balance changed in favour of the Allies when numbers of the American Expeditionary Force in France reached 430,000 men. The day of reckoning for the Germans occurred on 8 August, described by General Ludendorff in his memoirs as 'the Black Day of the German Army'. British, Australian and Canadian troops supported by the French, struck a blow at the German line east of Amiens.

Over the course of the War the British Army had come of age. The B.E.F. was 70,000 strong in August 1914 but by 1918, 5,700,000 had served with the British Army. To cope with such numbers it had to develop its organisational skills. It became a more effective fighting force due to improved communication, transport and better coordination between infantry, artillery, logistics, airpower, tanks and motorised units. Combined with better teamwork and the discarding of ineffective tactics, such as week-long bombardments, nearly eight miles of ground was gained on 8 August and 15,000 prisoners taken. It was the start of the 'Hundred Days' campaign when from September the Allies were engaged in an all out counter-offensive which quickly gathered pace due to the unrelenting pressure exerted by the British and Imperial troops.

Lille was liberated on 17 October. During the final days of the War there were a further 350,000 British casualties, more even than during the Third Battle of Ypres.

'Old Bill' remembering his lost pals at the Cenotaph.   *Barbara Bruce Bairnsfather*

🔸 *Ernest Farrar* . . . .*18 September*

Peace negotiations which had started in earnest in early October culminated with the unconditional surrender of Germany and the signing of the Armistice in a railway carriage at Compiègne at 5.10 a.m. on 11 November. It was ironic that on that morning, the Canadians entered Mons where the B.E.F. had fired its opening shots of the War.

🔸 *George Ellison* . . . .*11 November*

The precise overall cost of the War in human terms will never be known. The numbers of casualties for all the theatres of war are difficult to comprehend. They show that Britain and its Empire lost nearly 1,000,000 men to which must be added 2,300,000 wounded. France and her colonies lost over 1,400,000 and a further 3,600,000 were wounded. At least 1,800,000 Germans were killed and a staggering 4,250,000 wounded. Surely Europe and humanity had suffered enough? But then the Spanish influenza pandemic of 1918-19 ended even more lives than the War- estimates vary from 20 to 100 million.

In November 1918 there was an overwhelming collective sigh of relief. Victory was celebrated throughout Belgium, France and the British Empire. But a hundred years later the figures of deaths emphasise the enormity of what was perpetrated by the European rulers and their generals on humanity. There is no place now for celebration. We should just commemorate those of all nations whose lives were sacrificed.

Ypres in ruins: the cost in human and material terms   A - Cloth Hall   B - Cathedral   C - Menin Gate   25

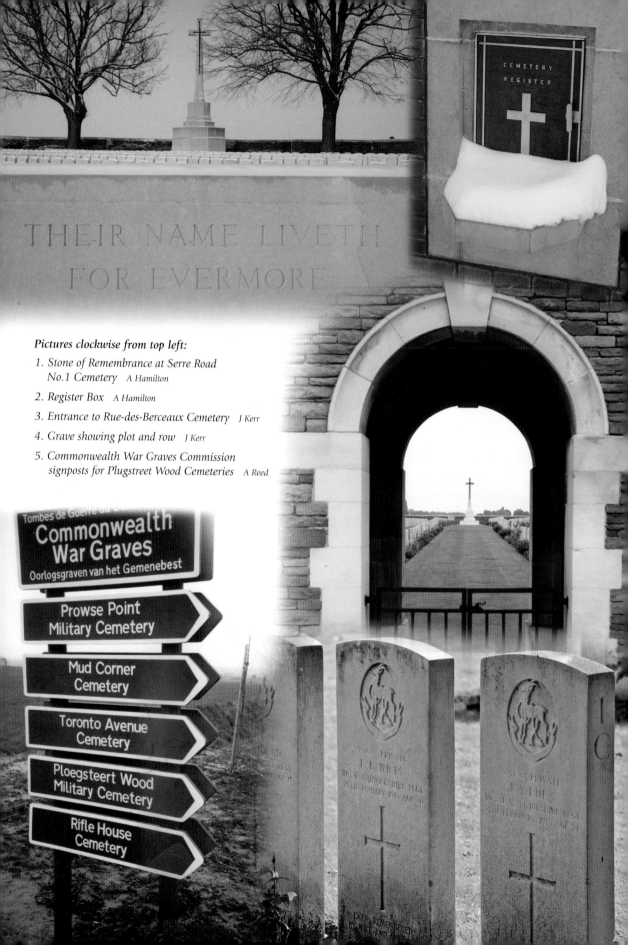

THEIR NAME LIVETH
FOR EVERMORE

Pictures clockwise from top left:

1. *Stone of Remembrance at Serre Road No.1 Cemetery* A Hamilton

2. *Register Box* A Hamilton

3. *Entrance to Rue-des-Berceaux Cemetery* J Kerr

4. *Grave showing plot and row* J Kerr

5. *Commonwealth War Graves Commission signposts for Plugstreet Wood Cemeteries* A Reed

Commonwealth War Graves

Prowse Point Military Cemetery

Mud Corner Cemetery

Toronto Avenue Cemetery

Ploegsteert Wood Military Cemetery

Rifle House Cemetery

IV

STOLEN LIVES

A Biographical Tour of Belgium and Northern France

The pen portraits that follow are in the order of the cemeteries and memorials recommended in five drives from the Ypres Salient down to the Somme. Each biographical study covers one main person of interest. In some cases, other soldiers are briefly mentioned if relevant to that person or their site of commemoration.

To do the sites justice, we suggest a five day tour but obviously it is not prescriptive and personalised itineraries can be chosen and adapted if, for example, there is a family member's grave to be visited. We hope that the itineraries are achievable but it is possible that the Day 3 Itinerary may be quite challenging!

There are three itinerary maps covering the Ypres Salient (p.28), Mons, French Flanders and Artois (p.154) and the Somme (p.204). They can be used in conjunction with a G.P.S. system, route finders or a Michelin map. We recommend use of Michelin Map number 301 Local (1/150,000) which covers all the relevant areas except for Mons. For each cemetery or memorial we have included its address, postcode and location co-ordinates.

Detailed routes to the sites can be found on the Commonwealth War Graves Commission's website: **www.cwgc.org**. Most of the sites are clearly marked by dark green directional signposts.

It is worth pointing out that some places you might visit in the area have different spellings, one Flemish, the other French e.g. Bergen and Mons, Ieper and Ypres, Mesen and Messines, Poperinghe and Poperinge, Rijsel and Lille.

Once you have arrived at a cemetery or memorial, look out for the register box in which you will find a visitors' book and a register in which there is a site plan and listed alphabetically are all the soldiers known to be buried or commemorated there. For each soldier's grave you will be given a plot reference in Roman numerals in the register but in Arabic numbers on the end grave of each row, then a letter for the relevant row and finally a number for the grave you are looking for. For example, Noel Chavasse, V.C. and Bar, is buried at Brandhoek New Military Cemetery in Plot III (3) Row B Grave 15. For a soldier remembered on a memorial, a panel, pier or bay number will be given.

If you want to photograph a grave, the details of which are faded or unclear, here is a little tip from a former head gardener of the C.W.G.C. the late Les Reed: pour some water from the top of the grave downwards across the gravestone… but only water!

Tyne Cot Cemetery   J Kerr

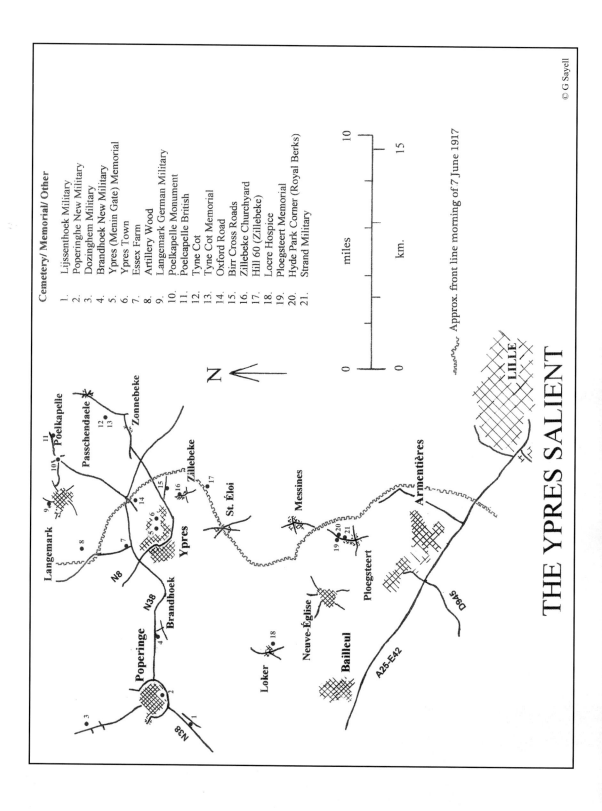

Cemetery/ Memorial/ Other

1. Lijssenthoek Military
2. Poperinghe New Military
3. Dozinghem Military
4. Brandhoek New Military
5. Ypres (Menin Gate) Memorial
6. Ypres Town
7. Essex Farm
8. Artillery Wood
9. Langemark German Military
10. Poelkapelle Monument
11. Poelcapelle British
12. Tyne Cot
13. Tyne Cot Memorial
14. Oxford Road
15. Birr Cross Roads
16. Zillebeke Churchyard
17. Hill 60 (Zillebeke)
18. Locre Hospice
19. Ploegsteert Memorial
20. Hyde Park Corner (Royal Berks)
21. Strand Military

N

miles

km.

Approx. front line morning of 7 June 1917

THE YPRES SALIENT

THE YPRES SALIENT
Day 1 Itinerary

Ypres (Menin Gate) Memorial J Kerr

THE YPRES SALIENT

Day 1 Itinerary

Much of the first day may be spent travelling to the Ypres Salient. Allow one hour from Calais to the first cemetery of interest, one of the largest British cemeteries, Lijssenthoek, where a 26 year old nurse and one of seven cousins to die are buried. On the way to Ypres, visit the graves of a West Indian Shot at Dawn at Poperinghe New Military and the Great War's only double V.C. at Brandhoek New Military.

An absolute must for a stay in Ypres is the Last Post Ceremony which is held every evening at 8.00 p.m. at the Ypres (Menin Gate) Memorial. When the laying of wreaths is finished and the crowds have melted away, look for the names of five of our subjects which include an England rugby international, an Olympic rowing gold medallist, a Canadian who was allegedly 'crucified' and an officer's batman who participated in the Christmas Truce of 1914.

Enjoy the rest of the evening in Ypres and admire the way in which, phoenix-like, the city rose from the charred ruins of four years of shelling.

	Cemetery/ Memorial	Address/Post code/Google map ref.	Name	Page
1	LIJSSENTHOEK MILITARY	Boescheepseweg, 8970 Poperinge, Belgium 50.82839,2.7016	Rev. Charles Doudney	31
			Samuel Sayell	39
			Nellie Spindler	44
2	POPERINGHE NEW MILITARY	Deken de Bolaan 94-98, 8970 Poperinge, Belgium 50.84738,2.73305	Herbert Morris	50
3	DOZINGHEM MILITARY	Leeuwerikstraat 6, 8972 Poperinge, Belgium 50.89244,2.70158	Edward Sayell	41
4	BRANDHOEK NEW MILITARY	Zevekotestraat 36, 8908 Ieper, Belgium 50.85273,2.78781	Noel Chavasse Double V.C.	54
5	YPRES (MENIN GATE) MEMORIAL	Menenstraat, 8900 Ieper, Belgium 50.8521,2.89138	Harry Band	61
			Gilchrist Maclagan	65
			Edgar Mobbs	69
			Milford Sayell	43
			William Tapp	74

REVEREND CHARLES DOUDNEY

'… even in his hour of trial, his consideration for others did not fail'

'One who has not been through it, could never hope to understand what this war is. It is just simply hell on earth, but a hell through which moves a race of heroes, whose bravery and self-sacrifice make one ashamed.' The Reverend Charles (Charlie) Doudney had experienced tough conditions in the South Australian outback when, early in his career between 1894 and 1906, he was a curate and then Chaplain to Empire troops; nothing, however, could have prepared him for what he encountered on the Ypres Salient in 1915.

At the request of Bishop John Taylor-Smith, the Chaplain General, Charlie Doudney joined the ranks of the Army Chaplains' Department in March 1915. His work in the parish of St. Luke, South Lyncombe near Bath, had made him eminently suitable for a chaplaincy role at the Front. In October 1914 he had been a captain in the Athletes' Volunteer Force based in Bath which, by March 1915, was 500 strong and in July was incorporated into the Somerset Light Infantry. On 20 March he preached a sermon to the Volunteers at St. Luke's, in which he forcefully advocated the desperate need to defeat the German Army.

His strong views were based on his experiences when returning from a holiday in Switzerland with his wife Zoë and daughters Esther and Joy. They travelled through France in late August 1914 and were caught up in the war fever. They noticed that in Paris 'the French soldiers were full of confidence. Whenever we encountered them they cheered us to the echo. It was *Vive l'Angleterre* everywhere.' Charlie's emotions were stirred when the family reached Amiens where they saw a train full of wounded British troops and two of Belgian refugees.

The Rev. Charles Doudney, vicar of St. Luke's Church, South Lyncombe near Bath
Doudney family photographs by kind permission of Rachel Horne

When he returned to his parish, he wrote an article for *The Bath Chronicle* of 5 September 1914: 'If they (the British) could only see what we have seen, those Belgian refugees, the homeless women weeping, the suffering little children and the awful destitution, there would be a great rush to join the colours.' His chilling and correct conclusion was that 'the nations know it is absolutely war to the death' and he believed strongly that there was a pressing need to fight for the liberty of Europe and for world peace. His parishioners soon began to realise exactly what war meant when, on 24 October, 50 wounded soldiers arrived at Bath railway station from Southampton.

Charles followed his father into the Anglican ministry; David Doudney was the was the much-loved vicar of the church of St. James in Carlisle, marrying Georgina who was the granddaughter of the famous prison reformer Elizabeth Fry. They brought up their seven children in Carlisle later moving to the parish of Ore, a village near Hastings, where Charles, the fourth of the seven children, attended the grammar school and went on to study at Corpus Christi College and Ridley Hall, Cambridge where rowing was one of his favourite pastimes.

He was ordained in 1894 and became curate at the church of St. John the Evangelist in Penge, South London. His next post was in West Hampstead, London and following the loss of daughter Noelle in 1907, Charlie took on the parish of St. Luke's where, as he did throughout his life, he endeavoured to foster community spirit and tend to the poor and needy. He set up a soup kitchen and worked for a Young Men's Club; he founded a Ladies' Working Party, reorganised the Men's equivalent and started a free parish magazine. So successful was he in generating interest in the church and its work that he and the church wardens decided to build an extension to the church but he found raising funds to pay for the work more challenging than expected.

Charles Doudney working on the church extension, 'helped' by daughter Joy and watched by his wife Zoë

When he left South Lyncombe to join the Army Chaplains' Department, *The Bath Chronicle* reported that 'the cheering for Mr. Doudney was hearty as the train pulled out of the station.' He was delighted to have been asked to contribute to the war effort in a spiritual capacity and wrote 'I feel I am the proudest yet humblest man in Bath and I never felt more elated than by this honour placed upon me and yet I feel very humble realising what little I can do.'

He was, of course, modest in the extreme; his reports from the Front for the Bath and district local newspapers and his parish magazine underline the monumental amount of work he and other chaplains achieved in the most trying of circumstances. At this stage of the War he was one of 40 or so temporary chaplains on secondment from their parishes and about 120 professionals- the numbers would increase dramatically as the War progressed so that by 1918 there were in the region of 3,500 on all fronts.

To introduce him gently to the action, Charlie was allocated to the No. 8 Base Hospital in Rouen which provided 650 beds for the sick and injured. He dreaded the arrival of the 'ghastly convoys' of wounded and dying men. In the first report of his experiences at the Front published by *The Bath and Wiltshire Chronicle* on 1 May 1915, he focused on a theme that recurs in his ensuing updates- he was deeply impressed by the uncomplaining and stoical nature of the wounded being treated in the hospital: 'All day motor ambulances rolled in and deposited rows of stretchers in the yard- in the shade- the poor torn fellows lay silent and patient till their turn came for the clean cool bed and the fresh dressing. And oh how they enjoyed it! I stroll around the wards seeking the worst cases and try to say some heartening word… I have spoken to many hundreds here but have not heard, as yet, one single word of complaint, seldom a groan.' The hospital received 1,000 casualties in one week in May, 458 of them in a 26 hour period. By now he admitted that he was 'getting inured' to the horrors he observed but his description of 'a poor Canadian' must have jolted his readers: 'Half his face has gone… his nose, one eye, all one cheek, upper jaw on one side, clean gone.'

He was inspired by the constant examples of 'true grit' as pain was endured without grumble, news that he disseminated to readers in the *Bath Chronicle* in vivid and expressive terms. 'And it's all so still! It's a breathless day, the masses of vivid green chestnuts there behind the offices are just murmuring, and two blackbirds are making liquid music, and a cuckoo is calling in the distance. And into this peace every two minutes comes the tramp of bearers and the silent heroes file past. You never hear a cry. Weary beyond words, aching and throbbing, these lads never murmur. Truly we don't know what they are. No words can describe their heroic patience, but in saying this, I do not mean to limit the credit to the patients. Nurses and staff are alike splendid. A hospital in war should be a certain cure for the "grumbles". They would be driven out for very shame!'

Unlike many of his profession the Reverend was happy to roll his sleeves up and help with treating the wounded. He was fascinated by the work being done to identify and deal with 'deathly microbes' and was full of admiration for a doctor in the hospital who was dealing with typhoid, tetanus and cerebral meningitis. 'Trenches and parapets and cover may save their hundreds but this quiet doctor had saved his thousands.'

By the first week of June he had served his apprenticeship. As he had predicted in the parish magazine, he would soon be called to the fighting near the front line. He received orders to join the 18th Brigade of the 6th Division and entrained to Ypres. When he entered the shattered city, he found the experience 'so unreal'. The sight was one he would never forget: 'As far as one could see there was not a house that was intact. All the buildings were deserted and it was literally the city of the dead. The sun had set and there was a weird twilight in which things looked ghastly and unreal.'

During the following month Charlie and four colleagues were fully stretched, either helping at the 18th Ambulance Advanced Dressing Station at the 'Hop Store' in Vlamertinge or conducting religious services. He held a communion service on 6 June for a dozen men in a hut, most of whom were officers. During the service 'a battery started up with shattering bangs, which added to the unreality of the service, but in a sense, also to its reality.'

The services he enjoyed most were small, voluntary and informal get-togethers when the 'congregation' would sit down, sing some hymns, say a few prayers and talk. On another occasion he recalled a service with a 'rough lot' at which no officers were present but they were attentive and involved. It must have been heart-warming for him to hold a service for two battalions in the 6th Division- 1/ East Yorks and 1/ West Yorks which was 'perfectly wonderful. And the singing!'

A talented artist, Charlie Doudney's water colour of Ypres in ruins

The Reverend found that a hop garden provided an 'excellent church' when a German aeroplane was circling overhead. Soldiers were standing in the lines of hops hidden by the fully-leaved hop plants and he maintained that the acoustics for singing were better than if they had been in the open.

He was in no doubt that the quality of services and life generally would be enhanced by a piano and it was incongruous that a padre should seek dispensation from higher authority to 'loot a piano'! One was transported back from a ruin in Ypres and one evening the Reverend joined the battalions for a concert in the woods: 'It was perfect. We sat in a big circle in the moonlight in a clearing and the singing was excellent, to the accompaniment of the looted piano!' He was amazed when one evening a pianist volunteered from the ranks and played a Rachmaninov Prelude beautifully! On 4 July a piano was used 'with a splinter right through it, which had smashed the middle notes and put them in the centre.' A discordant piano matched the atmosphere in the brewery hop store where the service was held: 'I shall ever connect the smell of hops (rather sour) with that of blood. Last year's hops have a very nasty sour smell.'

There are constant references in Charlie Doudney's writings to the number of burial services he had to perform. At Potyze Château (6th Division H.Q.) on 10 June, he noted 'we were standing by an open grave and I began the wonderful words: "I am the resurrection and the life", I have said them in strange places many times before but never had their ring come home so true.' Two funerals were held for men in the Durham Light Infantry on 29 June who were buried close to where they died: 'Two pathetic bundles in sacks- the poor limbs gathered up and put together as they could.'

For another chaplain, the popular Reverend Geoffrey Studdert Kennedy, the business of burying large numbers of soldiers was a depressing ordeal. When confronted with such a conveyor belt of death, he experienced great difficulty in remaining 'fresh' for each new burial which he considered so essential for the sake of the fallen soldier's comrades. His desire to do his best for them is conveyed in the poem *His Mate:*

All that week I'd buried brothers,
In one bitter battle slain,
In one grave I laid two hundred.
God! What sorrow and what rain!

…

There are many kinds of sorrow
In this world of Love and Hate,
But there is no sterner sorrow
Than a soldier's for his mate.

A chaplain holding a burial service in the field.   Australian War Memorial

Studdert Kennedy was, like Doudney, prepared to minister to British and German wounded. He had the common touch with 'other ranks' who appreciated his Irish sing-songs, use of language they understood (at times quite 'fruity'!) and most importantly, his gifts of Woodbine cigarettes: hence his nickname 'Woodbine Willie'. His experiences at the Front tested the strength of his beliefs and in sermons he did on occasions question the existence of God and denounce the inhumanity of the War. His relationship with the authorities was, at best, cool but he was nonetheless awarded the M.C.

One of Doudney's legacies was to paint an evocative and vivid picture of the total destruction of the fine medieval city of Ypres. He went there on 24 June 'to try and loot another piano. It was the first time we had been in the daylight and, though the impression was not so awesome, yet it was interesting to see clearer details. We went down street after street and into the Cathedral, which is, of course, absolutely wrecked. The walls are standing, though sadly torn. Huge stones are heaved about in all directions, pillars broken and the organ smashed. The beautiful Cloth Hall next door is still more done for. How I should like to loot some carvings for St. Luke's! One church had been occupied by French soldiers, and when the shelling began they had evidently gone out at once, for everything they possessed was littered over the floor. You never saw such a mess. We just picked our way through and did not stay as the smell was not good. We found some pianos and chose one, which the transports are sending for… It was pathetic to see decent houses, some quite splendid, torn to pieces, whole fronts gone, exposing the rooms on each floor like doll's houses, with all the details of civilised life open to the air. Inside everything was in utter confusion… But by far the greater number of houses are gone altogether, and nothing left but a heap of bricks and stones.'

The Rev. Charlie Doudney was influential in promoting the concept of founding a 'church club' or 'community of soldiers'. At the end of June 1915 he mentioned that five soldiers had talked about setting up a refuge for those in need of quiet spiritual contemplation away from the hell of the trenches. Only weeks after his death in October 1915, his replacement, the Rev. Philip 'Tubby' Clayton along with the Rev. Neville Talbot, set up such an establishment in a house in Poperinge, named in memory of Neville's brother, Lieutenant Gilbert Talbot, who was killed on 30 July 1915 when leading an attack at Hooge on the Ypres Salient. Charlie was saddened by Neville Talbot's loss: 'Poor chap, his brother was killed leading a charge. None of his party came back so Neville went out last night and crawled out of the front trench through the wire and actually found his brother and all others dead.' At first it was proposed that the new 'sanctuary' should be called 'Church House' but as Clayton asserted: 'the staff of our Division saw a scarecrow in the name and smelt tracts' so instead it was named 'Talbot House' in Gilbert Talbot's memory. It was a

The Reverend's radio equipment

popular destination for soldiers who were welcomed regardless of their rank. The refuge was affectionately known as 'Toc H', the British Army Radio Signallers' code for the initials T.H.

Doudney received news of a well-deserved leave and on 12 July returned home to 'take the waters' in Bath to treat an unpleasant outbreak of eczema caused, no doubt, by the stresses of war. He showed his family some of his watercolours of life at the Front and in some quiet moments indulged in his hobby of playing with his radio equipment which was, for the time, quite advanced.

More important to him, however, was the need to engage again with his parishioners. He gave a sermon in St. Luke's to a packed congregation and admitted that religion had been 'put to the severest test which any system could possibly be put to; and we have seen it come out absolutely triumphant.' He asked the question of his audience that doubtless some readers of this book will have been posing: 'Is it possible there can be a God who can allow these things to happen?' His answer was the standard response that must have been given on many occasions at the Front by the army of chaplains: 'We believe and teach that God will not stop these things unless men come and rank themselves with Him to do the work. It is the idea of co-operation in the work of God that the men reach for, and hold on to, and drink in so thirstily. And this idea gives a meaning to my work… They are not fighting alone for men, but it is a spiritual war they are fighting, side by side with God to get rid of sin in the world.' He went on to inform his flock of a miracle occurring day after day when 'tens of thousands of men, hard, rough working men, who perhaps never attended church at home, and never thought of it, are finding definitely that God is their close Friend… Oh if you the congregation could only see, only get a vision of one of those companies going into the trenches at night just in the fading light; or stand at the side of the road and watch them swinging past, and see the faces of those lads who know they are going to death!'

The Rev. Charlie Doudney in his Army Chaplain's uniform

Charlie departed for his final few weeks at the Front on 7 August and was soon dealing with the wounded. The men were in a terrible state, 'in some cases one or two limbs blown off and so on.' 35

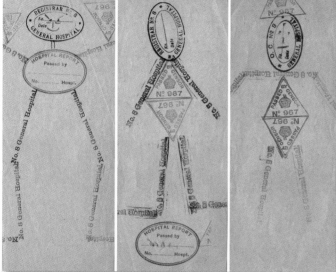

8 General
Hospital.

19th May
1915

Dear Joy,
Your Daddy
is behaving most
disgracefully, this
morning he ate all
my breakfast.
He has stolen all
my toffee, & I —
think he means
to eat my dinner
too.
Will I put a
label on him &
send him home?
With much
love
The Censor

Doudney was a friend of an official censor, Lieutenant K. Macnaughton,
who engaged in delightful correspondence with young Joy Doudney

Reverting to his oft-repeated theme, he commented: 'Poor chaps, they were as usual, marvellously brave.'

His reports from the Front cannot have failed to confirm the true horror of the conflict. He wrote in the parish magazine that 'I doubt if I shall ever get used to the shells; their scream is so vicious and their coming so unexpected and the crash so appalling that one's heart gets down into one's boots.'

Humour was never far from the surface of Charlie's portrayal of life in the trenches. On 14 August he was sitting on the edge of an old trench on his own while 'a good deal of awfulness was going on, but mostly passed overhead. One battery just behind me seemed to be playing tennis with a German gun. The shells came screeching over, backwards and forwards, quite evenly as if they were chucking them to each other in turns. I seemed to be the net, so was very glad they didn't serve any faults!'

The hard-hitting realism of his descriptions of the horrors and the overriding stench of death, begs the question as to how his reporting escaped the censor to reach its significant readership back in 'Blighty'. It did help that he had known the censor at No. 8 Hospital in Rouen well and had offered him a welcome helping hand to sift through hundreds of Tommies' letters and cards. The true situation in France and Belgium was hardly a secret.

On 13 October Doudney was accompanying an officer of the 18th Field Ambulance to an aid post by the railway line near Lijssenthoek. While he was talking animatedly about his interests in wireless telegraphy and X ray apparatus, a shell exploded, wounding him in the abdomen. He was taken to No. 10 Casualty Clearing Station at Lijssenthoek where he was ministered to by a chaplain, Canon Macnutt, the vicar of St. Matthew's, Surbiton. The Canon recalled a tribute to his fallen colleague that 'at the last, speech was beyond him and all he could do was just to smile on his friends, who among them would never forget his smile; and they could well understand how that smile uttered his faith, hope and affection more eloquently than any spoken word.'

It was tragic that he should have been mortally wounded just the day before he was due a spell of leave and that he should have been hit near the railway which would have taken him home. He died of his wounds at 9 p.m. on Saturday 16 October. The following morning a telegram was read out to the congregation of St. Luke's by a retired clergyman, announcing the tragic news of their beloved vicar. He was handed the role as no one else of the regular faithful felt they could deliver the news without breaking down.

The Rev. Charlie Doudney was buried on 18 October, appropriately enough St. Luke's Day, at Lijssenthoek near Poperinge. His wife Zoë received hundreds of letters of condolence which will

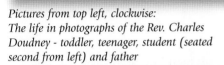

Pictures from top left, clockwise:
The life in photographs of the Rev. Charles
Doudney - toddler, teenager, student (seated
second from left) and father

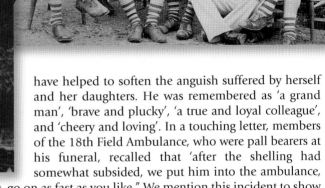

have helped to soften the anguish suffered by herself and her daughters. He was remembered as 'a grand man', 'brave and plucky', 'a true and loyal colleague', and 'cheery and loving'. In a touching letter, members of the 18th Field Ambulance, who were pall bearers at his funeral, recalled that 'after the shelling had somewhat subsided, we put him into the ambulance, and he remarked "Don't mind me lads, go on as fast as you like." We mention this incident to show that even in his hour of trial, his consideration for others did not fail.'

The Reverend Charles Doudney was a wonderfully energetic, talented and compassionate man. His death was a desperate tragedy for his family, parishioners, soldiers and comrades at the Front.

REVEREND CHARLES DOUDNEY:

Born:	13 March 1871 at Carlisle, son of the Reverend David and Mrs. Georgina Doudney, husband of Joanna (Zoë) and father of Esther and Joy
Education:	Hastings Grammar School, Corpus Christi and Ridley Hall, Cambridge
Occupation:	Clergyman
Unit/ Regiment:	Army Chaplains' Department attached to 18th Brigade, 6th Division
Rank:	4th Class (equivalent of a captain)
Died:	16 October 1915
Age:	44
Buried:	Lijssenthoek Military Cemetery, Poperinge I.A.32.
Inscription:	IN CHRISTO ET IN PACE (in Christ and in peace)

The cemetery was designed by Sir Reginald Blomfield; it is 12 kms west of Ypres near Poperinge and is the second largest Commonwealth cemetery in Belgium with over 9,900 burials including 223 Germans (a total of 1,100 Germans are buried in British cemeteries in Belgium). As it was generally out of the range of German artillery, several Casualty Clearing Stations were set up at Remy Siding named after the farmer Rémi Quaghebeur. They were situated along railway sidings on the line linking Poperinge to Hazebrouck in France, now the main road. The main entrance to the cemetery is located at De Boonaert which means 'bean field' in Flemish and was known as 'The Boneyard' by the troops. The majority of the headstones are of Hopton-Wood stone, a grey limestone also used in the construction of the Houses of Parliament and Westminster Abbey- unfortunately inscriptions are not as legible as those on graves of Portland stone

Reverend Charles Doudney's grave at Lijssenthoek   *A Hamilton*

Other Graves of Interest:

Chinese Labourers:	Plot XXXIV	About 100,000 served in the British Army - around 2,000 died
Major General:	Malcolm Mercer	3rd Canadian Division, died 3 June 1916 aged 57, VI. A. 38.
Shot at Dawn:	Private William Baker	26/ Royal Fusiliers, executed for desertion on 14 August 1918, XXV. B. 22.
Under age:	Private Donald Snaddon	1/ Royal Scots Fusiliers, died 18 January 1916, aged 15, II. D.37.

A Chinese Labourer's grave at Lijssenthoek   *A Hamilton*

SAMUEL SAYELL

One of seven cousins who fell

Few families escaped the grim death toll of the Great War. Some suffered more than others and when 33 year old Private Samuel Sayell was laid to rest at Lijssenthoek on 17 July 1917, he was one of seven cousins who died on the Western Front- the only soldiers by the name of Sayell to be commemorated by the Commonwealth War Graves Commission in the Great War. Seven Sayells fell in France and Belgium out of a total of 21 who served abroad, a family loss of 33%.

The family tree is traceable to Thomas Sayell a yeoman farmer who in 1700 married Elizabeth Rogers in the Buckinghamshire village of Ivinghoe. Generations of his descendants worked on the land. As fortunes changed after the depression of the 1830s, many became humble agricultural labourers in and around Ivinghoe and Cheddington.

Encouraged by the railways, the Sayells migrated further afield to London, the Forest of Dean and in time as far as Canada and Australia. Of the Sayells that were killed, four were employed on the land and the others were respectively a painter/ French polisher, an invoice clerk and a railway porter. The majority were Buckinghamshire-born and two hailed from north London and Watford.

Samuel Sayell was born at Horton near Cheddington in Buckinghamshire. He was the fourth of six children of cattleman Henry Sayell and his wife Elizabeth. Samuel started his working life as a farm waggoner and must have displayed ability and skill as he subsequently moved to Achurch, near Oundle in Northamptonshire where he is believed to have been a farm manager on Lord Lilford's private estate. He married Frances and they had two children, Harry born in 1908 and Lucy in 1910.

Samuel enlisted at Thrapston in Northamptonshire, giving his address as 'Lilford near Oundle'. He served in the 22/ Royal Fusiliers from the 29 June to the 12 October 1916 when he was transferred to the 32/ Royal Fusiliers (City of London Regiment).

The 32/ Royal Fusiliers took part in the Battle of Messines Ridge on 7 June 1917. It was one of the most dramatic days of the Great War when 19 mines laid under the ridge exploded simultaneously thus signalling the start of a major British offensive. His cousin Milford Sayell was in the 26/ Royal Fusiliers. Both men went 'over the top' in the early hours of the morning.

The 26/ Royal Fusiliers' War Diary describes what the cousins must have faced from 03.10 hours onwards: 'Promptly to the second our artillery opened up and our lines of waves went forward. About 5 seconds after zero the St. Eloi mine went up with a huge blaze and a rocking of the ground. This seemed to startle the men for they seemed to turn left handed. Fortunately the check was only momentary and the men soon settled down and were over the top and following the 32nd Royal Fusiliers who were in front in good order'. We can only wonder if the two cousins met that morning.

'The enemy defensive barrage came down on No Man's Land about 4 minutes after zero but it only caught our rear waves and caused little damage. The attack went off exactly as per schedule. The 32nd Royal Fusiliers took the enemy Front and Reserve trenches and at zero plus 35 minutes the Battalion were ready to advance on their objective the Damstrasse. This consisted of a sunken road which was thoroughly fortified and which was supposed to be a bit of a stumbling block. The Damstrasse was rushed and taken at 04.11 hours and a line made 50 to 100 yards beyond it.'

By early July 1917 when undergoing training at Méteren, the Battalion War Diary records that on 10 June the unit was commended by the Division Commander for 'the good work and cheerful and soldierly spirit shown by all ranks under the severe strain and during heavy and frequent hostile fire while holding the line for three weeks.' Two days later he presented awards and inspected the First Line Transport and commented on 'his satisfaction at the cleanliness of the vehicles and condition of the animals', credit for which may have been partly due to Samuel's experience in civilian life.

The Battalion returned on 13 July to dugouts at Ridgewood which they had occupied during the winter months. The following day Samuel was in a working party supervised by the 10th Royal Engineers Signal Corps burying cables and digging trenches in front of Spoil Bank and The Bluff, higher ground that provided a good vantage point and was the site of bitter fighting.

According to the Battalion War Diary this work continued and 'during the night of 15th/16th one party was caught by enemy shell fire and suffered 17 casualties consisting of 1 officer and 16 other ranks, two of the latter subsequently dying of their wounds.' Samuel was one of the latter. Every effort would have been made to save his life- firstly at a Regimental Aid Post, then an Advanced Dressing Station and, assuming his wounds were serious, at the Remy (Siding) Casualty Clearing Station which was adjacent to Lijssenthoek Cemetery. He may have been found dead on arrival or

Lijssenthoek Cemetery   *J Kerr*

died there. It was common practice for those unlikely to survive to be heavily dosed with morphine 'to help them on their way'.

Frances, Harry and Lucy received the news they must have dreaded of his death. They were led to believe that 'he was shot in the back whilst carrying a wounded soldier

to safety from the battlefield.' At least they could comfort themselves that he had died unselfishly helping a comrade in need.

The Northamptonshire Gazette of 17 August 1917 announced, inaccurately, that 'Pte. S. Sazell (sic) of the Northants Regiment (sic) whose home is at Lilford, has died of his wounds. Much sympathy is felt for his relatives.'

Like Annie Souls whose loss of five of her sons was compounded by the death of her youngest son of meningitis after the War, Frances Sayell was beset by further tragedies. In 1923 her daughter Lucy, at the age of 13, was struck by a motorcycle when on her way to Sunday school and suffered serious head injuries. She recovered but a year later said to her mother 'Mummy, I don't feel well. I want to lie down.' She was put to bed and later died.

In 1930 Harry who had only recently married was killed riding his motorcycle home one dark evening by a vehicle that did not stop. Frances's great nephew and author of this piece, George Sayell, remembers her as a smart and respectable lady who managed to bear her tragic losses with impassive stoicism.

Samuel is remembered on memorials in Mentmore, Buckinghamshire and Achurch in Northamptonshire.

by George Sayell

SAMUEL SAYELL:

Born:	1884, son of Henry and Elizabeth Sayell
Occupation:	Waggoner/ farm manager
Enlisted:	Thrapston, Northants
Unit/ Regiment:	22 and 32/ Royal Fusiliers
Rank:	Private
Died:	17 July 1917
Age:	33
Buried:	Lijssenthoek Military Cemetery, Poperinge XVI.F.20.

Samuel Sayell's grave   *A Hamilton*

The other members of the Sayell family to fall were:

ARTHUR SAYELL: (Samuel's first cousin)

Born:	1890, son of Jeffrey and Emma Sayell of Ford, Buckinghamshire
Occupation:	Farm labourer
Enlisted:	Aylesbury
Unit/ Regiment:	2/1 Oxfordshire and Buckinghamshire Light Infantry
Rank:	Private
Died:	19 July 1916, Battle of Fromelles near Sugar Loaf Salient
Age:	25
Commemorated:	Loos Memorial, Panel 85

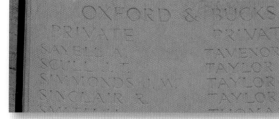

Arthur Sayell's name on the Loos Memorial   A Hamilton

Arthur was likely to have been one of 120 men of assault companies that moved into No Man's Land and lay down in four waves. At 6 p.m. 'with a cheer the four waves leapt up and assaulted the enemy's trenches. Even before 5.40 p.m. the enemies machine-guns had become busy; and at 6 p.m. they mowed down our advancing waves, so that only a few men actually reached the German parapet. These did not return.'

EDWARD THOMAS SAYELL: (Samuel's second cousin)

Born:	20 February 1892, son of painter and decorator Walter and Elizabeth Sayell, of 39, Springfield Road, Linslade, Buckinghamshire
Occupation:	Painter and French polisher
Enlisted:	Aylesbury
Unit/ Regiment:	Oxfordshire and Buckinghamshire Light Infantry then 143/ Machine Gun Corps
Rank:	Corporal
Died:	5 October 1917 at No. 4 Clearing Station, of chest wounds received during the Battle of Broodseinde, Third Battle of Ypres
Age:	24
Buried:	Dozinghem Military Cemetery V.H.2. The cemetery is 4 kms north of Poperinge in Belgium. It contains 3,174 burials and 65 German graves. It was near the sites of No. 4, No. 47 and No. 61 Casualty Clearing Stations. The architect was Sir Reginald Blomfield

According to the Linslade Parish Magazine, Edward was 'actually expected home on leave when the news came of his death from wounds.'

EZRA WILLIAM SAYELL: (Samuel's third cousin once removed)

Born:	1894, son of pork butcher Ezra and Sarah Sayell of Holloway, North London
Occupation:	Invoice clerk
Enlisted:	London
Unit/ Regiment:	29/ London and 11/ Hampshire, a pioneer battalion
Rank:	Private
Died:	4 April 1918

Edward Sayell's grave marker on the left in St. Barnabas Church at Linslade   A Hamilton

| Age: | 23 |
| Buried: | St. Sever Cemetery Extension, Rouen in Normandy P. IX.Q.5B. |

The cemetery was designed by Sir Reginald Blomfield. There are 9,348 burials, a large number because of its proximity to 15 hospitals- eight General, five Stationary, one British Red Cross and one Labour

Ezra is believed to have died in a hospital at Rouen having been wounded during the retreat preparing defences and destroying bridges around Péronne

GEORGE SAYELL: (Samuel's first cousin)

Born:	24 May 1891, son of shepherd Andrew Sayell and Ellen, of Cheddington, Buckinghamshire
Occupation:	Yard porter for the London North Western Railway Company
Unit/ Regiment:	'D' Battery, 36th Brigade, Royal Field Artillery
Rank:	Gunner
Died:	3 May 1917 at Roclincourt, supporting Canadians and XIII Corps
Age:	25
Buried:	Roclincourt Military Cemetery II.B.18.

George Sayell's grave in Roclincourt Cemetery G Sayell

The cemetery is situated east of the Arras to Lens road and was designed by Sir Reginald Blomfield. There are 916 burials and four German graves. A wooden memorial was erected by the 22/ Royal Fusiliers

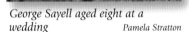

George Sayell aged eight at a wedding Pamela Stratton

JAMES SAYELL: (Samuel's third cousin once removed)

Born:	1896, son of bricklayer's labourer Jesse and Mary Sayell of Watford, Hertfordshire
Occupation:	Saw miller
Enlisted:	Hertford
Unit/ Regiment:	1/ Hertfordshire
Rank:	Private
Died:	30 October 1916 when in dugouts at Authuille, Battle of the Somme. The previous day the Battalion had been fighting at the 'Pope's Nose' in the Schwaben Redoubt near the present day Ulster Tower
Age:	20
Buried:	Connaught Cemetery XI.A.6.

The cemetery was designed by Sir Reginald Blomfield and is north west of Thiepval. Initially it contained 229 burials which increased later to 1,268 when more graves were brought in from 10 nearby cemeteries. Half of the burials are unidentified

James Sayell fought near the German observation post called 'The Pope's Nose' by troops from Ulster. It overlooks the Ancre Valley J Kerr

MILFORD SAYELL: (Samuel's third cousin once removed)

Born:	1895, son of Walter, a labourer in a railway carriage works and Sarah Jane Sayell
Occupation:	Wood yard labourer
Enlisted:	Bedford
Unit/ Regiment:	Bedfordshire then 26/ Royal Fusiliers
Rank:	Private
Died:	12 June 1917 after consolidation work in the Damstrasse on the Ypres Salient when five other ranks were killed
Age:	22
Commemorated:	Menin Gate Memorial, Ypres, Panel 6

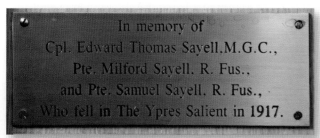

Plaque to three Sayells in St. George's Memorial Church, Ypres
J Kerr

A small brass plaque to the three Sayells who fell in the Ypres Salient, commissioned by George Sayell, author of this piece, can be seen on the wall to the left of the door as you enter St. George's Memorial Church in Ypres.

Six of the seven Sayells to die on the Western Front were descended from Humphrey (born 1812) and Jane Sayell. Three were their grandsons and three were great grandsons. Samuel's older brother Joseph was the great grandfather of the author of this piece.

Milford Sayell's name can be found on the Ypres (Menin Gate) Memorial - this view is from the ramparts   *J Kerr*

NELLIE SPINDLER

'A noble type of good, heroic womanhood'

Nellie Spindler was one of thousands of nurses who worked tirelessly behind the lines in Belgium and France. She was born in Wakefield, Yorkshire on 10 August 1891, the first child of Elizabeth and George Spindler who were married the previous year in Leeds. In 1896 Elizabeth gave birth to a second daughter, Lilly. George Edward was born in 1902 and May followed in 1904. Nellie was brought up in a loving family for whom duty, responsibility and caring for others were of great importance, qualities that can be seen in her father's career and character.

Lincolnshire-born George Spindler started his career as a police constable in 1889. The vicar of Caistor in Lincolnshire, the Rev. J.E. Wallis Loft referred to him in a letter of April 1889 as 'a good

The Spindler children- Nellie is standing behind baby May, Lilly is to the left and George on the right   *Vera Sheard*

officer and an intelligent man... very civil and obliging and anxious to get through an unpleasant duty with as little friction as possible'. Having moved to Wakefield he became a detective in 1892 and a sergeant in 1899, the year he won a First Aid competition. By 1903 he had achieved the rank of inspector. In his obituary it was stated that 'he was an expert ambulance-man, and on one occasion he saved a man's life in an extraordinary manner. The man had cut his throat, and when Mr. Spindler went to his aid, he treated him in such a manner that he was able to convey him to hospital, where he received medical attention. The man in question lived for many years and eventually died a natural death'. George also held office in the Oddfellows, a friendly society dedicated to the care of members of the community in need.

Nellie was educated at Eastmoor Council School in Wakefield. She was a diligent and conscientious pupil with a caring side to her character exemplified by a postcard she sent to her mother when staying with family in Leeds: 'I am enjoying myself up to the mark. Have you been having a dose of the indigestion cure?'

It is not surprising that Nellie, following the example set by her father, would wish to enter a profession for which she could be of help to others. The 1911 census tells us that she was a 'Servant' at Wakefield Fever Hospital. She trained at Leeds Township Infirmary from 1912 to 1915 and qualified as a staff nurse. In an extant set of lecture notes entitled 'Practical Details of Nursing' the contents, beautifully written up in neat and steady handwriting, demonstrate a desire for accuracy and attention to detail.

According to her niece Vera Sheard, the family was deeply religious. Nellie often carried with her pictures of churches and cathedrals she had visited. In one of her books a cutting was found of a poem by the American Edith Willis Linn (1865-1945) *Dear Restless Heart* which urges the reader to have faith and hope in God:

George and Elizabeth Spindler with Lilly and Nellie who is standing   *Vera Sheard*

> *'Just trust, and trust, and trust,*
> *Until His will you know'*

It was the kind of message that would offer much comfort to Nellie when tending to wounded soldiers at the Front.

In her spare time Nellie enjoyed sewing and tatting- a type of lace edging woven by the use of a

shuttle.

She applied to the Queen Alexandra Imperial Military Nursing Service Reserve which was formed in 1902 and the Queen, Edward VII's consort, was its first president. Between August 1914 and the end of the War more than 10,000 women served with the Q.A.I.M.N.S. Reserve.

In her formal application of 9 November she gave her year of birth as 1889 which is odd because she was actually born in 1891. She was claiming to be 26 rather than 24 years of age. In view of her upbringing and character, it cannot have been a careless mistake on her part and can probably be explained by a strong desire to do her 'bit for King and Country'.

To join Q.A.I.M.N.S., a nurse had to be single or recently widowed, of good social standing, to have completed a three-year training course in a hospital approved by the War Office and importantly in Nellie's case to be over 25 years of age. By falsifying her age, therefore, Nellie could qualify on all counts. Much is known about young boys under the age of 18 lying about their age in order to join the Army but it would appear that young women were also prepared to hoodwink the authorities. So was Nellie's 'slip of the pen', her little bureaucratic fib an exception or an example of a more widespread 'economy of the truth' used by young women keen to do their duty? One wonders whether she confided with anyone else. Unfortunately we shall never know.

From Nellie's book of lecture notes   Vera Sheard

Once accepted into Q.A.I.M.N.S., Nellie worked at Whittington Military Hospital in Lichfield from 10 November 1915 until 24 April 1917. It was a unit that specialised in venereal disease which could treat up to 800 officers and men. It was the most common ailment amongst soldiers, affecting 18 per 1,000. It was treated in over 30 hospital units throughout Britain. The second most prevalent condition was trench foot which afflicted 13 per 1,000.

During her service at Lichfield, Nellie was declared fit for service overseas and was given the necessary inoculations. She crossed over to France and worked in No. 2 General Hospital at Le Havre in Normandy at the end of May. After a week she transferred to No. 42 Stationary Hospital at Amiens in the Somme before being relocated to No. 44 Casualty Clearing Station (C.C.S.) with three other Staff Nurses at Brandhoek in Belgium. Nellie must have impressed those in charge: the nursing staff of a C.C.S. was specially selected.

What was the process for assessing and treating the wounded? Firstly, a wounded British soldier would be seen by the Battalion's Medical Officer (M.O.) at a Regimental Aid Post (R.A.P.) usually situated in a dugout or ruined house near the front line. If in need of further treatment he would then be taken to an Advanced Dressing Station (A.D.S.) which was located near a road for ease of access. The next stage, if required, was a Main Dressing Station (M.D.S.) normally beyond the fire of medium range artillery. A seriously wounded soldier was transported by Field Ambulance to a C.C.S. constructed close to a railway line or waterway further behind the lines. A Casualty Clearing Station could hold 800 to 1,000 beds and was staffed by members of the R.A.M.C. (Royal Army Medical Corps), the A.S.C. (Army Service Corps) and the nurses. Major surgical operations were carried out in tents or huts. Depending on the severity of his wound, the soldier would return to duty or be sent to a Base Hospital (Stationary or General), the majority of which like Étaples and Rouen were situated on or near the coast. Extreme cases were conveyed back to 'Blighty' to, for example, Craiglockhart War Hospital in Edinburgh which dealt with shell shocked officers and Queen Mary's Convalescent Hospital at Roehampton for limbless men.

Brandhoek, which translates as 'burnt' or 'burning corner' in Flemish, is a hamlet situated along a major road and rail link between Ypres and Poperinge, the major British base on the Ypres Salient. In preparation for the Allied offensive in July 1917, later known as the Third Battle of Ypres, it was the site chosen for three C.C.S.s- No.3 (Australian), No. 32 and No. 44.

About seven miles from the front line, Brandhoek was within range of some of the German artillery. The three C.C.S.s were located nearer than normal to the front line, the aim being to treat abdominal and chest wounds as quickly as possible to limit the loss of blood and the danger of infection. According to Kate Luard, the Sister in charge of No. 32 'this venture so close to the line is in the nature of an experiment in life saving' even if it could be argued that being in the range of German artillery endangered those endeavouring to save lives.

A doctor and nurses of No. 3 Australian C.C.S. relaxing at Brandhoek in 1917 Australian War Memorial

The diaries of nurses stationed at Brandhoek contain valuable details which provide us with a realistic and moving picture of the conditions endured by the medical staff and the tragic circumstances leading up to Nellie's death.

No. 3 Australian C.C.S. and No. 32 were the first to be set up at Brandhoek. May Tilton who worked in No. 3 Australian recalled in *The Grey Battalion* that 'there were acres of shells... we were a huge city of canvas, batteries and ammunition dumps'. She mentioned 'Big Bobs', 15-inch guns being fired at the German line and that the men were 'anxious about us being so close to the lines.' The tents and huts of the C.C.S. and the guns were camouflaged with canvas painted brown, green and yellow.

Kate Luard's entry for the opening day of the battle on 31 July, described her C.C.S. as consisting of 'huge marquees on both sides of a duckboard path'. The operating theatre was a long hut and the sisters' quarters were in bell tents. She recorded that the first cases arrived at 06.30, shells were exploding around the site and that 'we get cases an hour after injury'. On 1 August everything was 'a swamp... Water in some of the wards is half-way up the legs of the beds… 44 funerals yesterday and about as many today.' After a long day she concluded 'it is getting very ghastly; the men look all so appalling when

'… huge marquees on both sides of a duckboard path'- photograph taken in 1917 at Brandhoek
Australian War Memorial

they are brought in, and so many die. I don't see how the Break-the-News Letters are going to be written, because the moment for sitting down literally never comes from 7 am to midnight. It is a good thing we are all fresh and fit.' Four days later she commented that 'we are so much in the thick of war up here…' and ominously she warned that ' there's no sort of cover anywhere (i.e. from the shells) and it is purely beastly.'

The Australian Elsie Grant from Queensland wrote to her friend Rose that, when the shelling got bad, the sisters were put into dugouts but 'how cruel it was to leave those poor helpless patients'. Whether it was to do with her experiences during the War or not, the fact is that tragically Elsie took her own life in 1927.

Nellie Spindler in nurse's uniform
Vera Sheard

When Nellie arrived with the staff of No. 44 on 10 August, there was no time for them to get accustomed to the dreadful conditions- it was quite a 'baptism of fire' on the day she was celebrating her 26th birthday. By 13.30 they had received 50 wounded men from the battlefield. Four days later the C.C.S. was subjected to a bombing raid by a Gotha, a large twin-engine biplane bomber.

The three C.C.S.s were now taking it in turns to receive 50 casualties at a time. May Tilton graphically wrote that 'torrents of rain were falling... Many of our patients died as we lifted them from the stretchers... I was appalled by the immensity and hopelessness of the task before us'. These feelings were echoed by Kate Luard: 'I feel dazed with going round the rows of silent or groaning wrecks... One has got so used to their dying that it conveys no impression beyond a vague sense of medical failure. You forget entirely that they were once civilian, that they were alive and well yesterday, that they have wives and mothers and fathers and children at home.'

Another bombing raid on 16 August killed a Medical Officer, Captain Joseph Cecil Harris, who had just gone for a rest and was playing a gramophone. He was buried at Brandhoek New Military Cemetery No. 3. All the sisters' tents and the clothes hanging on the tent pole were, according to May Tilton, 'riddled with holes'. Nellie's C.C.S. received 153 casualties that day.

The B.E.F.'s Matron-in-Chief in France and Flanders, Emma Maud McCarthy, inspected the three C.C.S.s on 18 August. Her diary entry mentioned that 'the work had been, and still was, extremely heavy ... each unit had a staff of 35 Nursing Sisters, which included 4 Surgical Teams'. She asked for names of those 'showing signs of nervousness' with the intention of replacing them- an indication of the severity of the conditions in which the nurses had to work and her appreciation of the level of stress they were facing. Kate Luard recalled that Miss McCarthy was 'much distressed at the condition' and was concerned that they were working too near to enemy shelling, that 'she thinks we are too far up'.

Next day Kate went on a stroll along the Ypres to Poperinge road and recorded that 'there was an aeroplane caught in a tree and there was a model of the present offensive laid out in miniature in a field, with dolls' rails, trenches, cemeteries, farms and dugouts- a fascinating toy.' She complained that 'the mosquitoes are appalling tonight, so are the Gothas.'

By 20 August the workload had increased dramatically and May Tilton recollected that 'patients were carried in and out all night long. Some had been lying out for days; they still lived, but not for long'. Next morning the German shelling re-started. May mentioned a 'terrific explosion' at 10.30, followed by a second shell 'getting our QM stores'. The M.O. came to convey an order from the Commanding Officer: 'You have to get into a dugout at once'. The nurses were incensed that he would not allow them to change out of their night clothes. He impressed on them the need to move fast: 'Good God! That first shell killed a night sister at 44 in bed asleep. Come on!'

He was referring to Nellie Spindler. Kate Luard gave a fuller account of the events surrounding her death on 21 August in *Unknown Warriors*: 'The business started about 10 a.m ... The third (shell) crashed between Sister E's ward in our lines and the Sisters' Quarters of No. 44 ... I found Sister E. as white as paper but smiling happily and comforting the terrified patients ... I came on to the shell-hole and the wrecked tents ... A group of stricken MOs were standing about and in one tent the Sister was dying. The piece went through her from back to front near her heart ... She was in bed asleep. The Sister who shared her tent had been sent down the day before because she couldn't stand the noise ... The Sister who should have been in the tent which was nearest was out for a walk or she would have been blown to bits ... It all made one feel sick'. Three other nurses were concussed. Nellie died in the arms of Nurse Minnie Wood who, according to Nellie's family, was also from Wakefield.

A sister in each C.C.S. was awarded the Military Medal for their conduct. Sister Alicia Kelly of No. 3 Australian refused to go to the safety of the dugout and remained, handing out basins to protect the heads of the wounded from flying metal. The 'Sister E.' in Kate Luard's account was Staff Nurse Elizabeth Eckett of the Territorial Force Nursing Service in No. 32 who also received the Military Medal: 'Although the ward was riddled twice by enemy aircraft, she continued attending the patients'. The sister in charge of No. 44 was Minnie Wood. Her M.M. citation reads: 'This lady never lost her nerve for a moment and during the whole of a most trying day, carried out her duties with the greatest steadiness and coolness'.

A study of accounts by those present at Brandhoek fills one with admiration for all the staff, especially young nurses like Nellie who had to work under such intense pressure and in appalling conditions- evidence of their dedication, resilience, sense of duty and strength of character.

Following the events at Brandhoek, patients and personnel were evacuated to Remy Siding at Lijssenthoek, south of Poperinge, where the diary of No. 10 C.C.S. recorded receiving '312 patients, mostly bad cases'. The nurses of the three C.C.S.s were sent to St. Omer to recover.

Military funeral of a nurse killed by aerial bombing of hospitals in June 1918 at Étaples   IWM Q011035

Nellie's body was taken to Lijssenthoek. Her death was registered on a Casualty Form for Officers as having been 'killed in action'. She was buried with full military honours on 22 August and laid to rest in a row of officers. The 'top brass' were well represented at her funeral- in attendance were General Hubert Gough C.O. of Fifth Army, three other generals, the Director of Medical Services of the Army, the Surgeon General and over 100 other officers. The condolence card on General Gough's wreath read 'with deepest respect' and was sent to Nellie's mother on 3 September. In 'Our Roll of Honour' section of *The British Journal of Nursing* of 8 September, Nellie was mistakenly referred to as having been killed at Abbeville in the Somme: 'The Last Post was sounded over her grave... She was right in the danger zone, but while recognizing it, her letters were hopeful and cheery'.

Nellie had written a postcard to her sister on 14 July: 'Dear Lily, (sic) I have not forgotten your birthday, would you like one like I sent Mother. With love.' The 'one' received by her mother was a

'L'ange pleureur' in Amiens Cathedral- the subject of a popular postcard sent home by British troops   A Hamilton

pendant of 'l'ange pleureur', the weeping angel of Amiens Cathedral. Lilly received one and hers, with a surround, arrived after Nellie was killed, with the words: 'I hope you will like the pendant'. The weeping angel is a famous sculpture on a 17th century tomb behind the altar. It is a tragic coincidence that Nellie's last words were about an angel that holds in his left hand an hour-glass representing the brevity of life and whose right elbow rests on a skull: the symbol of death.

In Nellie's 'field will' she had appointed her mother as her legatee. Elizabeth Spindler received £20. 15s. and 3d. including a 'gratuity', a similar amount received in the case of a soldier.

A letter from Maud McCarthy gave the family information about Nellie's grave, reassuring them that it was being well looked after and that a small memorial had been placed by the wooden cross.

It seems that Elizabeth paid two visits to Nellie's grave, each time accompanied by one of her daughters. One visit is verified by the stamp on her passport: 'Calais, 30th June 28'. Her father apparently never visited his daughter's grave. The reason can be found in his obituary which stated that one of his legs was amputated. The family believes that there had been complications due to his diabetes and the leg had become gangrenous.

There was an interesting twist to the moving story of Nellie Spindler. At the Military Hospital in Lichfield she had been befriended by Eveline Reynolds who had sent Nellie a Christmas present in 1916- a little book by Henry Turner Bailey entitled *All For You* published in 1913 in the form of a card with the greeting 'A fairy allows me three wishes... for a friend.' On 27 February 1924, six and a half years after Nellie's death, Eveline sent Nellie's mother an unusual letter from Miami in Florida. In the second paragraph she wrote tentatively that 'there is a great deal of doubt in my mind as to whether I should write this letter or not but I feel the impulse to write stronger than not'. She then related that 'I had a special reading from a trance medium and at the end, Nellie came to me speaking her name as Spindler'. Eveline admitted that she had not expected this as she was consulting the medium about family matters. Via the medium, Nellie spoke to her of 'the time we

The original marker for Nellie's grave   Vera Sheard

48

had together in the army and how hard it was'. She asked Eveline to 'take good care of the medal you got', and twice urged Eveline to write to Nellie's mother Elizabeth to encourage her 'not to worry about the signing of the papers' and that 'she was helping and sent her love to you all'. Eveline then asked Nellie for her mother's address. Nellie replied that 'I had it in my little book' and, sure enough, Eveline found it when she got back home. Eveline added that 'the medium described Nellie afterwards very accurately to me and told me she had progressed well and was doing good work now.' In the final paragraph of her letter, Eveline remarked: 'Now you will have your thoughts about this. I really believe in it and I hated not to write it as she laid such stress on it' and ended by asking Elizabeth Spindler for her reaction. Sadly we do not know if and how she responded.

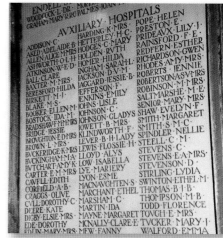

List in York Minster of women who gave their lives in the Great War- on the same panel are Nellie Spindler and Edith Cavell who was executed by the Germans for helping British soldiers to escape in 1915   A Reed

Two memorials commemorate Nellie Spindler, one in the Anglican Church of St. Andrew in Wakefield which she often attended with her family and the other in the Chapel of St James's Hospital in Leeds (originally Leeds Township Infirmary). There is also an inscription to her memory on her parents' grave in Sugar Lane Cemetery in their home town. Her name features on one of the 24 panels in the north transept of York Minster which lists the names of 1,501 women 'who gave their lives in the War 1914-1918' including 182 from Q.A.I.M.N.S. and 240 munitions workers. The C.W.G.C. which cares for Nellie's grave, commemorates more than 770 women who died in the Great War. Many of those died when ships were hit by a mine or sunk by U-boats. Others died through illness or accident. A number of nurses killed in France and Belgium, unlike Nellie, were well behind the lines when struck by aerial bombing at, for example, St. Omer or Étaples. The youngest recorded death was of a 17 year old nurse and the oldest to die was 66.

The contribution made by girls and women to the war effort cannot be underestimated, whether they for example made shells, nursed wounded soldiers or drove ambulances. Many of those who, like Nellie, served abroad, were confronted with appalling conditions and had to cope with terrifying experiences. Nellie did not return. Those who did, suffered greatly from mental anguish and emotional distress and like the soldiers who survived, they too had to adapt to a much changed society.

Staff Nurse Nellie Spindler's grave at Lijssenthoek   A Hamilton

NELLIE SPINDLER:

Born:	10 August 1891 in Wakefield, eldest daughter of Elizabeth and George Spindler
Education:	Eastmoor Council School, Wakefield and Leeds Township Infirmary
Occupation:	Nursing
Unit/ Regiment:	Queen Alexandra's Imperial Military Nursing Service Reserve (Q.A.I.M.N.S.)
Rank:	Staff nurse
Died:	21 August 1917, Third Battle of Ypres (Passchendaele)
Age:	26
Buried:	Lijssenthoek Military Cemetery, Poperinge XVI. A. 3.
Inscription:	A NOBLE TYPE OF GOOD, HEROIC WOMANHOOD (from H.W. Longfellow's poem Santa Filomena, a tribute to Florence Nightingale)

HERBERT MORRIS

'I am troubled with my head… I reported to the doctor and he gave me no medicine or anything'

Herbert Morris lived in the south east of Jamaica. His exact date of birth is unclear and little is known about his education and employment although he was competent enough to write letters home to his mother from France and Belgium. As he lived in an agricultural area of Jamaica, he may have been employed on a farm cultivating bananas or sugar cane.

Soldiers of the British West Indies Regiment in camp on the Albert to Amiens Road September 1916   IWM Q001202

After massive losses on the Western Front, the British Army was desperate for an increase in manpower and between November 1916 and March 1917 a recruitment drive in the Caribbean encouraged Herbert Morris to enlist with the British West Indies Regiment. Whatever his line of work, it was not as attractive an option as joining the war effort in defence of the 'mother country' and it would appear that he was prepared to conceal his true age. He was at least a year under the legal age for recruitment.

Herbert Morris was one of over 15,000 black soldiers to serve in the British Army in the Great War. Doubts have been cast as to whether Herbert was a black volunteer but 'whites' in the main were confined to the officer class and his place of birth and army rank would suggest it is unlikely that Private Morris was a white West Indian.

The British West Indian Labour Corps training in England
The Times History of the War 1915

He was assigned to the 6th Battalion of the British West Indies Regiment and attended training at the Swallowfield Military Camp in Kingston. The Regiment set sail for France in early April on *H.M.S. Briton* and arrived at Brest on the French coast on 17 April 1917. Herbert was fortunate to survive the journey during which troops died of measles or pneumonia. It was hardly a great start to their time at the Front- there were further deaths and the entire unit was isolated because of mumps and treated for hookworm.

The Battalion was soon posted to the Ypres Salient. Regulations in the 1912 *Manual of Military Law* stated that those not of 'pure European descent' in effect 'negroes and persons of colour', were barred from military service. Men of black skin were not considered reliable or disciplined enough for armed combat and their presence might affect 'white' morale; the 6/ British West Indies Regiment was tasked, therefore, with transport and communication duties and Herbert's 'B' Company was involved in back-breaking work handling and transporting ammunition at dumps, railheads and batteries throughout the Salient. Although the men in the photograph of the British West Indies Regiment are holding rifles, it would appear from the Battalion War Diary that they did not fight on the front line. During the Battalion's time at the Front, 17 men were killed and 87 wounded, a low proportion compared to units fighting in the trenches. When, for example, they were posted in 1918 to Taranto in Italy where they were engaged in loading and unloading ships, they were congratulated by the Base Commandant on the work they had been doing 'however unattractive and distasteful it might be' and that it was as 'useful towards winning the war as that of the troops in the firing line itself.'

Springtime on the Western Front in 1917 would have presented an unwelcome setting for a young man used to the sun and gentle pace of life in Jamaica where the temperature rarely dips below 20°C. The thunderous noise of shell fire and the ravages of war took their toll on the young man's mental stability.

On 20 August 'B' Company was ordered to travel by lorry to 'Essex Farm' and 'Burnt Farm' north of Ypres. When the lorry arrived, there was no sign of Herbert Morris. He was discovered the next day by Military Police wandering around Boulogne 'wearing a steel helmet and uniform but had no rifle, equipment or gas helmet.' His failure to produce a leave warrant led to his arrest and he was charged with 'desertion from active service near the front line' and his case came before a Field General Court Martial which convened on 7 September. It was chaired by Lieutenant Colonel Nutt of the 7/ Royal Warwicks and consisted of Major A. Lloyd-Baker of the 1/4 Oxfordshire and Buckinghamshire, Major M. Grimes of the Nottinghamshire and Derbyshire Regiment and Captain F.S. Baker of the 3/ Seaforth Highlanders. A trained barrister was in attendance to advise on procedural matters.

The Court Martial system allowed a defendant the support of a 'prisoner's friend' but for whatever reasons, Herbert had to face his prosecutors alone. After the finding Lieutenant Andrews asserted that 'the accused has never given me any trouble. He is well behaved. His intelligence is higher than that of the ordinary men in my platoon.' Lieutenant Burke 'heard no complaint of the accused's conduct except the two offences revealed in his conduct sheet.' Corporal Russell considered that Morris was a 'willing worker'.

Herbert Morris was in all probability depressed, frightened and isolated, yearning for a return home to the peace and warmth of Jamaica. In his defence statement, Morris contended that 'I am troubled with my head. I cannot stand the sound of the guns. I reported to the doctor and he gave me no medicine or anything. He gave me no satisfaction.' It is likely that the young man was suffering from shell shock. He was entitled to the production of medical evidence at his trial but none was forthcoming; he was also permitted a right of appeal but despite the presence of a monitoring legal officer, it was denied to him.

Two key factors counted against the defendant. Firstly his disciplinary track record was blemished-on 3 June he was fined for 'fighting in his billet' and for absenting himself without leave on 16 July, for which he received 14 days of Field Punishment Number No. 1. This entailed being tied to a post or wheel for two hours regardless of the weather, a practice known as 'crucifixion', a barbaric form of torture that was followed for the rest of the day by hard labour, punishments that failed to change Herbert's behaviour. He was in such a depressed and muddled state that he immediately reoffended.

The second factor that consigned Morris to an early death in 1917 was the desire to enforce discipline at a time when Field Marshal Sir Douglas Haig was planning a major September offensive. The authorities were nervous that rioting by disaffected Chinese and Egyptian labourers at Étaples might spread.

The Field General Court Martial passed the 'extreme penalty of death'. In many instances a Court's sentence of execution was commuted to a lesser punishment so did Herbert Morris stand a chance of being given a 'stay of execution'? Why was his age not taken into consideration? It would appear that he was only 17 and below the legal age. The authorities were unprepared to go through a time-consuming search for proof. The final stage of the process was when Haig duly signed the death warrant. Like the young Ulsterman James Crozier (see p.235), Herbert Morris would face the firing squad to deter other potential deserters.

Private Herbert Morris was shot in the courtyard behind Poperinge Town Hall at 6.10 a.m. on 20 September 1917. His gravestone in Poperinghe New Military Cemetery makes no mention of the fact that he was executed by his own side. He was commemorated in the same way as other soldiers but he was a young man whose life was sacrificed at the altar of military expedience... 'for the sake of example'.

In 2006 the Labour Government's Armed Forces Military Act granted a pardon to 306 British and Empire soldiers who were Shot at Dawn. It was officially recognised that Herbert Morris was 'one of the many victims of the First World War and that his execution was not a fate he deserved.' His sentence, however, was not overturned.

HERBERT MORRIS:

Born:	1898 at Riversdale, St. Catherine, Jamaica, son of William and Ophelia Morris
Education:	Unknown
Occupation:	Labourer
Unit/ Regiment:	6/ British West Indies
Rank:	Private
Died:	Executed 6.10 a.m. on 20 September 1917
Age:	17
Buried:	Poperinghe New Military Cemetery II. F.45.

This cemetery was set up near Casualty Clearing Stations. There are 677 Empire burials of which three are unidentified. It has the largest number of Shot at Dawn burials, a total of 17, including one officer, 2nd Lieutenant Eric S. Poole of the 11/ West Yorks for desertion and a Canadian of French descent for the same offence. Ironically he was called Private Come Laliberté. The architect was Sir Reginald Blomfield

SCHEDULE.

Number, Rank, Name and Unit of accused (a)	Offence charged	Plea	Finding, and if Convicted, Sentence (b)	How dealt with by Confirming Officer
no. 7429 Pte. Herbert Morris, 6th (S) Battn. British West Indies Regt. a soldier of the regular Forces	A.A. Sec. 12 (1 a) "When on active Service deserting His Majesty's Services" in that he, in the Field on the 20th of August 1917, when warned for duty, in the neighbourhood of the front line absented himself from his detachment until apprehended by the military Police at BOULOGNE on the 21st of August 1917.	Not Guilty	Guilty Death	£ Reserved. J.C. Blacklow Lt. Gn O.C. XVIII. Corps Confirmed D. Haig. F.M. 15 Sep. 17

The sentence of death by firing squad, confirmed by Sir Douglas Haig National Archives WO71/ 594

This document records that

Pte Herbert Morris of the 6th Battalion,
British West Indies Regiment

who was executed for desertion on
20 September 1917 is pardoned under Section
359 of the Armed Forces Act 2006.

The pardon stands as recognition that he was
one of many victims of the First World War
and that execution was not a fate he deserved.

Secretary of State for Defence

*The 2006 Armed Forces Act granted a pardon
to Private Herbert Morris signed by the
Secretary of State for Defence Des Browne*
National Archives WO/71/ 594

*The grave of one of only two
Army officers Shot at Dawn-
for desertion*   J Kerr

*Private Herbert Morris's
grave in Poperinghe New
Military Cemetery*
J Kerr

53

NOEL CHAVASSE, DOUBLE V.C.

'My blood is not that heroic'

When he first arrived at the Front in October 1914, Noel Chavasse wrote to his anxious mother and father and explained his likely role there. A member of the Royal Army Medical Corps, he was attached to the 1/10 King's (Liverpool Regiment), more commonly known as the Liverpool Scottish. He informed them that 'doctors are not allowed in the trenches, so really I shall run very little risk at all unnecessarily; my blood is not that heroic.'

Noel Chavasse of the R.A.M.C.
Master and Fellows of St Peter's College, Oxford

Noel Chavasse's personal 'risk assessment' would prove woefully wide of the mark. For nearly three years he would work tirelessly to tend to the wounded and dying in the most perilous of locations with no thought whatsoever to his own safety. He felt he had a duty to help the wounded: 'I could not bear to think of our wounded lying in trenches which would be shelled. They get so terrified.'

Noel and his twin brother Christopher were born on 9 November 1884 in Oxford where their father was Rector of St. Peter-le-Bailey. It was an anxious time for Francis and Edith Chavasse; their twins were so weak and poorly that their christening was delayed for seven weeks and soon afterwards they contracted typhoid fever.

The boys recovered and received instruction from a governess until the age of 12 when they went to Magdalen College School in Oxford. Noel excelled at athletics and performed well academically, even if spelling remained a mystery to him for the rest of his life. The twins were so similar that they were required to wear different coloured ties which they would swap to confuse their teachers!

Noel's school reports do highlight a propensity for showing too much interest 'in other boys' mischief.' Several years later his assessment of his school days was unduly harsh: 'I don't look back on my school days with any pride whatsoever. I see now I slacked terribly or rather worked without heart and so without any result.'

Francis Chavasse was appointed Principal of Wycliffe College, founded in 1877, for the training of Anglican ministers. The family enjoyed the space and freedom of the large house attached to the college in the Banbury Road but in 1900 their circumstances changed dramatically when Prime Minister Lord Salisbury nominated him to be the next Bishop of Liverpool.

Noel and Christopher attended Liverpool College from 1900 to 1904 and both were accepted by Trinity College, Oxford where Noel studied Natural Sciences and Christopher's chosen subject was History. The identical twins caused a stir in 1907 when they were awarded 'Blues' for athletics ; the twins were conspicuously successful in the 'Varsity' match- Christopher won the quarter-mile race against Cambridge. Noel came second and triumphed in the 100 yards. In 1908 they both participated in trials for the British Olympic athletics squad but fell short of the qualifying time.

Noel achieved a first class degree. With typical modesty he admitted to his sister Dorothea amusement and surprise at his achievement and how he was often met 'with incredulous smiles!' He could now start his medical studies at the Radcliffe Infirmary in Oxford. Christopher, however, failed to complete his degree, much to his brother's amazement, but despite this setback he followed his father into the Church, finishing his career as the Bishop of Rochester from 1942 to 1960.

Noel returned to Liverpool in 1909 as a newly qualified doctor and took up a post at the Royal Southern Hospital. He studied orthopaedics under the tutelage of Robert Jones, a renowned specialist in the field and passed his surgeon's exams on the second attempt in 1910.

In his university vacations Chavasse developed an interest in social work and philanthropy. Like the England rugby captain Ronnie Poulton Palmer, he considered it his duty to deter poor children from their 'wretchedness, vice and future criminality'. Now based full time in Liverpool he volunteered to help in the Grafton Street Industrial School, an institution for homeless boys in the Toxteth area of the city. Driven by his 'Muscular Christianity', he led bible sessions and introduced the boys to various sports. He was involved in organising and taking part in annual camps.

During his student days he joined the Oxford University O.T.C. Medical Unit with Christopher and their younger brother Aidan. Noel was underwhelmed by drills and training but was pleased to be doing his 'duty' rather than being a mere 'flannelled fool' or 'muddied oaf'.

He registered with the Liverpool Scottish as a surgeon-lieutenant in October 1912. His medical training covered bacteriology, infectious diseases and vaccination- knowledge of which would prove invaluable at the Front.

Noel had every reason to feel contented early in 1914. He was a qualified orthopaedic surgeon and a well-regarded medical officer. His philanthropic work with deprived children was richly fulfilling. Love for his cousin Gladys Chavasse had blossomed even if her father, the celebrated surgeon Sir Thomas Chavasse of Barnt Green near Birmingham, was lukewarm to the concept of marriage between first cousins.

He was disappointed to be sent by the R.A.M.C. to Chester Castle where he examined the medical condition of troops and vaccinated them. He was assiduously preparing himself for the day when his skills would be tested on the battlefield: 'I am really trying to train myself in every way I can to be useful and am reading hard.'

Noel was desperate to return to the Liverpool Scottish and plaintively wrote to his father: 'I have a great longing to take care of a regiment. When I go out with the Scottish boys I feel quite paternal and love keeping them fit and dressing their minor injuries… If ever I get sent to the Front with a regiment, I shall shed tears of joy.'

A 'tearful' Chavasse, therefore, was restored to the Liverpool Scottish at their camp in Edinburgh where he vaccinated the entire 1,000-strong battalion against typhoid. He was struck by the ill-health of recruits and in a letter to his mother suggested that 'the sickness, colds and influenza is due to them being clerks, unused to roughing it and unused to kilts.' He trained a squad of 16 stretcher-bearers and was keen to inculcate the importance of good hygiene in their work practices.

The Battalion started further training in Tunbridge Wells in October and on 1 November sailed from Southampton. 'Goodbye my dear father, I am going to do my best to be a faithful soldier of Jesus Christ and King George.' His twin brother Christopher was by now in France, acting as a chaplain to Number 10 General Hospital at St. Nazaire in Brittany.

The Liverpool Scottish arrived at the British front line on the Ypres Salient at Kemmel in late November. It was bitterly cold and an unforeseen medical problem he had to deal with was the effect of rain, followed by hard frost, on the pleated kilts worn by the Liverpool Scottish which froze into solid glass-like shards and, in many cases, caused lacerations to the men's legs followed by infection.

One of many problems he faced was 'trench foot' which badly affected his men whose feet suffered in the wet and muddy trenches of Flanders. Over 400 men were put out of action because of the condition. 'Doc' Chavasse, as he was affectionately known, was insistent that the men kept their feet clean and dry whenever possible and he requested his sisters in Liverpool to send out, at his expense, 1,000 pairs of warm woolly socks for the men. His treatments of 'trench foot' included the use of whale oil.

Chavasse insisted on cleanliness and basic hygiene: 'My orderlies are learning quite nice habits like washing their hands before each dressing.' An effective laundry and regular baths were essential- in one week 200 shirts and kilts were washed and ironed. He regularly checked the state of the men's skin, feet and hair. He often congratulated himself that for three years there were no outbreaks of scabies amongst his men which he put down to his régime.

The Battalion was based in Belgium during 1915 and fought in the Second Battle of Ypres when the Germans first used chemical gas. Noel's faith helped him through the horrors that confronted him: 'I ask God daily to give me courage and patience for naturally I am not overburdened with either.' He was pained by the continual loss of life. He was profoundly affected by the death of one of his party of stretcher-bearers who was 'a fine, upstanding, broad shouldered lad of twenty, the cheeriest and coolest of the party, strong, willing and wonderfully deft and tender with the wounded. I feel his death very much.'

Noel Chavasse dealt with many men who were suffering from the nervous and physical exhaustion of shell shock. He recommended, whenever possible, that they be transferred to lighter duties. The Battalion historian recorded: 'The Doctor had a genius for picking out those men who were near a breakdown, either in nerve or general health but not yet so run down as to be hospital cases. Rather than send them into the trenches, where their collapse sooner or later was inevitable, he kept them at his aid post as light duty men, where in comparative comfort they had a chance to rest and recover.' It was a philosophy that brought him into conflict with his commanding officers.

Officers were expected to act as role models but for many doctors and chaplains near the front line, the intensity of the warfare and its shocking effects on the combatants proved too much to handle- at least Noel was able to write on 19 April: 'I am now in the proud position of being the only regimental doctor who has not broken down.' In August 1916 he was once ticked off for entering front line trenches which, it was pointed out, were for soldiers not doctors but his reaction was typical: 'I think it cheers the men up if a man like myself who is practically a civilian is seen in the trenches.'

On a number of occasions the Chavasse twins met behind the lines. Many hours were spent discussing one topic which exercised them greatly- the execution of deserters and 'cowards'. Christopher was almost inconsolable about young men being Shot at Dawn. On 31 May Noel wrote to his father: 'Poor jaded and terrified boys of eighteen are shot for shirking the cruel hardships of winter; it fills us with dismay and rage.' A total of 306 British and Empire soldiers were executed by the authorities during the War, and by the end of April 1915, the number had reached 31, although none was from the Liverpool Scottish.

Before the War crowds would have flocked to county cricket matches to see great players like Colin Blythe and Percy Jeeves in action (p.112 and 253). At the Front the somewhat less talented Chavasse and members of the Battalion found a grassy area (quite a feat) and played a game of what they described as 'stump' rather than French cricket! He boasted to his father of 'terrific scores of 5 not out and 6 not out'! It was a 'curious game because there was an aeroplane watcher, and if he saw a Hun aeroplane he blew his whistle, and fielders and batsmen fled in a little copse in which the onlookers sat.'

The Liverpool Scottish were involved in the horrors of fighting at Hooge near Ypres in June and July 1915. German trenches were captured but at a considerable cost. Noel's surgical skills were in constant demand- the lip of one young private rescued from No Man's Land was badly cut in several places but after pulling out two teeth and bits of broken bone, Chavasse inserted stitches and was delighted when 'slowly a mouth reappeared from the ragged mess.' Another private had 'lost the whole side of his head and a large part of his brain.' Little wonder, therefore, that doctors and padres were being traumatised.

Sympathetic and caring as he was, Noel Chavasse was damning about 'shirkers'. He told his father in November 1915 that 'we always have the old soldier who wants a day of rest.' His reward was 'castor oil and duty if I can catch him'! He wrote on 24 September of a Highlander who had shot himself: 'When he gets well the poor fellow will be court martialled or given penal servitude I fear. It seems like tending a dead man but it cannot be helped. He seems a poor specimen of humanity.'

The young surgeon had been recommended for the M.C. for his efforts at Hooge for working in No Man's Land for 48 hours until 'he was satisfied that there were no further casualties.' Due to a bureaucratic hitch, it was not awarded until January 1916. Unusually there was no posting in *The London Gazette*. He played down his promotion to captain arguing that 'there is no glory attached to it.'

Chavasse continued to perform heroics but received no further promotions. He did not suffer fools gladly and his trenchant criticism of the *modus operandi* of the R.A.M.C. was not received with grateful thanks. His policy towards shell shock and his hostility to the official blind eye turned towards brothels and the consequent spread of V.D., ended his chances of further promotion.

Contrast his views with those of Frank Crozier who rose from being a private in 1914 to brigadier general in 1916: 'He who hopes to wage war without wine and women is living in a fool's paradise' and 'I think nothing of "throwing away" a thousand men in half an hour, providing a position is gained or held.' Chavasse and Crozier's paths probably never crossed- which was just as well…

After a year in the Ypres sector Noel Chavasse M.C. reflected that he was missing many 'jolly faces' lost in the actions at Hooge and Sanctuary Wood, particularly half of his 16 stretcher-bearers. He sent home a photograph of the 'stump cricket' match which he considered to be 'of great pathetic value as so many of the players are now dead.' By 16 October 1916 he could boast that his stretcher-bearers, 'strong as lions', had accumulated two D.C.M.s and two M.M.s.

Chavasse pointedly made every effort to improve morale. He begged books, magazines and copies of *The Liverpool Echo* which were kept in a common room and canteen he had established, warmed by a stove sent from his home city. He sent a £10 cheque home in April 1915 for a gramophone for his men, admitting a few weeks later that 'the gramophone still continues to be a great success and kind people are sending me records for it.'

His life was underpinned by his strong religious belief which offered him spiritual calm during the horrors of battle. 'The Holy Communion is the best comfort to the nerves I know.' He felt bereft when he lost his Book of Common Prayer which he had used at the graveside of many of the fallen Liverpool Scottish.

The Battalion was transferred in January 1916 from the 9th Brigade, 3rd Division to the 166th Brigade of the 55th (West Lancashire) Division. Noel went on a short leave in February during which

he visited Barnt Green and proposed to Gladys. He was delighted when she accepted: 'I can hardly believe my good fortune… because I used to think I should never get Gladys, I don't know why she is going to have me even now, for I am not much of a catch and she has been the prize of the neighbourhood.'

During another period of leave in the first week of June 1916, Noel received his M.C. at Buckingham Palace but without Gladys at his side, for she was not allowed to join him at the ceremony.

The Battalion spent the first month of the Battle of the Somme in reserve;

A reconstruction of an Advanced Dressing Station
A Reed photo by kind permission of Avril Williams

Chavasse was devastated by the wanton slaughter. They were involved in the action at Guillemont on 9 August at 4.20 a.m. when they attacked during a German bombardment. Casualties were heavy: 169 killed and 27 missing. Chavasse worked day and night with a team of stretcher-bearers to bring in the wounded. During the hours of darkness he whistled and called out to the wounded men to indicate to him their whereabouts. He ignored snipers' bullets and fearlessly carried out his duties, on one occasion just 25 yards from the German advanced trenches.

His 'conspicuous bravery' and 'devotion to duty' were acknowledged by the award of the V.C. as cited in the *London Gazette* of 26 October: 'During an attack he tended the wounded in the open all day, under heavy fire, frequently in view of the enemy'.

The Chavasse family at the Bishop's Palace in Liverpool were inundated with letters of congratulation and at the Front, Noel and friends celebrated at Elverdinghe Château. He dismissed his receipt of the British Army's highest award for bravery with typical self-effacing modesty: 'I don't think I really earned it as many have had to do, but deep in me I prize it more than I can say.' He accepted the 'prize' in February 1917 when on leave. Such was his newly-found fame that he featured in the V.C. set of Gallaher cigarette cards.

The tone of Noel's letters home changed noticeably in 1917. He was stressed and war weary. He was unguardedly hostile towards the 'top brass'. He was critical of the workload expected of the Liverpool Scottish: three days in the front line trenches and two in the support trenches was too demanding but 'of course this, I suppose must be a military necessity… our Higher Commands are so aloof that I doubt if they and their Staff are really in touch with and understand the battalions and I get the impression myself of a want of organisation and full mastery of detail.' Hardly a resounding endorsement!

The area where Noel Chavasse operated in August 1916 between what is now Guillemont Road Cemetery and Trônes Wood   *J Kerr*

He was unimpressed with the chaplains he encountered- particularly one who took leave in March 1916; Chavasse was angered that padres would take their allocation of the Battalion's leave at the expense of the more deserving infantryman. A year later he bemoaned his failure 'to galvanise our padre, the Rev. "Washout" into a little activity… He is absolutely useless and never visits the men unless they go to hospital.' Nor did his own profession escape Chavasse's barbed comments: 'The doctor has ceased to be considered the kindly, wise man, ever eager to help the sick and alleviate the suffering. He is looked upon as a lazy "cushy", windy man, who performs his job most perfunctorily and is often given to strong drink…' In fairness to padres and doctors who were not trained soldiers, the War was taking its mental toll.

Noel was looking over his shoulder, irritated that he had to be more of a disciplinarian than a doctor, required to speak sharply to potential malingerers at sick parades. He resented that some of the 'fatuous remarks' he would make as he strolled round tents, would be 'dished up again at a battalion concert, by a corporal who thinks he can take me off.' He was beginning to allow tittle-tattle to get to him. He too was being adversely affected by the strains of war.

He faced a thorny dilemma in June. He was offered the post of surgeon at a Base Hospital which would have offered him safety and the opportunity to employ his skills in a more hygienic environment and with better facilities. He was sorely tempted; by the end of the War he would be a skilled surgeon and would not have to go on refresher courses. It would do no harm for future job applications. He felt, however, that it was a job for an older man and it would be too comfortable: 'Young fellows like me ought to be with the fighting man and I am by no means done yet.' He admitted that 'I don't think I could leave the young lads here to fight it out while I luxuriated in a coastal town.'

There were contrasting fortunes for the Chavasse family. Noel's younger brother Aidan, of the same regiment, went missing in action on 1 July 1917 at Observatory Ridge, five miles from Ypres. His body was never found and his name is registered on the Menin Gate. His twin brother Christopher was awarded an M.C. Sadly, Noel never had a chance to congratulate him. Their sister May was Mentioned in Despatches by Field Marshal Douglas Haig for hospital work at Étaples and brother Francis Bernard was awarded the M.C. for actions at Passchendaele. Their cousin 28 year old Captain Arthur Chavasse of the R.A.M.C. had died the previous year of pneumonia and was buried at Ste. Marie Cemetery, Le Havre.

Gladys travelled to Paris to see her fiancé. She presented Noel with a dog called Jell to safeguard him from the ever present rat population, a role at which he would prove singularly unsuccessful. Marriage was a serious topic of conversation for the couple- Noel admitted that 'it's a bit pathetic to have to leave a bronze cross to a nephew or a cousin twice removed'. Their plan, therefore, was to marry at Christmas…

The Liverpool Scottish returned to the Ypres sector in late July and were based in the trenches at Wieltje. As part of the Passchendaele Offensive they advanced on 31 July at 3.50 a.m. and progressed towards Steenbeek stream supported by a tank which broke through the German barbed wire. By 7.45 a.m. trenches had been captured and Noel set up a Regimental Aid Post in a small captured dugout at Setques Farm where he could do no more than patch up the wounded. Ill-advisedly, Chavasse came out of the dugout to let his men know where he was located. He was hit in the head by a shell splinter. He went out to search for more wounded men despite his own injury and without a second thought set to work with a German doctor to assist the injured in hopelessly unhygienic conditions. He was wounded twice more but insisted on continuing. When he did stop for a rest, he was hit in the stomach by a shell and despite being fatally wounded, he managed to crawl on all fours slowly and agonisingly inched his way to a dugout occupied by men of the Loyal North Lancashire Regiment. He was stretchered to Casualty Clearing Station No. 32 at Brandhoek where he was treated. Sister K.E. Luard wrote that Noel was 'quickly X-rayed, operated on, shrapnel found, holes sewn up, salined and put to bed.' His abdominal injuries were so severe that on Saturday 4 August, the third anniversary of the outbreak of the War, Noel Chavasse died at 1.00 p.m.

He was treated by Ida Leedam who had worked with Noel at the Royal Southern Hospital in Liverpool. In a letter to Gladys, she comforted her with her fiancé's final words: 'Give her my love, tell her duty called and called me to obey.'

Sister Luard recorded in her diary that three other nurses and 'a lot of the M.O.s' were among those who attended Noel Chavasse's funeral on Sunday 5 August. Two of the M.O.s wheeled the stretcher and lowered him into his grave. 'His horse was led in front and then the pipers and masses of kilted officers followed. Our padre with his one arm, Father E.H. (Eustace Hill), looked like a Prophet towering over everybody and saying it all without a book. After the Blessing one piper came to the graveside (which was a large pit full of dead soldiers sewn up in canvas) and played a lament. Then his Colonel (Lieutenant-Colonel J.R. Davison) who particularly loved him, stood and saluted him in his grave. It was fine but horribly choky.'

Captain Noel Chavasse, the Great War's only double V.C. was buried in one of three cemeteries adjoining the Brandhoek Clearing Stations alongside men he had worked with and admired, not least his 20 year old batman Private Charles Arundel Rudd who died on 10 August 1917.

The Bar to Noel Chavasse's Victoria Cross was announced in the *London Gazette* on 14 September 1917. The citation described his final hours: 'Though severely wounded early in the action whilst carrying a wounded soldier to the Dressing Station, Capt. Chavasse refused to leave his post, and for two days not only continued to perform his duties, but in addition went out repeatedly under heavy fire to search for and attend to the wounded who were lying out. This devoted and gallant officer subsequently died of his wounds.'

His father poignantly wrote: 'Would that it had been God's will that he had lived to receive it.' The Bishop of Liverpool consoled himself that his son was 'a hero… a man of valour because he was a man of God.' He and Edith thanked God for their son's 'beautiful life spent in helping others, and crowned at last by his noble death, for the sure and certain hope that he is with Christ.' They chose an apposite epitaph for their son's grave from the King James Version of the Bible- St. John Chapter 15, Verse 13: 'Greater love hath no man than this, that a man lay down his life for his friends.'

Brigadier General Wilkinson, Commander of the 166th Infantry Brigade, wrote to the Chavasses: 'I constantly met your son and appreciated his work. He was quite the most gallant and modest man I have ever met, and I should think the best liked. What he did for his battalion of the Liverpool Scottish was wonderful, and his loss to them is irreparable. I do not believe a man of a more noble character exists.'

Noel's twin brother Christopher, who lost a leg at the Front, not surprisingly was heart broken by the news: 'My loss of my twin was like amputation- I felt half of me had gone for we were extremely close, so that I knew when he died, though he was 80 miles from me on the battle front… I still mourn my Noel every day of my life and have done so for forty four years… sometimes I wake in the morning, feeling I have been with him in my sleep and I believe that our spirits have been together.'

For Gladys there would not be a pre-Christmas wedding- she was inconsolable on receiving the news from Noel's brother Francis Bernard. Although she married the Rev. James Colquhoun in 1919, she nonetheless made her pilgrimage to Brandhoek New Military Cemetery and every year on 4 August recorded Noel's death in *The Times*.

The historian of the 1/10 King's (Liverpool Scottish) highlights the importance of 'duty' to Noel Chavasse; his bravery was not of the 'reckless or flamboyant type but the far finer bravery that sprang from his determination that nothing should stand in the way of whatever he considered his duty.' He saw himself as a doctor treating his patients who happened to be in the danger zone.

Noel Chavasse's parents received a letter from King George V who was 'grieved to hear of the death', recalling that he remembered with pleasure 'presenting the V.C. to your son and that he previously wore the Military Cross.'

Moving stealthily and athletically around No Man's Land, his 'electric torch' flashing round for wounded soldiers, Noel Chavasse did so without any consideration for his personal safety. He was selfless and modest about his achievements the greatest of which was to sacrifice his life for others. Deeply Christian, he was the bravest of men who rescued, saved and healed those in his beloved battalion but unlike the majority of V.C. holders, he did not kill a single enemy soldier. Contrary to what he self-effacingly claimed, his blood was indeed heroic.

The only gravestone on the Western Front to have two V.C.s engraved on it-Noel Chavasse's in Brandhoek New Military Cemetery   *J Kerr*

NOEL CHAVASSE Double V.C.:

Born:	9 November 1884, son of the Rev. Francis and Edith Chavasse of 36 New Inn Hall Street, Oxford
Education:	Magdalen College School, Oxford, Liverpool College, and Trinity College, Oxford
Occupation:	Surgeon
Unit/ Regiment:	Royal Army Medical Corps, attached to 1/10 King's (Scottish), Liverpool
Rank:	Captain
Died:	Of wounds, 4 August 1917 Third Battle of Ypres (Passchendaele)
Age:	32
Decorations:	V.C. and Bar, M.C.
Buried:	Brandhoek New Military Cemetery III.B.15. Noel Chavasse's gravestone is the only one on the Western Front with two V.C. medals engraved on it
Inscription:	"GREATER LOVE HATH NO MAN THAN THIS THAT A MAN LAY DOWN HIS LIFE FOR HIS FRIENDS" (King James Bible John 15:13)

Also buried in the cemetery is Chavasse's batman Charles Rudd in VI.B.11. with the inscription INTO THY HANDS O LORD I COME. Brandhoek is situated between Poperinge and Ypres and was used by Field Ambulances. There were 530 burials in July and August 1917 and there are 28 German graves. It was designed by Sir Reginald Blomfield

A record of the Chavasse family's contribution to the War effort. Clockwise from the top left: Noel, his father, Christopher, Francis, May and Aidan   *British Library Board (The Daily Sketch)*

HARRY BAND

'He was hacked to bits and spat on and his eyes gouged out'

Sergeant Harry Band of the 15th Battalion of the Canadian Infantry died during the Second Battle of Ypres in 1915 only seven months after enlisting. The exact date of his death is uncertain but evidence suggests it occurred on 24 April. He was one of 6,928 Canadians who died in the Ypres Salient and for whom there is no known grave but whose names are commemorated on the Menin Gate in Ypres. The nature of his death has caused great controversy ever since- did he die of chlorine gas poisoning? Was he shelled to death or was his demise of a distinctly more sinister nature?

From 25 April 1915 rumours were rife in the trenches on the Ypres Salient that one or more Canadian soldiers had been 'crucified' by the Germans in the St. Julien area. These were picked up by journalists and on 9 May, *The Times* ran a piece from their Paris-based correspondent entitled 'Torture of a Canadian Officer'. He reported that during the previous week, 'a large number of Canadian soldiers wounded in the fighting round Ypres, arrived at the Base Hospital at Versailles. They all told a story of how one of their officers had been pinned to a wall by bayonets thrust through his hands and feet, another bayonet had been driven through his throat, and, finally, he was riddled with bullets.' The wounded Canadians claimed that some Royal Dublin Fusiliers had witnessed the act 'with their own eyes' and their officers had been talking at length about the incident.

The episode was mentioned again seven days later in *The Times* by a 'special correspondent' who added more detail to the story in an article entitled 'The Crucifixion of a Canadian': 'The unfortunate victim was a sergeant, transfixed to the wooden fence of a farm building.' It was suggested that the man was dead before being pinned to the fence and that 'the enemy in his insensate rage and hate of the English wreaked his vengeance on the lifeless body of his foe.'

Sergeant Harry Band originally from Montrose, Scotland, served with the 48th Highlanders of Canada for three years then with the 15th Battalion of the Canadian Infantry

The Canadian's death was reported in Canada by *The Toronto Star* on 11 May 1915. Its report was based on evidence provided by Captain R.A.S. Allen who later died of wounds in a Base Hospital at Boulogne; he maintained that a Canadian sergeant was tied to a tree and pierced 60 times by German bayonets. *The Canadian Morning Post* reported that a body nailed to a door with hands and feet pierced with bayonets and riddled with bullets was seen by a group of Royal Dublin Fusiliers.

The Times report prompted Sir Robert Houston M.P. to raise the question of the 'crucifixion' in the House of Commons. He asked the Under Secretary of State for War, Harold Tennant, on 12 May whether he had received any information regarding 'the crucifixion of three Canadian soldiers recently captured by the Germans who nailed them with bayonets to the side of a wooden structure.' In reply Houston was told that the War Office had received no details of such an atrocity having been carried out by the Germans.

A week later on 19 May, Houston pressed for information to verify reports that about 40 wounded Canadians were bayoneted in a barn and that one of them, a sergeant, when alive, had been fastened to a large village crucifix from which the figure of Christ had been removed. Houston asked if 'crucifixion of our soldiers is becoming a practice of the Germans?' Again Tennant stonewalled, replying that no information had been forthcoming and that enquiries were ongoing.

After the War Germany was incensed by the crucifixion accusations and their ire was provoked by an exhibition held at the Royal Academy of Arts in London, sponsored by the Canadian newspaper **61**

The controversial sculpture Canada's Golgotha *by Francis Derwent Wood*   *Canadian War Museum*

magnate Lord Beaverbrook. The aim of the exhibition was to highlight Canada's contribution to the Allied Victory in 1918 and one exhibit, number 186, *Canada's Golgotha* by the British sculptor Francis Derwent Wood, depicted a Canadian soldier's crucifixion. The bronze statue represented German cruelty and criminality- the soldier was a Christ-like symbol of goodness destroyed by evil. The German authorities took umbrage. It was only a few weeks before the Conference at Versailles to draw up a peace formula; they officially demanded that detailed information be produced to support the allegations of a crime which they strongly refuted.

The British and Canadian Governments instigated enquiries which uncovered scanty and conflicting evidence. The contribution by the Canadian private, Arthur Bruell, was discounted as he was not actually at the Front in April 1915 and another, Lance Corporal Metcalfe V.C., reckoned to have witnessed a crucifixion on the St. Jan road rather than in St. Juliaan (the Flemish spelling). Sir Arthur Currie, the officer-in-command of the 2nd Canadian Brigade, was adamant that, to his knowledge, no such atrocity had been committed against any Canadian soldiers: 'I know of a great many who used endeavour to find out whether there was a justification for making this charge against the Germans, but nothing definite was ever ascertained.'

The British authorities failed to unearth any compelling evidence either and so, as far as the Germans were concerned, the case was unproven and to their satisfaction, the bronze statue was withdrawn from the exhibition. For nearly 70 years the story was dismissed as a myth, an example of war time propaganda to denigrate the Germans for their cruelty, an objective perpetuated by the Hollywood film *The Prussian Cur* released in 1918.

The identity of the crucified soldier was unknown and there were inconsistencies in the accounts concerning the numbers of those killed, and where and how the killings took place. It was not until 1987 that it was possible at last to verify the event and to identify the soldier. A letter was made public, written in 1916 by a Canadian private, William Freeman, to Elizabeth Petrie informing her of the death of her brother Harry. When she wrote to ascertain how he died, she was told that he had been crucified. On 20 June 1916 she informed her brother Martin: 'I have got another letter admitting the crucifixion of Harry… I have got it at last, the horrible details… they took him down alive. He was hacked to bits and spat on and his eyes gouged out.' She was told that the former fireman had died 'a soldier's and hero's death'.

Interestingly, the minutes of the Sons of Temperance, in Moncton, New Brunswick recorded on 14 July 1920 that 'Brother Band served in France, was taken prisoner by the Germans and met death by crucifixion in the hands of the enemy.'

Interviewed for a 2002 Channel 4 T.V. documentary, Elizabeth Petrie's niece, Lettie, was in no doubt that her great uncle Harry was the crucified soldier. The view that the incident was a myth or propaganda was debunked due to the research of Iain Overton who had discovered compelling evidence in the Leeds University Liddle Collection: a typed report by a Red Cross nurse, Ursula Chaloner, daughter of the future 1st Baron Gisborough, which gave details of an interview with a wounded Canadian soldier, Lance Corporal Clement Brown, who named the crucified soldier as Harry Band of the 15th Battalion of the Canadian Infantry.

Details of Red Cross nurse Ursula Chaloner's interview with Lance Corporal Clement Brown   *University of Leeds Special Collections*

The likelihood is, therefore, that the rumours and stories in circulation at the end of April 1915 contained more than a grain of truth, inconsistent and contradictory as they may have appeared at the time. Band's death may have been retribution for sniper attacks in some Belgian towns and villages. The Germans could have been making a point to the Canadians who on 24 April had defied their chlorine gas attack and ensuing advance, and had desperately managed to hold the Allied line in the absence of the retreating French and their colonial troops.

Another theory is that the crucifixion was another in a line of German war crimes similar to the outrages committed between 19 and 25 August 1914 against civilians in the Belgian towns of Aerschot, Dinant and Louvain when over 1,000 civilians were killed.

One element of mystery does remain- what happened to Harry Band's body? If so many soldiers allegedly saw Band's body, why did they not rescue it? If Canadian soldiers recognised their insignia on his uniform- why did they leave it bayoneted to a tree or barn door?

Behind the simple engraving of Harry Band's name on the Menin Gate lies a fascinating and controversial story about a Canadian soldier possibly suffering one of the most cruel and bizarre deaths perpetrated during the War. Was Sergeant Harry Band the luckless victim of German cruelty? Recently uncovered evidence suggests that there is a semblance of truth in the theory.

Harry Band's name on the Menin Gate- note the Canadian spelling of 'sergeant' (see below under 'Rank')

J Kerr

HARRY BAND:

Born:	August 1885 in Montrose, Scotland. One of seven children, he and his family emigrated to Canada
Education:	Unknown
Occupation:	Fireman
Unit/ Regiment:	48th Highlanders of Canada (15th Battalion of the Canadian Infantry)
Rank:	Sergeant. During the War British and New Zealander soldiers of this rank were spelled 'serjeant' but Canadians, depending on the unit, with a 'g' or a 'j'
Died:	Probably 24 April 1915 near St. Julien, Second Battle of Ypres
Age:	29
Commemorated:	Menin Gate Memorial, Ypres, Panel 24 The Memorial was unveiled in 1927, designed by Sir Reginald Blomfield and the sculpture by Sir William Reid-Dick. It commemorates over 54,400 British and Empire servicemen (apart from New Zealanders) for whom there is no known grave who died on the Ypres Salient. From 16 August 1917 onwards, missing British troops were recorded on the Tyne Cot Memorial. The Menin Gate site was chosen because thousands of troops would pass it on their way to and from the Salient

Also commemorated:

Brothers:	Major John Frederick Loder-Symonds, 1/ South Staffs, died on 1 November 1914 aged 40, one of four brothers who died in the War, Panel 35 Lieutenant Aidan Chavasse , 17/ King's (Liverpool), youngest brother of double V.C. winner Noel, died on 4 July 1917, aged 26, Panel 6
'Old Bill':	Lance Corporal T.H. Rafferty, 1/ Royal Warwicks, thought to be the inspiration for Bruce Bairnsfather's cartoon character, died on 25 April 1915, Panel 8
Name change:	Private Albert Atkinson 1/ King's Own Yorkshire Light Infantry is recorded on Panel 47: 'Served as Duty, A.' which he chose as his alias on joining up, for reasons best known to himself. He died on 8 May 1915, aged 21
Poet:	2nd Lieutenant The Hon. Gerald William (Billy) Grenfell, 8/ Rifle Brigade, son of Chairman of the 1908 Olympics Committee, Lord Desborough, died 30 July 1915, aged 25, Panel 46
Shot at Dawn:	Private Herbert Francis Burden, 1/ Northumberland Fusiliers, was executed for desertion on 21 July 1915, aged 17. His name can be found on Panel 60 entitled 'Addenda'. He was the inspiration for the statue in the Shot at Dawn Plot at the National Memorial Arboretum near Alrewas in Staffordshire

The Last Post Ceremony at the Ypres (Menin Gate) Memorial
J Kerr

GILCHRIST MACLAGAN

'One of the finest coxswains who ever handled the rudder springs of a rowing eight'

Six days after the murder of Archduke Franz Ferdinand in Sarajevo had set in motion an end to the fragile political equilibrium in Europe, Gilbert Gilchrist Maclagan completed his duties as steward of the Royal Henley Regatta on 4 July 1914 and returned to his home in Whitehall Court in the heart of London's theatre land.

He was also Honorary Secretary of the Amateur Rowing Association for which he was eminently well qualified, having won a gold medal at the 1908 Olympics when he coxed the Leander Club's eight to victory. The final pre-war committee meeting of the Association, for which he recorded the minutes, was held at 45 Parliament Street in Westminster on 9 July.

Gilchrist Maclagan's interest in rowing was fostered at Eton College between 1893 and 1898 although it would appear that a G.A. Lloyd was selected as cox for the main 'eight', Maclagan coxing the second string 'Victory' eight.

Gilchrist Maclagan, cox of the 1908 Olympic gold-winning Leander crew
River and Rowing Museum, Henley-on-Thames

He continued his interest in the sport at Magdalen College, Oxford, winning a 'Blue' in each of the years from 1899 to 1902. At only 8 stone 7 lbs, he was the ideal weight for a coxswain. His intelligent reading of the conditions and bold decision-making were important factors in Oxford's victory by 2/5 of a length in the 1901 University Boat Race. Conditions were very choppy and at a well-judged moment he dropped the crew to a paddle and riding the waves, coaxed the boat past Cambridge. He

was, however, in three losing Oxford crews but was selected for the Leander Club between 1899 and 1908 when they won the Grand Challenge Cup at Henley-on-Thames six times.

The Leander Club based at Henley is the most historic, successful and prestigious rowing club in the world, the rowing equivalent of M.C.C. or The All England Club at Wimbledon. Gilchrist Maclagan can be seen in photographs and on plaques throughout the magnificent clubhouse. He was on the Leander Club Committee in the early years of the century and was appointed to the Amateur Rowing Association's Committee of Selectors for the 1908 Olympics. They were to

Gilchrist Maclagan coxing Leander when they defeated Trinity College, Cambridge to win the Grand Challenge Cup at Henley in 1899   Leander Club, Henley-on-Thames

organise two eights, two fours and two pairs to represent the United Kingdom at the Olympic Regatta to be held at Henley-on-Thames. The Leander Club and Cambridge University were chosen for the eights. The Leander boat was full of experienced rowers, most of whom were in their 30s; Guy Nickalls, however, was 41 and described the crew as 'old crocks'! The Cambridge crew were younger and were expected to do well but failed against the Belgian Club Nautique de Gand.

Those selected received letters in January 1908. It was made clear what was expected of them- Guy Nickalls was faced with a challenge to get back to his rowing weight which he complained would entail giving up beer, spirits and wine and controlling his intake of potatoes, pastry and sweets! Modern rowing greats like Redgrave, Pinsent and Cracknell would be amused that a major feature of Nickalls's training was just a mile run before breakfast!

'Cockie', as Maclagan was affectionately known, was in control of the Leander eight at Henley. In the first heat they eased past the Hungarian crew and in the second, the Canadian 'Argonaut' crew posed more of a threat but Leander were easy winners by a length.

In the final Leander were to take on the 'redoubtable' Belgian Club Nautique de Gand, 'the terror of the then modern English oarsmen' who had beaten the young Cambridge University crew by a 'length and a third'. It was quite a showdown: for the rowing cognoscenti it would be a defining battle of different styles and methods.

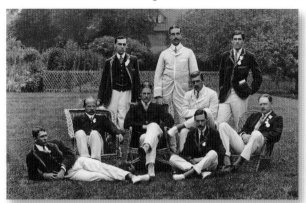

The Leander eight that won gold in 1908- Maclagan is sitting crosslegged on the ground and the 'stroke' F.S. Kelly (see p.260) is standing on the left   *River and Rowing Museum*

The feisty Guy Nickalls claimed that 'I had never been beaten by either a colonial or foreigner, and I certainly wasn't going to be in my old age…'!

Nickalls tells the story of the race: halfway along the one mile 880 yard long course (2.4 kms) Leander were leading by three quarters of a length when the psychological moment arrived: 'Cockie's clear voice rang out immediately after the Belgians' great spurt at Remenham Farm had subsided. "Now then, Leander, we'll have our ten strokes and let them know it! One…" The boat fairly leapt out of the water… we fairly sang along, cleared them at once and began sailing away… The race was over… We had them beat… Cockie looked back… "Take it easy and keep together Leander" shouted he, and we swung over the line easy winners, by more than two lengths in record time.'

Nickalls was delighted: 'Thanks entirely to the unselfish and patriotic action of the "old crocks" turning out again to show the younger generation how to row properly, I remained unbeaten by any colonial or foreigner. The victory of the orthodox, restored England's prestige as the greatest rowing nation in the world but straightened out the prevailing ideas on style and form…'

Gilchrist Maclagan's successes with Leander over the years at Henley earned him *The Rowing Almanac*'s assessment that it was 'a remarkable record and never likely to be equalled'.

Maclagan's Olympic Gold medal 1908   *Leander Club*

His leadership of many successful eights made him ideal officer material when war broke out on 4 August 1914. The Stock Exchange, where he had forged a successful enough career to have left £32,000 in his will, closed at the end of July. He might have enlisted with the Stock Exchange Battalion of the Royal Fusiliers but was gazetted on 15 August as a 2nd lieutenant in the Royal Warwickshire Regiment.

The Field reported in the third week of August that after Belgium had been invaded by the Kaiser's Armies, there had been a collection in Henley-on-Thames for the Belgian Ministers' Relief Fund for the sick and wounded. It was sponsored by the town's Mayor and Gilchrist Maclagan, Secretary of the Amateur Rowing Association. Not only had Maclagan coxed against the Belgians in 1908 but also in the final of the 1905 Grand Challenge Cup against the Club Nautique de Gand.

Plaque in the Leander clubhouse   *A Hamilton*

The Belgians had been popular and successful participants at the Henley Regatta for many years so it was natural that the rowing fraternity should contribute generously. *The Field* article concluded: 'The heroic defence of the Belgian nation has commanded the admiration of the world but nowhere has the gallant conduct of the Belgian army aroused more enthusiasm than amongst those who have in happier times watched the Belgian crews competing at the Henley Regatta.'

The rowing community enthusiastically answered the call to arms on behalf of their rowing comrades which is reflected by the deletion of many names from Leander's 1914 membership booklet.

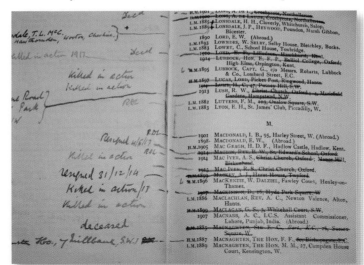

Maclagan enlisted immediately and in training displayed the right leadership qualities. The man who 'was quiet in manner and never bullied his crews' unsurprisingly soon caught the eye of the 'top brass' with his command of his platoon in late November and December when the 1/ Royal Warwicks were entrenched at St.Yvon in Belgium north east of Plugstreet Wood. Brigadier General Hull recorded in the Brigade War Diary in January 1915 that Maclagan was 'a promising young officer who has a thorough grasp of his men who would follow him everywhere.' He recommended him for a Mention in Despatches.

The Leander Rowing Club's membership book in 1914 shows on one page alone six deleted names of members killed in action including Gilchrist Maclagan's   Leander Club

The officers of the 1/ Royal Warwicks played hard when behind the lines and the leading morale booster was Lieutenant Bruce Bairnsfather who, as early as 1915, was achieving celebrity status for cartoons that depicted the trials and tribulations of the Tommy's life in the trenches.

Bairnsfather and Maclagan became the best of friends and used a ruined cottage at St.Yvon as a base. It was there that Bairnsfather drew his first cartoons on the walls. He somewhat self-effacingly wrote later: 'With some bits of coal, I made a mess on all the four walls of our back room.' The cartoon 'scribbles' as he described them, were the prototypes for *The Bystander* Magazine's *Fragments from France*, a collection of 41 cartoons first published in 1916, a year after Bairnsfather's return to 'Blighty'.

From the shell-shattered roof of the cottage at St.Yvon, Bairnsfather wrote that 'the view in short was this: one saw the backs of our own trenches, then the No Man's Land space of ground and beyond that the front of the German trenches.'

The Birth of 'Fragments'- Bruce Bairnsfather's sketch of himself drawing on the walls of a cottage in St. Yvon, Belgium
(Originally published in Bullets and Billets in 1916)
Barbara Bruce Bairnsfather

In *Bullets and Billets* about his experiences in the Great War, Bairnsfather referred to Maclagan as 'Hudson' but in real life referred to him as 'Mac'. Bairnsfather was in charge of the Battalion's machine-gun section and described his first meeting with the tiny Olympian at the cottage in St. Yvon: 'He came in and saw me examining the place. "Hello, you're here too are you? Are you going to stay here as well?" He did…'

The 1/Royal Warwicks suffered huge losses in the Second Battle of Ypres on 25 April 1915. The Battalion advanced to take St. Julien and Kitchener's Wood. Bairnsfather wrote that the orders were vague and the artillery back up was non-existent. The Battalion advanced to within 50 yards of the enemy in support of a Canadian unit that had been overwhelmed by German gas but were then mown down by machine-gun fire.

Gilchrist Maclagan's body was never recovered. He was one of seven Royal Warwicks' officers to lose their lives and in total, the Battalion lost over 500 soldiers during the Second Battle of Ypres. The names of those without a known grave are recorded on the Menin Gate.

"They've evidently seen me."

Bairnsfather's cartoon based on the time when he and Maclagan spied on German positions from the roof of Anton's Farm (originally published in The Bystander *of 21 April 1915)* Barbara Bruce Bairnsfather

Bruce Bairnsfather wrote of his friend 'Mac' in an article in *The British Legion Journal* of 1935 that 'no one in this war could have hated it more than he did and no one could have more conscientiously done his very best at it.'

Bairnsfather was invalided out of front line action after the Battle of St. Julien, suffering from what was clearly shell shock but he never forgot his own good fortune compared to that of his friend Gilchrist Maclagan: 'an excellent fellow, one of the best chaps I ever knew.'

Gilchrist Stanley Maclagan was one of 1,157 Old Etonians to lose their lives in the Great War. *The Eton Chronicle* of 13 May 1915 described Maclagan 'as gentle and manly a boy as ever was at Eton, he steered the eight here and afterwards when he was at Magdalen College, Oxford, the University eight. Keen-eyed, happy, bright and intelligent, both in work and play, he had a natural modesty and loveable disposition. It is written of him "he was the bravest of the brave and died gallantly leading his men." He has been invaluable and had endeared himself to all. We feel we have lost a great friend and a gallant officer.'

The editor of *The Eton Chronicle* was taken to task in the following edition when a correspondent pointed out that Maclagan did not steer the Eton VIII but the second-string Victory VIII. He added, though, that Gilchrist Maclagan was 'a keen fisherman, skater and a crack game-shot. "Cockie" as he was familiarly known, was beloved by innumerable friends and as *The Oxford Magazine* says "the loss of his vivid, winning personality is one very hard to bear"'.

42 Oxford and Cambridge rowing 'Blues' were to perish in the War. 'The rowing world sustains a very great loss' was how *The Rowing Almanac* of 1915 honoured his memory. 'He was one of the finest coxswains who ever handled the rudder springs of a rowing eight.'

All sports had to count their losses after the Great War. The rowing world appreciated that Gilchrist Maclagan's enormous contribution to their sport would be greatly missed.

GILCHRIST MACLAGAN:

Born:	5 October 1879, son of Dr. Thomas and Isobel Maclagan of 9, Cadogan Place, London
Education:	Eton College and Magdalen College, Oxford
Occupation:	Stockbroker
Unit/ Regiment:	'C' Company, 1/ Royal Warwicks
Rank:	Lieutenant
Died:	25 April 1915, Second Battle of Ypres
Age:	35
Commemorated:	Menin Gate Memorial, Ypres, Panel 8

Lieutenant Gilchrist Maclagan, one of 22 Royal Warwicks officers commemorated on the Menin Gate J Kerr

EDGAR MOBBS

'He did his duty even unto his death'

Edgar Mobbs was not a devotee of red tape and bureaucracy. Disappointed that at 32 years of age he was considered too old to enlist, he circumvented the problem by raising his own group of volunteers. Initially he encouraged 400 to sign up of whom 264 were fit enough for service which, as 'D' Company, was dubbed 'The Mobbs Own' and would provide the backbone of the 7th Battalion of the Northamptonshire Regiment.

A persuasive and strong character it was no surprise that Mobbs cajoled so many to enlist with him. He was a former England rugby international, described in 1909 by *The Times* as 'a determined runner with a strong "hand off" and whenever he got the ball he seemed dangerous.' His trade mark 'hand off' was so fearsome that opposing three-quarters wore protective caps. It was a tactic he honed when playing for Toulouse in south-west France where he was the crowd's favourite.

Sport was his main interest at Bedford Modern School but there were few pointers to his future success. Due to a knee injury he failed to gain selection for the 1st rugby XV and after leaving school in 1900, played hockey and cricket for Olney near his family home in Buckinghamshire.

He took up rugby again in 1903. Initially he played as a scrum half but then moved out to the wing where his performances for Olney attracted the coaches at Northampton Saints. He joined Northampton in 1905 and captained the Club from 1907 until 1913. He scored 177 tries and remarkably, six tries in a match on three occasions.

He was also selected for the East Midlands and was captain when the touring Australians were defeated 16-5 at Leicester on 2 December 1908, their only defeat of the tour. Mobbs's performance merited selection on 9 January 1909 for the first of his seven England 'caps', against the Australians

The England team that beat France 22-0 in 1909. Edgar Mobbs is in the back row second from the right and Ronnie Poulton Palmer (see p.141) is on the right of the front row World Museum of Rugby, Twickenham

at Blackheath in the days before Twickenham became the home of English rugby. Mobbs scored the first ever try against Australia after only two minutes of the match but it was not enough as England lost 3-9. He was appointed captain and inspired his team to an 11-3 win against France in Paris on 3 March 1910.

A victory in most sports generally confirms a captain's appointment but the Rugby Football Union decided otherwise and dispensed with Mobbs at the age of 28; his forthrightness was disliked by the authorities. It was an outcome that hardly came as a shock to him.

Mobbs represented the East Midlands on the Rugby Football Union Committee in 1909, a role he found stultifying and restrictive. He ruffled a few feathers with a vigorous and successful defence against charges of professionalism amongst Midlands clubs and in 1913 upset a few committee diehards with his criticism of the poor treatment of the visiting South African touring side whom he felt were treated like 'naughty schoolboys' and with little sensitivity towards their travel and accommodation needs.

He was a leading light for the Barbarians wandering side for whom he played in the traditional Boxing Day fixture against Leicester. He decided to hang up his boots at the end of the 1913 season at the age of 30. He followed his father into the motor trade and took a managerial job at a branch of the family's Pytchley Auto Company in Market Harborough.

Edgar's decision to enlist as a private on 8 September 1914 was a godsend for the Northampton Recruiting Committee. After his final match for Northampton Saints, wearing a straw boater, he addressed the assembled players and supporters and vigorously encouraged them to follow him to the recruiting station.

The owner of *The Northampton Independent*, W.H. Holloway used his pages to attack those who did not enlist and when 'The Mobbs Own' left for their training camp at Shoreham in Sussex, he warmly applauded them: 'The sight of Mr. Mobbs' Corps of recruits marching from the homes so dear to them, was a stirring sight, and a splendid example of the spirit which animated the best of our young manhood. They have left their situations and the comforts of home, conscious that in this hour of our national peril, it is the paramount duty of the young and strong to crush the monster of brutal militarism threatening our shores. This is the traditional spirit which had made England great and free and happy, and whatever Mr. Mobbs and his men have to endure for our sake, they may rest assured that they will for ever stand high in our respect and admiration, for the part they are so cheerfully taking in protecting our beloved country.' 'The Mobbs Own' were given an enthusiastic send off by flag waving school children who were thronging the streets of Northampton.

A natural leader on the rugby field, Mobbs was promoted swiftly from the ranks and within a few months of joining up he was promoted to lieutenant on 14 October 1914 and then captain on 1 July 1915. To raise funds and recruit rugby players into the Army, he arranged a number of Barbarians' matches in 1915 against among others, Leicester and a Wales XV at Cardiff, a match the Barbarians won convincingly. Over £200 was raised for war charities.

It was possible to arrange such matches because the Battalion's training lasted for a year. The success of Lord Kitchener's campaign to raise a new volunteer army took him and the authorities by surprise; at the training camp at Shoreham in Sussex, the 7/Northants were at first given blue uniforms which they agreed made them look like prisoners. Khaki uniforms before the War were sourced from Germany! The men were accommodated in bell tents with insufficient blankets but due to the efforts of Holloway in the pages of his newspaper, 300 blankets were raised and sent to the south coast.

The Battalion arrived at the Front in France on 25 September 1915 after a two-day 50 mile route march and was soon to experience the horrors of the warfare and the carnage that they had been hearing about. A Royal Engineer colleague recalled how Mobbs, in his inimitable style, bridled at the demand of a London-based civil servant that certain parts of a form were to be filled in with red ink. Captain Mobbs sent it back stating that red ink was scarce in the trenches but that he could find plenty of blood... 'if that would do?'

'The Mobbs Own' relieved trenches near Loos vacated by the Seaforth Highlanders, Gordons and Royal Scots. They remained in reserve while other battalions progressed through the coalmining area around Loos to Lens but any advantage was lost when Sir John French decided against a further 'push'. This gave the universally disliked Prussians the opportunity to regroup and counter-attack.

On 26 September the 7/ Northants were engaged in furious bayonet combat to keep the enemy at bay. Edgar Mobbs was at the heart of the action and at the end of the day returned to the trenches with his uniform torn to shreds. The Battle of Loos was the template for so many that followed: it was inconclusive and the British Army's six divisions incurred huge losses of 50,000 and little ground was taken. Mobbs's performance had merited promotion to the rank of major.

Mobbs led his men and fought with great courage and might have received an M.C. or a V.C. if, as was required, his exploits had been witnessed by a senior officer. 'The Mobbs Own' suffered serious losses and Mobbs admitted to being tired of having to write letters of condolence to the parents of the dead: he accepted it, however, as his duty. He was wounded during the battle but typically his injuries did not stop him from playing in an exhibition match between England and Scotland at Northampton when on leave over the New Year.

He was promoted to the dizzy heights of lieutenant colonel in 1916, commanding officer of the Battalion, due to the ill-health of his superior Lieutenant Colonel Skinner, a promotion path that before the

Mobbs recovering from his wounds

War would normally have taken about 15 years. It was an advancement that caused ripples amongst staff officers and regulars but Mobbs was an exception. He was a larger than life character and a fearless and inspirational leader of men. He was bemused by his rapid promotion: 'I am getting too big for words… I expect to get up to general then get killed. What a story it would make "From private to general and how to do it by E.R. Mobbs."' It was scarcely 18 months since he had raised his own 'company' of men as a private. He had achieved one of the highest of military ranks, a tribute to his energy and charismatic leadership. Edgar Mobbs was an appealing and energetic soldier who nonetheless found the action and responsibility challenging. By May he was in need of a well deserved break.

The 7/ Northants were fortunate to miss the first weeks of the Battle of the Somme in July 1916. Their turn for front line action came on 18 August when they attacked the village of Guillemont from positions east of Trônes Wood. 50 men were killed, 250 wounded and 50 were reported missing. Mobbs was hit by shrapnel in the shoulder badly enough to be sent back to 'Blighty' after initial treatment at the Red Cross Hospital at Rouen.

Two years after he had enlisted, Mobbs was declared unfit on 8 September and returned home again to recuperate. He was held in such high regard by his men that their morale was significantly boosted when he rejoined them. He was attracting jovial comment about his charmed life and invincibility and wrote: 'They tell me out here nothing would ever kill me. I do my best to keep everyone cheerful, it is the only way.' Not many British officers can have received and recovered from as many wounds as Edgar Mobbs and then return so dutifully to the trenches.

By mid-October the Northants were in action near Vimy Ridge. Mobbs was welcomed back by the Battalion as they moved on to Loos and Hill 70. He wrote on 23 November that 'we are in the trenches again, I am so sick of them, I never want to see another trench as long as I live.' By Christmas 1916 the Northants had been involved in trench warfare for nearly a year so it was hardly surprising that spirits were flagging.

The once powerful and athletic international rugby player was now a shadow of his former physical prowess. Over Christmas he was struck down by bronchitis and trench foot. His spirits must have been raised on 3 January 1917 when he was notified of his Distinguished Service Order in the New Year's Honours List.

Edgar Mobbs was back at Vimy Ridge near the river Souchez in March and by April even he, so positive and determined, was feeling the pressure of three years of the War: 'I shall not be able to stand the strain much longer, so they had better soon finish the war off. We have not been out of the front lines for 21 days, no bath or anything.' He had not been able to change his clothes for days so there would, he predicted, be 'some dirt I expect.'

Hill 60- *'a scene from Dante's Inferno'*

Antony of Ypres

Caterpillar Crater, on the Messines Ridge, caused by one of 19 mines that exploded on 7 June 1917

J Kerr

Mobbs's disenchantment was exacerbated by the never-ending loss of his men. He was particularly affected by the death of his 'runner', Private Hines, who was shelled to bits in front of his very eyes. Heavy casualties were suffered during the attempt on 7 June to take the Messines Ridge after 19 massive mine explosions 'like a scene from Dante's *Inferno*' had left huge craters and weakened the Germans' resolve. Mobbs was wounded in the hand during the offensive. Three days later he was hit by shrapnel in the chest and neck which entailed another 'Blighty' trip home for 12 days.

He returned to the Front on 26 June for the final time to join the 7/ Northants in what would be known as the Battle of Passchendaele. The Battalion's objective on 31 July was the capture of the high ground of 'Tower Hamlets'. Mobbs was behind the lines at Battalion Headquarters when news came through that the majority of his officers had been killed. He felt he had no option but to lead from the front himself despite being warned it was an unwise move.

Zero hour was 3.50 a.m. The surprise attack was hindered by rain. The Lieutenant Colonel led a small group into No Man's Land near Zillebeke which included his new 'runner' and a young subaltern, 2nd Lieutenant Berridge. The aim was to take out an enemy machine-gun post at 'Shrewsbury Forest' which he had discovered was holding up the advance and causing great numbers of casualties. The Battalion War Diary recorded that he ran with a grenade towards it 'with his familiar long, high stride that had held him in good stead on the rugby field.' As he dashed into a hail of machine-gun fire, Berridge shouted 'For God's sake, sir, get down.' Mobbs persisted but the odds were stacked against him and he never delivered his hand grenade. Hit by a salvo of bullets, he crawled into a muddy shell hole and in his final moments wrote a message to Battalion H.Q. detailing map references of the machine-gun's location. He requested reinforcements and stated he was seriously wounded. It was an act, as a fellow officer wrote, that showed 'his devotion to duty at the last' but one can discount the romanticised version of his death- that during his charge, he punted a rugby ball towards the enemy.

For Edgar Mobbs's family there was no grave to visit. His body was never recovered and all that remains of one of the most courageous characters to have died in the Great War is his name engraved on the Menin Gate. His bravery throughout the War was legendary. His death and the failure to find his body were used as a morale-boosting exercise. The Battalion War Diary asserted: 'The fact that his body could not be recovered and buried, as all ranks would have wished, was perhaps a good thing, as it helped keep alive his memory in the Battalion, and inspired in everyone the resolve to avenge his death and to end the war that had already caused so much misery and suffering.'

A former Bedford Modern School pupil wrote a eulogy for *The Times*, choosing not to dwell on the details of his death: 'I have seen men and good men, but for a man of his standing and rank it was magnificent. I sat afterwards in a captured post, and instead of that picture, I saw the old three-quarter in his own 25 yards get the ball from a crumpled scrum and get clean through and on. The same man, the same determination, a born leader. Thank God for such men.'

Edgar's father, Oliver, received huge numbers of letters of condolence. Alexander Allen, one of his teachers at Bedford Modern School, asserted that 'his record in this awful struggle is one that the school can never forget.' Earl Spencer, the Lord Lieutenant of Northamptonshire, considered Oliver Mobbs's son to have been 'a true patriot and born leader of men.' A letter from Captain Farrer whom Mobbs had encouraged when his nerve had gone, gave an example in his letter of Mobbs's great strength of character and moral rectitude: 'Edgar had rather dramatically saved the lives of two German prisoners by interposing himself between them and a burly Gordon Highlander, who, fired up with fury, was charging at them with his bayonet.'

Vision of E. R. Mobbs and his Corps at the Front.

Reproduced from the " Northampton Independent."

Cartoon in the The Northampton Independent *of Edgar Mobbs 'handing off' the Kaiser* World Museum of Rugby, Twickenham

W.H. Holloway who had lauded Mobbs's efforts so vigorously in *The Northampton Independent*, in effect accepted that modern weaponry proved too great for even the indomitable Edgar Mobbs. He declared in his obituary: 'All the horrors of modern warfare failed to quench his brave and buoyant spirit.'

After the War the townsfolk of Northampton raised over £2,000 for a memorial to the dashing ex-England rugby international. It was unveiled in July 1921 but was later moved from Market Square in 1937 to Abington Square with a plaque inscribed: 'In memory of Edgar R. Mobbs D.S.O., erected by subscriptions of admirers the world over, to the memory of a great and gallant soldier sportsman… He did his duty even unto his death.'

The Boxing Day fixture between the Barbarians and the East Midlands was first played at Northampton in 1921 in memory of Edgar Mobbs and the fixture continued until 2007. A larger than life personality, he was almost invincible on the rugby field but even he was unable to hand off the deadly bullets of German machine-gunners during the Battle of Passchendaele.

EDGAR MOBBS:

Born: 29 June 1882, son of Oliver and Elizabeth Mobbs of Olney, Buckinghamshire

Education:	Bedford Modern School
Occupation:	Manager at the family's Pytchley Auto Company in Market Harborough and England rugby international
Unit/ Regiment:	7/ Northants, known as 'The Mobbs Own'
Rank:	Lieutenant Colonel
Died:	31 July 1917, the first day of the Third Battle of Ypres (Passchendaele)
Age:	35
Decoration:	D.S.O.

Edgar Mobbs's name on the Menin Gate A Hamilton   Commemorated: Menin Gate Memorial, Ypres, Panel 43

WILLIAM TAPP

The Christmas Truce: 'It was like a clock that has stopped ticking"

Private William Tapp could scarcely believe his eyes. In his diary he wrote 'it is a strange sight and unbelievable... we are mixed up together... we exchange souvenirs, I pull a button off my coat, a German does the same so we exchange also cigars.' He was describing one of the most iconic of events of the Great War- the Christmas Truce at St. Yvon in Belgium between the 1/ Royal Warwicks and the 134th Saxon Corps.

Like many of the soldiers in the Battalion, Tapp's formative years

TIPS BIRMINGHAM F.C. FOR PROMOTION.

'A happy group of Birmingham men of the 1st Warwicks in the trenches. They have experienced heavy fighting, but have repulsed the Germans. Private Tapp (second from left) was a recipient of one of the "Picture World" Christmas Boxes.

Private Tapp, photographed in the trench he has so gallantly helped to defend. He is a keen Birmingham F. C. supporter, and has tipped them for promotion. His forecast, however, has caused a lot of argument in the trenches.

Printed and Published by the BIRMINGHAM GAZETTE, LTD., at 106 and 103, Ch. and 51 and 67 Corporation Street, West Bromwich. 1

William Tapp featured in The Birmingham Post's Picture World *on 10 March 1915*

were spent in Birmingham and he joined the Regiment in 1905. He was considered reliable enough to be chosen as an officer's 'servant' or batman by 22 year old Lieutenant Richard Tillyer.

Most Great War diary accounts were written by well-educated officers. Tapp, in contrast, had received a comparatively basic Three R's education; his diary account may lack finesse in its grammar, punctuation and spelling but its content is remarkable for its perceptive and humorous account of the challenges faced by the 1/ Royal Warwicks in the first six months of the War. It is quoted below as it was originally written.

He arrived in France in late October and commented in his first diary entry that 'C' Company had been in action without a break for a month during which time they had suffered 'all kinds of weather, sometimes the water was up to our ankles.' The fighting in October and November 1914 was intense. Tapp mused that 'once or twice I had a glimpse of hell'. The Warwicks had been involved in checking the German advance on Paris but the warfare left its mark. Another private, Charlie Pratt, recalled that 'at times, it is like living in hell.'

Bruce Bairnsfather's sketch of the Christmas Truce between the 1/ Royal Warwicks and the 134th Saxons   Barbara Bruce Bairnsfather

One night when it was raining hard, Tapp and his officer were surprised by the ferocity of a German attack. Tapp allowed himself grudging respect for Tillyer but considered him 'rather reckless' and 'prone to taking too many risks.'

His diary entry for 24 November highlights the ever-present dangers but also the comical aspect of life on the front line. Humour and the tales of amusing events relieved the stress of living through the 'hell' they faced. A soldier was, after all, a sniper's bullet away from death: 'I go with mate in search of water, after going to a few farms we find pumps all out of order, some broken, some froze, we have to go along the road and are exposed to the enemy as it is a bright moon light night they have got a maxim gun trained on us, bullets whistle past our ears continually, we at last get water by breaking ice on a pond, the water smells bad, we must boil it. I am determined to get good water tomorrow if I have to go miles for it... I have found a pump at last... the enemy can either see us or hear us working the pump, as their shots are frequent and close as they are hitting round the pump, my mate sees someone crouching towards us from the field in front, make plans etc... I trip over some barbed wire, up again, and get within a few yards suddenly I stop it is only a young calf... the noise is deafening carn't hear ourselves talk.'

Tapp was joined in 'C' Company on 20 November by machine-gunner Lieutenant Bruce Bairnsfather who in 1916 received acclaim for his morale-boosting cartoons or 'sketches' as he preferred to describe them, of the exploits of 'Tommies' he worked alongside- 'Berts', 'Alfs' and

The Fatalist.
" I'm sure they'll 'ear this damn thing squeakin'."

The Fatalist- *most of Bairnsfather's cartoons were based on real events*   *Barbara Bruce Bairnsfather*

'Bills'. It is possible that Bairnsfather's 'Fatalist' sketch was inspired by Tapp's tale of the water pump incident, as told to Lieutenant Tillyer.

Many of the Warwicks had been in action without leave since late August 1914. They had suffered heat exhaustion in September, rain and damp in October and cold, frost and snow in December. As Christmas approached and with it no sign of any chance to celebrate a family Christmas, soldiers on both sides were understandably gearing up for some sort of celebration. Tapp commented: 'Well the trenches have their bright side, for instance the Germans in their trenches have just sang our national anthem and then shouted "hurrah" and then several boos so then we give them a song and a cheer, sometimes one of our fellows shouts "waiter" "sausages" and then send 5 rounds rapid over. The Germans seem to know who we are for they shout "Good old Warwicks" and our officer always tells us to give them a song back...' Tapp was correct in his assumption that 'I think we shall be pals by Xmas.'

On 22 December Tapp and three other servants were fortunate- they were billeted in a private house having in previous weeks been consigned to barns or, after an eight mile march on 23 November, in some pigsties. They all received parcels from home and 'we are making this our Xmas day, we had bacon, one egg each and chipped potatoes for breakfast, eggs are a luxury now they are 3d each and hard work to get any at all. Dinner roast beef, potatoes, Brussels sprouts, which we had seen on the way down, also plum duff and mince pie and a couple of jugs of beer, cigarettes, for tea we are hoping to have a milk loaf which has some English butter, cake, sweets, ect. I hope everyone in England has as good food for their Xmas day, we shall be back in trenches dodging the shots. We go back to trenches tonight Xmas Eve[1] it is going to be a moonlight night so I think we shall lose a few

1   *We go back to trenches tonight Xmas Eve:*
   - Captain Hamilton of 'A' Company wrote in his diary: 'We set off for the trenches at 6.30 p.m. a little sad at spending Xmas day in them. Crossing the well worn danger zone to our consternation not a shot was fired at us.' Leutnant Kurt Zehmisch of the 11th Company of the 134th Saxons marched his men to the German front line and ordered his men not to fire that evening or on Christmas Day.

men while we are relieving the other regt.[2] we get near the trenches but carn't hear any firing now we hear some singing from their trenches and ours, we have got settled now, it is about 7 pm and one of the Ger's who can speak Eng is shouting over to us to go over, we shout back "Come half way"[3] it is agreed on, our sergeant goes out[4] their man takes a lot of coaxing but comes at the finish and we find they have sent two we can hear them talking quite plain they exchange cigarettes and the German shouts to wish us Merry Xmas we wait for the Sergeant's return, he gets back and tells us they are not going to fire tonight and not tomorrow if we don't, they have got lights all along their trench and also a Xmas tree lit up they are singing so we give them one,[5] it is funny to hear us talk to one another our stretcher bearers have nothing to do no wounded to carry tonight, so they have all come from headquarters and are going round carol singing, they sing several in our trench before going, the Ger's give

One Night in Flanders- *Bruce Bairnsfather's sketch of the fraternisation on Christmas Eve at St. Yvon in 1914*   Barbara Bruce Bairnsfather

2   *the other regt:*
  • Tapp is referring to the 2/ Royal Dublin Fusiliers, who along with the 1/ Royal Warwicks, 1/ Royal Irish Fusiliers and the 2/ Seaforth Highlanders, made up the 10th Brigade.

  • In his diary entry for Christmas Eve, Captain Robert Hamilton recorded that 'the Dubs told us as we relieved them that the Germans wanted to talk to us.'

3   *"Come half way":*
  • a similar sequence of events occurred for 'A' Company as described by Captain Hamilton:'The Germans said "You come half way, and we will come half way, and bring you some cigars". This went on for some time, when Pte. Gregory, Double Ginger, my late servant came and asked if he might go out half way. ('late' because Hamilton had sacked him for making appalling cups of tea!). I said "Yes, at your own risk". Pte. Gregory stepped over the parapet, and got half way, and was heard saying, "Well here I am, where are you?" "Come half way" they said so on went Gregory, until he came upon two unarmed Germans, and one fully armed, lying down just behind, with his rifle pointed at him, typically German. Gregory was unarmed and alone. Typically British. He got his cigar and spun them some magnificent yarns about the strength of his company, which amused us all very much when he told us later. They wanted me to meet their officer, and after a great deal of shouting across, I said I would meet him at dawn, unarmed.'

4   *our sergeant goes out:*
  • Tapp's account is corroborated by the machine-gun officer attached to 'C' Company, Lieutenant Bruce Bairnsfather, who described how Serjeant Rea met two Germans by 'the remnants of a hedge and ditch that ran out at right angles from our trenches to the Germans', and exchanged gifts and lit cigarettes.

  • Zehmisch referred to a natural field ditch 'from which one Englishman emerged and met two of my men.'

5   *they are singing:*
  • Private Day recalled that at 'about 1 o'clock they struck up with a band of concertinas and a cornet; they played Home Sweet Home first, then a lot of other tunes finishing up with God Save the King.'

them a cheer for singing, this night I would not have missed for a lot I don't go to sleep till 2.30 Xmas morning, get up at 6.30, see all the Germans walking about on top of their trenches, now some of them are coming over without rifles, of course our fellows go to meet them including myself, it is a strange sight and unbelievable,[6] we are all mixed up together, there are quite a lot can talk English[7] they all say it is a pity to fire while we are up to our knees in mud, their trenches are worse than ours, we exchange souvenirs[8] I pull a button off my coat a German does the same so we exchange also cigars. I have got 2 buttons one cap badge and 2 cigarettes, 9 am Xmas morning, a mist come over and their men and ours are ordered to the trenches, about an hour after the mist suddenly lifts and we catch them putting barbed wire out, and they catch us doing the same thing, but there is not a shot being fired, here today we have another gathering of Germans and us it was one mass, about 150 of them and half as many of us all in a ring laughing and talking we are trying to arrange a football match with them for tomorrow.[9]

Boxing Day, they say they are not going to fire if we don't, but of course we must, and shall do, but it dosent seem right to be killing each other at Xmas time, I carn't realise this being mixed up with Germans it is certainly go as you please today, we have arranged not to shoot till 4.30 pm Boxing Day

6   *it is a strange sight and unbelievable:*

   The armistice and fraternisation that took place at St. Yvon definitely left their mark on those involved:

   - For Captain Hamilton, it was: 'A very merry Xmas and a most extraordinary one' even if he did double the sentries after midnight and in capital letters he wrote that it was 'A DAY UNIQUE IN THE WORLD'S HISTORY'.

   - Lieutenant Bruce Bairnsfather believed 'there had not been an atom of hate shown by either side… it was a punctuation mark on all the combatants' lives of cold and humid hate.'

   - Private Harry Morgan succinctly observed there had been 'No guns, no bullets, no voices'. He was amused, however, when the silence at dawn was broken by a Saxon's attempt at a cockcrow!

   - Across No Man's Land, Leutnant Zehmisch declared the ceasefire had been 'marvellous and strange… how wonderful that the Christmas Festival of Love should have caused enemies to be friends for a short time.'

7   *there are quite a lot can talk English:*

   - There is evidence to show that this and other fraternisations along the Western Front were initiated by the Germans and that their English was far superior to the English soldiers' mastery of German!

   - Private Layton: 'There were a good many amongst them that could speak broken English all right and they said "you make it no shoot, we make it no shoot". They belong to a Saxon Corps and I believe they would not fire again unless they were compelled to for I think they are almost fed up with flying bullets.'

   - Private A. Smith: 'Some of the Germans speak English very well, so they shouted "No shoot" and we said the same.'

8   *exchange souvenirs:*

   - Private Day recalled that 'we exchanged cigarettes for cigars, a gift from the Kaiser. I have got some of their post cards which they signed and addressed.'

   - Private Harry Morgan was pleased with the bargain he negotiated- a cigarette case for a tin of bully beef.

   - Lieutenant Bairnsfather asserted that 'our men were a light hearted, open, humorous collection as opposed to the sombre demeanour and stolid appearance of the Huns in their grey-green faded uniforms, top boots and pork pie hats.'

9   *we are trying to arrange a football match with them for tomorrow:*

   - According to Bruce Bairnsfather 'a football match was suggested and a kick about ensued with a football received by one of the soldiers as a Christmas present'

   - Captain Hamilton- "A' Coy would have played the 134th Saxon Corps tomorrow only that the company was relieved.'

   - Zehmisch recorded that 'a couple of English brought a football out of their trench and a vigorous football match began… towards evening the English officers asked whether a big football match could be held on the following day.' Zehmisch was unable to agree to a match as his company were due to be relieved. There were many fraternisations along the 450-mile Western Front at Christmas 1914, and there were instances of 'international' football matches- but only a spontaneous 'international' kick around in the St. Yvon area of Belgium.

I don't know what our General would say if he knew about this,[10] food is pretty good today, beef, potatoes and plum duff for dinner,[11] toast and butter stewed prunes and custard and Xmas cake for tea the Germans all have electric lights and lots of cigars and a watch each which I guess is loot, they seem a decent lot of fellows in front of us,[12] I think they know they are beaten, one fellow says he has only fired 3 shots and them at an aeroplane, they say if they are ordered to fire they will fire in the air, one fellow says the war is not good to them, or us, says he wishes he was back in Manchester,[13] it gets dusk so we all get to our trenches, its Xmas night how different to the Xmas nights I remember, especially the one four years ago when I stood under the Miseltoe with the girl I married later. I never thought of all this happening, I have been down to headquarters tonight to see my friends 3 other servants. I have been down other nights and the bullets have simply rained past me, but not a shot tonight, although they can see me, their trenches are about 180 yards from ours[14] one trench is better than the last time in fact it is a new trench as the other one fell in on account of the wet, this one is built higher, so that we can drain it, we have filled 1000s of sandbags with earth and piled them up instead of digging down, to bed at 10 pm, quite early for Xmas night, get up at 7.40 has to be called to as the officer was waiting for breakfast. I am supprised to see the Germans and our fellows still walking on top its too ridiculous for words, we are all mixing up again 8.49 am one of our Officers tells them to get back in their trenches as our artillary are going to shell them at 9 am, some of them say "we will get in your trenches we will be safer", this will stop the football match, shells are exchanged for a few hours but we will stand up at intervals no fear of being shot with a bullet, of course our artillary are a long way from us, same as theirs is from them so they know nothing about our little holiday, I forgot to say that both sides took advantage of the holiday

---

10   *I don't know what our General would say if he knew about this:*
- Captain Hamilton had been an instigator of the truce in his sector and to have met an enemy officer could have been construed as a major breach of military discipline. Interestingly, initial advances were made by privates or N.C.O.s. Hamilton wrote that 'I am told the General and staff are furious but powerless to stop it' and indeed late on Boxing Day General Smith-Dorrien was seeking details of officers and units who had taken part in the Christmas Truce 'with a view to disciplinary action'.
- The Battalion War Diary recorded that Christmas Eve was a 'Quiet day. Relieved the Royal Dublin Fusiliers in the trenches in the evening.'
- The Brigade War Diary: 'A quiet day. No firing. The Germans appear to think that an armistice exists for Christmas Day. An informal interchange of courtesies took place between troops in the fire trenches of both belligerents. Some valuable information was gleaned during the intercourse. The trenches seem fairly strongly held, the enemy cheerful and well fed.'

11   *beef, potatoes and plum duff for dinner:*
- Private Walter Cooke: 'The plum duff and mince pies were a treat. We had a real good feed on Christmas Day; we had a duck for our Christmas dinner which we bought off a Belgian farmer for 5 francs. We plucked it and cleaned it ourselves and roasted it in bacon fat.'
- Private Alfred Smith: 'I dare say you will be surprised at me writing a letter on a paper serviette, but you will be more surprised when I tell you it contained cake given to one of our men by a German officer on Christmas Day and I was given some of it.'

12   *they seem a decent lot of fellows in front of us:*
- The British were generally better disposed towards the Saxons than Prussians whom Captain Hamilton described as 'treacherous'.

13   *he wishes he was back in Manchester:*
- Many Germans lived in Britain prior to the War and there were many instances during the Christmas armistices of friendships and acquaintances being rekindled, albeit briefly. When he was an officer with the Norfolk Regiment, Captain Hamilton had attended a regimental dinner at the Trocadero restaurant in London and was amazed to meet the German chef in No Man's Land on Christmas Day! 'The chef of the Trocadero was among the Saxons in front of us, and he seemed quite delighted to meet some of his former clients.'
- Serjeant Philpotts spoke to a German who had been a chef in Birmingham and had left his wife and five children there when he travelled to the Front.

14   *their trenches are about 180 yards from ours:*
- Sometimes the distance was less- Serjeant Philpotts remembered that 'our line was only 70 yards from the Germans with turnips growing between the wire.'

yesterday to bury the dead,[15] some of the bodies had been there more than a month, dinner over I took a stroll to a cottage near their trenches where neither side dare to go at ordinary times. I am out after coal, meet a few Germans on the way they have come to buy one of our army knives, I don't want to sell mine so we exchange coins, I have got 3, also five rounds of ammunition I give one a pkt of cigarettes get cigars in return then I go for the coal, a German comes in with a bag to get some too, he helps me fill my bag so it was only polite to help him fill his, it didn't take long to clear all the coal out of that cottage we have fires night and day, we could not have done that last time we were here, one fire would have caused vollies to be sent over. My officer has taken advantage of the lull, he has kept the men working and made our trench like a fort, they do not seem to be doing so much at theirs, we asked them when they get relieved and they say "never" so we say the same, their regiment is the 134th and they are Saxons, they say if they are ordered to fire they will fire in the air. I do not think there will be any firing till this relief is finished. I carn't bring myself to shake hands with them, as I know I shouldn't if they were in our country I have not forgotten Belgium and I never did like the word German.

27th Dec: another day and night gone and still they walk about on top of their trenches but they don't come over we have been told that this friendliness has to stop, so we keep apart, although we walk about on top without fear of being shot, the Scotch won't have anything to do with them[16]... I forgot to mention that last time we were here they put a target up for us to shoot at, so we did the same, and signalled to each other a hit or a miss. About the weather it set in frosty Xmas Eve there was an inch of ice on the stream where we get our water from on Xmas Day, we had a little snow Boxing day which at night turned to sleet, and now this morning has turned to rain, there are only a few walking around now, I miss the sound of the shots flying over, it is like a clock which has stopped ticking.

28th Dec: at 2 am this morning we were working on our barbed wire of course they could hear us and I guess they thought we had been at it long enough, so they sent one of their lights over but no bullets which I think was very sporting of them, as they could have easily sent a volley over instead, 8 am the bounders are still walking about on top. Our officer wants to send a few shots over the top of them to make them keep in their trenches as we carn't shoot them without warning them, it is settled that we shall do nothing till after we come back from our rest, we get relieved tonight, spend a night in the reserve trenches we call it starvation trench as there are no dug outs, and we have to stand up to sleep, which is rotton tonight as it is raining hard.

29th Dec: 5 am we march to the pigaries, have a day there, the reserve trenches are only occupied at nights, 5 pm we march ten kilometres to La Cresse, (La Crèche) where we are having our 3 days rest. I am glad we are down for New Years Day. Well the last few days are the best I've had since I been out. I carn't understand the friendship between our fellows and Germans. It may be they are short of ammunition, if so, it is a clever trick of theirs it was hardly believable that we should be both working on wire, fifty yards from each other, they are Saxony though, and different to the Prussians and I think a little persuasion and they would all surrender.

30th Dec: we are at our billet, have a bath and change, receive a Xmas card from King and Queen also one from the General of our Division, am sending them home for souvenirs, my collection now is 5 rounds of their ammunition.

15 *both sides took advantage of the holiday yesterday to bury the dead:*
- The Brigade War Diary: 'Men of the Somerset Light Infantry, 134th Saxons, Hampshires, a Prussian and an Uhlan were all buried. The Germans helped in the digging, the 1/ Warwicks supplied the tools, the Germans stating they had no spades.'
- Serjeant Philpotts: 'there was a mass burial of British and German bodies and a military funeral on the edge of Plugstreet Wood'.
- Leutnant Zehmisch corroborates the description of burials: 'My people buried the fallen English and Germans whose bodies were already completely decomposed.'

16 *the Scotch won't have anything to do with them:*
- The commanding officer of the Seaforth Highlanders, who were to the left of the Royal Warwicks, refused to sanction any fraternisation. He ordered that the Seaforths were not to fire unless the Germans left their trenches.
- When Serjeant Philpotts' recollection was of seeing a German standing on the parapet, shouting and waving his arms and promptly being shot down, he may well have witnessed the order being duly carried out.

1st Jan.1915: We return to the trenches after 3 days rest, the war has started again, as they soon knocked one of our fellows over, but we soon have one for one, as one of the Germans stood up a bit too long he went over like Aunt Sally at the fair, they sent a little dog over with a message which read "how are you nicey Englishmen, we are all well, please send the dog back" but we gave the dog some bully beef, he would not go back, he surrendered next day we found a German drunk laying on our barbed wire he said they all wanted to give in, but were afraid to come over he said "Look at me I'm not frightened am I?" It is still raining our dug out leaks, my blanket is wringing wet weighs twice as heavy, and it has got to be carried besides an oilsheet, top coat, fur coat, cooking utensils they begin to get heavy after doing about 8 miles, we are having 5 days in trenches and 3 out, much better than 6 in and 2 out, as we do get two clear days rest, I hear that the Pigaries where we stayed has been shelled killing 17 of the kilties.

12th Jan: I am getting fed up, as there is no excitement we can fetch water without being sniped at.

26th Jan: I have just finished my breakfast got inside my dugout when they started shelling. I thought my time had come as I dropped two yards away a Jack Johnson making a hole as big as a cellar if it had have come a few minutes sooner there would have be no more diary. We can dodge bullets, but if these things come, there is not much chance...'

William Tapp's diary entries were becoming less detailed and for some reason, he ended his diary mid-sentence but lived for another three months- it is possible that he was exhausted physically and mentally or perhaps felt that his life had become repetitive and that he had little of interest to record.

Life for the Warwicks from 1 January 1915 was fairly quiet and the author of the Battalion War Diary recorded some light-hearted moments like the issue on 20 January of 'gooseberry jam in lieu of plum and apple'. Another entry records that there was no shelling all day and very little sniping: 'Lieutenant Tillyer reported that a boring machine had been heard in German lines. They were probably mining our trench. This was later discovered to be a bull frog which was heralding the approach of spring!' One might be forgiven for assuming the entry was for 1 April but it was in fact for 24 March.

'Very heavy firing' was heard from the Ypres direction all night on 23 April. There had been 'a lot of training' so an offensive was obviously afoot. The Battalion marched to Ypres as part of the 10th Brigade and on 25 April at 4.30 a.m. attacked St. Julien. The diarist recorded that there was insufficient support-shelling of the German trenches so the decision was taken to retire at 7.00 a.m. It was a disastrous day; casualty numbers were comparable to those sustained by many battalions in the Somme on 1st July 1916: 17 officers and 500 other ranks were killed, wounded or missing. More than half the Battalion was lost. Lieutenant Tillyer was one of the missing officers as was his batman William Tapp. Bruce Bairnsfather was taken to hospital 'suffering from shock.' On 13 May there was an influx of 15 new officers to replace those lost.

There were no known graves for Tillyer and William Tapp- their names are to be found on the Menin Gate Memorial. Tapp left a widow Edith and two very young children.

The report of the Warwicks' involvement in the Second Battle of Ypres concludes with a withering appraisal of the action, counter-signed by the commanding officer Major A.J. Poole: 'It is inadvisable to attack an enemy's position unless properly supported by Artillery fire and a thorough reconnaissance made beforehand.'

William Tapp was one of thousands of British soldiers who lost their lives as a result of questionable tactics by their superiors.

WILLIAM TAPP:

Born:	1884 in Birmingham, married to Edith, with two young children
Education:	Unknown
Occupation:	Professional soldier
Unit/ Regiment:	'C' Company, 1/ Royal Warwicks
Rank:	Private- officer's servant or 'batman'
Died:	25 April 1915, Second Battle of Ypres
Age:	Unknown
Commemorated:	Menin Gate Memorial, Ypres, Panel 8

NOON W.
NORBURY A.
O'BRIEN T.
O'DELL F.
O'DOWD M.
OLIVER F.
OSBORNE J.

SULLIVAN
SURCH T.
SWAIN G.
TAPP W.
THOMAS
THOMAS
THOMPSON
THORNHIL

Private William Tapp's is one of nearly 500 Royal Warwicks names on the Menin Gate
J Kerr

THE YPRES SALIENT
Day 2 Itinerary

Advanced Dressing Station at Essex Farm   J. Kerr

THE YPRES SALIENT
Day 2 Itinerary
(see map of the Ypres Salient p.28)

The itinerary for the second day explores the commemorative sites of the Ypres Salient starting with the graves of a grandson of Queen Victoria buried at Ypres Town Cemetery and a 15 year old under-age volunteer at Essex Farm. Here there is a good example of a British bunker, used as an Advanced Dressing Station, which can be approached along the path to the left of the entrance. A Welsh poet lies in Artillery Wood. A highlight of the Ypres Salient is Langemark, a brooding and atmospheric German cemetery where the name of an air ace can be found on a memorial block above a mass grave for nearly 25,000 Germans.

On your way to Tyne Cot Cemetery and Memorial, drive to the roundabout in Poelkapelle where there is a statue dedicated to a French air ace. A short drive out of the village is Poelcapelle British Cemetery where controversy surrounds the grave of a young Irish boy soldier.

The memorial and cemetery at Tyne Cot commemorate the thousands who died on the Ypres Salient, stark reminders of the huge loss of lives during the Great War but a marvellously designed tribute by Sir Herbert Baker, one of the four main architects used by the Imperial War Graves Commission.

After visiting the grave of one of the finest England Test cricketers in Oxford Road Cemetery, a fascinating and very different site is the 'Aristocrats' Plot' at Zillebeke Churchyard where in November 1914, 15 officers of aristocratic descent were buried during the First Battle of Ypres.

A spectacular site is to be found at Hill 60 where there are two large craters caused by massive explosions prior to the Messines offensive. The Hill 60 crater is in a Memorial Park and the Caterpillar crater is on the other side of the railway line.

One of the most interesting of graves on the Western Front is that of an Irish Nationalist M.P. His solitary grave outside the Locre Hospice Cemetery sadly reflects his misguided conviction that Catholic and Protestant soldiers fighting together would help facilitate a peaceful political transition to Irish Home Rule.

There is much to see and do in the Plugstreet Wood area, not least refreshment in Claude Verhaeghe's wonderfully welcoming hostelry, 'The Auberge', near the Ploegsteert Memorial and Hyde Park Corner Cemetery where you can find the graves of one of the youngest boys to die in the Great War and of another England rugby international. A short distance away is Strand Cemetery where one of the five Souls brothers is buried.

If you are then in need of a gentle walk, take Mud Lane from 'The Auberge' to Prowse Point Cemetery, the only one to be named after an individual. If you have time, take a stroll in Plugstreet Wood and visit the picturesque cemeteries there- Toronto Avenue, Ploegsteert Wood Military and Rifle House where if you are lucky you may see a beautiful flight of butterflies.

By which time you will be ready for your return to Ypres!

Cemetery/ Memorial/ Other	Address/Post code/ Google map ref.	Name	Page
6 YPRES TOWN	Zonnebeekseweg 49-51 8900 Ieper, Belgium 50.854,2.89616	🌺 Prince Maurice of Battenberg	85
7 ESSEX FARM	Mccraepad, 8900 Ieper, Belgium 50.87138,2.87247	🌺 Joe Strudwick	243

8	ARTILLERY WOOD	Poezelstraat 4, 8904 Ieper, Belgium 50.89966,2.87252	🌺 Ellis Evans	89
9	LANGEMARK GERMAN MILITARY	Klerkenstraat 84, 8920 Langemark-Poelkapelle, Belgium 50.92016,2.91747	🌺 Werner Voss	95
10	POELKAPELLE MONUMENT	Roundabout- Guynemerplein 1-23, 8920 Langemark-Poelkapelle, Belgium 50.917537,2.956984	🌺 Georges Guynemer	101
11	POELCAPELLE BRITISH	Brugseweg 275-277, 8920 Langemark-Poelkapelle, Belgium 50.92104,2.97188	🌺 John Condon	243
12	TYNE COT	Tynecotstraat 22-28, 8980 Zonnebeke, Belgium 50.88699,2.99771	🌺 Clarence Jeffries V.C.	104
13	TYNE COT MEMORIAL	as above	🌺 Frederick Millins	109
14	OXFORD ROAD	Wieltje 6-10, 8900 Ieper, Belgium 50.86928,2.91606	🌺 Colin Blythe	112
15	BIRR CROSS ROADS	2/9 Meenseweg, 404-414, 8902 Ieper, Belgium 50.84757,2.92856	🌺 Raymond Lodge	116
16	ZILLEBEKE CHURCHYARD	Zillebeke-Dorp 1-7, 8902 Ieper, Belgium 50.83553,2.92226	🌺 Baron Alexis de Gunzburg 🌺 Avenel St. George	121 125
17	HILL 60 (Zillebeke)	Zwarteleenstraat 36-40, 8902 Ieper, Belgium 50.823737,2.929951	⬤ Two large mine craters	72 84
18	LOCRE HOSPICE	Godtschalckstraat 30, 8958 Heuvelland, Belgium 50.77921,2.78066	🌺 William Redmond	131
19	PLOEGSTEERT MEMORIAL	Rue de Messines 150-160, 7782 Comines-Warneton, Belgium 50.7378,2.88228	🌺 Geoffrey Donaldson	137

20	HYDE PARK CORNER (Royal Berks)	Rue de Messines 159, 7782 Comines-Warneton, Belgium 50.73765,2.88251	Albert French	145
			Ronald Poulton Palmer	141
21	STRAND MILITARY	Rue de Messines 115-157, 7782 Comines-Warneton, Belgium 50.73277,2.88025	Alfred Souls	147

Caterpillar Crater (Hill 60) on the Messines Ridge

J Kerr

PRINCE MAURICE OF BATTENBERG

'A most gallant and capable officer, beloved by his men'

The message imparted by several Great War recruitment posters was the urgent need for men to join up to save the King and his Country from the belligerent 'Hun'; the ranks of the British Expeditionary Force, described by Kaiser Wilhelm II as 'a contemptible little army', struggled against the might of von Kluck's 390,000-strong army at Mons and it was imperative that numbers should be increased rapidly.

Lord Kitchener's pointing finger and stark stare permeated all ranks of society. The pressures to take part were immense and no one would have felt this more keenly than Prince Maurice of Battenberg, King George V's first cousin and 40th and youngest grandchild of Queen Victoria. *The Times History of the War* maintained that: 'The Battenbergs were hereditary enemies of the Hohenzollerns and had been treated by Bismarck and Wilhelm II with peculiar insolence.'

The Prince was an Army regular; he had attended the Royal Military College at Sandhurst, was gazetted to a 2nd lieutenancy in the 1/ King's Royal Rifle Corps in March 1911 and was promoted to lieutenant in February 1914. According to *The Daily Sketch*'s obituary he was affectionately nicknamed 'Pip-Emma', the Army Signallers' code for P and M- i.e. Prince Maurice. With the threat posed by Germany to his cousin King George V and to his country, Prince Maurice was determined to be fully involved with the B.E.F. to halt the progress of the German armies.

A 1914 recruitment poster emphasising the importance of defending King and Country
IWM PST 011745

Maurice's mother Beatrice, the youngest daughter of Queen Victoria, married the German, Prince Henry of Battenberg in 1885. On the day of their wedding Queen Victoria conferred on her son-in-law the title of *Royal Highness* to give him equal rank with his wife and the couple adopted the style, *Their Royal Highnesses Prince and Princess Henry of Battenberg*. Prince Henry was created a Knight of the Garter and appointed to the Privy Council.

During Queen Victoria's reign, British imperialism had spread its influence throughout the world and Prince Henry of Battenberg, a colonel in the Army, played his part in defending British interests during the campaign against the Ashanti tribe in modern-day Ghana. He died of an illness contracted during the operation when Maurice was only four years old,

2nd Lieutenant Prince Maurice of Battenberg of the King's Royal Rifles in 1912

coincidentally the same age as his mother, Princess Beatrice, when her father, Prince Albert, died in 1861.

Prince Maurice of Battenberg, the 40th and youngest grandchild of Queen Victoria, sitting cross-legged to her right
National Portrait Gallery X8489

Over the years ties between the German and British Royal families had become close through marriage. In a bizarre turn of events, various relatives of the British and German Royal families ended up on different sides. King George V was a cousin of Kaiser Wilhelm II who was a grandson of Queen Victoria and

SEND UP THE 100,000 QUICK; LET LORD KITCHENER SEE WE TRUST HIM.

DAILY SKETCH.

No. 1,760.　　　　LONDON, THURSDAY, OCTOBER 29, 1914.　　　[Registered as a Newspaper.]　ONE HALFPENNY.

THE JOLLY PRINCE WHO DIED FOR HIS COUNTRY.

The only death of a member of the Royal Family during the Great War was headline news.
British Newspaper Library, Colindale　F60118-43

Pictures　　　*Left: Princess Beatrice who has now given both husband and son.*
　　　　　　Centre: Prince Maurice who has died of wounds
　　　　　　Right: The happy uncle- with one of Queen Ena's (Victoria Eugenie) children

ironically held the rank of Field Marshal in the British Army- but not for long! The Duke of Saxe-Coburg-Gotha was George V's cousin and served in the Prussian Army. The Duke of Brunswick was a nephew of Queen Alexandra and Prince Albert of Schleswig-Holstein was a grandson of Queen Victoria and served in the Prussian Army.

The young prince was sent to Wellington College where he was a lance corporal in the Officer Training Corps; he excelled as a fine marksman and was in the College's Shooting VIII. He suffered from haemophilia which, however, did not prevent him from embarking on a military career.

He was tall, dark and humorous with, according to *The Daily Sketch*, a 'boyish jollity of manner'. He enjoyed cricket, boxing, football and was a 'capital golfer'. He often visited Hendon Aerodrome and inspired by witnessing pilots at work, his great ambition was to own an aeroplane.

He was a Royal with a common touch- he loved 'motoring' to the East End of London where he paid surprise visits to the Port of London Sea Scouts. In a tribute to the Prince, The Rev. Everard Digby of

St. Agatha's Church recalled his popular personality and his personal qualities: 'He was kindness itself at all times. When an accident happened to our yacht off Gravesend and several of our sea scouts were drowned, the first letter of condolence received was from Prince Maurice who also sent telegrams of sympathy to all the parents of the boys.'

The 1/ King's Royal Rifle Corps was soon in the thick of the action, arriving in France on 13 August 1914 and was based in the Mons, Marne and Aisne areas in August and September.

During fighting in the area round the river Marne, a Corporal Jolley told of the Prince's intrepid approach: 'On the morning of 7 September, the King's Royal Rifles were the advance guard. We traversed a wood and found that the enemy had camped on the other side. We could see the Germans making blockages on the bridge, preparing to blow it up, but on seeing us they made off, and as we had no artillery with us, they got off free. The order then came that the bridge must be taken at once.

When we got there we found that the bridge had three blockages, comprised of carts, furniture, glass, wire etc. Prince Maurice of Battenberg was first man over, searching the house beyond all by himself. This was a brave act for an officer alone.'

Prince Maurice and the 1/ King's Royal Rifles were involved in a particularly successful action on 10 September, when, after crossing the Marne, they engaged the enemy on the Vierley-Chézy road for 90 minutes when 80 Germans were killed or wounded. Towards the end of the month the Battalion suffered many casualties.

In October the 1/ King's Royal Rifles moved to the Ypres Salient and on 27 October, 'A' and 'B' Companies advanced from Zonnebeke to Broodseinde and once over the Passchendaele-Becelaere road, came under heavy fire.

Prince Maurice of Battenberg's grave and marker in 1914

Prince Maurice was hit by shrapnel. A serjeant tried to help him but to no avail. The Prince and 32 year old Captain W. Wells, son of Admiral Sir Richard Wells, K.C.B., were killed along with 24 other ranks. *The King's Royal Rifle Corps Chronicle* reported: 'To the sincere sorrow of all who knew him in the Regiment, he died of wounds on October 27th, received in action whilst gallantly leading his men. The late Prince Maurice had endeared himself to all ranks of the Regiment by his charming personality and thoughtfulness for others. He was a most gallant and capable officer, beloved by his men, his last words being to wish them goodbye. The funeral took place at Ypres on the 31st October, and the following eulogy was passed upon the Prince by Field-Marshal Sir John French, (Commander-in-Chief of the B.E.F.): "The army has lost a gallant officer, who was a fine example to all around him."'

The French President Poincaré was keen to acknowledge the efforts made by the British monarchy and in a telegram to Princess Henry of Battenberg, consoled her by recalling that 'I had quite recently the great pleasure of seeing Prince Maurice in the midst of the splendid British troops and today I learn that he has fallen on the field of honour. I beg that Your Highness in this great trial will accept my sincere and respectful sympathy.'

The Prince's obituary in *The Daily Sketch* praised him for his 'instinctive soldierliness and complete absence of "side" which had made him immensely popular… His genial comradeship in the officers' mess, his kindliness and unaffected naturalness among his men' had won him general affection. 'The Prince was fond of leading his men at the double when there was a charge to be made, and his unquestionable pluck and enthusiasm were only equalled by his physical vigour and power of endurance.' The newspaper reported that 'even the Kaiser is said to have had an especial regard for his young cousin.'

On news of Prince Maurice's death Lord Kitchener suggested that the Prince's body should be

A haunted look on the face of King George V during a visit to Maurice's grave in 1921
IWM Q003427

brought home but his mother refused, insistent that her son would have wanted to be buried with the men of his company.

King George V was distraught on hearing the news of his cousin's death- his sadness would have been tempered by the knowledge that Prince Maurice's attention to duty and his courage warranted a Mention in Despatches. The King visited Maurice's grave in May 1921.

Lieutenant H.H. Prince Maurice of Battenberg K.C.V.O. (Knight Commander of the Royal Victorian Order awarded by George V on 19 June 1911) of the King's Royal Rifle Corps was buried in the Ypres Town Cemetery aged 23. Had he died three years later, his name would have been recorded on his gravestone as Prince Maurice Mountbatten; for understandable reasons, George V decided in 1917 to airbrush German connotations from the family names, so Saxe-Coburg-Gotha changed to Windsor and Battenberg to Mountbatten.

Maurice of Battenberg was a popular member of the Royal Family so it was hardly a surprise that his death should have been headline news on 29 October 1914.

PRINCE MAURICE OF BATTENBERG:

Born:	3 October 1891 at Balmoral Castle, son of Their Royal Highnesses Prince and Princess Henry of Battenberg
Education:	Wellington College and the Royal Military College, Sandhurst
Occupation:	Royalty and Army
Unit/ Regiment:	1/ King's Royal Rifle Corps
Rank:	Lieutenant
Died:	27 October 1914 at Broodseinde during the First Battle of Ypres
Age:	23
Buried:	Ypres Town Cemetery I.B.
Inscription:	GRANT HIM WITH ALL THY FAITHFUL SERVANTS A PLACE OF REFRESHMENT AND PEACE

The cemetery is located near the Menin Gate and was established in October 1914. It was in use until May 1915. There are 145 Great War burials amongst locals' graves

Prince Maurice's grave in the Ypres Town Cemetery   J Kerr

ELLIS EVANS

Hedd Wyn (Blessed Peace)

The 1917 National Eisteddfod was held at Birkenhead in Cheshire. During the second day of the ceremony on 6 September, the eisteddfodic sword was placed across the arms of the Chair ready to be awarded to the winner of the poetry competition. In the presence of the Prime Minister, Welshman David Lloyd George, the Archdruid Dyfed announced that *Fleur de Lys* had won the Chair. There was a pause- the recipient of the prize had not come forward. His name was called two more times. The Archdruid then announced that the winning poet had been killed on the field of battle. The sword was removed and the Chair draped in black. *Fleur de Lys* was the pseudonym of Ellis Evans, one of 31,500 casualties on 31 July 1917, the first day of the Battle of Passchendaele.

The Evans family- Ellis is standing far left
Alan Llwyd Collection

Ellis Humphrey was born on 13 January 1887, the first child of Mary Ellis, a serious and solemn maidservant who married Evan Evans, a hillside farmer from North Wales. They lived at Yr Ysgwrn, a farmhouse just outside Trawsfynydd in Merionethshire, North Wales. Between 1888 and 1907, Mary gave birth to four more sons, six daughters and two still-born babies. Two of the children died- a boy aged five and a three year old girl.

Although he received only a basic education, Ellis developed an early interest in poems, encouraged by his father who enjoyed poetry and bought him a book of Welsh verse. The young Ellis was happy to escape the noisy household and enjoy the solitude of his job as a shepherd. In the still of the night when everyone had gone to bed, he would write poetry, in much the same way as another poet from a similar background- Will Streets, a miner from Sheffield (see p.228)

Ellis was awarded the main literary prize when only 12 at the Ebenezer Chapel where the family worshipped. The minister, J.D. Richards, became a close friend and Ellis befriended another

Ellis and sister Mary   *Meirionnydd Archives*

minister R. Silyn Roberts with whom he often went fishing and discussed religion and politics. Roberts was a committed socialist and his views helped to shape Ellis's attitude to the War. Ellis's poetry was inspired by the romanticism of Percy Bysshe Shelley's work and his themes tended to

Ellis Evans standing next to his second Chair presented at the Llanuwchllyn Eisteddfod of 1913
National Library of Wales

focus on nature and religion. He won his first Chair at the Bala Eisteddfod in 1907. Encouraged by his family, probably wishing to improve himself and keen to seek independence, he went south in 1908 to work in the Abercynon colliery. An *englyn*, a strict metre four-line stanza written when in the coalfields, highlighted that his heart and soul belonged in Trawsfynydd and not surprisingly after only four months, he returned to the relative freedom and tranquillity of shepherding on the hills overlooking his family home. He could now concentrate on his poetry.

Ellis's ultimate goal was to win the National Eisteddfod and to fulfil his ambition, he competed in many literary competitions; each time he gained in confidence and competence and benefited from the opportunity to swap ideas with the poets he met.

It was at a bardic gathering in Blaenau Ffestiniog in 1910 that the local poet Humphrey Jones gave him his bardic name of Hedd Wyn: 'Hedd' the Welsh for peace and 'Wyn' blessed although it can mean white or pure. Jones recalled that Ellis 'had the appearance of a dreamer and he moved slowly and calmly.'

His fame began to spread in 1913 amongst literary circles when he won his second Chair at the Llanuwchllyn Eisteddfod as well as his third at Pwllheli and lesser prizes. Although shy and overawed amongst educated people, he enjoyed their company.

In photographs Ellis gives the impression of someone serious or even sullen. The poet Evan Williams (1897-1937) whose bardic name was Glyn Myfyr paints a vivid picture of the young poet: 'His thick hair was more or less untidily parted'; of his upper lip: 'We can't recall noticing anyone with such a thin lip as his' and of his thin nose 'its tip angling slightly towards the right cheek and when he spoke, especially if conversing with someone who shared his interests, he would instinctively get hold of his nose, and twist it in the above mentioned direction. We are unable to decide whether or not it was the effect of this habit that made his member more or less crooked'!

Ellis Evans 'Hedd Wyn'
National Library of Wales

Ellis partied hard on his prize money! On one occasion he won a prize for a poem in memory of a Methodist deacon and spent all his money on drink. On seeing him staggering out of a local pub, a minister scolded him for his lack of temperance: 'What a disgraceful state to be in. What have you got to say for yourself?' to which Ellis replied: 'I wouldn't be in this state if some Methodist deacon hadn't died!'

His mischievous streak reached a high when judging a poetry competition in Trawsfynydd. As there was not a single entry, he wrote a poem and got his good friend Morris Davies to submit it. Ellis duly awarded it first prize and spent his winnings on more beer!

His drinking got him into trouble with one of his girlfriends, Jini Owen, an orphan three years his junior. She regularly carried out her threat to leave him unless he moderated his drinking, but they soon made up. At the same time as he was courting Jini, he was seeing Mary Catherine Hughes who was ten years younger than him. She was teaching at the village school attended by Ellis's youngest sister Enid who acted as a message carrier for them. Another of his girlfriends, Lizzie Roberts, died of tuberculosis in 1916 in whose memory he wrote an *englyn*:

She bowed down in the prime of her life to the grave	*Gwyrodd yn ei hoed hawddgaraf – i'r bedd*
When the world was in beauty,	*A'r byd ar ei dlysaf;*
And now, through the summer breeze,	*O'i hôl hi, trwy'r awel haf,*
I hear the song of longing.	*Alawon hiraeth glywaf.*

Alan Llwyd in *The Story of Hedd Wyn- The Poet of the Black Chair* suggests that Ellis's relationship with Jini would have flourished and become permanent.

When war was declared in August 1914, unlike thousands of his generation, Ellis was not caught up with the propaganda and patriotic fervour for enlisting. There is a similarity here with another poet from humble beginnings- Isaac Rosenberg (see p.193). Evans did write some patriotic verse in the same vein as Rupert Brooke's but the tone soon changed in poems written in memory of friends killed in battle. The mood of some of them was dark and critical exemplified in *War* and *The Black Spot*:

Jini Owen   *Alan Llwyd Collection*

War

Man raised his sword, once God had gone,	*Pan deimlodd fyned ymaith Dduw*
To slay his brother, and the roar	*Cyfododd gledd i ladd ei frawd;*
Of battlefields now casts upon	*Mae sŵn yr ymladd ar ein clyw,*
Our homes the shadow of the war...	*A'i gysgod ar fythynnod tlawd...*

The Black Spot

We only have a right to exist	*Ni does gennym hawl ar ddim byd*
On earth in its vast devastation	*Ond ar yr hen ddaear wyw;*
And it's only man's strife that destroys	*A honno sy'n anhrefn i gyd*
The glory of God's creation...	*Yng nghanol gogoniant Duw...*

Ellis continued to compete in spite of the War. In 1915 he won two Chairs but his entry for the National Eisteddfod held at Bangor- *An Ode to Snowdon*, was savaged by the critics. Undeterred he entered the Aberystwyth competition in the following year where one of the three judges voted for his poem *Strata Florida* about the ruins of a Cistercian Abbey.

It was inevitable that the shadow of war would envelop the Evans family. Ellis's mother warned him against going into the village and receiving criticism for having not enlisted or worse still being handed the symbol of cowardice, a white feather by a young girl. His father tried to save him and his brothers from military service on the grounds of essential war work in the fields.

In 1916 Ellis and his father were summoned to appear before several tribunals investigating his sons' failure to 'take the King's Shilling'. According to the Minister J.D. Richards, 'Hedd Wyn could have remained at home without violating any law. He wasn't a soldier by nature... To quarrel angrily was not his way.' Ellis volunteered to join up instead of his 18 year old brother: 'One of us has to go and Bob is too young.'

He enlisted at Blaenau Ffestiniog, joining the 15/ Royal Welch Fusiliers at the time when he was working on his entry for the 1917 Eisteddfod- *Yr Arwr* (The Hero). Private Simon Jones who travelled with Ellis to Litherland camp near Liverpool in January 1917 recalled that Ellis was fond of his pipe and was wearing red shoes which were stolen (or maybe destroyed!) at the depot. Jones also   91 mentioned that Ellis Evans was not a natural soldier and was often ticked off by officers. In a letter to his friend Morris Evans, Ellis wrote: 'Well I am quite well, considering that I'm only a Private. There is little poetry here, but plenty of poets, because most of the men and officers are Welshmen. I have committed quite a few transgressions since arriving here, but I have been pardoned every time and that is quite an achievement in the army.' The poets Robert Graves and Siegfried Sassoon were officers in the Royal Welch Fusiliers- a mere private, Ellis probably never encountered them.

He was released in March 1917 for several weeks to work on the family farm. He harboured doubts about his Eisteddfod poem *Yr Arwr* which he was working on but his friends and Jini in particular, encouraged him to continue. The Military Police arrived to return him to barracks as he had over extended his leave!

Ellis arrived at Rouen in Normandy to undergo more training in June. He wrote to Morris Evans from 'Rowen, France... Heavy weather, a heavy soul and a heavy heart.' In late June he wrote to H.O. Evans of Trawsfynydd: 'This is a very beautiful country from what I have seen of it up to now- the trees high and full-leaved and their leaves shaking, quivering and murmuring as though they were trying

Shell cases   *J Kerr*

to say something mysterious, or as though some nostalgic spirit from Wales was returning sadly after failing to find someone who is lying in a grave "Somewhere in France" ...the most beautiful thing I have seen since coming here is an old shell-case that had been adapted to grow flowers ... doesn't that prove that beauty is stronger than war and that loveliness will outlive the sadness?'

He joined his battalion at Fléchin north of Agincourt in July. It was there that he completed *Yr Arwr*. The poem arrived late in Wales, probably because his commanding officer, not understanding Welsh, had to be convinced it was not propaganda or criticism.

Attached to the 38th (Welsh) Division, the 15/ Royal Welch Fusiliers had already experienced heavy fighting in the Somme the previous year at Mametz Wood. The Battalion was now to be involved in yet more momentous events in Flanders where hopes were high for a breakthrough following the successful taking of the Messines Ridge in early June. Their objective was to reach the so-called 'green line' approximately two miles from the start line in order to allow the 17/ Royal Welch Fusiliers to capture the village of Langemark. On 30 July they assembled in their trenches near the canal at Boesinghe, north of Ypres. Their attack commenced at 03.50 the next day. The 10 and 13/ Royal Welch Fusiliers achieved their objective with little difficulty but the 14th and 15th Battalions encountered stiffer opposition in the Iron Cross area. Every officer, including Lieutenant-Colonel C.C. Norman of the 15th, was killed or wounded. As a result, command had to be handed over to an N.C.O., Regimental Serjeant Major Jones whose order was to consolidate their position.

Accounts differ as to what happened to Ellis Evans but it is generally agreed that he was struck by a shell fragment when the fighting was at its fiercest at about 8.00 a.m. Badly wounded, he was taken by stretcher bearers to a Dressing Station where a Doctor Day quickly established that Evans was mortally wounded. According to the Reverend R. Peris Williams, a chaplain with the Royal Welch Fusiliers who had interviewed soldiers in the 15th Battalion, Ellis asked the doctor and those around him: 'Do you think I will live?' in a cheerful manner, a reaction to the dose of morphine that would have been administered to him. One of the soldiers comforted him: 'You seem to be very happy' and at about 11.00 a.m. he uttered his last words: 'Yes I am very happy.' The Battalion's chaplain, the Reverend D. Morris, conducted a burial service at Ellis's grave; his wooden cross was draped with the Red Dragon Flag. His body was later moved to Artillery Wood Cemetery (II.F.11.) where another Celtic poet, Francis Ledwidge, is buried (II.B.5.)- a lance corporal of the 1/ Royal Inniskilling Fusiliers, from County Meath in Ireland. Francis was killed, aged 29, on the same day as Ellis whilst taking a break with a mug of tea during plank-laying over the battlefield. He was self-educated with a political conscience and joined up 'to fight an enemy common to our civilisation'. He became disillusioned with the War and homesick. He describes himself in one of his most famous poems, *Soliloquy*, as 'The helpless child of circumstance'.

Ellis Evans's Eisteddfod winning poem *The Hero* features the Daughter of the Tempests who represents the beauty of nature and the symbol of love. The Hero symbolises freedom, goodness and justice. The end of the Ode looks forward to a better age.

It was ironic that the 1917 Chair was crafted by Eugeen Vanfleteren a Flemish carpenter who fled from the German armies as they invaded Belgium in 1914. After the 1917 Eisteddfod a committee was established in Trawsfynydd to preserve the poet's works and in 1918 an anthology was published entitled *The Shepherd's Poems*.

His mother unveiled a bronze statue of her son dressed as a shepherd in 1923 which received criticism in some quarters for over romanticising the shepherd poet. Fittingly the statue bore an inscription written by Ellis himself in memory of a friend killed during the War.

His sacrifice was not in vain, his face	*Ei aberth nid â heibio, - ei wyneb*
In our minds will remain,	*Annwyl nid â'n ango',*
Though the Hun has stained his fist	*Er i'r Almaen ystaenio*
Of steel in his blood.	*Ei dwrn dur yn ei waed o.*

Ellis Evans's grave in Artillery Wood Cemetery   *A Hamilton*

After the statue had been unveiled, Ellis's friend Silyn Roberts, acting on the wishes of the Evans family, asked the Imperial War Graves Commission to engrave on his headstone the inscription: 'Y Prifardd Hedd Wyn' (The Chief Bard Hedd Wyn). Roberts presented Ellis's original wooden cross to the Council School at Trawsfynydd.

If he had survived the War, would Ellis Evans have continued as a shepherd and occasional poet or would he have gone on to greater things? It was remarkable that someone who had received such a modest education should have been awarded the coveted Eisteddfod Chair for poetry. In his tribute to the fallen poet, William Morris, a younger friend of Ellis's, pointed out that 'one could easily pass him by on the street and mistake him for an ordinary farmhand. But when conversing with him… one soon realised that a very rare spirit stared through those lively blue eyes. He was the most unassuming and most decent person I have ever known.'

ELLIS EVANS:

Born:	13 January 1887, son of Mary and Evan Evans of Trawsfynydd, Merionethshire, NorthWales
Education:	Village and Sunday school
Occupation:	Shepherd
Unit/ Regiment:	15/ Royal Welch Fusiliers (1st London Welsh). Before the War the Regiment was spelled 'Welch'- during the War, the War Office changed the spelling to 'Welsh' but the original spelling was reintroduced in 1920
Rank:	Private
Died:	31 July 1917, the first day of the Third Battle of Ypres (Passchendaele)
Age:	30
Buried:	Artillery Wood Cemetery II.F.11.
Inscription:	Y PRIFARDD HEDD WYN (The Chief Bard Blessed Peace)

The cemetery was established 4 kms north of Ypres after the Battle of Pilckem Ridge in July 1917. There are now over 1,300 burials, 500 of them unidentified. The designer was Sir Reginald Blomfield

Langemark German Cemetery   J. Kerr

WERNER VOSS

'A daredevil first class'

There was no major offensive on the ground in the Ypres Salient on 23 September 1917 but there had been much activity high above in the skies which ended in one of the epic fights of the War. It involved machines flown by 56 Squadron, one of the most successful in the Royal Flying Corps, whose pilots encountered one of the greatest German air aces. The British air ace and future V.C. holder, Captain James McCudden, recalled in his memoirs that 'the German pilot saw us and turned in a most disconcertingly quick manner… (he) seemed to be firing at all of us simultaneously… none of us could hold him in sight at all for any decisive time.' Captain Geoffrey Bowman noted that 'his machine was exceptionally manoeuvrable and he appeared to take flying liberties with impunity.' The odds were stacked against the German pilot who found himself amongst six R.F.C. planes. Lieutenant Arthur Rhys Davids, a 19 year old Classics scholar from Eton College, would be credited with bringing down the enemy aircraft. The German airforce lost one its finest pilots- Werner Voss. In about ten months as a fighter pilot, he had claimed 48 'scalps'.

Werner Voss was born into a wealthy family of three sons and two daughters on 13 April 1897 in the Rhineland mill town of Krefeld. His father Max managed a successful dyeing business where Werner and his brothers Otto and Max were destined to work. Their mother Mathilde was a principled Evangelical Lutheran. Werner was a conscientious student at school and passed his exams with distinction. He was a happy child but was prone to behave in an impetuous and obstinate way, traits that would characterise his attitude as a pilot.

He had volunteered before the War to join the local militia in Krefeld so it was not surprising that when Germany went to war, he enlisted in the No. 11 Hussar Regiment which was sent to the Eastern Front to fight the Russians.

Werner Voss and a motorbike given to him by his parents on his 18th birthday　　　　Dennis Hylands

The young cavalryman soon had to get accustomed to fighting as a foot soldier now that more effective weaponry had rendered the cavalry virtually obsolete. He was swiftly promoted to gefreiter and then unter-offizier, ranks similar to those of lance corporal and corporal, but without the powers accorded to similar ranks in the British Army.

His bravery was recognised in May 1915 with the award of the Iron Cross 2nd Class, also received by another gefreiter, Adolf Hitler, for helping to save the life of his commanding officer in November 1914.

He applied successfully to join the Imperial German Air Service: it was preferable to continuing with the infantry on the Eastern Front. He was soon recommended for training as a pilot and was considered an exceptionally able pupil. When only 18, he became the youngest instructor in Cologne and by March 1916 was deployed as an observer over the Verdun battlefield. Two months later, he received his pilot's badge and moved to the Somme.

One month into the Battle of the Somme he was the only pilot in his unit to have survived the air offensive. Ambitious for promotion, he applied for a commission and was sent to East Prussia for advanced instruction. As a leutnant der reserve, he then trained in single-seat machines.

At the end of November he joined the most successful German squadron in the Somme: Jasta 2 (an abbreviation for Jagdstaffel, the equivalent to an R.F.C. fighter squadron) which had been formed by the legendary Oswald Boelcke, the 'Master and Father' of the German Air Service. Boelcke had been killed in a collision with one of his pilots before Werner's arrival.

Voss benefited greatly from the experience of his commanding officer the aristocrat and uhlan Manfred von Richthofen, later known as 'The Red Baron', who downed 80 allied aircraft during his fighting career.

Werner's first success was remarkable as it marked the first of several doubles for which he was awarded the Iron Cross 1st Class. Although he shot down three aeroplanes of the French Aviation Militaire, his time in the air was generally spent in combat with the R.F.C. General Ernst von Hoeppner of the German Army Air Service was of the opinion in 1917 that 'because of their number and their sporting audacity, the English continue to be our most dangerous enemies.'

There is often talk of chivalry and respect shown between the fighter pilots but it was not in Voss's nature to show such reverence to his enemies. However, in February 1917, when he claimed his fourth victim over Achiet-le-Grand in the Somme, he visited Captain Albert Daly who had been hospitalised after managing to land his damaged machine behind German lines. Werner brought him cigars and, characteristically, a signed photograph of himself!

He was becoming increasingly daring by the time he scored his 19th victory on 18 March. On this occasion Captain Guy Thorne, although badly hit by an explosive bullet in the back, succeeded in landing his BE2d (a two seater reconnaissance plane) behind German lines before dying of his wounds. His observer, 2nd Lieutenant Philip van Baerle came through unscathed but was taken prisoner. After his release he recalled that Voss had fired on the BE2d after it had landed. According to the combat report, Werner landed next to the British plane, took its Lewis guns and set fire to it. He referred to the two-seater crew as 'poor devils' explaining that 'I know how they felt. I have flown in such a type. They must be destroyed because they spy out our secrets but I would prefer to shoot down fighters' which echoes Georges Guynemer's sentiment (see p.101)

Voss with his 'Pour le Mérite' medal
Alex Imrie Collection

Voss accounted for his 23rd and 24th victims during the Battle of Arras in April, described by the British as 'Bloody April' when the R.F.C. lost more aircraft (151) and aircrew (316 casualties) than in any other month of the War. The life expectancy of an R.F.C. pilot that month was reckoned to be a mere 23 days.

Voss's 23rd victory on 1 April revealed a disquieting trait- the observer Lieutenant Adrian Mackenzie was killed instantly and the pilot, Captain Arthur Wynne, although wounded, crash landed his machine and was thrown out of the cockpit just before Voss, flying low, strafed the wreckage. Wynne did survive and fought in the Second World War in the R.A.F. Volunteer Reserve.

Voss was now being recognised for his exploits. He received the Order of the Knight's Cross on 27 March and on 8 April he learnt that he had been awarded the highest decoration for gallantry, the 'Pour le Mérite' which had been initiated in 1740 by Emperor Frederick II who was a French speaker. It was affectionately known as 'The Blue Max' by German airmen, so-called because when it was awarded to Max Immelmann in January 1916, the sun caught the royal blue on the medal and reflected a blue hue on his face

Werner Voss notched his 25th victory on 7 May 1917 when, east of Arras, he shot down and killed the 18 year old 2nd Lieutenant Roger Chaworth-Musters who had been at the Front for just over a month with 56 Squadron which, on that day also lost their famous ace, Albert Ball, north of Lens (see p.182).

Voss was appointed acting commander of Jasta 5 and on 5 June he took out his 33rd plane and again he strafed a grounded machine. The Canadian observer 2nd Lieutenant Herbert Harris, lost the index finger of his left hand and the pilot, Captain Francis Don, had to have his shattered left arm amputated. Both became prisoners of war. After the War ended, Don was promoted to Air Vice-Marshal and posted to the British Embassy in Berlin as Air Attaché. A female relative of Werner, perhaps his sister Margrit, asked to be introduced to Don who flatly refused, no doubt smarting at having been raked by him.

By mid-1917 Voss and Manfred von Richthofen were fêted as heroes back home in Germany. Although 'rivals' in the air, they were great friends on the ground. They spent some leave together, von Richthofen staying at the Voss family's hunting lodge in the Black Forest. There were rumours of the Red Baron's love for Werner's younger sister Margrit, who may have been the mysterious writer of long letters to him. As airmen, the two were quite different: Voss was the more skilled pilot whereas Von Richthofen was more of a leader of men. Modesty did not prevent Voss describing his rival as 'a great fighter… he has done wonderful work for the Fatherland but I do not believe that he is better than I am'! Von Richthofen was killed by ground-fire over the Somme on 21 April 1918.

Voss was a calculating pilot whose strength lay in his belief that the best way to ensure a 'hit' was to fight as close as possible to the enemy aircraft before shooting- a manoeuvre that required great skill, nerve and aggressive spirit. When flying, he would wear his best tunic with a silk shirt rather than the regulation woollen one which would have been rougher on the skin but, more importantly, he wore the silk one so that if he were unlucky enough to be shot down he would, sartorially, be ready to entertain the girls in Paris! Slim and blue-eyed he would no doubt have been a 'hit' with the local girls.

Like other German pilots he personalised the decoration of his plane- he painted a red heart with a white border and a white swastika on his Albatros II, a good luck symbol with at that time no Nazi connotation. It is possible he was in that plane when he crossed swords with the British air ace Edward Mannock who recorded in his diary details of the dog fight on 19 August: 'Ran into my old friend a few weeks ago. No luck. He's a marvel. For ten minutes… he manoeuvred so cleverly that I was unable to get my gun on him once': quite a tribute from the highest scoring British pilot with 73 victories in 14 months whose account closed in July 1918 when he was brought down by ground fire.

Voss painting a heart on his Albatros in April 1917   *Alex Imrie Collection*

German losses were escalating during the summer of 1917. The R.F.C. had taken delivery of the SE5 (Scout Experimental), the variant SE5a and the F1 Sopwith Camel which were superior to the German Albatros. The Germans were forced into a re-think and organised themselves into larger units, Jagdgeschwader which were equivalent to R.F.C. Fighter Wings, consisting of four Jastas. The first, JG1, was not surprisingly commanded by Manfred von Richthofen and dubbed the 'Travelling Circus' by the R.F.C. pilots who were, at the time, crossing freely over the German lines. Von Richthofen commented on their bravery which had 'a touch of foolishness about it' whereas 'in a Frenchman, bravery is quite exceptional and if you do meet it, it is like a glass of lemonade and very soon goes flat.' His colleagues on the receiving end of the French air aces' fire would have begged to differ.

Voss was given permanent command of Jasta 10 in July. He was bored by paperwork and disliked being restricted by battle plans. It would appear that the strain of constant combat was starting to show. Some men in his unit recalled his ageing appearance and how nervously 'he continually slid around on his chair.'

Prior to taking command of Jasta 10, Voss went on leave, during which he visited a factory owned by

A Fokker triplane of the kind flown by Manfred von Richthofen, 'the Red Baron'   *Aerospace Publishing 1997*

the Dutchman Anthony Fokker at Schwerin where he tried a newly designed triplane which impressed him greatly. It was sturdily built, manoeuvrable, good for zooming moves and able to rise to 3,000 feet in under three minutes. However it was not as fast as the SE5 and Sopwith Camel and not as easy to handle in a steep dive.

Jasta 10 was moved to Courtrai in Belgium, in readiness for the forthcoming British offensive. At the end of August Voss took delivery of the new Fokker triplane on which the Germans were pinning their hopes. He achieved a hard won triple on 10 September, bringing down three machines over Langemark- two R.F.C. and one Aviation Militaire and managing to kill all three pilots.

The following day he scored another double, taking out both pilots, including Lieutenant Oscar McMaking of 45 Squadron whose commander, Captain Norman Macmillan, gave chase and in his memoirs *Into the Blue*, described the fight: 'This fellow was of a different breed… The range was so close that I could almost read the man's expression. I gave him another burst and saw a stream of tracer miss his head by inches as he swerved outward from my line of sight.' Macmillan had managed to do what no other R.F.C. pilot had done before: to be just 20 feet from Werner Voss. That close encounter proved too much for Voss and that evening he signed his own leave warrant and travelled to Germany. During his time away he tried out a new triplane at the Fokker factory and it is said that his last night of leave was spent at a reception in Berlin at the invitation of Anthony Fokker. It was a reunion, admittedly unsubstantiated, of air aces including the von Richthofen brothers, Manfred and Lothar and one Hermann Göring who would notch 22 victories, receive the 'Blue Max' award and become Commander-in-Chief of the German Air Force in the Second World War.

Werner, centre, with his brothers on the day he died, 23 September 1917 Alex Imrie Collection

Voss returned to the Front. His day started auspiciously for him on 23 September when, in the morning, he added a 48th and final enemy plane to his tally. Both crew were killed. He lunched with his brothers Otto and Max and the three of them were photographed. The strain of ten months' of air combat is plain to see in Werner's eyes.

Late in the afternoon he took to the sky in his Fokker triplane with eight other planes but true to his reputation as a loner, he peeled away from them over Zonnebeke. He was spotted by two planes from 60 Squadron who were returning from a patrol. The encounter ended when the two R.F.C. pilots coaxed their badly hit planes westwards to the British lines. From further above, the engagement had been observed by pilots of 56 Squadron including the leader of 'B' Flight, Captain James McCudden, the R.F.C.'s ace of aces at the time who was killed in a flying accident in July 1918, having scored 58 victories. He signalled to the other six to attack. The next 10 to 15 minutes would mark one of the greatest air battles of the War. The R.F.C. pilots were frustrated in their efforts to shoot at the German who took evasive action with spectacular dives and turns while still managing to hit their machines. V.P. Cronyn, a Canadian lieutenant, complimented Voss in his memoirs: 'I take my hat off to that Hun as he was a most skilful pilot, but he did give me a rough passage.' His machine badly hit, Cronyn had to 'limp' home. Machines of 'C' Flight, led by Captain G. Bowman arrived on the scene at the same time as a German Albatros which was seen off by Lieutenant R.A. Maybery. It is believed he drove off a triplane, probably the one of Oberleutnant Oskar von Boenigk of Jasta 4 who later admitted: 'Hell, the sky was full off damned English, so I stuffed my nose down and cleared off'.' Witnessing Werner's action from above, Major R. Stuart-Wortley wrote that he watched 'with profound admiration this display of skill and daring… He was in and out and round about our Scouts, zigzagging like forked lightning through the sky.' Voss momentarily disengaged from the fray and joined a dozen German machines which had appeared on the scene. He may have thought that they would support him but they did not. Without hesitation, he returned to the action and then was seen to fly in a straight line (a major flying error) which may have been because he had been hit. Lieutenant Rhys Davids was able to fire his Vickers gun at the triplane which crashed west of Zonnebeke. Davids was killed in the same area a month later, aged 20.

The 56 Squadron pilots noticed, on their return to base, that all their machines were riddled with bullets. At dinner, the mood was sombre. Bowman remarked: 'It was an amazing show on the part of Voss. I remember at the time feeling rather sorry it had to end the way it did. Our elation was not nearly as great as you might have imagined.' Davids confessed to McCudden: 'If only I could have brought him down alive.' McCudden's appraisal of Voss was complimentary: 'His courage was magnificent… in my opinion he is the bravest German airman whom it has been my privilege to see fight.'

The careers of Albert Ball and Werner Voss were remarkably similar. Their backgrounds were comparable, they operated as loners, were unsuited to the responsibilities of command and were the most skilful of pilots. They showed tremendous courage as well as a recklessness which, in addition to the nervous stress of combat, could only end in one way.

Werner Voss's crash site was close to Plum Farm near Frezenberg. His body was identified the next day and buried in the nearest shell hole by gunners of the Royal Field Artillery.

It was ironic that Werner Voss, the 'lone wolf', was transferred to a huge mass grave in the German Cemetery at Langemark which is one of four German cemeteries in Flanders where by the end of the conflict there were 128 German burial sites. The

A student soldier by a comrade's grave in Langemark Cemetery www.greatwar.nl *(Rob Ruggenberg)*

cemetery incorporates three original front line German bunkers and the first burials there date from 1915. Following a signed agreement in 1954, 9,500 bodies from 18 smaller sites were reinterred at Langemark. More than 44,000 are now buried in an awesome site, known to the Germans as 'Der Studentenfriedhof' (The Students' Cemetery). About 3,000 students are buried here, casualties of the First Battle of Ypres when they faced the regulars of the B.E.F. Such was the strength of feeling about the deaths of these young men, some as young as 17, that Adolf Hitler visited the cemetery during his tour of newly occupied northern France and Belgium in June 1940 and in their memory one of the Waffen-S.S. divisions, consisting of Flemish volunteers, was named the 'Langemark Division'.

A visit to Langemark makes an interesting contrast to typical British cemeteries with their space, white stone graves, green lawns and colourful borders. The site is entered through a bunker-like structure constructed in heavy dark stone which evokes a sombre mood and the melancholy of the site is reinforced by the shade thrown by a number of sturdy oak trees, the national tree of Germany. Inside the dim room to the right are wooden panels inscribed with the names of the men known to have been buried in the cemetery but do not have identifiable graves.

Special plaque to the British Privates Carlill and Lockley on the first block to the left of the Langemark mass grave A Reed

The focus of the cemetery is the central mass grave in which nearly 25,000 bodies were buried of whom over 7,500 were unidentified. Those known to be buried in the Comrades' grave are inscribed on bronze tablets that surround it. They include air ace Werner Voss and, on a separate plaque, two British soldiers: Private Albert Carlill aged 19 of the Loyal North Lancashire Regiment and Private Leonard Lockley of the Seaforth Highlanders who both died in the last two weeks of the War. Their names are also recorded on the German bronze tablets but incorrectly spelled as Carhil and Lookley.

Small burial plots with horizontal stone markers bearing the names of those buried surround the Comrades' grave. The group of three basalt lava crosses are architectural features only and represent the crosses motif of the Volksbund Deutsche Kriegsgräberfürsorge, the German counterpart of the Commonwealth War Graves Commission.

A feature of the cemetery is the eerily evocative group of four bronze statues of soldiers mourning at a comrade's grave. The Münich sculptor Professor Emil Krieger took his inspiration from a photograph of soldiers mourning at Langemark in 1918.

Catch a glimpse of an inscription above the lintel of the rear doorway of the entrance building: 'Deutschland muss leben und wenn wir sterben müssen' which translates as: 'Germany must live, even if we must die', a patriotic sentiment expressed in his 1914 poem *Soldiers Farewell* by Heinrich Lersch (1889-1936) who later in 1933 was one of 88 writers to swear allegiance to Adolf Hitler.

Langemark Cemetery is well worth a visit, not just to find Werner Voss's place of burial but also to experience one of the most haunting memorials to the dead of the Great War.

Voss's name on one of the blocks that surround the mass grave at Langemark Cemetery   *J Kerr*

WERNER VOSS:

Born:	13 April 1897 in Krefeld, son of Max and Mathilde Voss
Education:	Real Gymnasium, Krefeld
Occupation:	Family dyeing business
Unit/ Regiment:	Jagdstaffel 10 (Fighter Squadron) of the Imperial Air Service
Rank:	Leutnant der Reserve
Died:	23 September 1917, Third Battle of Ypres (Passchendaele)
Age:	20
Decorations:	Iron Cross 2nd Class, Iron Cross 1st Class, Knight's Cross with Swords (Hohenzollern Order), 'Pour le Mérite'
Buried:	Mass grave, Langemark German Cemetery, commemorated on Block 63

The four bronze statues in Langemark Cemetery   *J Kerr*

GEORGES GUYNEMER

'If one has not given everything, one has given nothing'

An unusual memorial of a stork in full flight commemorates a French air ace, Georges Guynemer in the middle of a roundabout in the village of Poelkapelle. By the time of his death on 11 September 1917, he had brought down 53 officially confirmed German aircraft. There is no hard evidence but it is possible that on the same day, the German air ace Werner Voss was also in action and that one of his two victories may well have been the prized scalp of Guynemer.

Georges Marie Ludovic Jules Guynemer was born in Paris into a wealthy aristocratic family on 24 December 1894. His mother claimed descent from Kings Louis XIII and XIV. A weak and unhealthy child, Georges was educated at home until the age of 14 when he was strong enough to attend the lycée in Compiègne and later the Collège Stanislas in Paris where his reports described him as 'wilful'.

When war was declared he was not deemed fit enough to join the cavalry or infantry. His interest in flying led him to apply for a place in the Aviation Militaire. He started as a mechanic but with perseverance obtained his pilot's licence in March 1915.

His first mission was in June in a Morane Saulnier L two-seater when he was described by his observer as fearless, ignoring fire from the ground and from enemy planes. In July he scored his first victory for which he was awarded the Médaille Militaire. In early December he was flying a Nieuport 10 which was a better and faster machine and sent an enemy plane into a downward spin having fired at 15 metres range. Low on fuel and on a tight schedule to meet his parents for Sunday Mass, he landed and told his father to find 'my Boche' while he reported to his H.Q. His father obligingly found the German pilot's body! His Christmas and 21st birthday treat, was the news that he had become Chevalier de la Légion d'Honneur, France's highest award instituted by Napoleon I.

Georges Guynemer featured in Le Miroir *on 20 May 1917*

In 1916 his squadron 'Les Cigognes' (Storks) was operating in the skies over the notorious Verdun battlefield. Storks were symbols of French determination and were associated with Alsace and Lorraine, regions which had been lost following humiliating defeat in the Franco-Prussian War of 1870-71. In March Guynemer was wounded in the left arm when flying a newer and faster Nieuport. He crash-landed and took three months to recover from his injuries.

He was involved in a famous 'scrap' with ten enemy planes after his return. He survived despite his Nieuport showing signs of more than 80 hits and accounted for a two-seater observation plane. Reminiscent of Voss's reaction, Guynemer confessed that 'it was simply murder for the fast fighter planes to bring down the poor old observation planes.'

He moved to the Somme in September and was flying a sturdier machine equipped with a synchronised Vickers machine-gun, a Spad VII (Société Anonyme Pour L'Aviation et Ses Dérivés). He achieved three victories on 23 September- two confirmed and one unconfirmed but when returning to base, he was hit by anti-aircraft fire from his own side but managed to crash-land. He wrote to his father that 'only the fuselage was left, but it was intact!'

By February 1917 he was a lieutenant and became the first allied airman to force down a large twin-engine Gotha bomber near Nancy in eastern France. The three crew members were taken prisoner. The following month the French President, Raymond Poincaré, presented him with the Russian Order of St. George, 4th Class on behalf of the Tsar. He was also promoted to capitaine. During May he downed four aircraft in one day.

Guynemer affectionately called the planes he flew 'Vieux Charles' after his fellow pilot Charles Bonnard from whom he inherited his first plane. A German ace, Ernst Udet, credited with a tally of 62 hits by the end of the War, recounted in his *Memoirs* that he must have encountered the French ace because he had spotted the word 'Vieux' on the Frenchman's plane: 'Only one man flies like this on our front… with lightning speed he anticipates all my moves… I realise his superiority.' When Udet did have the chance to fire at Guynemer, his machine-gun jammed. Appreciating the German's plight, Guynemer flew alongside his enemy and waved at him before moving away. Udet was of the opinion that it was an act of chivalry by the Frenchman who could have easily shot him down.

Guynemer alongside his Spad- note the Stork symbol and the name he gave his planes- 'Vieux Charles'   *www.herodote.net*

Pilots of all sides were subjected to great stress and when at home on leave Guynemer's father recognised that the pressure was beginning to tell. He encouraged him to consider moving away from fighter planes but his son was adamant that 'it will be said that I have ceased to fight because I have won all the awards… If one has not given everything, one has given nothing': prophetic words.

Like Voss and the British ace Albert Ball, success meant that Guynemer was allowed an involvement in the design of fighter planes. He was flying the Spad XII in July which he described as his 'avion magique'. By the end of the month he had become the first French ace to score 50 victories.

The Storks were sent in August to Flanders to join the French First Army in their support of the British offensive in the Ypres Salient. Capitaine Guynemer's Spad was suffering from mechanical problems heightening his stress levels which were not helped by tuberculosis. He fainted twice when in the air and a doctor advised him to rest but, never one to stay still, Guynemer returned to action a few days later. Aware of his nervous condition, he bluntly confided in a friend that 'I shall not survive.'

There was little action on the ground in the Ypres Salient on 11 September and it was not raining. Disappointed that on the previous day a number of problems had forced him to land away from the base, he was determined to overcome his bad luck and with the inexperienced Bozon-Verduraz he took off to patrol the skies above Langemark. At about 9.30 a.m, while Guynemer was busy engaging a two-seater near Poelkapelle, Bozon-Verduraz had to deal with a group of enemy planes which scattered. When he returned to join his superior, Guynemer was nowhere to be seen.

After two days the French authorities declared that Guynemer was missing. Several weeks later, the Germans announced that he had been shot down by 2nd Leutnant Kurt Wisseman who was unable to confirm this as he himself had been brought down by Captain G. Bowman who fought Voss on the day the German ace was killed.

A sergeant in the German 413th Regiment claimed to have identified Guynemer's body. He reported that the French ace had received a bullet in the head, sustained a broken leg and had lost a finger. Unfortunately it was not possible to rescue the body because of intensive shelling.

Georges was denied a proper resting place which was ironic because when asked what decoration he was still to be awarded, he had answered 'the wooden cross'.

Georges Guynemer was a national hero and in death his name was used by the French Government to boost flagging morale.

Portrait of Guynemer by Lucien

He is remembered in the Panthéon in Paris where the great of France are honoured. The wording of his plaque typifies the mood of the time: 'A legendary hero fallen in glory from the sky... he will remain the purest symbol of national ideals for his indomitable tenacity of purpose, his ferocious verve and sublime gallantry... he has bequeathed to the French soldier an imperishable heritage which consecrates the spirit of sacrifice...'

GEORGES GUYNEMER:

Born:	24 December 1894 in Paris, son of Paul and Julie Naomi (née Doynel de St-Quentin) Guynemer
Education:	Lycée at Compiègne and Collège Stanislas, Paris
Unit/ Regiment:	No. 3 Squadron, Aviation Militaire
Rank:	Capitaine
Died:	11 September 1917, Third Battle of Ypres (Passchendaele)
Age:	22
Decorations:	Médaille Militaire, Croix de Guerre, Officier de la Légion d'Honneur, D.S.O. (British), Order of St. George (Russian) and awards from Belgium, Portugal, Romania and Serbia
Commemorated:	His body was never found. He is commemorated by a monument in Poelkapelle

The 'Stork' monument at Poelkapelle in memory of Georges Guynemer   *J Kerr*

CLARENCE JEFFRIES V.C.

"… it was entirely due to his bravery and initiative that the centre of the attack was not held up for a lengthy period'

Lieutenant Clarence Jeffries
Australian War Memorial PO1920.028

Clarence Jeffries or 'Clarrie' as he was known to his family, spent many of his working hours underground, surveying coal mines in the Newcastle area of New South Wales, Australia. He had followed his father Joshua into the Abermain Collieries which were owned by his mother Barbara's family and where his father was the General Manager. By 1916, 22 year old Clarence was working in the Surveying Department.

He performed well academically firstly at a primary school in Dudley, a seaside suburb of Newcastle, and then at Newcastle Boys' High School. He loved playing cricket and developed a keen interest in breeding thoroughbreds. His military career started at the age of 14 when, in 1908 he volunteered for the local militia and in 1912, under the compulsory training scheme, he joined the 14th (Hunter River) Infantry Regiment as a private; a year later he was promoted to sergeant and was successful enough to merit promotion to the rank of 2nd lieutenant by 1914.

Most Australians were of British descent; strong family ties resulted in great enthusiasm for the war effort when hostilities broke out in 1914. Jeffries's enlistment papers described him as a 'Naturalised British Subject' which helps to explain his enthusiasm to join up.

During the first year of the War he trained volunteers in Newcastle and Liverpool (New South Wales) for the newly created Australian Imperial Force which had been established to implement the Fisher Government's initial offer to Britain of 20,000 troops. This number multiplied

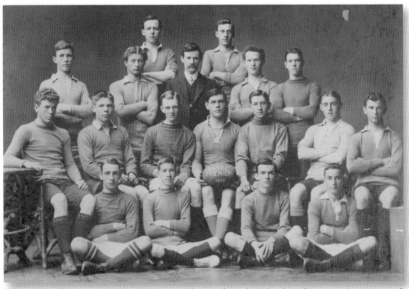

Clarence Jeffries aged 16 in the Newcastle Boys' High School rugby team. He is seated on the ground on the far right   *Bill Storer*

greatly in the next four years; by 1918 Australia had contributed approximately 322,000 troops to service overseas of whom 60,000 never returned.

Clarence had to hang up his cricket boots and leave his thoroughbred horses to the tender care of others in May 1916. He embarked from Sydney on the *Hororata* with the 34/ Australian Infantry at the head of 'B' Company. They disembarked in Plymouth at the end of June. After a four month spell of training at the Chelsea Officers' School in London he was promoted to lieutenant and on 4 November he and the Battalion were despatched to the Armentières sector.

Life was relatively quiet there until the Battle of Messines. On 9 June 1917 Clarence suffered an injury to his left thigh which was serious enough for him to be transported back to Britain. After an operation at the 3rd General Hospital in London he was sent to recuperate firstly at the Perham Downs Camp in Wiltshire which was near Tidworth Military Hospital and then at Cobham Hall in Kent where during the War, 1,300 Australians were able to convalesce in marvellous surroundings thanks to the generosity of the Darnley family. During his convalescence Clarence received the news that he had been promoted to captain. He re-joined his comrades at the Front in early September.

In October 1917 the 34/ Australian Infantry were involved in the Battle of Passchendaele. The muddy conditions on the front line were appalling. The Australians achieved their objective of taking the ground below Broodseinde Ridge on 4 October. A week later they resumed their offensive, aiming to drive the Germans down the other side of the ridge towards Passchendaele village. Jeffries and 'B' Company were near the current location of Tyne Cot Cemetery and the railway line at Dash Crossing. Their progress was being obstructed by machine-gun fire from a number of German pill-boxes which were targeted by a series of audacious attacks, one of which was led by Jeffries to a pill-box located near the Zonnebeke to Passchendaele road, north east of Hillside Farm and at the highest point of the Broodseinde Ridge.

According to the 34th Battalion's War Diary 'machine-gun fire at the start came from the ruined house near Defy Crossing on its centre from "Hillside Farm" and on its left, from Augustus Wood. The pillbox opposite the centre was supported from the rear by a trench in which were Germans with machine-guns, and here there was a delay which threatened to wreck the whole attack. It was not until an hour after programme time that these places were rushed by the neighbouring portion of the line under Captains Carr and Dixon of the 35th Battalion… Part of the line was also held up by a pill-box close to the Passchendaele road near the highest point of the ridge. Here there was practically no shelter for the attack, but Captain Jeffries of the 34th managed to organise a party, with Sergeant Bruce and another N.C.O. and a dozen men, and outflanking it, charged the place from the rear, capturing 25 Germans and two machine-guns. These actions set free the advance. The pill-box captured by Jeffries being not far short of the first objective, the 34th dug in there.' During the attack Clarence was fatally wounded in the stomach by shell fire. His efforts were to no avail as the Australians were later forced to retreat.

In recognition of his exploits Captain Clarence Jeffries was posthumously awarded a V.C. The citation from *The London Gazette*, dated 18th December 1917, records that 'this gallant officer was killed during the attack, but it was entirely due to his bravery and initiative that the centre of the attack was not held up for a lengthy period. His example had a most inspiring influence.'

Like thousands of parents Joshua and Barbara Jeffries visited the battlefields in the hope of identifying their son's final resting place. They made the long journey from New South Wales in July 1920 to no avail. Tragically, only two months after their return to Abermain, Clarence's body was located and exhumed from a field grave near Hein House on 4 September and buried in Tyne Cot Cemetery.

The authorities could at least reassure the Jeffries that their son's body had been identified: 'A set of Captain's stars, "Australia Numerals" and the initials C.S.J. pencilled on the groundsheet in which the remains were wrapped, constituted the means by which the identification was arrived at. The fact that no other Australian Captain who bore the initials "C.S.J." was killed in the neighbourhood of Passchendaele further supports the conclusion that the remains were those of Captain Jeffries V.C.'

The Jeffries did make the long trip again in 1924 and were now able to pay their final respects to Clarrie. According to Clarrie's second cousin Carol Calderwood, her aunt Barbara was inconsolable until her death. She chose the inscription for her son's grave: ON FAME'S ETERNAL CAMPING GROUND THEIR SILENT TENTS ARE SPREAD from *Bivouac of the Dead* by Theodore O'Hara which Carol believes her grief-stricken aunt, 'truly related to'.

In memory of Sergeant Bruce who helped Clarence before being killed himself, Joshua made a point of employing his two sons as mining surveyors at the Abermain Colliery.

When the War ended it was decided that Australian towns where V.C.s were brought up, should receive as memorials, cannon captured by the Australian Infantry on 8 August 1918 near the German Hindenburg line. A newspaper in 1931 described the howitzer awarded to Abermain: 'Standing on its solid concrete block…with its weather-beaten, ugly barrel pointing in the air… a silent emblem of the dark days of 1914-18… what a story it could tell if only it had the power of speech…'

Tyne Cot Cemetery- Barbara Jeffries found her son had been buried in a beautiful park with a well-tended garden   J Kerr

A massive granite monument was erected in 1919 in memory of those who had enlisted from Abermain. The fund-raising committee admitted that 'it could never hope to repay the living or express adequate appreciation of the dead, but they could, by engraving on that granite, hand down to their children's children the names of the gallant soldiers of Abermain who had won a glory that could never die.' The inscription on the monument reads: 'On the altar of their country's good they laid the incense of their fortunes and their lives.'

Appropriately the V.C.'s mother Barbara was invited to unveil the memorial. She thanked the committee for their efforts in funding a memorial to those 'who volunteered for active service abroad to defend our liberty, and all that we as Britishers, hold dear.' She thanked those who had played their part in ensuring that Australia remained 'a free country'. She observed that 60,000 of 'the flower of Australia' lay buried in foreign countries and that 'they made the greatest of sacrifices, and it is our duty to make ourselves worthy of their sacrifice…'

She made another pilgrimage to Tyne Cot Cemetery in August 1933. In an interview with *The Sydney Morning Herald* she admitted to having returned from Belgium much happier than when she left: 'I found the cemeteries more like beautiful parks with well-tended gardens. No Australian mother need fear that her son's sacrifice has not been fittingly remembered'- a glowing tribute to the work of Sir Fabian Ware and the cemeteries' architects and gardeners.

The grave of Clarence Jeffries V.C. in Tyne Cot Cemetery. A German pill-box is in the background   J Kerr

Captain Clarence Smith Jeffries was one of over 60 Australians to receive the V.C. in the Great War, some consolation at least for his family and the Abermain mining community. The medal was bequeathed by Barbara Jeffries to Newcastle's Christchurch Cathedral and is exhibited in the Warriors' Chapel. She was also the driving force behind an unusual memorial to the fallen of the Hunter Valley. When the War ended, she suggested to the Bishop that widows be requested to donate their fallen husbands' wedding rings to be made into a fitting tribute- the Cathedral's *Book of Gold*.

Clarence Jeffries was a typically selfless member of Britain's Imperial forces, who considered it was his duty to defend the 'mother country'.

CLARENCE JEFFRIES V.C.:

Born:	26 October 1894 at Wallsend, New South Wales, Australia, only son of Joshua and Barbara Jeffries
Education:	Dudley Primary and Newcastle Boys' High School
Occupation:	Mining Surveyor, Abermain Colliery
Unit/ Regiment:	14th (Hunter River) Infantry Regiment and 34/ Australian Infantry known as 'Maitland's Own', Australian Imperial Force
Rank:	Captain
Died:	12 October 1917, Third Battle of Ypres (Passchendaele)
Age:	23
Decoration:	V.C.
Buried:	Tyne Cot Cemetery XL.E.1.
Inscription:	ON FAME'S ETERNAL CAMPING GROUND THEIR SILENT TENTS ARE SPREAD (from a poem *Bivouac of the Dead* by Theodore O'Hara written during the American-Mexican War 1846-48)

The cemetery is located 9 kms north-east of Ypres and was designed by Sir Herbert Baker. According to the C.W.G.C. the Northumberland Fusiliers named a barn near the level crossing on the Passchendaele to Broodseinde Road 'Tyne Cottage' or 'Tyne Cot' for short. At the site of the barn the Germans had built six pill-boxes which were captured by the 3rd Australian Division on 4 October 1917. The largest pill-box was turned into an Advanced Dressing Station. Some 300 who died there were buried in the cemetery but numbers increased dramatically after the War when remains from the Passchendaele and Langemark battlefields were interred in Tyne Cot Cemetery which is now the largest Commonwealth War Cemetery in the world with nearly 12,000 burials of which about 8,000 were unidentified. The Cross of Sacrifice is to be found on the original A.D.S. pill-box, placed there on the suggestion of King George V during his visit to Tyne Cot in 1922

Other Graves of Interest:

Brigadier General:	James Riddell, 149th Infantry Brigade, died 26 April 1915, aged 52, XXXIV.H.14.
	Inscription: KILLED LEADING HIS BRIGADE BUT FIVE DAYS LANDED SOLDIER AND GREAT GENTLEMAN
Brothers:	Hatt, C. and F., 25/ Canadian Infantry (Nova Scotia Rifles), died within two days of each other, on 6 and 8 November 1917, II.E.10 and II.E.11.
Inscription:	2nd Lieutenant Arthur Conway Young, 4/ Royal Irish Fusiliers, died 16 August 1916, aged 26, IV.G.21. SACRIFICED TO THE FALLACY THAT WAR CAN END WAR

The grave of Arthur Young. Note an absence of a religious symbol and there is a rare anti-war comment
A Hamilton

Tyne Cot Cemetery and Memorial   J Kerr/A Hamilton

FREDERICK MILLINS

A romance that died in the mud of Flanders

At the outbreak of war three Buckinghamshire-born brothers, John, Dennis and Frederick Millins, along with thousands of other working-class country boys, joined queues at recruiting stations throughout the country, eagerly volunteering their services to their King and Country. After months of training they left for the Western Front in 1915- John with the Royal Field Artillery and Dennis as a driver in the Royal Engineers. The youngest and tallest, Frederick, was selected to serve with the prestigious Grenadier Guards in their 2nd Battalion.

Frederick faced constant danger for over a year. Accounts in the 2/ Grenadier Guards' War Diary highlight the nature of the warfare that he and his fellow soldiers had to endure in a two week period between 12 and 26 September 1916 on the Somme when it was intense, dangerous, brutal and relentless.

The Battalion was involved in two major actions in September 1916. On 12 September they moved into trenches in the Ginchy line and the following night drove the Germans out of Ginchy Orchard with the loss of 100 casualties. This prepared the ground for a forthcoming major attack. They were then relieved in preparation for that assignment scheduled for the 15 September. At 06.20 on that day they fought their way into Ginchy village under heavy machine-gun fire losing many men. The centre of the Battalion rushed the German trenches and 'bayoneted all the Germans they found.' This was followed by intense fighting with each side trying to bomb the other out of the trenches. When the Guards had exhausted their supply of 'bombs' (hand grenades), they carried out another bayonet charge, killing the enemy bombers and taking over 40 prisoners. Fighting continued until the evening, the Guards managing

The three Millins brothers, John, Frederick and Dennis with their mother Dinah G Sayell

to hold their line during 16 September against further enemy attacks. They were relieved on the following day but the action had been at great cost to the Battalion.

Frederick and his comrades were congratulated on their efforts by General Rawlinson, Commander of the Fourth Army. The Guards Brigade Commander, Brigadier General Pereira complimented them on 'their splendid discipline' when advancing through a heavy artillery barrage 'as if on parade'. No doubt with the intention of boosting their morale, he praised them for having shown the Germans 'what they have to expect when they meet the pick of the British Army'.

On 21 September, before the second action, the Battalion camped in Bernafay Wood. Where possible they erected bivouacs using any sacks and corrugated iron they could lay their hands on for shelter and protection from the weather. Two days later fatigue parties moved stores and ammunition to the front line in preparation for the impending battle. The following morning they relieved the 2/ Coldstream Guards opposite Lesboeufs village. The Guards Cemetery now stands on this front line where they fought and died.

The relief was completed on 25 September at 01.00 despite heavy shelling which continued throughout the day. At 12.35 the Battalion advanced towards Lesboeufs and took the first objective despite the wire being unaffected by the support shelling. During this phase enemy rifle fire and hand grenades caused many casualties including most of the officers. A number of Germans were killed or taken prisoner and a machine-gun captured. An hour later the Guards continued their advance towards the village, bombing well-defended dugouts in the Sunken Roads; they killed many Germans and took some prisoners. The advance had to be delayed for an hour due to the Guards progressing faster than the supporting artillery fire. The village was then taken and the enemy was seen to be retiring over the next hill. Despite further shelling and sniper-fire, they held the village until they were relieved after five days of bitter fighting by which time they were ready for a well-earned rest and marched back to Citadel Camp.

When billeted at Aumont on 4 October, their actions drew further praise from the Commander-in-Chief, Sir Douglas Haig who awarded decorations to officers, N.C.O.s and other ranks. Private Frederick James Millins was awarded the Military Medal.

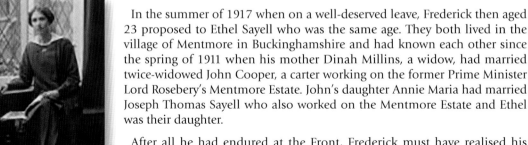

In the summer of 1917 when on a well-deserved leave, Frederick then aged 23 proposed to Ethel Sayell who was the same age. They both lived in the village of Mentmore in Buckinghamshire and had known each other since the spring of 1911 when his mother Dinah Millins, a widow, had married twice-widowed John Cooper, a carter working on the former Prime Minister Lord Rosebery's Mentmore Estate. John's daughter Annie Maria had married Joseph Thomas Sayell who also worked on the Mentmore Estate and Ethel was their daughter.

After all he had endured at the Front, Frederick must have realised his chances of survival were slim and that he may never have another chance to propose to his true love. He was not deterred by the fact that Ethel had a five year old illegitimate son, Joseph William Burnett Sayell. Given the social mores of the time, for him to take on an unmarried mother reflected a kind and understanding nature and his offer emphasised the close bond between the families.

Ethel Sayell, Fred Millins's fiancée   *G Sayell*

Ethel had been employed as a domestic servant in St. John's Wood, London and it was generally understood that her employer's son had forcibly 'had his way' with her and was baby Joseph's father. His name was included in the child's birth certificate.

She had been fortunate in obtaining a position locally despite her circumstances. Joseph was brought up by his grandparents Joseph and Annie Maria Sayell and for many years he was led to believe that Ethel was his big sister.

Frederick asked for her hand in marriage and was delighted when she gladly accepted. He gave her a ring and said he also wished to buy her an engagement present, sensing perhaps that he might never return from the Front and she would have something to remember him by in the future.

Ethel's son Joseph   *G Sayell*

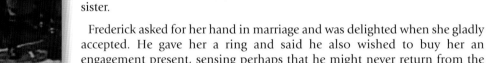

For Ethel, an engagement ring was the perfect token of their love and a happy future together. She replied that all she wanted was for him 'to come back safely from the War'. Frederick was insistent and, undecided on what to give her, discussed it with the families. His mother Dinah suggested that a sewing machine would be an ideal present as Ethel was keen on sewing and she 'could make little Joe's trousers with it.' For a mere private in the Army and a humble railway porter in civilian life, it was a remarkably generous present. So Ethel became the proud owner of a brand new state-of-the-art Singer 66 manual sewing machine.

His short leave over Frederick soon had to bid farewell to his fiancée and Joseph. It was to be his final spell at the Front.

The Third Battle of Ypres had been underway since 31 July and in early October the 2/ Grenadier Guards were preparing for further action. The Battalion moved on 7 October to Charterhouse Camp between the Yser Canal and Elverdinghe. Stores were issued and in the evening they marched to take over their battle positions, parallel to and about 250 yards back from the Broenbeek. This line passes through the Langemark German Military Cemetery. It was a cold and windy night, the march long and troublesome due to the sodden and shattered state of the ground.

On the following afternoon the weather broke and steady rain turned into a soaking downpour which continued until the early morning of 9 October. The positions occupied by the troops, at best shell holes, were miserable in the extreme. Fortunately they had been issued with rum and hot tea which would be their only comfort in what would be for some of them, their final night.

The Battle of Poelkapelle commenced at 05.20. Under cover of an intense bombardment by 18 pounder guns and Stokes mortars, the 2/ Grenadier Guards began their attack. They were to cross the Broenbeek with a line of attack parallel to the Staden to Langemark railway some 300 yards to their right. Their final objective was the southern fringe of Houthulst Forest. The Broenbeek had flooded and it was feared that it might be impassable. With great ingenuity the Grenadier Guards managed to cross the swollen brook by using fallen trees, planks or duckboards. Some waded through, at great risk of disappearing into hidden shell holes. The advance continued virtually unchecked and the objectives were achieved. The Guards were relieved and returned to Larrey Camp near Elverdinghe.

Private Frederick James Millins M.M. was one of 33 of the Battalion to fall in the action. He has no known grave and is remembered on Panel 9 of the Tyne Cot Memorial. Little Joseph was woken in the early morning when his grandfather Joseph came into the cottage and shouted up the stairs 'Fred Millins is dead.' Ethel and the families were devastated by the news. She was informed that 'he had been blown to bits' and her distress was unlikely to have been alleviated when told that 'he had not suffered.'

Frederick's brothers survived. John Millins married in 1915 and when he departed to France in September he had been promoted to the rank of serjeant and by the end of the War was a Warrant Officer 1, 'Battery Quartermaster Serjeant.' He and his wife lived in London.

Dennis was a lance corporal by April 1917 and after the War was transferred to the Reserve in 1919, the year he married. Later in life he lived in Watford and worked as a caretaker for the public library.

In time Ethel found a new love in Fred Humphrey who was released from a German prisoner of war camp in 1919. They married in 1921 and six years later young Joseph was joined by his half-sister Mary.

Ethel never parted with her sewing machine, a tangible and touching reminder of her first love. It served her well throughout her lifetime and in due course was handed down to Mary, who in turn passed it on to her half-brother Joseph's son George Sayell. This treasured item is a family heirloom and a reminder of the doomed romance.

Frederick Millins's bravery at the Front had merited a Military Medal and it is sad that his family will never know the exact reasons for it as only officers' exploits were cited for awards of medals.

A kind-hearted and generous man, Frederick's life was cruelly stolen from Ethel by a war of extraordinary inhumanity.

by George Sayell

George Sayell with the sewing machine Frederick Millins gave Ethel Sayell as an engagement present, passed down to him by his aunt Mary   A Hamilton

FREDERICK JAMES MILLINS:

Born:	1894, son of William and Dinah Millins, Cheddington, Buckinghamshire
Occupation:	Railway porter
Unit/ Regiment:	2/ Grenadier Guards
Rank:	Private
Died:	9 October 1917
Age:	23
Decoration:	Military Medal
Commemorated:	Tyne Cot Memorial, Panel 9
	The Memorial lists the names of almost 35,000 New Zealand and British missing who died in the Ypres Salient after 16 August 1917. Its semi-circular design by Sir Herbert Baker is reminiscent of the shape of the Salient
Also commemorated:	Father and Son: Lieutenant Colonel Harry Moorhouse D.S.O., T.D., Légion d'Honneur and Captain Ronald Moorhouse, M.C. both of the 4/ King's Own Yorkshire Light Infantry who died within half an hour of each other on 9 October 1917. Both are to be found on Panel 108

Frederick Millins M.M. is commemorated on the Tyne Cot Memorial   J Kerr

COLIN BLYTHE

'… as cricketer and soldier patriot, he played the game'

The home in St. James's Road, Tunbridge Wells of Colin Blythe, one of the greatest of English cricketers
A Hamilton

A caricature of Colin 'Charlie' Blythe in Vanity Fair's, *'Man of the Day' for the edition on 3 August 1910 by an unknown artist*

The moment Serjeant Blythe returned home from his interview, he excitedly told his wife Gertrude the good news. He had been offered the post of cricket coach at Eton College which gave the couple much needed security once the War concluded. It would be a wrench to leave their homely terraced house in St. James's Road, Tunbridge Wells but it was a challenge that they both looked forward to.

For Colin Blythe it was a reward for being one of the finest cricketers of the early 20th century. He had played as a professional for Kent County Cricket Club since 1899 and had taken 100 wickets every season since 1902. His career haul of 2,503 first-class wickets would be bettered by only 10 bowlers in the history of the game. The journalist Neville Cardus described 'Charlie' Blythe as 'the prettiest slow left-handed bowler of his, or surely any other period.'

He played for England 19 times, a total that would have been higher but for being in the shadow of another fine spin bowler, the Yorkshireman Wilfred Rhodes whose batting was superior to Blythe's. His England career was hindered by epilepsy- ironically it afflicted him after triumphs like his match figures of 15 wickets for 99 runs against the South Africans at Headingley in 1907; he also suffered a seizure when he took 11 Australian scalps at Edgbaston two years later.

Nervous exhaustion triggered epilepsy and fearful of a recurrence, the selectors were reluctant to choose him after two undistinguished performances in South Africa in March 1911. He never played for his country again and in the comparatively stress-free environment of county cricket, his left-hand spin bowling flourished for Kent until the outbreak of war.

At international level, 100 wickets constituted serious under achievement for such a fine bowler. One of the greatest batsmen of the period, the England star Kumar Ranjitsingh, claimed that he would far prefer to face Rhodes than the wily Colin Blythe.

To secure the coach's position at Eton was a source of pride for the cockney boy from a family of 12 brought up in dockland Deptford to the east of London. He left school at 13 and took an engineering apprenticeship at the Woolwich Arsenal. In his spare time he played cricket on pitches somewhat inferior to Agar's Plough at Eton; Blythe's natural talent caught the eye of several Kent players when he turned up to bowl in the nets during a county game at Blackheath in July 1897. Within two years he was a professional cricketer.

'Charlie' to his colleagues, Blythe was a model professional who worked hard to improve his skills. He believed in the team ethic and treated cricket as a game to be enjoyed and won. A chirpy cockney, he derived almost as much pleasure from an opposing batsman's fine shot as trapping him with guile and perseverance.

Unusually for a professional sportsman he was also a talented musician. He learned the violin from an early age and displayed a talent that enabled him to play for a Music Hall orchestra in London. When he moved to Kent, winter evenings were spent performing for local orchestras and he was happiest when playing Mozart symphonies. Before the days of air travel, M.C.C. touring parties would

The painting that hangs in the Long Room at Lord's Cricket Ground of Colin Blythe bowling for Kent against Lancashire at Canterbury in 1906 by A. Chevallier Tayler

Andrew Brownsword Foundation

sail to Australia and South Africa and Blythe entertained his team mates. His musical talents helped to while away many an hour on the long voyages.

As storm clouds gathered over Europe, Blythe's final first class match was played at Lord's on 27 and 28 August 1914; unfortunately his 7 wickets failed to save Kent from a two day trouncing by Middlesex. Caught up in the prevailing war fever, Blythe stood down from the last match of the season and enlisted with the Kent Royal Fortress Engineers. An epileptic, he should not have been accepted on medical grounds but Blythe was a patriot, desperate to be involved as soon as possible. Keen to welcome a celebrity into the ranks for recruiting purposes, it suited the authorities to overlook his medical problem and making use of his fame, Blythe encouraged 25 men to join up with him, including five county cricketers.

A well-orchestrated press campaign resulted in an impressive crowd gathering at Tonbridge station to send off four Kent cricketers and Claud Woolley, originally from Kent but who played for Northamptonshire. Once on the train the cricketers, as if in the pavilion changing room during a rain break, organised a sweepstake- the winner would be the first to gain promotion. 'Charlie' scooped the pool within weeks when he was promoted to corporal!

Colin Blythe remained on the Kent County Cricket Club payroll during the War. He and other professionals who enlisted were rewarded with a supplement to their Army pay. The Club Committee frowned on those who failed to volunteer, docking their pay and warning them that 'in the event of a Benefit being granted to any one of them, their popularity with the public might be adversely affected.'

Blythe spent over two years at Gillingham with the Fortress Engineers manning coastal defences. It was a safe existence but for a cricketer who had enjoyed the excitement of combat on cricket fields at home and abroad, he yearned to be more actively involved.

In October 1916 he learnt that his younger brother Sidney had been killed. It was news that further confirmed his desire to make a more positive contribution to the war effort. Nearly twenty years his junior, Sidney served with the Hampshire Regiment in the Dardanelles and was fortunate to survive the torpedoing of the *Royal Edward* troopship on 13 August 1915 after being in the Aegean Sea for nearly five hours. He survived the Battle of Suvla Bay but his luck ran out when the 1/ Hants were sent to the Western Front. Sidney Blythe was killed in action on the Somme on 23 October 1916. His commanding officer wrote: 'He went over the top with the others and got back safely, and after that he went out again to help a wounded colonel. He bandaged him up and had just finished his job when he was shot through the head; he died at once, and it must have been practically without pain… no man could hope for a better death than to give his life to save another.' The death of 20 year old Sidney Blythe is recorded on the Thiepval Memorial in the Somme.

Colin Blythe was transferred to the Royal Engineers' camp at Marlow in Buckinghamshire in June 1917 and in July he announced his retirement from first class cricket at the age of 38 after securing the cricket professional's job at Eton College.

The carnage on the Somme in 1916 meant there was now a desperate shortage of physically able men and in August 1917, 8,000 Royal Engineers were transferred to units that had been depleted. Blythe was posted to the King's Own Yorkshire Light Infantry but his engineering skills were regarded highly enough for him to be drafted in to build trenches, roads, railways and gun emplacements.

Aware that his chances of survival at the Front were limited, he made a will when on leave on 24 August, in which his estate was left to Gertrude and his two violins to his father, Walter. On 25 September, he sailed to France and October was spent training. In early November the K.O.Y.L.I. was part of the final push at Passchendaele. Serjeant Blythe was behind the allied lines building a railway on 8 November when a German shell killed him and four colleagues. He was buried in the Oxford Road Cemetery near Ypres.

The Sporting Life announced on 16 November that 'the cricket world has suffered a great and almost irreparable loss, by the death in action of Colin Blythe, the famous Kent and England slow bowler, one of the best left hand bowlers this country has produced. Though Mrs. Blythe has not received an official notification, there seems no reason to doubt the sad news.'

'It is my painful duty to inform you …' Gertrude Blythe did indeed receive the dreaded news of her loss. Tributes to her famous husband helped to ease the pain. Lord Harris, the President of Kent County Cricket Club wrote of Colin Blythe's 'sterling character', his fine judgement of the game and to modern eyes rather patronisingly 'his positive influence amongst his class'. Lord George Hamilton, the Chairman of the Club described 'Charlie' Blythe as a 'remarkable personality and although fragile in physique, he had the heart of a lion.'

The celebrated cricket writer Neville Cardus eulogised the fallen Kent and England cricketer in his inimitable style: 'He lost his life fighting for England, one of the first to join up. A shell made by somebody who had never known cricket and directed by eyes that had never seen a Kent field, fell on Blythe and killed him. On any of those quiet distant delicious afternoons at Canterbury, when Blythe bowled his gentle spin and the summer blossomed all around, could even the ironic Gods have discerned the course of events which was to take Blythe overseas and leave him there as part of the foreign dust?'

Colin Blythe was an unassuming and talented man who entertained crowds throughout the cricket-playing world. The memorial tablet in Tonbridge Church records that 'as cricketer and soldier patriot, he played the game.' After a visit to Blythe's grave in 2009 by the England cricket team, the captain Andrew Strauss confessed it had been a 'deeply moving and humbling experience.'

Colin Blythe's shrapnel-riddled wallet with German and Belgian bank notes and a photo of his wife, recovered from his body on 8 November 1917

David Robertson, Hon. Curator Kent C.C.C.

114

COLIN BLYTHE:

Born:	30 May 1879, son of Mr. and Mrs. Blythe of New Cross, London
Education:	Duke Street Infants School, Alverton Street School, Deptford, London
Occupation:	Professional cricketer
Unit/ Regiment:	Royal Engineers then 12/ King's Own Yorkshire Light Infantry
Rank:	Serjeant
Died:	8 November 1917, Third Battle of Ypres (Passchendaele)
Age:	38
Buried:	Oxford Road Cemetery I.L.2.
Inscription:	IN LOVING MEMORY OF MY DEAR HUSBAND THE KENT & ENGLAND CRICKETER

The cemetery is 2 kms north east of Ypres and was designed by Sir Reginald Blomfield. It contains 851 burials, 297 of which are unidentified. Oxford Road was the name of a road that ran behind the support trenches between Wieltje and the Potijze to Zonnebeke Road

Colin Blythe's grave in Oxford Road Cemetery near Ypres- note the simple inscription by his wife Gertrude J Kerr

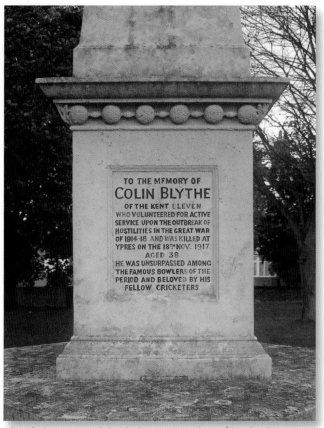

The Blythe Memorial (with the incorrect date of his death) at Kent County Cricket Club's St. Lawrence Ground in Canterbury
David Robertson, Hon. Curator Kent C.C.C.

Stuart Broad, the England Test cricketer, at the grave of Colin Blythe in 2009
Getty Images

RAYMOND LODGE

'Death is not the end'

At midday on 27 September 1915, a gentleman in his mid-sixties made an anonymous visit to a Mrs. Leonard, a spiritualist medium, in London. At the same time, his wife had her first 'sitting' with a Mr. A. Vout Peters. Both husband and wife claimed that they had been 'put in touch' with their son who had been killed on the Western Front two weeks earlier. They were Sir Oliver and Lady Lodge. He was one of the most respected scientists of the time, a physicist and inventor best remembered for his part in developing wireless telegraphy. In November 1916 he was prepared to put his reputation on the line by publicly making a case for life after death in his book *Raymond or Life and Death* which by May 1918 was in its ninth edition. He declared in the introduction that 'I have thought it my duty to speak out.' Oliver Lodge had been President of the Society of Psychical Research from 1901 to 1903 and was now keen to investigate the subject with a scientific and critical approach.

Sir Oliver Lodge, physicist and inventor
Sir George Reid, National Portrait Gallery 3952

The subject of spiritualism during the Great War is a controversial one and many historians have opted not to refer to it or to mention it briefly in passing. It became increasingly popular as the War progressed and the number of spiritual societies nearly doubled after 1916. Understandably hundreds of thousands of grieving families were desperately trying to find ways of coping with the death of a loved one. Some sought comfort in conventional religion; others were hoping to receive assurance that their son, husband or brother was 'safe' after a horrendous death. Spiritualism provided an answer for many, especially those who were questioning their faith as a result of the horrors and mounting casualties.

Sir Arthur Conan Doyle, the creator of the super-rational Sherlock Holmes, embraced spiritualism wholeheartedly and like Sir Oliver Lodge, was a member of the 'Ghost Club'. He devoted his final years to promoting the 'movement' in books and lecture tours at home and abroad. His son Kingsley who had been wounded during the Battle of the Somme, died of influenza in the 1918 pandemic. It was unfortunate that Sir Arthur was naïvely uncritical and fell prey to charlatans but until his death stuck to his beliefs in spite of the mockery and condemnation of his stance.

Raymond Lodge aged two
from Raymond or Life and Death *by Sir Oliver Lodge*

Although he showed some interest in the occult and had a sister Trix who professed to be a medium practising under the name of Mrs. Holland, Rudyard Kipling, a friend of Conan Doyle, does not appear to have tried to 'contact' his son John. When Maxine Elliott, the actress, returned to London in May 1916 after supporting wounded and refugee Belgians from her specially converted barge, she asked a friend with spiritualist beliefs to introduce her to a medium in an attempt to 'meet' again the man of her life, the Wimbledon tennis star Tony Wilding (see p.173).

Raymond Lodge was born in Liverpool on 25 January 1889, the seventh of the Lodges' twelve children, six girls and six boys of whom Raymond was the youngest. His father was Professor of Physics and Mathematics at University College, Liverpool. Raymond was a solitary child who disliked parties and even Christmas time festivities.

He was sent to Bedales the unconventional school in Hampshire where he unwound and became well known for his sense of humour which sometimes interfered with his and others' studies.

After reading Engineering at Birmingham University, he undertook his practical training at the Wolseley Motor Works in Birmingham for two years and then joined his brothers Brodie and Alec in the family business, the Lodge Plug Company, which manufactured sparking plugs for aeroplanes and cars.

A military career would have been, according to his father, 'quite foreign to family tradition' but when war broke out, Raymond volunteered in September 1914 'through a sense of duty'. He was commissioned in the 3/ South Lancashire Regiment and trained at Great Crosby near Liverpool. He was attached to the 2nd Battalion when he was sent to Flanders in March 1915. His engineering skills were utilised on the front line for trench and shelter construction. He was sent on a machine-gun course in June.

Raymond was an assiduous and conscientious letter writer and his correspondence offers a detailed and interesting insight into his life at the Front and behind the lines. When referring to conditions in the billets and in the trenches he claimed 'there is not much difference, here we "pig" it pretty comfortably in a house, and there we "pig" it almost as comfortably in a dugout' but during a spell of duty in the trenches 'shaving and washing is usually dispensed with (even by the Colonel).'

2nd Lieutenant Raymond Lodge in uniform
from Raymond or Life and Death *by Sir Oliver Lodge*

He referred to life in June 1915 as 'full of interest… Bad times do come along occasionally… It is most like a long picnic in all sorts of places with a sort of constraint and uneasiness in the air. This last is purely mental and the less one worries about it the less it is, and so one can contrive to be light-hearted and happy through it all.' Soon after arriving at the Front, he had written: 'If it wasn't for the unpleasant sights one is liable to see, war would be a most interesting and pleasant affair.' By August he had worked out his method of survival: 'As long as you smile and don't care a hang about anything, well the war seems to go on quite well.'

He took pleasure in circumventing the censors by the use of acrostics in poems in which the first or last letters of each line spelled the name of a place that he could not mention, for example he told the family where he was billeted i.e. Dickebusch

My first is speechless and a bell	*D um B*
Three letters promising to pay	*I o U*
There's nothing gross about this act	*C ares S*
A General less his final 'k'	*K lu Ck*
Our Neenie who is going west	*E dit H*

His academic father and family did not take long to work out the answer!

Raymond's caring nature is exemplified in a letter to one of his brothers in which he enquires about whether morphine could be dispensed in tablet form as he considered 'injection too complicated.' Of some German prisoners he wrote: 'Poor devils, I do feel so sorry for them. One officer of sixteen with six weeks' service. Old men with grey beards too, and many of the student type with spectacles- not fit to have a fight.'

One of the great wonders of organisation during the War was the Mail Service. A letter from the family in Edgbaston, Birmingham reached him at the Front with extraordinary speed: 'The postmark is 2.30 p.m. on the 16th at Birmingham and here it is in my hands at 4 p.m. on the 18th!'

Rats and mice were regular topics in letters from the Front and Raymond entertained his family on the subject: 'You can hear them directly you lie still' and admitted to being terrified that a rat might run over his face when asleep, but as his servant slept in the same 'outhouse' he amusingly consoled himself that 'the chances are just even that they won't choose me. I wish he wouldn't snore though he is lowering the odds... By the way, they say these rats "stand-to" at dawn as we do.'

Lodge's love of engineering and his skills feature regularly in his letters. Once in a support trench he arranged to dam a stream to use the water for boiling and to keep the trench dry. His officer friends awarded him the 'honorary' position of 'O.C. Works'. He was attached temporarily to a pioneer battalion deepening trenches and improving parapets at the notorious Hill 60, a tactical strongpoint where the Passchendaele and Messines ridges meet. He was glad to re-join his unit and by the end of August they were on duty opposite Hooge Château on the Menin Road under which both sides were busily mining. Above ground opposing positions were as little as '40 or 50 yards away'.

Raymond was unimpressed with the Germans' laying of mines and use of explosives: 'When one of their mines went up recently a lot of Germans went up with it!'

He announced in his letter of 6 September that he was now commanding 'C' Company as his Captain had 'sprained his ankle by falling from his horse. Hope not for long. Too responsible at the present time...'

He told his family on 12 September that 'we are going into the front line trenches this evening at 5.00 p.m. for an ordinary tour of duty. We are going up in motor buses!'

Five days later Raymond's parents received a telegram from the War Office informing them that their son 'was wounded 14th Sept. and has since died. Lord Kitchener expresses his sympathy.' Four days later another telegram arrived from the King and Queen commiserating with them on their loss.

Raymond was struck in the left side of his back by a shell fragment at Hooge and died an hour or so later in a dugout. According to a colleague, Lieutenant George Case, Raymond was ensuring that his men went down safely to the rear of the trenches during German shelling. His servant, Private George Gray, aged 23 from St. Helen's, Lancashire, was hit in the head and died later. He is remembered on the Menin Gate, as is Lieutenant Case who was killed at the age of just 19, three weeks after Raymond.

Lieutenant William Roscoe of the 2/ South Lancashires and attached to the Machine-Gun Company wrote to Sir Oliver about his son's dying moments: 'I was going up to the line to visit the guns, when I saw Ventris, who was killed, laid out ready to be carried down, and presently I saw your son in a dugout, with a man watching him. He was then quite unconscious, though still breathing with difficulty. I could see it was all over with him.'

Captain Cheves of the R.A.M.C. did his best to reassure the family about their son's last moments: 'When his body was brought down in the evening, the expression on his face was absolutely peaceful... He was buried in our cemetery just outside the aid post.' This may have been the Union Street graveyard 1,000 yards north of Zillebeke. Later, Raymond was re-interred at Birr Cross Roads Cemetery where he rests next to his friend 2nd Lieutenant Alan Ventris, the 18 year old son of Major General Francis Ventris.

Among the many letters of sympathy received by the family, the one that stands out was sent by fellow officer Lieutenant Eric Fletcher: 'Raymond was the best pal I've ever had... through it all he was always the same, ever ready to help anyone in any way he could, whilst his men were awfully fond of him and would have done anything for him.' Fletcher would die on day three of the Battle of the Somme on 3 July 1916 and is buried at Delville Wood Cemetery. Lieutenant William Roscoe praised Raymond for his practical bent: 'Being of a mechanical turn of mind, he was always devising some new "gadget" for use with the gun- for instance, a mounting for firing at aeroplanes... Those of my men who knew him still quote him as their authority when laying down the law and arguing about machine-gunning.'

Many grieving parents turned to spiritualism as a comfort and to make contact with their lost loved ones. The Lodges' first experience of spiritualism was when Lady Lodge took pity on a French widow who had been hospitable to the Lodges' daughters during winters spent in Paris. She was staying with Lady Lodge at Edgbaston and was in great distress having lost both her sons within a week of each other. To comfort her, Lady Lodge anonymously arranged some 'sittings' for her with a medium and during the first one on 25 September, Raymond communicated that he had been helping the two sons and sent a message to his father: 'Tell father I have met some friends of his.'

The Lodges attended 'sittings' independently of each other on 27 September. During Sir Oliver's, Raymond claimed to have 'got a great deal of work to do… helping those who are passing over in the war… I have teachers and instructors with me.'

During her 'sitting' Lady Lodge was asked via the medium about a photo of her son in a group- she was sceptical about this, as the family did not possess a photo of Raymond in a group. Raymond, however, was insistent that his mother should be told of the existence of this photo.

The family forgot about the matter until 29 November when Lady Lodge received a letter from a Mrs. Cheves, who was completely unknown to the Lodges. She was the mother of Captain Cheves of the R.A.M.C. who had written to the Lodges following Raymond's death. In her letter Mrs. Cheves mentioned a photo of a group of officers her son had just sent her and asked the Lodges if they knew anything about it. They promptly replied requesting a copy. At his next 'sitting' on 3 December Sir Oliver asked his son about the photo and Raymond explained that he was sitting in the front row with a walking stick and that a row of men were standing behind him. He mentioned three particular details- that one of the men standing behind wanted to lean on him, that the photo was taken outside and that there were vertical lines on a black background.

The photograph sent to the Lodges by Mrs. Cheves. Raymond is in the front row second from the right
from Raymond or Life and Death *by Sir Oliver Lodge*

The photo arrived on 7 December at the Lodges' house. Raymond's description via the medium was correct. The Lodges saw their son sitting cross-legged on the ground with a walking stick he had mentioned. One row of officers is seated behind him and another standing in front of a dark shed with distinct vertical lines on its roof. What made an impression on the Lodges was that the officer sitting behind Raymond was resting a hand on his shoulder, which by his expression, was clearly annoying him.

For Sir Oliver Lodge, the celebrated scientist, the photograph was prime evidence that it was possible to communicate with the dead through spiritualism. Nonetheless he needed to check the photo's provenance and he found that the negative had indeed been received in England on 15 October, two weeks after its existence was revealed through the medium. This reinforced his belief in life after death and what decided it for him was the fact that Raymond had been so insistent that the medium should tell his father about the photo. Uppermost in Sir Oliver's mind would have been the encouragement he received from Raymond during a 'sitting' on 29 October: 'For God's sake, Father, do it. Because if you only knew, and could only see what I see… you would throw the whole strength of yourself into this work.'

In his attempts to find incontrovertible evidence, Sir Oliver was joined by his other sons who devised questions about trivial matters which would be known to Raymond but not his parents. They suggested that at his next 'sitting' their father should mention the words 'Argonauts' and 'Dartmoor'. Raymond's answer was 'Telegram'. Once when the parents were away from home, all the boys had motored to Devonshire and Raymond had sent a telegram to their sisters, signing it 'Argonauts', something that the parents would have been unaware of.

On another occasion a humorous incident puzzled the medium. Raymond laughingly 'sent' the seemingly random words: 'Mr. Jackson', 'a fine bird' and 'a pedestal'. They made sense to Sir Oliver- their pet peacock 'Mr. Jackson' had just died and as he was leaving home for the 'sitting', he recalled his wife showing a wooden pedestal to the taxidermist who was about to stuff the bird!

Sir Oliver Lodge's biography *Raymond or Life and Death* is a celebration of his son's life but he was

aware that he would lay himself open 'to harsh and perhaps cynical criticism.' He presents the case in Part III of the book that 'life after death' is a subject worthy of study and he was 'as convinced of continued existence, on the other side, as I am of existence here'. In one of his concluding remarks he issues an appeal to 'the educated of the younger generation' to refrain from 'accepting assertions without severe scrutiny', and to approach the subject of the 'afterlife' with an open mind.

Whether one regards spiritualism as bunkum or not, it certainly offered many grieving parents solace and comfort during and after the Great War. That such an eminent scientist as Sir Oliver Lodge should have embraced the existence of an 'afterlife' with such conviction, encouraged many other families to attempt communication with their lost loved ones via spiritual mediums.

The graves of Raymond Lodge and Alan Ventris   *A Hamilton*

RAYMOND LODGE:

Born:	25 January 1889 at Liverpool, son of Sir Oliver and Lady Mary Lodge
Education:	Bedales School, Hampshire and Birmingham University
Occupation:	Engineer
Unit/ Regiment:	2/ South Lancashire
Rank:	2nd Lieutenant
Died:	14 September 1915
Age:	26
Buried:	Birr Cross Roads Cemetery II.D.5.
Inscription:	RAYMOND WHO HAS HELPED MANY TO KNOW THAT DEATH IS NOT THE END

The cemetery is 2 kms east of Ypres and was designed by Sir Edwin Lutyens. It was established in 1917 near an Advanced Dressing Station and was enlarged after 1918 when graves from smaller cemeteries were introduced. There are 833 burials of which 336 are unidentified

Baron Alexis de Gunzburg

'... a victim of his own heroic bravery'

A graveyard in the Ypres Salient that should feature high on the list of Battlefield Guides' itineraries is to be found at Zillebeke Church in Belgium. It contains the so-called 'Aristocrats' Plot' where 15 officers of aristocratic descent were buried during the First Battle of Ypres in November 1914. The church is two miles south east of Ypres and lay just behind the front line. It suffered severe damage by shell fire and was near enough to the fighting for the unfortunate officers to be buried immediately in the graveyard.

The 'Aristocrats' Plot' in Zillebeke Churchyard   *J Kerr*

Baron Alexis de Gunzburg was one of the 15 officers buried in Zillebeke Churchyard. All were members of the Army's most prestigious regiments: seven were members of cavalry regiments- the Royal Horse Guards ('The Blues'), the Hussars ('The Cherry Pickers') or the Life Guards ('The Donkey Wallopers'). Eight officers were attached to infantry regiments- six of them to the Grenadier Guards ('The Bill Browns'), one to the Coldstream Guards ('The Lilywhites') and the other to the less glamorous Gloucestershire Regiment ('The Glorious Glosters').

The Army was the chosen career step for many aristocrats with limited interest in further academic study or positions in the Law and the Church; seven of the officers buried in the graveyard received their military training at the Royal Military College, Sandhurst. Seven were regulars who had been commissioned before 1905 and were veterans of the Boer War between 1899 and 1902.

Only five were descended from ostensibly 'landed' families with an aristocratic lineage boasting dukes and earls. Several were sons of successful ennobled industrialists whose wealth had been based on the exploitation of minerals and shipping during the growth of Britain's Empire and industry in the 18th century.

In *Aristocrats Go to War*, Jerry Murland has established that buried in Zillebeke churchyard in 1914 are 10 Etonians, two Harrovians, one Glenalmond old boy and two Carthusians (Charterhouse). After their schooldays four of the 15 continued their studies at either Trinity College, Cambridge or New College, Oxford- with varying levels of enthusiasm and success.

121

Baron Alexis de Gunzburg

Baron Alexis de Gunzburg who fell near Zillebeke was not of true British 'blue blood' but was educated at Eton College and Oxford University. He was born in Paris in 1887, the youngest son of Baron Salomon de Gunzburg and Baroness Henriette. The de Gunzburgs were a Russian Jewish family described by *The Times* in 1912 as financiers and bankers who had accrued much of their wealth from Russian mining companies. The 'I. Ye. Guenzburg' Banking House was opened in St. Petersburg in 1859, one of the most significant institutions of its kind in the Russian Empire. It had a broad network of business and family connections with banks in Hamburg, Berlin and Paris. The family owned sugar factories and shares in gold-mines, joint-stock companies and in a steamship company; several joint-stock banks and insurance companies were established with their financial backing. The de Gunzburg Banking House enjoyed favour in Court circles and managed the finances of Tsar Alexander II's brother-in-law, the Grand Duke of Hesse who in 1870 granted Horace de Gunzburg the title of Baron. The Russian Imperial permission to transmit these titles to his heirs followed in 1879, the only occasion when Jews were allowed to adopt a noble title in Russia.

In 1876 Horace's son, Baron Salomon, married the 17 year old Henriette, daughter of the influential Jewish financier Saloman Goldschmidt; they had four children, the youngest of whom was Alexis. They lived in Paris but it was decided to educate Alexis in England at Eton College. Little is recorded about his five years at the College; he was in Mr. Booker's House for whom he played the Eton version of football and in his final year according to Mr. Booker, managed 'to conquer a bad habit of cooling. Has an off day which occurs rather frequently. Works hard.' His efforts academically secured him a place at Oxford University on leaving Eton in 1904.

Alexis followed in the family tradition of working in finance and was successful enough to become a partner in the London stockbroking firm of Basil Montgomery, Fitzgerald and Company which suggests the description of his profession on his Army form as 'Gent' may have been a little wide of the mark.

The 27 year old stockbroker answered the call to arms of his adopted country in early August 1914. He enlisted with the 11/ Hussars whose colonel-in-chief since 1911 had ironically been Wilhelm Crown Prince of Germany. He was gazetted as a 2nd lieutenant on 14 September. His lack of height did not count against him but a major problem surfaced when training with the Regiment started. It was discovered that Alexis was not a British national. The family's connections, however, came to the rescue via the Rothschild family. Overtures were made to Winston Churchill, the First Sea Lord and by 18 August, Alexis's naturalisation papers were in order even if the authorities found it impossible to spell his surname correctly- gazetted as 'de Gunzturg' and in other records referred to as 'de Gunsberg'. Now officially a British subject, Baron Alexis de Gunzburg was free to resume his training.

The 11/ Hussars were in the 7th Cavalry Brigade that sailed for France in October. Alexis's command of the French language was a valuable asset. He was attached to the Royal Horse Guards as 'galloper' or aide-de-camp and acted as a translator, liaising with French generals and carrying messages to and from the front line. He was not required to undertake front line duties as he was an interpreter but his sense of adventure was such that he embarked on a series of dangerous missions.

2nd Lieutenant Alexis de Gunzburg died on 6 November near the village of Zillebeke when he and four other cavalry officers were engaged in a counter-attack which successfully halted the German advance. Fellow officers to fall were Lieutenant William Wyndham of the 1/ Life Guards, Lieutenant William Petersen of the 2/ Life Guards, Captain Norman Neill of the 13/ Hussars and the Royal Horse Guards' commanding officer, Lieutenant Colonel Gordon Wilson. All were buried in Zillebeke

Church's 'Aristocratic Plot'.

Confusion surrounds the precise circumstances of Alexis de Gunzburg's death. The most likely explanation is that he was carrying a message from Major General Kavanagh, the Brigade Commander, to Lieutenant Colonel Wilson, which is corroborated by the report in the Battalion's War Diary that he died when 'running across an open field'.

Tributes included in de Ruvigny's *Great War Roll of Honour*, emphasise that de Gunzburg had been running messages 'under threat of enemy fire'. It was possible that he had returned with a message and was with his commanding officer when they were both killed.

When Alexis's mother Henriette, widowed in 1905, received the news of Alexis's death, she may have been comforted by commiseration from George V who had 'learnt how gallantly Baron de Gunzburg fought with his comrades of the Royal Horse Guards, although his duties as an interpreter did not necessitate his presence in the firing line.'

Tributes highlighted Alexis de Gunzburg's qualities. Captain Cyril Potter, aide-de-camp to Major General Kavanagh noted, patronisingly perhaps, that 'Alexis was killed, poor little chap, on 6 November whilst behaving with great gallantry. Indeed, all the time he has been out here he has been more brave than words can tell you. My General was devoted to him and felt his death terribly. During the day that he was killed he had been carrying messages under heavy fire all over the place, and always came back with a cheery smile. He was very gallant, too, the day Alastair Innes-Ker was wounded; he insisted on going back into the trenches to look after him, again under heavy fire. Truthfully, nobody in the Brigade displayed more courage at all times, and he was universally beloved by all the Brigade. I saw a great deal of him during the last few weeks, and learnt during that time to realise and appreciate all his sterling qualities. Active Service, as a rule, shows the best and worst of a man's character. We found nothing but that was good and loyal in poor little Alexis. We managed to regain his body yesterday, and have buried him in the churchyard at Zillebeke with Colonel Wilson and Reggie Wyndham. I am sure he cannot have suffered much as he was killed almost instantaneously.'

'Alexis', the brass bell given to Zillebeke Church by Baroness Henriette de Gunzburg in memory of her son
A Hamilton

Major Brinton maintained that 'he was a victim of his own heroic bravery. At the time he was shot, he was carrying messages. He was most popular with everyone in the Brigade and is universally mourned for. Had he been content to merely carry out his ordinary duties as an interpreter, he might have been alive now. But he knew no fear, and was always anxious for some work in the firing line. We have lost many gallant fellows but no one is more deserving of our honour than Alexis de Gunzburg.'

The attack near Zillebeke 'rather failed' in the view of Captain Arthur Foster: 'At one place the Germans stopped in some houses and shot several of our men, among them Alexis and Colonel Wilson… When I told General Kavanagh about it at the time, he said how well he had done, and how much he had helped in explaining the situation to the French general who was co-operating with us.'

Despite the glowing tributes to an officer who clearly performed beyond the call of duty, his exploits were not acknowledged by a posthumous award. His family spared no expense in their memorial to Alexis after the War. A large bell, cast in Luxemburg and weighing 397 kilograms was placed in the belfry of Zillebeke church alongside a larger 774 kilogram bell called Catherina. It was inscribed 123 with the words: *'De profundi clamavi ad te Domine. Je m'appelle Alexis. J'ai été donnée par la Baronne Henriette de Gunzburg en souvenir de son fils soldat Baron Alexis de Gunsburg tombé à Zillebeke l'année 1914'*. (From the depths, I have cried out to You, O Lord. My name is Alexis. I was given by Baroness Henriette de Gunzburg in remembrance of her son soldier Baron Alexis de Gunsburg, fallen at Zillebeke in 1914).

According to Zillebeke's churchwarden Frans Deleye, 'the smaller bells in the campanile are rung with Catherine and Alexis, and have commemorated at exactly 20.30 on every evening since November 11, 2002, all the fallen soldiers from both world wars and all those buried in the churchyard. The bells also mourn the futility of war.'

Alexis was buried next to his commanding officer Lieutenant Colonel Wilson and initially a small wooden cross marked his grave which was destroyed by shell fire. Henriette later provided an ornate tombstone for her son which was erected before the Imperial War Graves Commission insisted on a uniformity of headstone 'to avoid class distinctions'.

Baron Alexis de Gunzburg became a British subject 'to do his bit' in the conflict against Germany. He was of an aristocratic Jewish and Russian ancestry and had been brought up in France- he was a European who recognised the magnitude of the German threat to the continent's balance of power. Energetically and enthusiastically he threw himself into the defence of his adopted countries against the Kaiser's drive for German domination of Europe. He paid the ultimate price for doing so.

BARON ALEXIS DE GUNZBURG:

Born:	6 May 1887 in Paris, youngest son of Baron Salomon and Baroness Henriette de Gunzburg of 199, Boulevard St. Germain, Paris
Education:	Eton College
Occupation:	Partner in stockbroking firm Basil Montgomery, Fitzgerald & Co, London
Unit/ Regiment:	11/ Hussars (Prince Albert's Own); he was attached to the Royal Horse Guards as an intelligence officer and interpreter for the Staff of the 7th Cavalry Brigade
Rank:	2nd Lieutenant
Died:	6 November 1914
Age:	27
Buried:	'Aristocrats' Plot', Zillebeke Churchyard
Inscription:	None- but a bell rings out from the belfry in his memory and there is a special tombstone in the churchyard

Zillebeke Churchyard is 3 kms south east of Ypres. It contains a plot of 32 burials of whom 15 were officers of aristocratic descent; its design was by W.H. Cowlishaw

J Kerr

AVENEL ST. GEORGE

'He was splendid out here, always cheerful and never losing his head, even under the most trying circumstances'

The youngest of the officers buried in Zillebeke Churchyard was 19 year old Howard Avenel Bligh St. George, known to his family as Avenel or 'Ave'. He left Eton College in July 1913 and joined the Army in January 1914 when he was commissioned as a probationary officer into the Life Guards, the élite regiment of the Household Cavalry. Just ten months later he was shot when returning to his front line trench near Zwarteleen Wood in Belgium.

Evelyn St. George
Baker Family Papers, Baker Library Historical Collections, Harvard Business School

The origins of his family are traceable to the Norman Conquest, Burke's Peerage stating that 'the origin of the family in England has always been ascribed to one Baldwin St. George who came to England *tempore* William the Conqueror.' By the 18th century, a branch of the St. George family were substantial landowners in County Galway on Ireland's west coast. Howard Bligh St. George, a J.P. in Galway and son of the 2nd baronet, married in 1891 a beautiful American heiress, Evelyn Baker, the daughter of one of the wealthiest financiers in New York- George Fisher Baker was reputed to have a fortune estimated at 200 million dollars and was acerbically described by *Time Magazine* as 'the richest, most powerful and most taciturn commercial banker in U.S. history'.

Their first child, George Baker, was born in 1892 and Howard Avenel Bligh followed in 1894. The family moved to England in 1912 to south Warwickshire, an area that attracted a number of wealthy Americans at the turn of the century such as Charles Tuller Garland who built a mansion at Moreton Morrell. He also built two courts, one for real tennis and the other for the precursor of squash- American squash tennis. Evelyn and her children regularly availed themselves of the facilities. Garland was so keen to display his credentials as a landed English gentleman that he volunteered for the war effort and joined the Life Guards in 1915.

When a third son Frederick Ferris was born in 1908, 13 year old Avenel entered Eton College. According to his obituary in the December 1914 edition of *The Eton Chronicle*, he had 'no taste for book learning and was happiest when following the College beagles' and he was their Whip from 1912 to 1913. Despite his preference for sport and the outdoor life, he was, nonetheless, President of his House Library.

Avenel St. George was an all-round sportsman. He came third in the College steeplechase in 1913 and was an accomplished exponent of rackets, one of the fastest of all racquet sports but he irritated his housemaster Mr. Martens who blamed him for losing the House rackets doubles final in 1912: 'Hill was easily the best player on the court but St. George gave him the most feeble support, never having taken the trouble to play once during the half (term) before the ties.' He

The St. George family in 1913.
From back left: Avenel, Howard and George and in the front: Gardenia, Evelyn and Vivien, and Ferris
Baker Family Papers Baker Library Historical Collections, Harvard Business School

performed for his House football team, not the football now played by millions world-wide but Eton's special, older version, played by boys of all ages in the spring term. 'He kicked well in the bully and tackled well… a little slow perhaps but very keen', and when performing for the House cricket team he 'could hit the bowling about very effectively.'

Avenel displayed qualities at Eton that would serve him well as an officer: 'He showed to a marked degree a practical sagacity and common sense… whilst there was a charm about him which made him much liked and appreciated by all who came across him.' He was gregarious by nature, reflected by his membership of 'Pop', a prestigious society for the College's prefects. Captured on camera in his Life Guards' uniform, the young St. George exudes a self-confidence imbued in him by his five years at Eton.

Avenel St. George in his Life Guards'
uniform in 1914 Frans Delaye- copy of photo
given to the citizens of Zillebeke by Colonel Ferris St.
George, Avenel's younger brother, in 1968

The 1/ Life Guards reached Belgium in early October 1914 after training on Salisbury Plain and were part of the rear guard action south of Ypres to prevent the German 4th and 6th Armies driving through Belgium to the Channel ports. Avenel was unimpressed with the 'terrible weather' and the general state of war-torn Belgium. He did not pull any punches and wrote with venom: 'I hate this country.'

He asked his parents to 'tell me when you write again the war news as I have no idea how matters stand.' Confusion reigned: on 14 October the Life Guards were involved in street fighting with a patrol of uhlans but they had difficulty discerning between friend and foe; his squadron was hit by 'friendly fire' and also mistakenly fired on by Belgians. Avenel complained that 'the guns never cease' and that there was a 'continuous roar all day and sometimes night.'

'Words can't describe the hell it is' he wrote to his family on 23 October. He reported heavy casualties and complained that 'the French are rotters, leaving it all to us.' At least he derived some satisfaction from the destruction of a Zeppelin which was 'a fine sight.' His family had cause for increasing concern for their son's safety- on 27 October, he bemoaned the loss of his servant and many of the Life Guards' horses: 'By Jove, we are dirty and smattered with blood… don't worry for Heaven's sake', he unconvincingly tried to reassure them.

His brother George was in New York working for bankers J.P. Morgan and Co. He may have envied Avenel's exciting adventure on the Western Front but would have felt somewhat safer at his home in Madison Avenue. 'Well it would open your eyes a bit if you could see what is going on here. Words can't express the inferno it is…The worst part of it all is the ghastly sight of wounded men.' Avenel told of how he took a rifle and opened fire on about 500 Germans crossing a field advancing 1,200 yards away. He was satisfied that he 'picked off about seven, not bad… I am not exaggerating at all in anything I tell you' and along with most soldiers at the Front, he would 'not be sorry when this foul affair is over.'

Avenel was at pains to inform his family of the importance of his Life Guards' role: 'The Belgian army is nearly done. They have had an awful hammering' and the French were 'doubtless doing their share further south.' He wrote to his parents on 1 November, admitting 'it is no good telling you about the battle as I'd have to write volumes, but it will give you an idea if you imagine a ceaseless roar of thunder day and night and have to roar to the person next to you to hear at all.'

By 7 November, the 7th Cavalry Brigade was under intense pressure. The Germans had broken through British lines on 6 November when many casualties were incurred including Avenel's superior officer, Captain Hon. E.H. Wyndham. Avenel wrote with pride about the Brigade's action on 7 November which 'is said to be the finest thing yet done in the whole war.' The 1/ Life Guards were suddenly ordered to support the infantry who were in retreat- the Germans were driven out of the trenches and three were retaken, held all night and returned to the infantry in the morning. 'General Byng commanding our Division said it was the finest thing he'd ever seen.' Byng later master-minded the capture of Vimy Ridge at Easter 1917.

Avenel allowed himself 'a little tale' about himself: 'During this advance I was dashing thro' a wood in front of my troop with my head down to avoid branches going into my eyes and ran into three Germans with fixed bayonets. They got such a fright that they flung down their arms and surrendered to me- which I may tell you was rather a relief. Of course', he concluded, 'we do all our fighting dismounted.'

He wrote to 'Darling Mama and Papa' on 13 November addressing his letter from 'Hell'. The cavalry 'invariably come to the rescue and drive them back… we were out all last night in the heaviest rain I have ever seen.' It was virtually the last action he would see.

A numbing cable was received by his brother George at 258, Madison Avenue, New York on 22 November from his father: 'Our dear Avenel was instantaneously killed in action at Zillebeke November fifteenth leading his men in a charge. Lawrence Straker buried him under heavy fire in a churchyard there. St. George.'

Evelyn St. George had received the news she must have dreaded and half expected, from Straker, Avenel's friend and fellow officer. 'Poor Ave is dead. I saw his body in the church here today. It had been left there to await burial. I am awfully cut up, but looked in his pockets to find any letters and all I found were some for other people which he was carrying, some revolver cartridges and the enclosed pocket handkerchief. I am sending a letter to his Headquarters to say that I wish to be present at his burial and will let you know where he has been buried and I will do anything that I can to see that everything is properly done, and will, contrary to the regulations, let you know *exactly* village and spot where the grave is, and get a "censor" stamp to stamp the letter with as they are awfully strict.'

Grandson of George Baker, one of the richest men in America, Avenel St. George's death was worthy of mention in the The New York Times *on 26 November 1914*

Straker comforted Evelyn by declaring her son was 'quite the nicest fellow' he had met during his time at the Front. He commended Avenel for his honesty and kindness 'to all no matter who they were' and expressed his admiration for the way in which Evelyn always 'gave him his head. I feel most awfully for all of you. I thought you would like to have his handkerchief so I send it; it's all he has on him.'

The Church of St. Catherine, Zillebeke before the War and in ruins in 1918   *Frans Delaye photographic collection*

True to his word, on 16 November, he enclosed directions to Avenel's grave in Zillebeke Churchyard: 'I got some nice large boards and burnt the inscription on myself. I put his grave on the north side of the Tower as the Germans are shooting from the south side, so his Grave will not be disturbed. I could only bury him 3 ft. deep as the Germans are shelling the Church; and one of the men of my machine-gun section (who was helping me) was knocked on the head by a small stone and made

'The Beanstalk'- Evelyn St. George painted by William Orpen c. 1912

unconscious, but will recover. I think someone in his regiment must have got his identification badge, revolver etc. to send home as only the things I mentioned were on him.'

2nd Lieutenant Howard Avenel Bligh St. George's obituary in *The Eton Chronicle* asserts that he 'did extremely well with the 1st Life Guards… he was killed on 15 November… he had driven the German Imperial Guard out of their trenches and was following them up when a wounded German left behind by his retreating comrades, seeing him right in front and that he was an officer, shot him dead through the heart at point blank range. A senior officer (Captain Hon. E. H. Wyndham who had by now recovered from his wounds) wrote that "he is a terrible loss to us and the regiment. He was splendid out here, always cheerful and never losing his head, even under the most trying circumstances. I never saw him whinge, he was always just the same. I don't believe he had any nerves at all."'

Accounts in the *Eton Chronicle* and by Lawrence Straker maintain that Avenel was killed by a shot to the heart by a German lying in front of him- the biographer of Avenel's grandfather, George Fisher Baker, chose to engage in some post-war 'Hun bashing' by claiming that Avenel was 'shot from behind by a wounded German in the customary fashion of that "chivalrous" race.' As was often the case, the obituary did not quite match the truth of Avenel St. George's death. The Life Guards' War Diary more prosaically reported that after arriving at Headquarters to report that the Germans had retreated from Zwarteleen Wood, he was shot by a sniper based in a house not far from the British forward trenches.

Despite being sent away to boarding school, Avenel may have accepted that his parents' marriage was under strain. By the final two years of his time at Eton, it appears to have been little more than a 'marriage of convenience'. His mother Evelyn's first meeting in 1906 with the Dublin-based painter, William Orpen, developed into a long lasting affair to which her husband turned a blindish eye, content to concentrate on the thrill of the chase with the hounds in Ireland and later in Warwickshire.

Evelyn bought a flat in London's Berkeley Square where she and Orpen conducted their relationship in the public eye. Evelyn was a socialite with a wide circle of acquaintances in 'high society'; the couple were an interesting pairing- she was tall and stunningly beautiful, Orpen was short and characterful rather than handsome. They were playfully described in society circles as 'Jack and the Beanstalk'! When playing a charity show at the Drury

Illustrated letter from William Orpen to Mrs. St. George with a sketch of the artist and Mrs. St. George roller skating
National Gallery of Ireland, Dublin

Major William Orpen sketching in Amiens in August 1918
IWM Q 008258

Zillebeke Church
October 1918.

Mud
Everywhere
Nothing but mud
The very air seems thick with it
The few Tufts of grass are all smeared with it
Mud
The church, a heap of it
One look, and weep for it
Thats what they made of it
Mud
Slimy and wet
Churned and upset.

Here Bones that once mattered
with crosses lie scattered
Broken and Battered
covered in mud
Here where the Church's Bell
Tolled when our Heroes fell
in that mad start of Hell
Mud
Thats all thats left of it.

Mud by William Orpen written in effect as an epitaph to Avenel after a visit to Zillebeke in 1918
National Gallery of Ireland, Dublin

Lane Theatre, the actress Elsie Janis (see p.210) stayed at 'the country house of Mrs. Evelyn St. George- present was William Orpen- that small, gentle, wickedly witty young man whom the family called "Woppy"'. She pointed out in 1933 that 'for a portrait today we have to pay thousands of pounds…' and referring to his knighthood conferred in 1918, 'he has a new name- Sir William Orpen.'

William Orpen was a painter of renown who was commissioned as an official war artist in 1915 thanks to members of Evelyn's influential circle of friends, not least Sir John Cowans, the Quarter-Master General and Field Marshal Douglas Haig whom Orpen would later describe as 'one of the best friends I ever had.' At first he composed portraits of luminaries like Haig and Winston Churchill but increasingly his deep seated disillusion with the War was reflected in paintings that capture the devastating effect of it on man and nature. The influence of Evelyn's loss of Avenel was a factor in changing Orpen's perception of the War and his poem *Mud* composed after a visit to Zillebeke in 1918 was inspired by Avenel's death and was an epitaph to him.

In a letter written on 7 November, a week before his death, Avenel complimented his mother on her contribution to the war effort: 'You are too good taking so much trouble about hospitals etc.' In his memory Evelyn financed the St. George Ward of the American Women's War Relief Hospital at Paignton in Devon, described in a diary entry by Renie Hamilton, the wife of Royal Warwicks officer Captain Robert Hamilton, as 'a wonderful place'.

Evelyn had the financial wherewithal to mark her son's death in a way that Annie Souls from a different stratum of society (see p.147) could not. After the War she

Zonnebeke by William Orpen   Tate Gallery, London

Stained glass windows in memory of Avenel St. George in St. Catherine's Church, Zillebeke　　　*J Kerr*

arranged for a memorial to be built in the graveyard of the church of St. George at Newbold Pacey in Warwickshire for her son and villagers who lost their lives; she also paid for stained glass windows to be installed there and in the church of St. Catherine in Zillebeke.

Avenel Bligh St. George was the archetypal young officer, always in the firing line and fiercely patriotic. He epitomised a generation and class that were destroyed in the front line of battle during the Great War.

AVENEL St. GEORGE:

Born:	16 December 1894, son of Howard Bligh St. George and Evelyn St. George of Ashorne Hill, Warwickshire
Education:	Eton College
Occupation:	Professional soldier
Unit/ Regiment:	1/ Life Guards
Rank:	2nd Lieutenant
Died:	15 November 1914
Age:	19
Buried:	'Aristocrats' Plot' in Zillebeke Churchyard
Inscription:	FIRMITAS IN COELO
	(Strength in heaven- the St. George family motto)

Avenel St. George's grave　　*A Hamilton*

The 'Aristocrats' Plot' Zillebeke Churchyard　　*J Kerr*

WILLIAM REDMOND

*'It would be a fine memorial to the men who have died
so splendidly if we could, over their graves build up a bridge
between North and South'*

William Redmond was a fervent Irish Nationalist and Roman Catholic who fought for Irish Home
Rule. He sat in the House of Commons from 1883 until his death in 1917 as a member of the Irish
Nationalist 'Home Rule' Party. He loathed British rule and land ownership in Ireland and was a
passionate proponent of self-government for the Irish, working assiduously for an end to English
landlordism. He was imprisoned three times in 1882, 1888 and 1902
for methods he adopted in advocating his anti-British stance.
A passionate politician, he was evicted a number of times from the
floor of the House of Commons, often for over-zealous confrontation
with Protestant Unionist M.P.s.

It was a great surprise, therefore, when in 1914, at the age of 54, he
volunteered for service with the British Army and actively encouraged
his constituents in East Clare to volunteer for the British war effort.

At the outbreak of war Redmond expressed the wish that 'every Clare
man will be ready, Protestant or Catholic, to stand shoulder to
shoulder for the benefit and protection of all our people, of all creeds,
classes and parts.' He made clear his support for the conflict with
Germany in a speech from a window at the Imperial Hotel in Cork to
a large gathering of Irish Volunteers, a Catholic group dedicated to
the introduction of Home Rule for Ireland, exhorting them to follow
him to Flanders and France 'to do what is right for Ireland.'

Willie Redmond's passion for Irish Home Rule was instilled in him
from an early age by his father William who was a Home Rule M.P.
for Wexford between 1872 and 1880. William junior followed in his
father's political footsteps as an M.P. He was elected to represent
Wexford in 1883, Fermanagh North in 1885 and East Clare in 1892
which he represented until his death in 1917. His brother John, a
barrister, was more moderate and conciliatory by nature and assumed
leadership of the Irish Nationalist Party in 1900.

*Willie Redmond M.P. for East Clare
in 1898*
National Portrait Gallery, London x35016

Willie took great pleasure from 'sticking thorns in the side of the British Lion'. In 1881 he was
involved with the Land League's agitation against English landlords, the aim of which was to bring
about a reduction of rack-rents and to obtain 'ownership of the soil' by tenant farmers. He was
engaged in encouraging them to organize themselves more effectively and defended those threatened
with eviction for refusal to pay 'unjust' rents.

For their efforts, Redmond and Charles Stewart Parnell, leader of the Irish Nationalist Parliamentary
Party since 1875, found themselves sharing a cell in Dublin's Kilmainham Gaol.

On his release he and John travelled to the United States and Australia where they raised £15,000
from Irish *émigrés* for the Land League's campaign which was now 'boycotting' English landlords.
Willie Redmond wrote in 1885 that 'unless you boycott, you will never beat landlordism out of the
country. Unless you boycott, you will never be able to put up the green flag permanently over the
castle.' He was using the word 'boycott' in common parlance only five years after Captain Charles
Boycott, the British land agent for the County Mayo landowner Lord Erne, had been ostracised for
trying to undermine the Land League's action to protect tenants from exploitation by landlords.

Redmond was imprisoned a second time in 1888 for inciting a tenant to resist a sheriff's eviction
order in County Wexford. When arrested, he considered it 'the highest honour in being prosecuted
by Mr. Balfour', the Chief Secretary for Ireland, who had earned himself the sobriquet 'Bloody

Balfour' after the shooting of three Land League campaigners in September 1887: 'I undoubtedly cheered those men when they were defending their homes against unjust eviction and I shall continue to cheer every man who does so.' Both Redmond brothers were imprisoned in Kilmainham Gaol.

Redmond was at his rhetorical best in debates over the Boer War which he described as 'cruel, unnecessary and unjust' for which he was ejected from the floor of the House of Commons. He received his third prison sentence on 4 November 1902 for an inflammatory speech in defence of the newly formed United Irish Land League.

After the general election of 1910 the Irish Parliamentary Party found itself holding the balance of power in the House of Commons. In the years preceding the War, Home Rule was becoming a distinct possibility. However, there was a significant development in Irish politics that Willie Redmond stands accused of failing to appreciate fully. A 'Solemn League and Covenant' was signed by 250,000 Protestants in the north against Home Rule and in 1913 the Ulster Volunteer Force was founded. It was a military outfit, hell-bent on resisting by force if necessary, the introduction of self-government for Ireland. Ominously, a rival body, the radical Irish Nationalist Volunteer Force, was set up to ensure the passage of Home Rule. Nonetheless, Redmond was gratified that the 3rd Home Rule Bill was making steady progress through Parliament and on 18 September 1914, nearly two months into the War, the Home Rule Bill received royal assent but was temporarily suspended.

So why was it that Willie Redmond, a firebrand whose political life had been spent for over 20 years working against British rule of Ireland, should have enlisted with the British Army? His great fear was that Ireland would suffer the same fate as Belgium at the hands of the Germans: 'There may be a few who think that Germany would not injure Ireland, and might even benefit from her. I hope the Clare people will rely on no such rash statements. If the Germans come here… they will be our masters, and we at their mercy. What that mercy is likely to be, judge by the mercy shown to Belgium. I am far too old to be a soldier, but I mean to do my best, for whatever life remains in me, to show that Ireland at least is true to her treaties, and not in any way ungrateful to her friends throughout the world. No Irishman worth his salt would be beholden for any favour to the men who have ruined Belgium.'

Redmond was not alone in his desire for retribution for the bombardment of Scarborough and other coastal towns by a German cruiser squadron on 16 December 1914 when 130 lives were lost and nearly 600 wounded. Winston Churchill, then First Lord of the Admiralty, referred to the Germans as the 'Baby Killers of Scarborough'. The incident galvanised Redmond, despite his advancing years, to join in early 1915 the Royal Irish Regiment with whom he had served as a young man from 1879 to 1888, when he had achieved the rank of 2nd lieutenant. He had gained military experience that would prove invaluable many years later: 'It would be ungrateful and inhuman if we stood idly by while English, Scottish and Welsh people were in danger, and their women and children killed in cold blood, as happened at Scarborough.'

Redmond's eagerness to volunteer for Kitchener's Army was partly as a result of his brother John's espousal of the cause and their view that if Catholics and Protestants fought alongside each other, the attainment of self-government for Ireland would be easier to achieve. It was a theme that Willie developed and returned to on many occasions in 1916 and 1917.

Willie Redmond enlisted despite fruitless efforts by some of the 'top brass' to dissuade him- a man of his age could not be expected to cope with the dangers and discomforts of fighting in the front line… but to no avail. As far as he was concerned 'if I am too old to fight at least I will not sit comfortably in an armchair and read what other men are doing and suffering.'

Redmond was gazetted on 22 February as a temporary captain in the 6/ Royal Irish of the mainly Catholic 16th Division. Training at Fermoy in County Cork and then Blackdown, Surrey was, as the majority of volunteers were to find at training camps throughout Britain, irritatingly monotonous. When the 6/ Royal Irish eventually sailed from Southampton on 17 December 1915, Willie absented himself temporarily from his Parliamentary duties. Christmas Day was spent in the Festubert and Loos area where Redmond's 'B' Company was on duty with the 10/ Gordon Highlanders.

Older than most at the Front, Redmond struggled physically with the conditions and general hardship but was accepted as a father figure and inspiration to those younger than himself. He was much loved and respected by his men and made a point of marching on foot with them rather than overseeing them on horseback.

The notion that a leading politician might have popped back in more recent times to the green benches of the House of Commons from military action in the Falklands, Iraq or Afghanistan, is inconceivable but William Redmond caused quite a stir in the Chamber when from March 1916, the silver-haired soldier in his army uniform returned on several occasions from the Front to take his seat and speak passionately in debates.

More than any exploding shell, the greatest blow that Redmond suffered at the Front was the unwelcome news of the Easter Uprising in Dublin between 24 and 30 April 1916 by Irish Republicans whose aims were to end British rule in Ireland and to establish a republic. Disappointing though this was for Redmond, it reinforced his view that the War would bring the two factions in Ireland closer together in a self-governing framework similar to those he had witnessed and approved of in Canada and Australia. He wrote to the celebrated novelist Arthur Conan Doyle after the worst of the Battle of the Somme arguing that 'it would be a fine memorial to the men who have died so splendidly if we could, over their graves build up a bridge between North and South. I have been thinking a lot about this lately in France- no one could help doing so when one finds that the two sections from Ireland are actually side by side holding the trenches!' The Easter Uprising and its potential ramifications induced him to remain at the Front with his beloved company.

Major William Redmond M.P. in military uniform　　The Times History of the War

He was promoted to the rank of major in July 1916 but much to his annoyance, was removed from the front line. He had the opportunity to record his observations of the War anonymously in articles he wrote for *The Daily Chronicle* entitled *Trench Pictures from France*. In one, *A Garden Trench*, he contrasted trenches in winter and summer: 'A trench in winter is… a veritable lane of agony where weary feet fall and where no single bright spot redeems the dullness or catches the eye. In contrast, in summer, the trench is transformed- poppies red and cornflowers blue spread along the trenches in marvellous profusion… Now and again a gust of wind will blow the petals of the flaming poppies down, and they lie at the bottom, looking again on the brown clay like bright red drops of blood. Whilst human beings day and night slaughter each other, Nature marches her course unruffled.'

When blades of grass began to peep through the mud and destitution in No Man's Land, for Willie Redmond it was a case of Nature transcending war. He wrote lyrically of spring awakening above the trenches of the Somme: 'But with the dawning of Sunday there was a change. The fog disappeared. The sky, glowering and dark for so long, turned into an expanse of purest blue. A lark, rising from God knows where on the dismal war-seared plain, rose high over the trench and sang, and sang and sang blithely. The screaming of the shells, the roar of the guns seemed silenced by the song. The men looked up and listened, pausing in their work, pausing even in taking their hasty meal. It was a wonderful song. The trench-stained men were transported by it. They were no longer amidst ruin and misery and war. The song brought them back to their homes, and they stood in the pleasant fields of Ireland, and listened as they had so often done to the skylark on high.' (See p.284 for Redmond's beautifully written tribute to 'Jack' the fox terrier of the 6/ Royal Irish).

Redmond was Mentioned in Despatches on 13 November. It was with great authority that, when on leave, he informed the House of Commons about how Catholic and Protestant troops were fighting together: 'If it be possible for men with divergent views in politics, religion and everything else to agree and stand shoulder to shoulder in face of the common enemy in the trenches and camps of France and Belgium, it must be possible, and it should be possible, that men of these opinions should learn to agree, and to come to an arrangement and settlement which would make it possible for Ireland in the future to be governed in a satisfactory way.'

Redmond's expectations for the future of Ireland were, sadly, unrealistic and naïve. Terence Denman asserts in his biography *The Life and Death of William Redmond* that he expressed 'an almost mystical belief in a new Ireland forged in the trenches' and it was idealistic in the extreme to consider that 'the hatred of centuries could be abrogated by a few years' shared privations on the Western Front.'

Willie Redmond spoke memorably in the House on 7 March 1917 on a motion to introduce Home Rule. Dressed again in his soldier's uniform, he was listened to intently. He argued that the Irish were sympathetic to the Allies' cause and the French efforts to repel the German Armies. They were outraged by the nature of the German occupation of Belgium. He passionately believed that the resolve of the Irish troops would be stiffened if they knew they were to be granted self-government; Ireland was the only part of the British Empire engaged in the War without such a constitutional freedom. When British and Irish soldiers were fighting side by side, was it not time, he asked, that memories of William of Orange's victory at the Battle of the Boyne be forgotten?

He returned to the Front in May, desperate to be with his 'splendid' men. 'We are pulling famously with the Ulster men.' Maybe he was suffering pangs of self-doubt claiming 'I shall never regret I have been out here.' His dreams were gradually eroding; siren voices in his East Clare constituency were calling for his resignation and an Irish Convention was being mooted by Prime Minister Lloyd George, in which parts of Protestant Ulster would be excluded. The Home Rule scheme which Redmond had proposed so ardently, was gradually being transformed into something completely different to the political ideal he had been fighting for in Parliament and on the Western Front.

The 6/ Royal Irish were due to launch an attack on Messines, on 7 June, arguably the first salvo in the Third Battle of Ypres or Passchendaele, which lasted until November at a cost of 250,000 British casualties. Redmond rallied the Battalion with an impassioned speech and also rallied the 7th and 8th Battalions. Not for the first time, Redmond had to plead with his commanding officer to allow him, despite his advancing years, to 'go over the top'.

Father Edmond Kelly, chaplain to the 6/ Royal Irish described how miserable Redmond was at the prospect of not being allowed to join his men: 'He had used every influence with the General to get over the top with the men, and he had little hope of succeeding. He spoke in the most feeling manner of what awaited the poor fellows, and longed to share their suffering and their fate. However, he was not to be denied, and to his extreme delight was given leave by fellow Irish nationalist Major General William Hickie to charge with his old battalion of the Royal Irish. He put on his equipment in Father O'Connell's room and was simply bubbling over with joy. While fastening the belts over his shoulders, he was laughing with good humour. He went up to the trenches accompanied by his servant Organ.' At 10.00 p.m. the political firebrand went round every man under his command to steady their nerves and prepare them for the next morning's offensive.

At 3.10 a.m. on 7 June, the 6/ Royal Irish of the 16th (Irish) Division in conjunction with the 36th of the Protestant Ulstermen set off for an area north of Wytschaete (known as 'White Sheet' to British soldiers) on the Messines Ridge after mines, laid by miners under German positions, exploded.

Two of the craters on the Messines Ridge at Kruisstraat caused by mines exploding on 7 June 1917   J. Kerr

Major Redmond had advanced only a few paces when he was mortally wounded by shell fire in his wrist and leg. The chaplain who attended Willie Redmond when he was dying wrote to Eleanor Redmond about her husband's last moments. She replied 'I am indeed grateful to you for your kind letter and especially for your goodness to my dear husband in his hour of need. How glad I am that you were able to be with him and I am sure he was pleased to find himself so tenderly cared for by the 36th Division. It was always to him a source of joy that there was such a friendly feeling between the two Irish Divisions. I wish you could please thank for me all your friends who helped him in his last hours. Is the soldier who first carried him alive and where is he, also the stretcher-bearers? I would like especially to thank them. Perhaps sometime you would be good enough to let me have their names. At first when I heard from you I felt sorry to think my husband had been conscious and suffered, but after I felt it was all for the best. If he could have known how great the victory was I should have been glad- but God's ways are not our ways and He knows best and I think takes us when we are most ready.' This was the second major tragedy she had suffered- the Redmonds' only child, a five year old son, had died in 1891.

The wounded soldier who came to Willie Redmond's rescue was Private Meeke of the 11/ Royal Inniskilling Fusiliers and the stretcher-bearers who took him to the 36th Division's Advanced Aid Post at Dranoutre were also from the Protestant 36th (Ulster) Division. It was there that he spoke his last words to the Anglican chaplain also coincidentally called William Redmond. He asked him to pass on a message to his wife Eleanor: 'Give her my love and thank her for all the help she has given me and tell her that if we do not meet in this world, I hope we shall meet in the next.' He left in the Field Ambulance but died of his wounds and shock. It was fitting that Ulstermen should have been so caring in his final moments. His namesake, the chaplain wrote: 'Is it too much to hope that his noble sacrifice for the cause of God and our Empire and the touching incidents surrounding his death may yet bear a better understanding and a greater sympathy between North and South in Ireland? God grant it may!'

Redmond and his wife Eleanor British Library Board (*The* Daily Sketch)

Redmond's body was taken to the convent chapel at Locre. He was buried on 8 June in the convent garden in a coffin (in general most soldiers were buried in groundsheets)) found for him by Major General Hickie. His grave was not moved to the Locre Hospice Cemetery but remained in the convent garden. After the War, the Sisters of Mercy returned to a rebuilt convent and took on the care of the Major's grave. From the time that Eleanor visited her husband's grave for the first time in the autumn of 1919, the location of the grave was the subject of a tug-of-war. The nuns and the local people of Locre wanted the grave to continue *in situ* whereas the Belgian Government decreed that it was unlawful for a grave to remain on private property. The Imperial War Graves Commission, which was founded on the principle that no soldier should receive special treatment, argued that Redmond's grave should be moved into the nearby Locre Hospice Cemetery. Although agreement was reached in 1967 to move Redmond's grave, the Belgian Government relented and bowed to local pressure masterminded by Father Rafael Debevere. Major William Redmond was allowed to rest in peace on his own outside the military cemetery.

When Eleanor paid her visit, she at least did so with tributes to her husband fresh in her mind. Protestant Unionists like M.P. James Campbell admitted to being emotionally affected by Redmond's 'courageous and eloquent speeches.' The Unionist Sir Edward Carson sent his condolences to John Redmond, commenting favourably on his brother enlisting at such an advanced age. Days after Redmond's death, Prime Minister Lloyd George referred to him during a speech outlining details of the proposed Irish Convention. A Sinn Fein member of the Athlone District Council informed Eleanor that, however much his members disagreed with her husband, they admired him for his bravery. The French Government awarded Redmond posthumously the Légion d'Honneur.

Eleanor Redmond must have been touched by the comments from the men who served with her husband. His batman Private William Organ wrote: 'Mrs. Redmond, don't fret for the master will have a bed in heaven'; his company serjeant major assured her that 'the whole company felt his loss as a true father' and three other N.C.O.s commiserated with Eleanor and assured her that the Major was

Willie Redmond's grave stands on its own outside the
W.H. Cowlishaw-designed Locre Hospice Cemetery   *J Kerr*

Nuns from the Locre Hospice at Redmond's grave, 11 June 1917
IWM   Q005475

'a soldier of the highest honour- we loved and adored him.'

Eleanor was informed that her husband had been buried 'at the south end of the garden of the Hospice Locre, south west of Ypres'. His grave is now at the end of the path beyond the Locre Hospice Cemetery. Its alienation symbolises the failure of William Redmond's hope of an Ireland governed by Catholics and Protestants. The way in which die-hard Unionists, who would have taken his name in vain in peacetime, sensitively cared for him in his final moments, collected £100 for his Memorial Fund and provided a guard of honour at his funeral, was testament to his personality, generosity of spirit, indomitable attitude, charm and selflessness.

A requiem mass was held for Redmond on Saturday 22 June 1917 at St. Mary's Catholic Church, Clapham. J. Nolan, an Irish Home Rule M.P. requested that buglers of the Irish Guards attend to sound the 'Last Post' as many members of the Irish Nationalist Party would be present and a large number of Irishmen resident in London.

In the by-election caused by Redmond's death, his old constituency of East Clare elected Sinn Fein's Eamon de Valera with twice the number of votes polled by the Irish Nationalist candidate. William Redmond had foreseen his own death and perhaps that of the Irish Nationalist Parliamentary Party. Had he survived the War, the partition of Ireland into two parts in 1921, the six mainly Protestant counties of Ulster and the remaining 26 predominantly Catholic counties of the south, would have broken his heart.

WILLIAM REDMOND:

Born:	13 April 1861 at Grassendale, Liverpool, son of William and Mary Redmond, husband of Eleanor of Delgany, County Wicklow
Education:	Clongowes Wood College
Occupation:	Irish Nationalist Member of Parliament, 1883-1917
Unit/ Regiment:	'B' Company, 6/ Royal Irish
Rank:	Major
Died:	7 June 1917, Battle of Messines
Age:	56
Decoration:	Légion d'Honneur (France)
Buried:	Close to the path leading to the Locre Hospice Cemetery, one of very few British burials not in a cemetery
Inscription:	MAJOR W. H. K. REDMOND 6TH BATT. ROYAL IRISH RGT KILLED IN ACTION 7-6-17 R.I.P.

Soldiers from both religious divides paid their respects at Major
William Redmond's grave at Locre on 21 September 1917
IWM   Q003043

GEOFFREY DONALDSON

'It is too hard to bear this terrible sacrifice of all our best boys, and of all the best of the nation- such a fine boy, so keen, so good'

Geoffrey Donaldson was an academic high flyer. In June 1914 he celebrated the award of a 1st Class in Part 1 of his Natural Sciences Tripos at Gonville and Caius College, Cambridge; his summer vacation was spent with four fellow students studying the *flora* of Provence in southern France under the tutelage of the renowned Cambridge botanist Arthur Tansley. Botany was Donaldson's great love and the signs were that he would pursue a brilliant career in botanical research.

On his return to England he answered Lord Kitchener's call to arms. He had been a member of the O.T.C. in his first year at Cambridge in 1913 and rejoined a year later in late August. Training started at Royston in Cambridgeshire and in October he joined the 2/7 Royal Warwicks, a Territorial battalion based in Coventry. He was soon promoted to lieutenant but the next 17 months were spent training.

For several months he was trained to be a musketry instructor and his potential was recognised when in November 1914, he attended the Staff College at Camberley. Donaldson was keen to see action at the Front and felt that training was conducted in an atmosphere of 'discontent and impatience' which he believed would not be dispelled 'until we cross the Channel.' At least his mood was ameliorated by a trip to the Norfolk Broads in the summer of 1915.

Captain Geoffrey Donaldson sporting the officer's facial uniform of a moustache. Note the Antelope Badge of the Royal Warwicks Oundle School Memorial Book

The 2/7 Royal Warwicks sailed at last to France in May 1916 and were first engaged in the Neuve Chapelle area. They were fortunate to avoid the carnage of 1st July at the Somme. Donaldson had seen and learned enough to conclude in a letter to his mother Florence on 31 May that 'what impressed me most about the whole thing was the hopelessness of it all.' He was convinced that 'fighting will never end the war.'

The young student assured his mother that unlike others, he was coping with the constant assaults on his nerves: 'I don't think anything will affect my nerves now, so don't worry about me dear, because I shall pull through all right and I am strong enough to stand any amount of fatigue.'

The pressures on soldiers of all ranks were immense and shell shock was a major consequence of the static trench warfare. Geoffrey Donaldson was sensitive to the effects of battle fatigue on the men under his command in 'C' Company and he appreciated that one soldier's nerves gave way due to lack of sleep, exhaustion and diarrhoea. Rather than take punitive action, Donaldson sent him back behind the lines to take on lighter duties. He believed shell shock was a disease 'which they themselves are unable to prevent. It just depends on the way you are made.'

His sense of duty as a role model is evident in the letter he wrote to his mother on 23 June: 'The night before last I took out a patrol of four men about half way across No Man's Land. There is comparatively little risk attached to this work but it is of course a considerable strain on the nerves. Last night, I went out with Wakefield and a wiring party, that is to say, with about six men improving our wire entanglements. I consider on the whole this is as nerve-racking a job as any, more so than 137 patrol work. You must not think I shall go out like this every night. I have been out the last two nights as much to set an example and get the thing going.'

Geoffrey Donaldson was a popular officer- 'Dunlop' as he was affectionately known, enjoyed the humour and comic situations engendered by the typical 'Tommy' in the trenches, perceptively and wittily observed by Captain Bruce Bairnsfather in his contemporaneous cartoons or 'sketches'. Geoffrey informed his mother on 24 June that 'there is a second volume of Bairnsfather sketches out which are really excellent for they have caught the atmosphere of the trenches exactly… like the Bible and Shakespeare, they should be on every bookshelf.' Geoffrey was referring to the 2nd edition of *Fragments from France* published in 1916. Officers and men serving at the Front were great fans of Bairnsfather's work.

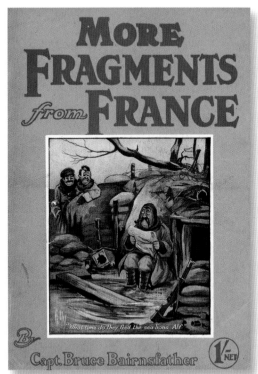

A cartoon of 'Bert', 'Alf' and 'Old Bill' by Bruce Bairnsfather on the front cover of the 1916 2nd edition of Fragments from France
Barbara Bruce Bairnsfather

A responsibility that he found most irksome was trawling through stacks of letters written by the men in his 'C' Company to censor sensitive material; he considered it 'such a waste of time censoring them as there is scarcely anything to cross out.' The letters did, however, offer him frequent amusement like the unintended irony of one missive: 'We have had some narrow escapes. One sergeant-major lost his arm and I have lost my mess-tin.'

The excesses of war failed to dampen the young botanist's enthusiasm for the natural world around him: 'The water in which you have your daily wash is drawn from a ditch and contains a pleasing medley of snails and gnats.' On 25 May the Battalion marched to billets at Busnettes and La Vallée and the soldiers marched past 'many dykes and damp spots, with marsh *flora* (Iris, Comfrey, Holtonia, Hydrocharis, Equisetum and Palustre), nightingales, black caps and frogs croaking'. Pencil and paper in hand, Geoffrey immersed himself in the sights and sounds of the nature that surrounded him like 'a brown warbler, about the size of a reed warbler… singing from a tree a very sweet song with notes rather like that of a starling.'

Geoffrey Donaldson's religious beliefs remained intact, unsullied by the horrors and excesses of war. In a quiet moment he wandered into the churchyard at Neuve Chapelle where 'there stands a huge black Calvary with the figure of Christ hanging intact upon it, a silent reminder of the ideals of Christianity and I suppose, that just as that pathetic figure has been spared by the bursting shells and still remains there in the scene of desolation, so the ideals of Christianity remain unshattered.'

Nature also could still transcend the charred and muddied landscape of the Western Front: 'The grass grows high round the dilapidated gravestones and everywhere there is a profusion of garden and wild flowers, poppies, roses, larkspur, monkshood… I enclose a piece of lysimachia from the churchyard. I only wish photographs could be taken here. The ruined château with its fine clematis-covered gateposts and Church and Calvary would make wonderful pictures. They impressed me more than most things I have seen.'

The 2/7 Royal Warwicks moved up to the Fauquissart sector on 15 July to take part in what would later be known as the Battle of Fromelles. Florence Donaldson's concern for the safety of her 22 year old son would have been heightened by receipt of one of Geoffrey's last letters written on 16 July: 'I can tell you that in the 30 minutes before the attack started, I came nearer to "having the wind up" or in other words losing my nerve than has ever been the case before. At 8.30 p.m. the show started. I had all the men in the trench out of the dugouts and we all had our helmets (gas) on. It was like an appalling nightmare as you look like some horrible kind of demon or goblin in these masks.

There were words of commands along the line from the R.E. and then a loud hissing sound as the taps were turning on and the deadly greenish white vapour poured out of the jets and slowly blew in a great rolling cloud towards the opposite line of trenches. In the next fire bay to me, an idiot of a sapper turned the jet in the wrong direction and filled our trenches with gas. I was OK.' Donaldson dryly remarked that 'a number of dead rats were lying about killed by the gas, as they have no gas helmets.' The attack on 19 July was a disaster, described by Sir Basil Liddell Hart, the military historian, who himself was gassed in 1916, as 'incredibly muddled'. The Battle of Fromelles saw an attempt by the newly-arrived Australian 5th Division and the 61st (South Midland) Division, which included the 2/7 Royal Warwicks, to break 400 yards of the German line which had been held around the village of Fromelles for most of the War by the 6th Bavarian Reserve Division. The aim was to divert German troops from the Somme area.

At dawn on 19 July there was a low lying mist which dissipated as the sun rose but was replaced by the fog of dust and mud caused by the pre-attack bombardment which lasted for eight hours. At 5.30 p.m. Captain Donaldson of 'C' Company and Captain Bethell of 'D' Company led their men into No Man's Land to attack a strong point known as 'Sugar Loaf'. They found that the bombardment had failed to destroy the barbed wire entanglements and intelligence had failed to establish that the Germans had retreated from their front line trenches. At 7.00 p.m. a runner returned with a message from Donaldson reporting that he and 20 men were holding a German second line trench but were being heavily shelled. They were the only units of the whole 61st Division to reach the enemy trenches, but there were too few of them to hold their position.

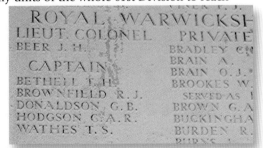

According to the Battalion War Diary 'it was entirely due to the excellent organisation and coolness of Captain T.H. Bethell and Captain G.B. Donaldson that the attack was successful and I regret to say that both these officers were reported killed. Major A. Welch reports to me that the waves went over in perfect order and that the final rush from about 40 yards of the German line was carried with great dash and exactly as it had been arranged.' Donaldson was hit by a German

Geoffrey Donaldson commemorated on the Ploegsteert Memorial   *A Hamilton*

grenade and was officially reported to have 'died in German hands'. At 8.50 p.m. the Battalion was ordered to retreat, the attack hardly a great success and in fact quite the opposite- the 2/7 Royal Warwicks lost 210 men killed and 173 were reported missing.

By the end of the two day Battle of Fromelles, about 5,500 Australian and 1,500 British troops had been killed, wounded or captured. Poor Dunlop's body never surfaced but his identity disc was returned from Germany on 4 December 1916 via a neutral embassy. His wallet followed some time later on 22 June 1917 with its meagre contents of 1.5 francs.

The Ploegsteert Memorial, one of the finest on the Western Front was designed by Harold Chalton Bradshaw and unveiled in 1931. Two lions designed by Gilbert Ledward guard the Memorial; one is placid and this one is sneering   *A Hamilton*

There is a possibility that Geoffrey Donaldson's was one of the bodies found in mass graves dug by the Germans and discovered at Pheasant Wood on the edge of Fromelles in 2009. The cemetery built there is the first to be built in France by the Commonwealth War Graves Commission for 50 years and contains 250 Australian and British soldiers reinterred from the mass graves. Only 111 have been formally identified.

Florence Donaldson had lost her husband Eben in 1904 and on 21 July suffered the ordeal of learning of her only son's death. A major who fought with Geoffrey may or may not have consoled her with the thought that 'he died for his country- what more could he do?'

Company Serjeant Major Griffith wrote that 'his methods, treatment of men, and unconcern for danger have been the admiration of all his N.C.O.s and you can think of him conducting the grim business of war, as calmly as his studies at home.' The letter sent by the Headmaster of Geoffrey's Public School, Oundle, in Northamptonshire, was an oft repeated *cri de coeur*: 'It is too hard to bear this terrible sacrifice of all our best boys, and of all the best of the nation- such a fine boy, so keen, so good.' His Science master spoke of 'his brilliant promise' which had been 'a source of pride and pleasure to me'. The Master of Gonville and Caius College, Cambridge, Sir Hugh Anderson, bemoaned the loss of 'the ablest and nicest man in the College who had a brilliant career ahead of him.' For the eminent botanist, Arthur Tansley: 'Three of the five men whom my wife and I took to France in the summer of 1914 are now dead. The War has been very hard on our young botanists but it makes one glad to think how splendidly they responded to the call.'

Geoffrey's cousin Eben Hamilton wrote from the trenches on the Somme: 'The flower of the flock- the only one of my relations, outside my immediate family for whom I ever cared.' When his son was born in 1917, he named him Geoffrey after his cousin.

Geoffrey Donaldson's response to the call was his own death sentence. He wrote that 'on March 10th, I became that very common product of the war, a very young captain.' As an officer regularly on front line duty, his chances of survival were limited. In *Six Weeks* John Lewis-Stempel maintains that an officer below the rank of major had a life expectancy of six weeks at the Front. The officer class lost a disproportionately high number of men.

Despite a loathing of the War, Geoffrey Donaldson led his men with 'dash' and courage in a woefully planned action which they had little chance of surviving. He was one of many young volunteer officers with brilliant careers ahead of them who were callously cut down before they had reached their prime.

It was ironic that a man dedicated to the study of the natural world, should have had his life so tragically curtailed in such an unnatural and brutal manner.

GEOFFREY DONALDSON:

Born:	25 November 1893, son of Dr Eben Donaldson, Medical Officer and pharmacist of Burt near Londonderry and Florence Donaldson
Education:	King Edward VI Grammar School, Stratford-on-Avon, Oundle School, Northamptonshire and Gonville and Caius College, Cambridge
Occupation:	Natural Sciences student, Cambridge University
Unit/ Regiment:	'C' Company, 2/7 Royal Warwicks
Rank:	Captain
Died:	19 July 1916, Battle of Fromelles
Age:	22
Commemorated:	Ploegsteert Memorial, Panel 2

The Ploegsteert Memorial was designed by Harold Chalton Bradshaw. Over 11,300 soldiers for whom there is no known grave are commemorated on the panels of one of the finest of the British memorials, including Serjeant Barnard Beechey, 2/ Lincolns, one of five Lincolnshire brothers who died in the War, killed on 25 September 1915, aged 38 (Panel 3). Those listed on the Memorial lost their lives in a large surrounding area which included Ploegsteert Wood, Dranoutre, Estaires, Hazebrouck, Bailleul, Armentières and Nieppe. Originally the I.W.G.C. hoped to build a memorial at Lille but the French were reluctant to agree to another being erected. On either side of the Memorial is the Berks Cemetery Extension which contains 876 burials including twin brothers, Riflemen Leonard and William Crossley, aged 31, of the 21/ King's Royal Rifle Corps, believed to have been killed by the same shell on 30 June 1916. Their graves are E.20. and 21.

RONALD POULTON PALMER

'A Brave Soldier and a Gentleman'

On 1 August 1914 Ronald Poulton Palmer returned to his small house in Reading, after spending a week with a Reading Boys' Club at New Romney in Kent. Since his undergraduate days at Oxford, wherever he had been based, he made a point of supporting the local boys' club, offering his interests and enthusiasm to those less fortunate than himself. He would spend two evenings a week in the College Boys' clubs in Reading after a long day at the factory, where he was learning about the workings of the world famous biscuit making firm, Huntley and Palmers.

His uncle, George W. Palmer, was the company's chief executive and as he did not have an heir, he was lining up his nephew Ronald to assume the reins of power. Since 1911 Ronald had started work at 6.30 a.m. gaining experience of the factory's financial and manufacturing systems. A condition of George Palmer's will, was that on his death, Ronald should take over the business but change his surname to Palmer, which he did when his uncle died on 30 September 1913. He changed his name officially to 'Ronald William Palmer'. His friend the Rev. Walter Carey joked: 'I see you've got to change your surname. Luckily "Ronnie" will remain!' Ronald and his father agreed that it would be simpler to have one surname, 'Palmer', in accord with his uncle's wishes but the press, in particular, thought otherwise and for the rest of his life, he was generally known as Ronnie Poulton Palmer.

Ronald Poulton Palmer when a student at Balliol College, Oxford Balliol College Roll of Honour

He was one of the Edwardian era's leading sporting icons and was rarely out of the public eye. In the year that war broke out, he was appointed captain of the England rugby team. His first match in charge was a thrilling 10-9 triumph over Wales on 17 January 1914 at Twickenham. *The Times* rugby correspondent considered that the victory was due to the 'soundness and resource of the greatest three-quarter back that this country has had for a quarter of a century.' He held the team together with a 'wonderful kick' or an 'electrifying cut through' and was a steadying influence amongst the backs. Poulton Palmer led by example, with flair and calmness under pressure.

Poulton Palmer, seated in the middle of the front row, captain of England for the match in March 1914 versus Scotland at Inverleith World Rugby Museum, Twickenham

In the following home match against Ireland, England won 17-12 and the pundits were agreed that Poulton Palmer was the best player on the pitch. The final international match to be played in Britain before the outbreak of war was the Calcutta Cup clash between Scotland and England at Inverleith, **141** when, once again England squeaked home 16-15. His team completed the season, with, in effect, the 'Grand Slam', trouncing France 39-13 in Paris. Poulton Palmer confirmed his place in the sport's hall of fame with four tries and an unbeaten record as captain. His tally of four tries in the match remained a record until broken by Brian Ashton against Italy on 12 February 2011.

Ronnie Poulton Palmer played as an amateur in an era when sport was played in a corinthian spirit. Rugby did not experience the kind of sharp practices which have at times been seen in the modern professional game. It was a time when batsmen 'walked' and sportsmen played the game for enjoyment above all else and he was a paragon of this spirit. During his five-year international career, according to the journalist A.C.M. Croome, he never played a bad game for England and no opponent 'caused him to lose his temper or any referee found him question the correctness even of an obviously wrong decision.'

He played rugby before analysis by television replay. There is no archive film footage of his 'dexterous swerve and deceptive speed'- only the word of the watching correspondents. His finest tries, like the brilliant solo effort for Oxford in the 1909 Varsity match at Queen's Club in West London, will never be drooled over and dissected by slow motion replay.

Poulton Palmer displaying the infamous 'electrifying cut through' against France on 13 April 1914 *World Rugby Museum, Twickenham*

From an early age when at the Dragon Preparatory School in Oxford, young Ronnie displayed the ability to leave an opposing three quarter for dead with a dummy or a body swerve and was commended for his coolness under pressure and an ability to take the right option in the heat of a match.

It was fitting that he should move on to the birthplace of the game at which he excelled. He started at Rugby School in Warwickshire in 1903 and in the school magazine's report of a match in 1903, Poulton was reported to have 'made a good dribble' and a team mate of his, successfully 'intercepted a punt'. His team mate was the son of a master at the school, who would achieve fame as a poet, Rupert Brooke (see p.265), who succumbed to septicaemia on the way to the Dardanelles in Turkey aged 27. He died on 23 April 1915 on a French hospital ship off the Greek island of Skyros and was buried in an olive grove on the island.

Poulton's play was not above reproach. For much of his career he was criticised for defensive frailty, a perception that dogged him until his international status was established. It was a factor in his being overlooked for a 'Blue' in his first year at Oxford in 1908. Disappointed by his omission, he won a hockey 'half Blue' instead!

Despite not playing for Oxford University in the 1908-09 season, he was signed up by the Harlequins Club in London on the recommendation of his friend Adrian Stoop, the influential international full back. On the basis of his inspirational performances for Harlequins, Ronnie was selected to play for England at Leicester in a 22-0 defeat of France in 1909 (see photo p.69). Initially he made little impression and failed to impose his authority in defeats at the hands of Ireland at Lansdowne Road and Scotland at Richmond in the final game before Twickenham became rugby's national venue.

It would have been a travesty if Poulton had not been selected to play for Oxford in the Varsity match in 1909, having already played for his country. It was not a cut and dried decision but it was vindicated by a stunning performance when he scored five tries in front of 13,000 spectators at Queen's Club. He made only one international appearance in 1910, paying the price for a missed tackle which resulted in a match-losing try against Wales in an 11-6 defeat. Poulton Palmer was awarded 17 caps for England between 1909 and 1914 and scored 28 points.

He played for the Liverpool Rugby Club in 1913 while on work experience at the Mather and Platt Engineering Company in Manchester. He impressed the Chief Director Sir William Mather, who wrote to his friend George W. Palmer in glowing terms: 'We have never had so charming a personality in our works.' Ronnie threw himself into researching the provision of boys' clubs in Manchester and Salford, areas with greater poverty than Reading and Oxford. He discovered a network of provision that had been instigated by the philanthropic involvement of several successful entrepreneurs. The clubs there were run on the principles of 'muscular Christianity', with an emphasis on religious instruction, sport and education.

Poulton Palmer was a genuine all-rounder. At Balliol College, Oxford, he led a full and energetic life; he was a member of the University's Officer Training Corps and participated in the College's debating society. He committed himself to working at the St. Ebbes' Boys' Club where the boys were somewhat boisterous- after one of his first sessions with them, he told his father that they 'were fairly quiet- that is to say they whistled and talked and threw chairs about'!

He was on the Junior Common Room Committee and developed his mediation skills when attempting to resolve major differences between the college's mainly Old Etonian 'bloods' and those unhappy with their excessive behaviour. Despite the plethora of interests, he found sufficient time for his academic studies, achieving a 2nd class degree in Engineering.

Ronnie's upbringing was comfortable and could best be described as upper middle-class. His father, Sir Edward Poulton was Professor of Zoology at Oxford University, specialising in animal and insect camouflage; he was a supporter of Darwin's theory of natural selection and wrote a mere 200 books and essays; titles included the snappily entitled *The Colours of Animals: Their Meaning and Use, Especially Considered in the Case of Insects* (1890), *Charles Darwin and the Theory of Natural Selection* (1896) and *Essays on Evolution* (1908). Ronnie's mother Emily was from the biscuit-making family and her brother George saw in her son the potential to succeed him in the family business.

The Poultons lived in Oxford at Wykeham House on the Banbury Road which was spacious enough to house six servants to see to the needs of the family of five children- Edward, Ronald, Hilda, Margaret and Janet who were brought up to be respectful of all people regardless of their station in life. In his *For Poulton and England*, James Corsan describes the Palmer family of Reading as 'enlightened, philanthropic investors in the Berkshire community, keen on education and charitable "good works" who took their public responsibilities most seriously.' Ronald's interest in supporting boys' clubs emanated from his philanthropic heritage.

On evenings when he visited the Reading Boys' Club, he would play a hymn, then read from the New Testament. He would finish by saying a few prayers. Walter Dimbleby of the Club summed up Ronald's contribution to it: 'Ronald's fame as a rugby international gave him a great hold over the boys in the early years of their acquaintance…this fame receded into the background and his sympathy and charming personality made him beloved by all the boys.'

Ronnie Poulton Palmer was a 2nd lieutenant in the territorial 1/4 Royal Berkshire Regiment and on 2 August 1914, he volunteered his services as a transport officer. He was posted to Corsham in Wiltshire and then Chelmsford in Essex. Interminable route marches, drill and weapon training, bored and frustrated the men who were desperate for action at the Front.

It was not until 30 March 1915 that the Regiment left for France, ironically sailing on the same ship that had ferried the England rugby team to Paris a year earlier. The Royal Berkshires marched from Boulogne to join the 1/ Royal Warwicks, 2/ Seaforth Highlanders and 1/ Royal Irish Fusiliers at Plugstreet Wood in Belgium, passing through places that those regiments knew only too well- Cassel, Flêtre, Bailleul and Le Romarin.

Poulton Palmer's No.13 Platoon of 'D' Company was in the thick of the action by 9 April, entrenched half a mile from the Germans near La Douve Farm. The grim reality of the warfare affected Ronald who described the shelling as 'very frightening' and after shell bursts, left him wondering 'if you are alive'.

Since November 1914 the officers of the regiments based in the Ploegsteert and Steenwerck areas had played hard when behind the lines. At Steenwerck during the four days away from the trenches, Poulton Palmer organised a truncated game of rugby which included a number of leading lights in pre-war club rugby. Physically challenged by their time in the trenches, a full 80 minute game was out of the question!

Poulton Palmer's platoon was based in trenches near Anton's Farm from 19 April where they worked on defences that were located just a long 'punt' away from the enemy trenches. 'The whole thing as a war is a screaming farce' he wrote. 'The joke is we are 120 yards from the German trench and about 80 yards from German working parties... and we make a hell of a row, laugh, talk, light pipes...' He noted that snipers were a constant threat, apart from one he described to his mother as 'Sir Charles', who was famed for his inaccuracy and failure to do any damage.

He was in reserve at Ploegsteert at the end of April 'in a beautiful wood, living in log shanties'. On the penultimate Sunday of his life he attended an unusual church service: 'It is Sunday today, and we had Holy Communion in the school yard- the altar a pile of ammunition boxes, covered with a mackintosh sheet. It was not quite ideal because we could not kneel down.'

Ronald Poulton Palmer's grave and wooden marker
from The Life of Ronald Poulton *by Edward Poulton*

Ronald was now in front line trenches- he had installed a 'splendid French oven stolen from Anton's Farm, in a kitchen dugout by the officers' mess'. His aunt learned that, on what would be his final day of life, the weather was perfect: 'I am sitting in our dining room, which is dug well down and faces the rear. I am getting a little tired of this view of the cabbage patch to our rear!'

In an unguarded moment on Wednesday 5 May, shortly after midnight when in charge of a fatigue party, Ronnie stood above the parapet of a dugout and was shot by a sniper. He was the first officer of the 1/4 Royal Berkshires to die. In *The Life of Ronald Poulton*, Professor Poulton wrote in 1919 that his son's 'expression in death was peaceful and happy.' It was ironic that in a letter home a few days earlier, Ronald had recounted that 'the Germans shout out "Don't shoot, we are sick of this."'

A special funeral was conducted on 6 May by a family friend of the Poultons, the Bishop of Pretoria, at Hyde Park Corner at Plugstreet Wood. The Bishop consoled Professor Poulton that 'it was tremendously touching to see the men's faces as I spoke, and I felt it such a privilege to be there.' The esteem in which Lieutenant Poulton Palmer was held by his men was so strong that many broke down in tears when informed of his death. One of them, Private Hambridge of Ronald's platoon, composed a letter of condolence which must have been of great comfort to the Poulton family: 'He was a real gentleman and to each one of us not only our leader but our friend.'

The former England rugby captain was buried in a special burial plot for the 1/4 Royal Berkshires which his father visited 20 December 1918. It must have been a miserable scene: 'Ronald's grave was uninjured, although there were four shell holes within a few feet of it; the oak cross was intact save for two scratches from shell splinters.'

The Battalion's commanding officer, Colonel Serocold, who attended the funeral, comforted the Poultons with soothing words: 'His death has been a terrible loss to us: he was the very best type of young officer, always ready to do a bit more than his share of the work and always with a smile and a joke for the men, who adored him.'

The tributes to Ronald Poulton Palmer underline that he was a remarkable and special 'people person' who commanded respect from all those with whom he came in contact. He was charming, gracious and courteous; he was admired by rugby players and soldiers under his command for his warm hearted and open approach and modestly charismatic leadership. A private in the Royal Berks was adamant that 'we would have followed him into the jaws of death for he was a brave soldier and a gentleman.'

E.B. Osborn in *The New Elizabethans* considered that 'a Poulton try was by far the most fascinating thing in Rugby football. His father the famous professor once complained that his most important lecture might get a paragraph here and there in the newspapers, whereas any try scored by Ronald would be sure of a column everywhere.'

At a memorial service held in St. Giles's Church, Oxford on 29 May 1915 the Rev. William Temple in his tribute highlighted the consequence of his foreshortened life: 'He will not do the work on earth that we had hoped' and that his rugby career was 'a mere fraction of his activity and had he lived… he would have been known for far greater things.'

What 'greater things' might he have achieved if he had been spared the sniper's bullet? He could have played several more seasons of international rugby and club rugby for even longer. He could have slotted seamlessly into an administrative role in rugby. His penchant for social work might have taken him down a political route- as an M.P. for Reading and then perhaps a ministerial post… or he was ideally suited to being an inner city clergyman. Maybe he would have taken the helm at Huntley and Palmers and continued his philanthropic works in his spare time.

Ronnie Poulton Palmer's will is a lasting testament to his desire to help those less fortunate than himself- organisations that benefited from his bequests included the Workers' Education Association, the Rugby School Mission, the Huntley and Palmers' Benevolent Fund and the St. John's Church Boys' Club in Reading.

Ronald Poulton Palmer's grave in Hyde Park Corner (Royal Berks) Cemetery   *A Hamilton*

One thing we can be certain of- Ronald William Poulton Palmer's death was typical of the Great War- it was a total waste of a man who had so much to offer... to so many.

RONALD POULTON PALMER:

Born:	12 September 1889, son of Professor Sir Edward and Lady Emily Poulton, of Wykeham House, Banbury Road, Oxford
Education:	The Dragon School, Oxford, Rugby School and Balliol College, Oxford
Occupation:	Trainee at family firm, Huntley and Palmers of Reading and England rugby captain
Unit/ Regiment:	1/4 Royal Berkshire
Rank:	Lieutenant
Died:	5 May 1915
Age:	25
Buried:	Hyde Park Corner (Royal Berks) Cemetery, B.11.
Inscription:	HIS WAS THE JOY THAT MADE PEOPLE SMILE WHEN THEY MET HIM LT. S. L. REISS

(from a letter by Lieutenant Stephen Lacy Reiss of the same regiment)

Buried just nine graves (B.2.) from Ronnie Poulton Palmer is a young man from a very different background. **PRIVATE ALBERT FRENCH** was only 16 when he took the 'King's Shilling', two years under the legal age for enlistment. He looked mature enough to be 18, and such was the desperate need for new recruits, that no searching questions were asked by the recruitment officer of the King's Royal Rifle Corps at St. Pancras in Middlesex.

145

Albert was an apprentice fitter at the Wolverton Railway Works in Buckinghamshire. He left his job on 16 October 1915 without giving notice. It was the start of what he hoped would be a great adventure: 'I shall rise like the early morning dew to be a Major-General' he confidently predicted.

The 18/ King's Royal Rifles left Aldershot for Southampton on 2 May 1916 arriving in Le Havre the next day. The Battalion trained at Steenje for a month before moving up to the trenches at Plugstreet Wood. By this stage disenchantment was setting in. Provisions were so poor that Albert and his colleagues were spending most of their money on coffee, ginger beer and chocolate. 'We still get our 3/6d a week but that does not go very far.' He was so disillusioned that he predicted 'I shan't stop in the army after the war, it's just not good enough.'

Life in the trenches was harsh for the sixteen year old: 'We have to do our grub up securely or half of it disappears to the rats and mice!' On 4 June he posed his father a question born of desperation: 'The war will have to end sometime won't it?'

Only nine days before his death, Albert's sister May wrote: 'Dad and the boys send their love, you will soon be sweet 17 and never been kissed, on the 22nd of this month. Well, cheerio and keep on smiling. I will close now with all my fondest love. Hurry up and send me a line as you know you owe me one. Your loving sister…'

Albert French, 16, two years below the official recruitment age

A typically uninformative Field Post Card arrived on 12 June at the family's small terraced house in Young Street, New Bradwell (now part of Milton Keynes) in Buckinghamshire. Three days later, Rifleman French was dead. His widowed father, Aunt Jane, brothers William and George and sister May received a letter from the Battalion's chaplain M.A.O. Mayne: 'Dear Mr. French, I am very sorry to have to inform you that your dear son was killed in action on June 15th. He died as every true soldier wishes to die- doing his job nobly for King and Country. He was doing some sandbagging on the parapet of the trench when four bullets from a machine gun hit him and he died instantaneously. He lies buried amid brave comrades in a wood, and his grave is carefully tended by his friends in his battalion. I offer you my deepest sympathy and pray that Almighty God in his mercy will give you comfort and strength to bear up under this great blow. May I remind you of that text in Chapter 15, verse 14 of St. John's Gospel *Greater love hath no man than this, that a man lay down his life for his friends.'*

Albert French's commanding officer, Captain Pennell appears to have accepted the youth of his former charge: 'He was a very good soldier, although so young, and a willing worker who made many friends in the Company.'

Albert French's grave   *A Hamilton*

ALFRED SOULS

One of five sons who never returned

'We regret to inform you…' was the start of a communication that thousands of mothers dreaded receiving in the course of the Great War. Mrs. Annie Souls' world collapsed in April 1918 when she opened and read the official letter informing her of the death of her twin son Arthur. What made her experience so shattering was that Arthur was the fifth son of hers to die fighting on the Western Front.

She and her husband William, a carter, were married on 19 October 1885 at his home village of Sherborne in Gloucestershire when they were both 27 years old. Their marriage took place there as Annie, classed as 'illegitimate' in the 1891 census, had been raised in the workhouse at Maugersbury. They brought up most of their family of six boys and three girls in the small Gloucestershire villages of Farmington and then Great Rissington where the children attended the little school across the village green, opposite their small four-room tied cottage.

The outbreak of war offered the young Souls boys an exciting alternative to their humdrum existence working, like their father, as labourers on local farms. The sense of adventure would have been immense for young men for whom a major trip might have been to the nearby town of Burford.

By Christmas five sons had enlisted- the youngest Percy, was still at school and William at the age of 50 was too old for service. The youngest volunteers Albert and Walter, enlisted with the 2/ Worcesters. The identical twins Alfred and Arthur, and Frederick, who was a year younger, had joined the 16/ Cheshires.

The 16/ Cheshire Battalion was formed on 3 December 1914 at Birkenhead in Cheshire after the town's M.P. Alfred Bigland had obtained permission from the War

Cottages in Great Rissington, Gloucestershire, where the Souls brothers were raised
A Hamilton

Office to form a 'Bantam' battalion of men who failed to reach the British Army's minimum height requirement of 5 feet 3 inches. 'Small men with big hearts'- about 3,000 volunteered for the Battalion, many of whom had been rejected by other regiments. It is not known, however, if Alfred, Arthur and Frederick had been rejected by the Worcestershire Regiment for being too short in stature.

Annie Souls's four year nightmare began with news of the death of her youngest son Albert, who had sailed with Walter to France with the 2/ Worcesters in June 1915 after six months of training. The Battalion suffered heavy casualties at the Battle of Loos in September and the brothers were among the survivors who received special praise for their efforts and were paraded before King George V. The King's visit on 28 October did not go as planned. He was usually transported to the Front by car. However, according to the Prince of Wales and future King Edward VIII, Sir Douglas Haig 'suggested that the men could see the King better if he were mounted and in the morning had produced his own horse, guaranteed to be completely quiet and crowd-trained. My father acquiesced and rode among the troops... The officer in charge called "Three cheers for His Majesty the King." The men's response to the order was so lusty that Sir Douglas Haig's charger took fright, reared up, lost its balance, and fell back on top of my father.'

In his diary, Haig recalled that: 'It was a most unfortunate incident. We were within 50 yards of the place at which he (the King) was to dismount and look round the airoplanes (sic). The mare was so quiet all through the day, too, but the waving caps and the sudden cheering would have upset any horse at such a close distance.' The King had damaged his pelvis and was confined to bed for a day

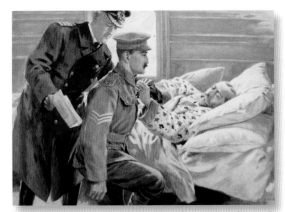

The injured King George V awarding the V.C. in a hospital train at Aire on 1 November 1915 to Lance Serjeant O. Brooks of the Coldstream Guards
R.H.Q. Coldstream Guards 2000

or two to recover. He sent a message to Haig to reassure him that he knew that the mare had never done such a thing before and that Haig was not to feel perturbed at what had happened.

In January 1916 Albert and Walter were transferred to the 5th Company/Machine-Gun Corps which on 14 March was in action at Bully-Grenay near Béthune. The Unit War Diary reported one death- that of the 20 year old Private Albert Souls, the first of the brothers to die. He was buried in the French military plot in the civilian cemetery at Bully-Grenay. Walter was in the vicinity when Albert fell and was overcome with grief. In July he and the Machine-Gun Corps were heavily involved in the first days of the Battle of the Somme. The evidence suggests that on 20 July he suffered a leg wound and was taken to one of the hospitals at Rouen but died on 2 August after an unsuccessful operation. His mother received a touching letter of condolence from the hospital matron who wrote that her son Walter 'came to us with a wound in the upper part of his left leg, and had to undergo an operation, but he rallied from that all right and he seemed to be better. In fact, he was quite cheery, but in the evening on the next day, he suddenly collapsed and died instantly from an embolism in the heart. I am enclosing a postcard which he wrote on the day he died. He will be buried in the little British cemetery just outside Rouen where lie other brave lads who have fallen in the dreadful war. This will be a dreadful blow to you and you have our deepest sympathy in your great loss.'

The hospital chaplain's note to Annie Souls may not have had such a soothing effect: 'You have both made a great sacrifice- you have given your only son, he his life. It was only the day before I had a talk with him. He seemed quite happy and little did I think that he was so near the end.' The 'little British cemetery' where Walter Souls was buried, is St. Sever at Rouen- by the end of the War it was no longer 'little' but one of the largest British cemeteries with 3,082 burials and a further 8,658 in an extension. The number was so high because of the nearby hospitals which took in soldiers, who like Walter Souls, died of their wounds.

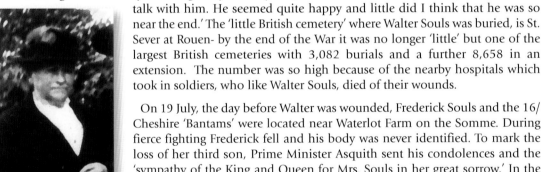

Annie Souls, mother of five sons killed in the War

On 19 July, the day before Walter was wounded, Frederick Souls and the 16/ Cheshire 'Bantams' were located near Waterlot Farm on the Somme. During fierce fighting Frederick fell and his body was never identified. To mark the loss of her third son, Prime Minister Asquith sent his condolences and the 'sympathy of the King and Queen for Mrs. Souls in her great sorrow.' In the forlorn hope that Frederick might return, his mother kept a candle constantly burning in the window of her cottage. Without an identifiable grave, his name was recorded on the Thiepval Memorial.

During the ensuing campaigns of 1916 and 1917 Annie was spared further family losses. Her 30 year old identical twins, Alfred and Arthur, were still in the thick of the action at the Front. The Cheshires suffered hugely during the Battle of the Somme. The 11th Battalion was so badly decimated that the twins were transferred from the 16th Battalion to bolster their numbers.

Appalling casualties were suffered by their new battalion but the twins survived the conflict centred on the Messines Ridge and Ypres in 1917. The Cheshires were forced to retreat in the face of the Germans' Spring Offensive in April 1918. Private Alfred Souls may have been killed on 20 April during desperate defensive action at Plugstreet Wood and was buried in the Strand Military Cemetery on the edge of the wood.

The twins had been inseparable and Arthur was greatly affected. According to those who knew the family, he lost the 'will to live'. By early April 1918 he was transferred to the 7/ Royal West Kents whose orders were to hold the Villers-Bretonneux plateau near Amiens 'at all costs'. They succeeded but lost six officers. The last surviving Souls brother, Lance-Corporal Arthur Souls, was among the 228 other ranks killed, wounded or missing and one of 550 men buried at the Hangard Communal Cemetery Extension. He died on 25 April and because of his action he was awarded the Military Medal for courageous conduct.

Once hostilities ceased on 11 November 1918, Annie Souls could be forgiven for having felt bitter about the destruction of her family; she and William moved from Great Rissington a few miles to Great Barrington near Burford. As if her suffering was not enough, it has been alleged by family members that she suspected there was a local whispering campaign about the fact that she received a shilling a week pension for each of her five dead sons. Embittered by her losses, who can blame her for her firm but quiet refusal to stand for 'God Save the King' whenever it was sung. Nor did she harbour a desire to keep any record of her sons' military careers; family recollections suggest that various documents and the postcard written home by Walter, were consigned to a bonfire.

Annie Souls must have questioned the value of her family's sacrifice every day for the rest of her life. Fate would decree that her pain and anguish were not yet over. Too young to have fought at the Front, her sixth son Percy was struck down by meningitis and died in 1923. Little is known of Annie Souls's final days- she died on 8 January 1935 and was buried next to her husband William in an unmarked grave in the churchyard of St. Mary's, Great Barrington.

Tablet in the church of St. John the Baptist in Great Rissington, commemorating the five Souls brothers and eight others　　　　　*A Hamilton*

To appreciate the Souls family's tragedy further, the Cotswold village of Great Rissington is well worth a visit. Many of the sites so familiar to the Souls still exist: the Lamb Inn, the school, the former bakery and the family cottage surround the neatly tended village green. One can imagine the small boys rushing across the green to spend their day at school and later in their short lives, leaving their cottage at first light on cold winter mornings to work with their father in the rolling countryside nearby and later in the evening perhaps downing a well-deserved pint or two in the 'Lamb'...

Then walk down the hill to the church of St. John the Baptist, sturdily constructed in Cotswold stone with a large square tower, adjacent to an imposing Jacobean manor house and the Rectory which no longer houses the vicar.

Unusually for a British village, unless they were a 'Thankful Village', like Halford in Warwickshire that escaped any fatalities, there is no outside war memorial. The church is in effect the memorial; in an understated but effective way, it remembers the fallen of Great Rissington. Inside a white marble tablet is dedicated to the five Souls brothers and eight others who died. Photographs of the brothers, smartly dressed in their military uniforms, stare out hauntingly at the onlooker. The story of the Souls family is indeed one of the saddest and most poignant of the Great War.

CENSUS OF ENGLAND AND WALES, 1911.

Before writing on this Schedule please read the Examples and the Instructions given on the other side of the paper, as well as the headings of the Columns. The entries should be written in Ink.

The contents of the Schedule will be treated as confidential. Strict care will be taken that no information is disclosed with regard to individual persons. The returns are not to be used for proof of age, as in connection with Old Age Pensions, or for any other than the preparation of Statistical Tables.

	NAME AND SURNAME	RELATIONSHIP to Head of Family	AGE		PARTICULARS as to MARRIAGE				PROFESSION or OCCUPATION				BIRTHPLACE	NATIONALITY
			Ages of Males	Ages of Females			Total Children Born Alive.	Children still Living.	Personal Occupation	Industry				
1	William Souls	Head	46		Married	25	9	9	Farm Labourer	Labourer		Worker		
2	Julia Annie Souls	Wife		47	Married	25	9	9						
3	Fredrick George Souls	Son	24	24	Single				Farm Labourer			Works		
4	Alfred Ernest Souls	Son	23		Single				Farm Labourer					
5	Arthur William Souls	Son	23	23	Single				Farm Labourer					
6	Kit Lizzie Souls	Daughter		20	Single				Domestic Servant					
7	Walter Paris Souls	Son	19		Single				Farm Labourer					
8	Albert Souls	Son	15		Single				Farm Labourer					
9	Hilda Mary Souls	Daughter		13										
10	Percy Souls	Son	9						School					
11	Iris Emily Souls	Daughter		4					School					
12														
13														

Total: Males 4, Females 4, Persons 11

SMITH R. 10019
SMITH R. 16085
SMITH 2163
SMITH W.
SOPER H
SOULS F G
SOUTHERN
SPARROW
SPEAK T
SPEDDING

In order of death, the Souls brothers were:

ALBERT SOULS:

Born:	6 September 1895, son of William and Annie Souls
Education:	Great Rissington School
Occupation:	Farm labourer
Unit/ Regiment:	2/ Worcestershire, transferred to 5th Company, Machine-Gun Corps (Infantry)
Rank:	Private
Died:	14 March 1916
Age:	20
Buried:	Bully-Grenay Communal Cemetery, French Extension, A.41. The cemetery is 20 kms north of Arras. In the French Extension there are 91 British graves. This is not to be confused with the British Extension designed by Sir Edwin Lutyens where there are over 803 graves

FREDERICK GEORGE SOULS:

Born:	1886, son of William and Annie Souls
Education:	Great Rissington School
Occupation:	Farm labourer
Unit/ Regiment:	16/ Cheshire
Rank:	Private
Died:	19 July 1916, Battle of the Somme
Age:	30
Commemorated:	Thiepval Memorial, Pier 3 Face C

WALTER DAVIS SOULS:

Born:	29 March 1892, son of William and Annie Souls
Education:	Great Rissington School
Occupation:	Farm labourer
Unit/ Regiment:	2/ Worcestershire, transferred to 5th Company, Machine-Gun Corps (Infantry)
Rank:	Private
Died:	2 August 1916, Battle of the Somme
Age:	24
Buried:	St. Sever Cemetery, Rouen, B.29.33. There are over 3,000 burials in this cemetery, a large number because it was situated near 15 hospitals. It was designed by Sir Reginald Blomfield. Also buried in this cemetery is one of four brothers, Captain Robert Loder-Symonds 1/ Cheshire who died 3 March 1915 aged 31 (Officers A.1.13.) In the cemetery extension lies one of another set of five brothers who fell, Rifleman Leonard Beechey 18/ London Regiment (London Irish Rifles) who died of wounds 29 December 1917 aged 36 (P.V.H.12B.)

ALFRED ERNEST SOULS:

Born:	4 September 1887, son of William and Annie Souls
Education:	Great Rissington School
Occupation:	Farm labourer
Unit/ Regiment:	16 and 11/Cheshire
Rank:	Private
Died:	20 April 1918
Age:	31
Buried:	Strand Military Cemetery, IX.B.9. This cemetery was designed by Charles Holden and is 13 kms south of Ypres. It began with only two burials in 1914 at the end of the 'Strand' trench on the edge of Ploegsteert Wood and was not used again until 1917 and 1918 when graves were brought in from smaller sites. There are 1,143 burials, 354 of which are unidentified

ARTHUR WILLIAM SOULS:

Born:	4 September 1887, son of William and Annie Souls
Education:	Great Rissington School
Occupation:	Farm labourer
Unit/ Regiment:	16 and 11/ Cheshire, then attached to 7/ Royal West Kents
Rank:	Lance Corporal
Decoration:	Military Medal
Died:	25 April 1918
Age:	30
Buried:	Hangard Communal Cemetery Extension, 1.G.7. (see photo p.300)
	The cemetery, 13 kms south east of Amiens, contains 141 burials, 39 of which are unidentified. It was designed by Sir Edwin Lutyens

The village school at Great Rissington, Gloucestershire   A Hamilton

The **Beechey** family from Lincolnshire also lost five of their eight sons. Their mother Amy, the widow of the Rev. Prince William Thomas Beechey, when presented to Queen Mary informed her that the loss of her five sons 'was no sacrifice, Ma'am, I did not give them willingly,' a similarly poignant reaction to Annie Souls's refusal to stand for the National Anthem. One of the three brothers who survived, Christopher, was severely disabled for the rest of his life after falling down a ravine during action in Gallipoli.

To emphasise how the Great War cut across class boundaries, the **Loder-Symonds** family lived about 20 miles from the Souls in Hinton Manor near Faringdon. Captain F.C. Loder-Symonds lost four sons- Major John aged 40, Captain Robert 31, Lieutenant Thomas 22 and Captain William 32.

Five French brothers of the **Jardot** family from the village of Evette-Salbert three kms north west of Belfort in north east France were all killed within nine months of each other. A sixth brother Aimé survived.

Four **Etcheverry** brothers also lost their lives. They came from the hamlet of Harambels eight kms south of Saint Palais in the Basque country of southern France:

TO THE MEMORY OF AMY BEECHEY,
A BRAVE MOTHER WHO LOST FIVE SONS DURING
THE GREAT WAR
SGT. BARNARD REEVE BEECHEY 25 SEPT. 1915
2nd/LT. FRANK COLLETT REEVE BEECHEY 14 NOV. 1916
L/CPL. HAROLD REEVE BEECHEY 10 APRIL 1917
PTE. CHARLES REEVE BEECHEY 20 OCT. 1917
RF/M. LEONARD REEVE BEECHEY 29 DEC. 1917
AT THE GOING DOWN OF THE SUN AND IN THE MORNING,
WE WILL REMEMBER THEM

*Plaque to five Beechey brothers and their mother
in Newport Cemetery, Lincoln*

Passant, souviens-toi !

Dans cette maison sont nés 5 garçons
qui ont donné leur vie pour notre liberté :

Les cinq frères JARDOT

Léon-Emile   1885 - 27 septembre 1914
Eugène-Armand   1887 - 2 octobre 1914
Joseph-Alfred   1892 - 3 janvier 1915
Aristide-Justin   1886 - 8 février 1915
Jules-Paul   1883 - 16 juin 1915

Pense un court instant à ces 5 jeunes hommes, fauchés en pleine jeunesse,
morts pour la France en l'espace de neuf mois.
Nous leur devons une éternelle reconnaissance.

Il était autrefois
Evette et Salbert

*Plaque to five Jardot brothers at
Evette-Salbert*

A LA MÉMOIRE
DE RAYMOND ETCHEVERRY
SOLDAT AU 234ᴱ D'INFᴺᴵᴱ
TUÉ LE Iᴿ AOÛT 1918
AU COMBAT DE CRAMAILLE (AISNE)
ÂGE DE 20 ANS

*Plaque to one of four Etcheverry brothers
in the church at Harambels*
D Bryant

Thiepval Memorial where Frederick Souls's name can be found   J Kerr

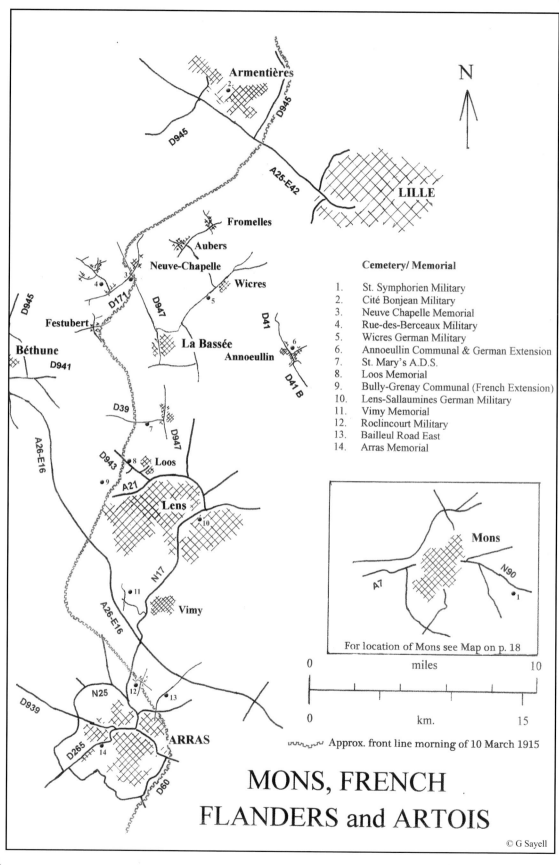

N

Cemetery/ Memorial

1. St. Symphorien Military
2. Cité Bonjean Military
3. Neuve Chapelle Memorial
4. Rue-des-Berceaux Military
5. Wicres German Military
6. Annoeullin Communal & German Extension
7. St. Mary's A.D.S.
8. Loos Memorial
9. Bully-Grenay Communal (French Extension)
10. Lens-Sallaumines German Military
11. Vimy Memorial
12. Roclincourt Military
13. Bailleul Road East
14. Arras Memorial

For location of Mons see Map on p. 18

0   miles   10

0   km.   15

〜〜〜 Approx. front line morning of 10 March 1915

MONS, FRENCH
FLANDERS and ARTOIS

© G Sayell

MONS, FRENCH FLANDERS AND ARTOIS
Day 3 Itinerary

Neuve Chapelle Indian Memorial J Kerr

MONS, FRENCH FLANDERS AND ARTOIS
Day 3 Itinerary

Although off the beaten track, St. Symphorien Cemetery near Mons is definitely worth a visit. The graves of the first and last British soldiers to die in the War can be found there.

At Cité Bonjean Cemetery in Armentières is the grave of an officer of the Royal Warwicks who was one of the first to suffer from shell shock. The centre of Armentières is an interesting place to stop for lunch.

Do not miss the Neuve Chapelle Memorial to over 4,700 Indian soldiers who died for the 'mother country', a beautiful design incorporating oriental features by Sir Herbert Baker.

One of the early 'greats' of lawn tennis, four times Wimbledon winner, is to be found in the Rue-des-Berceaux Cemetery. On your way to Annoeullin, we recommend you stop off at the atmospheric Wicres German Cemetery which is of typically Teutonic design but provides a marked contrast to archetypal British cemeteries. One of the great characters of the War, a 20 year old air ace, is the only British burial in the German Cemetery at Annoeullin- an unusual and interesting British grave.

There has been significant controversy surrounding the truth about Rudyard Kipling's son. It was assumed that his body was never found, hence his name appearing on the Loos Memorial. However, the C.W.G.C. decided that a grave in St. Mary's A.D.S. Cemetery was his. As a result, you have the opportunity to pay tribute to the 18 year old officer twice.

The youngest boy to die in the Great War is thought to be a 14 year old German- he was laid to rest in the German Cemetery at Lens-Sallaumines, also worth making a special effort to visit. Look for the sign 'Carré Militaire' in the civilian cemetery.

On your way to Arras, make a point of stopping off at the impressive Canadian Memorial at Vimy Ridge and then visit the grave of, in the authors' view, one of the best of the Great War poets in Bailleul Road East Cemetery. Final stop of the day is the Arras Memorial designed by Sir Edwin Lutyens. The name of one of the subjects of the book is to be found on the walls there- one of Britain's first black officers and footballers.

Arras is a fine French cathedral city with an excellent assortment of bars and restaurants to relax in after a busy day!

	Cemetery/ Memorial	Address/Post code/ Google map ref.	Name	Page
1	ST. SYMPHORIEN MILITARY	Avenue de la Shangri, 7032 Mons, Belgium 50.43271,4.01102	Maurice Dease V.C.	160
			George Ellison	159
			John Parr	158
			George Price	160
2	CITE BONJEAN	48-54 Avenue Roger Salengro, 59280 Armentières, France 50.68574,2.863	Charles Bentley	163
3	NEUVE CHAPELLE MEMORIAL	407-437 Rue du Grand Chemin, 62136 Richebourg, France 50.57514,2.77526	Manta Singh	169

4	RUE-des-BERCEAUX MILITARY	4-6 Rue du Haut Chemin, 62136 Richebourg, France 50.57227,2.74444	Anthony Wilding	173
5	WICRES GERMAN MILITARY	N41, 59134 Wicres, France 50.564875,2.849903	✝ Unusual German cemetery	314
6	ANNOEULLIN COMMUNAL & GERMAN EXTENSION	739-925 Rue du Vent de Bise, 59112 Annoeullin, France 50.5245,2.94237	Albert Ball V.C.	182
7	St. MARY'S A.D.S.	D39, 62138 Haisnes, France 50.48573,2.78906	John Kipling	189
8	LOOS MEMORIAL	Chemin du Mont de Vermelles, 62750 Loos-en-Gohelle, France 50.461,2.77173	John Kipling / Arthur Sayell	189 / 41
9	BULLY-GRENAY COMMUNAL (French Extension)	Rue Fernand Marché, 62160 Bully-les-Mines, France 50.44698,2.71722	Albert Souls	147
10	LENS-SALLAUMINES GERMAN MILITARY	24 Rue Constant Darras, 62430 Sallaumines, France 50.42516,2.84287	Paul Mauk	243
11	VIMY MEMORIAL	Chemin des Canadiens, 62580 Givenchy-en-Gohelle, France 50.3795,2.77385	✝ Canadian Monument	314
12	ROCLINCOURT MILITARY	2-12 Voie du Rionval, 62223 Roclincourt, France 50.32469,2.78525	George Sayell	42
13	BAILLEUL ROAD EAST	Chemin de Bailleul, 62223 Saint-Laurent-Blangy, France 50.31993,2.81669	Isaac Rosenberg	193
14	ARRAS MEMORIAL	2 Boulevard du Général de Gaulle, 62000, Arras, France 50.28697,2.76065	Walter Tull	200

JOHN PARR

'The First'

John Parr left his job as a caddy at the North Middlesex Golf Club before the War broke out to join the Army as he considered it offered him a more exciting future. It would appear that he overstated his age to meet the legal age requirement and was assigned to the 4th Battalion of the Middlesex Regiment.

John Parr's grave in St. Symphorien Cemetery- the first British soldier to be killed in the Great War   *A Hamilton*

Based at Devonport when war was declared, on 13 August the 4/Middlesex travelled by train to Southampton and sailed to France on the *SS Mombasa*. Parr disembarked at Boulogne and after a spell at a rest camp, on 20 August the Battalion marched to Monceau, arriving at Bettignies on the following day.

Private Parr was ordered to go by bicycle to scout for information about enemy activity but was shot by a German sniper. In the ensuing chaos of the Battle of Mons and the British retreat after a failed rearguard action when nine officers and 453 other ranks were killed in the first major action of the War, Parr's body was not recovered.

Unbeknown to the British authorities John Parr was buried by the Germans in St. Symphorien Cemetery which remained in their hands until 1918. His parents Edward and Alice did not receive any news of their missing son for several months because at this early stage of the War, it was believed there was a chance he had been captured. They learned of his death from one of their son's fellow soldiers.

Young John Parr holds the dubious honour of being the first British soldier to be killed by enemy fire during the Great War. In the euphoria of the opening shots of a war which it was thought would be 'over by Christmas', only the most pessimistic would have predicted that nearly 1,000,000 British and Imperial soldiers would die for their King and Country. In a bizarre coincidence two of the last men to die in 1918 were buried only yards from John Parr's grave.

The first British serviceman to die in the Great War is thought to have been 51 year old Major Arthur Hughes-Onslow, a Boer War veteran of the 10th (Prince of Wales's Own Royal) Hussars who died on 17 August aboard a ship transporting the B.E.F. to Le Havre. He was so depressed by what he feared might happen to the horses in his charge that he took his own life. His family only found out the truth later, having been led to believe he had died of sickness during the crossing. He was buried in Ste. Marie Cemetery at Le Havre. (64.VI.B.1.)

For the British the Great War started in earnest with their first casualty, John Parr at Mons on 21 August 1914 and ended there 1,544 days later and after 1,000,000 deaths.

JOHN PARR:

Born:	1898 London, youngest son of Edward and Alice Parr of 52 Lodge Lane, Finchley, London
Occupation:	Golf caddy and professional soldier
Unit/ Regiment:	4/ Middlesex
Rank:	Private
Died:	21 August 1914, two days before the Battle of Mons
Age:	Gravestone records his age as 20 but it was more likely to have been 16
Buried:	St. Symphorien Military Cemetery, Mons I.A.10. The cemetery was started by the Germans in late August 1914 after the Battle of Mons. It remained under German control until after the Armistice was signed in November 1918. There are 164 identified casualties out of 230 British Empire graves, together with 284 Germans. It was designed by W.H. Cowlishaw

GEORGE ELLISON

'The Last'

The Armistice was signed in a railway carriage in the forest of Compiègne at 5.10 a.m. on 11 November 1918. At a time when communications were not as advanced as they are 100 years later, it would take time for all front line units to receive the news so it was decided that the formal cessation of hostilities would take place at 11.00 a.m. For many, though it would be business as usual.

Private George Ellison was the last British soldier killed in action on the Western Front. He was buried just seven yards from Private John Parr, the first British casualty. It might appear that this was cleverly planned but it was in reality, an accident of fate. The Commonwealth War Graves Commission's records suggest that Ellison was buried in the first available plot in the St. Symphorien Cemetery before it could have been established that he was indeed the last British serviceman to fall before the Armistice came into effect.

When George left his elementary school in Leeds he became a miner but chose to escape the nearby pits to join the 5/ Royal Irish Lancers, a cavalry unit, with whom he fought in South Africa against the Boers.

Remarkably Private Ellison was in action on the Western Front from August 1914 when he took part in the retreat from Mons through to 11 November 1918. Once the use of cavalry had been nullified by improved weaponry, he fought as an infantryman. He took part in the campaign in 1914 to push the Germans back over the River Marne and was involved in the Second Battle of Ypres in April 1915 where he may have experienced the use of gas by the Germans; he survived the Somme offensive and the *dénouement* of the War in 1918. On 11 November 1918 George Ellison must have been counting down the days, if not hours, to a reunion in Leeds with his wife Hannah and their four year old son James.

George Ellison, the last British soldier killed in the Great War, was buried in St. Symphorien Cemetery opposite John Parr   A Reed

At 9.30 a.m. rumours must have been rife on both sides of the divide of an impending armistice. Nonetheless George Ellison was part of a patrol that was sent out to gather information on the outskirts of Mons. Just 90 minutes before the cessation of hostilities, he was hit by a German sniper. Once the Germans had relinquished control of St. Symphorien he was buried opposite John Parr.

After surviving more than four years of some of the most intense warfare on the Western Front, it was a tragic and cruel irony that Private George Ellison should have lost his life when hostilities were brought to an end.

GEORGE ELLISON:

Born:	1878 Leeds, son of James and Mary Ellison; husband of Hannah Maria Ellison, of 49, Edmund Street, Bank, Leeds and father of James
Occupation:	Miner then regular soldier
Unit/ Regiment:	5/ Royal Irish Lancers (The Redbreasts)
Rank:	Private
Died:	9.30 a.m. on 11 November 1918 near Mons
Age:	40
Buried:	St. Symphorien Military Cemetery, Mons, I.B.23.

Also buried in the St. Symphorien Military Cemetery is the last of the British Empire's soldiers to have been killed in military action on the Western Front. **PRIVATE GEORGE LAWRENCE PRICE** was born and bred in Port Williams, Nova Scotia, Canada. He was conscripted in 1917 and served with the 28th Battalion (The Saskatchewans) of the 6th Canadian Infantry Brigade. The 25 year old was engaged in street fighting to the north of Mons on 11 November 1918 and was shot in the head by a German sniper at 10.58 a.m. His grave reference is V.C.4.

Another notable burial in the cemetery is that of the first British officer to receive a posthumous V.C. The 24 year old **LIEUTENANT MAURICE DEASE V.C.** of the 4/Royal Fusiliers was killed in action on 23 August 1914 during the Battle of Mons. *The London Gazette* of 16 November 1914 described his courageous exploits: 'Though two or three times badly wounded, he continued to control the fire of his machine-guns at Mons on 23 August, until all his men were shot. He died of his wounds.' The inscription on his grave (V.B.2.) is REQUIESCAT IN PACE (May he rest in peace).

The graves of John Parr, George Ellison, George Price and Maurice Dease make St. Symphorien Military Cemetery well worth a visit. It is an unusual cemetery in that more Germans (284) were buried there than soldiers from Britain and her Empire (230).

The site was gifted to the Germans in 1914 by a local resident, Jean Houzeau de Lehaie. It was designed to give a sense of being in a secluded wooded garden. It is overlooked by a seven metre high granite obelisk erected by the Germans to the memory of both the German and British who fell in the Mons area.

The Canadian, Private George Lawrence Price, died three minutes before the Armistice came into effect
A Hamilton

The communal cemetery at Nouvelles, 5 kms south of Mons is of further interest. There are eight identified graves, four of soldiers who were casualties on 23 and 24 August 1914 at Mons and four who also died there on 11 November 1918. Another coincidence is that the four 1918 deaths were of an Englishman, an Irishman, a Scot and a Welshman.

The United States of America declared war on Germany in April 1917 following German submarine activity against American shipping. Feelings had been running high since the sinking of the *Lusitania* and the loss of 128 American lives in May 1915. Inevitably the hawks in Congress pressed for revenge.

The U.S.A. was the last major power to enter the European conflict and a 23 year old American from Baltimore is thought to be the final soldier to die before the Armistice. **PRIVATE HENRY GUNTHER** was born on 6 June 1895 and brought up in a German enclave in East Baltimore; his family experienced anti-German racism once war had been declared so, not surprisingly, he was

Maurice Dease V.C. with German graves in the background
A Hamilton

an unenthusiastic draftee. His career in a bank in Baltimore was progressing well and he and his fiancée Olga Gruebel were planning to marry.

Gunther was serving with the 313th Battalion of the 157th Brigade and arrived in France on 18 July 1918. His lukewarm attitude to the war effort was underlined in a letter he wrote to a friend back home whom he advised strongly to do everything possible to avoid being drafted into the Army. Unfortunately for Gunther, his advice was uncovered by a censor and he was stripped of his rank of supply sergeant.

On 11 November at 10.44 a.m. news reached Brigadier General William Nicholson commander of the U.S. 157th Infantry Brigade that the Armistice would soon be implemented. Rather than taking a common sense decision, he ordered that 'there will be absolutely no let up until 11.00 a.m.'.

At 10.59 a.m. German machine-gunners, fully aware that the War was over, could not believe their eyes when they saw American soldiers advancing towards them. They fired in the air as a warning but Gunther, perhaps trying to prove himself after his demotion, pressed on regardless. He was urged to halt by his comrade Sergeant Powell but to no avail. The Germans had no choice but to defend themselves. Private Gunther was shot in the head and died instantly at the very moment when hostilities were due to cease. The Divisional record is a chilling epitaph for the final American death of the War: 'Almost as he fell, the gunfire died away and an appalling silence prevailed.' His remains were returned to the U.S. and were buried in a cemetery in Baltimore. His rank of sergeant was restored posthumously.

French Army records show that the final French casualties were on 10 November. The facts point, therefore, to a systemic cover up by the authorities.

German graves in St. Symphorien Cemetery   *A Hamilton*

The 163rd French Infantry Division on 11 November 1918 attacked the élite Hannetons German unit. There has been speculation that Maréchal Foch intended to end any German vacillation and pressurise them to sign the Armistice by ordering an advance on the Germans in the Meuse area.

During the early hours of 11 November the Division was ordered to find a way across the Meuse despite the Germans having blown up the bridges. A number died when falling off sluice-gates into the frozen waters of the Meuse and others were killed by machine-gun fire. Action continued at 8.00 a.m. but by 10.00 a.m. news of the peace negotiations was received and an order was sent out for a bugle to announce the end of the War. A bugle was blown at 11.00 a.m. by the French and the Germans to herald the end of 'the war to end wars' but only minutes before at 10.50 a.m., a messenger, **AUGUSTIN TREBUCHON**, was shot near the railway line three kilometres from the Meuse. In his hand he was clutching a message which read 'Muster at 11.30 for food'. He was the last named French death of the Great War, a 40 year old community shepherd from the Lozère region who fought against the invading Germans way back in August 1914. During that time he went on leave only once, in 1917. He was due to marry Hortense Brun after she had given birth to a daughter Marie. He was reluctant to go back to the Front but according to his niece Augusta Trébuchon, his mother insisted he return.

161

Trébuchon's date of death on his death certificate is recorded as 10 November, bearing the hallmarks, therefore, of a clumsy misrepresentation of the truth by an establishment ashamed of having allowed 75 French soldiers to die unnecessarily. Another explanation for the incorrect date is that the military authorities and doctors were keen to ensure that widows of those who died on Armistice Day would definitely receive a war pension. On the cross that marked his grave in the Vrigne-Meuse Cemetery in the Ardennes, the inscribed date is 10 November 1918. It marked a death in the name of an action with no strategic importance.

LEUTNANT TOMA is thought to be the final German death of the War. He is mentioned in Joseph E. Persico's 2004 book, *Eleventh Month, Eleventh Day, Eleventh Hour: Armistice Day, 1918, World War I and Its Violent Climax* as having been shot after 11 a.m. by an American whose unit was unaware of the order to cease hostilities as communication lines may have been destroyed.

The casualty list for the last morning of the War makes for depressing reading. There were an estimated 2,700 deaths and 7,300 wounded or missing. The C.W.G.C. records show that 863 British and Imperial soldiers died on 11 November but some died of wounds received earlier. More than 3,000 casualties were incurred by the United States of America whose generals were determined to fight to the bitter end.

St. Symphorien Cemetery, one of the British plots   A Hamilton

CHARLES BENTLEY

'Poor Bentley'

Captain Charles Bentley's grave is one of 2,619 in the Cité Bonjean Cemetery on the outskirts of Armentières. His last days, like those of most of the other soldiers buried there, would have remained an untold story but for the discovery of a diary written by Captain Robert Hamilton, a fellow officer in the 1/ Royal Warwicks. In conjunction with the Battalion War Diary and the memories of the future Field Marshal, Bernard Montgomery, who also served in the Battalion, it has been possible to uncover the truth surrounding the final days of an officer who was fighting not just the Germans but his own inner demons.

Charles Bentley was born in 1878, in Kirkliston, Linlithgowshire, the eldest son of Dr. George Herbert Bentley, a physician and surgeon who practised in Edinburgh. Charles was a boarder at the Callander School in Perthshire which was founded thanks to the munificence of Donald McLaren, a wealthy merchant banker. The school was open to children, whatever their parents' means, in the West Perthshire area. Following in his father's footsteps, Charles enrolled to study medicine at Edinburgh University in 1896 but it would appear that, as he failed to graduate, he had decided that the Army offered a more exciting career prospect.

In 1898 he joined one of the most prestigious of Scottish regiments- the Royal Scots Greys and served with distinction during the Boer War when he received the Queen's medal with six clasps and the King's medal with two clasps for operations in the Orange Free State and Transvaal. Just before the War ended he joined the Royal Warwickshire Regiment and was gazetted 2nd lieutenant on 22 April 1902 and lieutenant in 1905. In 1910 he was selected as a Staff Officer of the Local Forces and Adjutant of Constabulary in Trinidad, a post which his grandfather had also held, having acted 'bravely in the suppression of a meeting of the local troops' in 1837.

Charles Bentley

Bentley was recalled to England in 1914 to prepare for action across the Channel and when he sailed to France on 22 August he may have optimistically hoped that he would be home to celebrate Christmas with his wife Geraldine and their children Charles aged six, Sybil five and two year old Hester.

The intensity of the warfare, far more dangerous and demanding than any previously experienced, provided many challenges for the British Expeditionary Force. For the Scottish commanding officer of 'A' Company of the 1/ Royal Warwicks, who had fought so successfully in South Africa, the warfare in northern France proved so challenging that on 12 September he was placed under arrest for drunkenness. Thereafter his life was a tragic descent into bouts of inebriation that affected his ability to lead the men of his company.

When the 1/ Royal Warwicks arrived at Le Havre on the way to engaging with the Germans, Captain Hamilton commented several times on the heat- on 24 August 'it was stinking hot' and on 29 August it was 'very hot during a route march'. Officers and men were short of sleep after standing-to all night and three days later were on 'marching order' for 20 hours. On 3 September it was 'awfully hot' during a night time march and two days later, Hamilton recorded another long march 'in the heat and dust'.

A recurring theme in his diary entries is his concern for the men in 'A' Company, admitting that by now 'the men were on their last legs.' Hamilton enjoyed his first good sleep for days on 7 September. It would appear that his immediate superior, Captain Charles Bentley, was also 'on his last legs', affected by the physical demands of long route marches in the heat. The Battalion manoeuvred into battle formation on 8 September to take the village of Jouarre, advancing 'over red hot fields and in the heat of the day.' It was, Hamilton claimed, 'an extraordinary show' but for the first time, he comments on Bentley's performance: 'Should not have thought Bentley would have been so jumpy.' A combination of factors suggests he was suffering from mental and physical exhaustion.

Bentley's general condition would not have been improved by 'six of the stiffest miles' Hamilton had ever experienced in his career and 'awful sights' witnessed in the wake of the German Army's retreat over the River Marne. 'This is the hell' he commented, noting 'numerous dead Germans and spies shot at any old wall.' Another nine mile march further exhausted all concerned but by the evening Bentley had calmed down enough to grab some sleep under straw in a barn with fellow officers Hamilton, Wood and Wasey.

Hungry and exhausted 'A' Company was subjected to fire from long distance guns. They reached a farm at Villers-le-Petit which had been set ablaze by the Germans. The farmer and his wife had been burnt alive. The soldiers were met by their traumatized children. Did the full horror of the episode trigger a reaction from Charles Bentley, parted from his own three children and only too aware of the possibility of them losing their own father? Did this incident bring back haunting memories of farms set ablaze by the British Army during the Boer War?

Unfortunately for those around him Captain Bentley stumbled across the perfect antidote to his problem: 'The owner had left a lot of wine in the cellars. Bentley got hold of some and filled both his flasks and water bottle.' He had 'an awful nightmare during the night'.

At dawn when the Battalion moved off, Bentley was 'drunk as an owl'. The company serjeant major was placed in charge of him at the rear of the column. Drunkenness was a permanent problem for the authorities particularly amongst the 'other ranks'. Later on 12 October for example, Hamilton's batman Private Wilkes got 'helplessly drunk' for which he was unceremoniously sacked as a batman but not court martialled. For an officer, however, to be incapacitated when in charge of a unit, was a major problem for his fellow officers. Montgomery, the master of brevity, summed up the day in his diary with one word: 'Bentley'. How sad and humiliating it must have been for the company commander to be consigned to the rear of the marching order. Hamilton wrote that he was now placed in charge of the company which 'was very much out of hand.'

The 1/ Royal Warwicks pursued the retreating Germans over the river Aisne on 13 September and halted at the pretty village of Bucy-le-Long. The Germans were positioned above the heights overlooking the village. Robert Hamilton was promoted to captain on 16 September which may have been an emergency measure given the state of Charles Bentley's health.

The following day Bentley attended a court martial at which he was treated leniently and allowed to return to action, to the chagrin of the newly promoted Captain Hamilton who expressed the wish that 'I might command this Company or had a captain I could trust to keep sober.' The senior commanders were clearly making allowances for Bentley who was, despite his recent difficulties, a highly regarded officer.

The problems faced by Bentley's fellow Royal Warwicks officers were not dissimilar to those portrayed by R.C. Sherriff in *Journey's End* in which Captain Stanhope's drinking causes difficulties amongst the officers of the company- Captain Hardy sympathises with the avuncular Lieutenant Osborne: 'Poor old man. It must be pretty rotten for you, being his second in command, and you such a quiet, sober old thing.' After three years at the Front, Stanhope was a hardened drinker. One former captain claimed that during the War he 'never drew a sober breath' in the trenches. It was a matter of degree. Bentley was more of an uncontrolled drinker, incapable of hiding the physical and mental effects of his state and was thus a danger to the safety of the men under his command. One can assume that he resorted to drink to help him overcome the problems he faced.

The dangers from the enemy guns, the uncertainty caused by Bentley's personal problems, the rain and muddy conditions, prompted Robert Hamilton to observe wearily: 'Am quite sure I look 50, feel 70'.

The Germans vacated two large caves just above the village of Bucy-le-Long, once stone quarries with huge chambers and seemingly never ending tunnels. They offered the 1/ Royal Warwicks welcome shelter from the rain and shells but the atmosphere created by cigarette smoke, cooking and general odour must have been putrid. The severe overcrowding caused by 300 men in the 'foul cave' was unlikely to have improved Charles Bentley's state of mind.

At another court martial on Sunday 4 October, Bentley was 'given a chance and told that if his conduct was alright for the rest of the war, the entry would be washed off his records altogether.' Hamilton wished that his superior officer could be found a 'staff job'; he spent the night outside the cave overseeing the digging of trenches and on his return he found Bentley in a state of talkative hypertension. Hamilton was an Anglican churchwarden at the church of St. Thomas à Becket in Sourton on the edge of Dartmoor and considered that Bentley's views on religion were 'most extraordinary. He believes in there being an Almighty God thoroughly, but not in his son, or in the story of the Cross and in the sacrifice. I am afraid his home life is not a happy one, and I feel sorry for him, but can never forgive him for the risks he runs when drunk. The men will not follow him, but nothing will induce him to believe this.'

Charles Bentley was in desperate need of help and support. Had he been back in England his condition would have been diagnosed as neurasthenia, caused by severe fatigue, the cure for which was

Co-author Alan Reed in the 'foul cave' at Bucy-le-Long   A Hamilton

The WARWICKS are "holding their own."

'He kissed them all twice'- a contemporary postcard captures action behind the lines...   Alan Reed collection

rest. The evidence is clear that he was in a disturbed state: restless and troubled by nightmares. For an officer in the firing line, however, the remedy was a simple case of 'pulling himself together' and resolving his problems with a 'stiff upper lip'. At least his colleague Robert Hamilton was concerned enough to engage with him by candlelight in the 'foul cave' and attempt to calm him down.

Charles Bentley had received a traditional religious upbringing; he was baptised at St. Mary's Episcopal Church near Rathgo, Edinburgh, so why and when he decided to adopt a Unitarian religious outlook are questions unlikely to be answered.

It is mere speculation but if he was as troubled by his home life as Hamilton suspected, it may have been because his wife was unhappy that the family had returned to England from the sun and gentle pace of Trinidad. Adjusting to the climate and new living accommodation in England may have been causing difficulties...

Bentley bet Hamilton a bottle of wine on 7 October that 'at least 100 dead Germans would be found in our barbed wire,' not the most sensible of bets in view of Bentley's troubles but perhaps taken, as it was a manifestly foolish wager that would at least save Bentley another bout of over indulgence. In the event of course, not a single German was to be found in the barbed wire in the morning!

165

Bentley was a convivial character who enjoyed life to the full. On 8 October 'all the farm girls lunched with us and we had great fun. We kissed them all.' Bentley excitably went one step further as 'he kissed them all twice. They didn't in the least mind, and only said "Eh bien, c'est la guerre."' Was this typical behaviour or an example of his instability?

Bentley, Hamilton and two other officers whiled away the rest of the evening in an *estaminet* where they composed their version of the nursery rhyme with its title, so unacceptable for the 21st century: *The Ten Little ....* Their version was about ten German soldiers wearing their Pickelhaube spiked helmets:

'Ten little Pickelhauben advancing in a line
Bum crack, bum crack
And then there were nine'

The doggerel amusingly and inexorably wends its way to the penultimate stanza about:

'The last little Pickelhaube thinking about his wife
Raised his hands, dropped his gun
And thus saved his life'

and finally to the 'moral' of the rhyme:

'So...Remember little Pickelhauben, altho' we be but few,
In future be more wary
Of French's deadly crew.'

Charles Bentley would have been in his element but when the Battalion arrived in St. Omer in French Flanders, the two men's relationship was tense. Hamilton had secured a private car for the 'A' Company officers, but Bentley insisted on them getting into a *charabanc* full of French officers.

The 1/ Royal Warwicks suffered heavy losses at the Battle of Méteren on 13 October, the first major engagement since Le Cateau. The Battalion War Diary recorded '42 killed, 85 wounded' which included the 26 year old Lieutenant Montgomery who, once recovered from his wounds, returned to the Front as a staff officer at the Headquarters of the 33rd Division. It had been 'very wet all day. A perfect advance by Companies concerned and dash and spirit shown by all concerned' and in particular by Captain Bentley who was commended in the War Diary: 'Early in the day he had led his Company to within 200 yards of the enemy trenches and established himself there until reinforced by the general attack of the brigade; all men near this officer were killed or wounded and he himself had two bullets through his clothes.'

Charles Bentley was involved with the retreat from Le Cateau which was followed by the relentless campaign in the Marne and Aisne areas. The fighting at Méteren had taken its toll mentally; when the Royal Warwicks officers assembled on 17 October at a large hotel for 'a feed', Hamilton recorded that 'Master B. was at his old games again... and at about 2.a.m. there was a wild alarm with shells dropping everywhere and nothing could wake Bentley until the adjutant came down to see why we were not standing-to.' Hamilton was irritated that Bentley was 'once more allowed to get off.'

The situation was spiralling out of control. Bentley was drunk again on 22 October and had to be taken in hand by two N.C.O.s. At 11 a.m. the next day, the noise of guns and shells exploding was deafening. Major Bannerman, the Battalion's temporary commander, on being told about Bentley's state, had come down to the trenches to put him under arrest. Hamilton states that Bentley saw Bannerman and 'staggered' out of the trench to meet him. At which point a shell landed between them killing Bentley and wounding Bannerman. With a chilling finality, he concluded: 'So that was the end of poor Bentley and I took complete command of 'A' Company much to my joy.'

'Poor Bentley': Robert Hamilton was undoubtedly sad to lose a colleague with whom he had enjoyed banter and high jinks in the quiet times behind the lines. Did Hamilton himself have a personal agenda? Was his use of the word 'staggered' biased or a true description of Bentley's physical state? Robert Hamilton was ambitious but throughout his diary, he voices concern for the men of 'A' Company. He and Montgomery were unhappy that they were being commanded by someone who was too ill to cope- he was relieved, therefore, to be responsible himself for the direction of 'A' Company's future operations.

There is little reason to question Hamilton's version of events- his diary was for private consumption only. Contrast his description of Bentley's death with that sent by a relative for publication in the *Daily Graphic* and later *The Times*. The account was by Private S. Harper of the Royal Warwicks who at the time was recovering from wounds in Craigleith Military Hospital in Edinburgh:

"Captain Bentley took splendid care of his men, and always went well ahead cheering them on. We said he must have had a charmed life. He did not seem to know what fear was, and that made them all brave, too. It was at the little village (Houplines) near Armentières, where he was killed. The Warwicks were told this village must be taken at any cost, so four companies were sent out, and Captain B's Company had to lead. They had to make a turning movement to get round the village. 270 set out to do it, and when they took the place, there were only 20 left- 100 were killed and 150 wounded. The captain was at the head of the twenty when he fell. He was sniped in three places. He never seemed to think of his wounds and just went on cheering the men, and almost the last words he said were "Go on my men. Keep up the good name of the Warwicks. Don't give in." They took the village and they held it against 800 Germans until the Fusiliers came up to help them.'

Alan Tucker, a historian of the Royal Warwickshire Regiment, questions the veracity of the account- he argues that only a handful of soldiers were killed at Houplines, in routine trench warfare and that the Royal Warwicks did not hold the village against as many as 800 Germans. He is sceptical about the manner of Bentley's death and indeed his final words.

If Private Harper had fought with Bentley he would have known about his captain's problems and the time spent under arrest with the company serjeant major and may have decided to put a positive spin on his demise for the benefit of his family- that it was indeed a heroic and courageous death leading his men. *The Times* later printed a touching poem inspired by the romanticised account of Bentley's death:

'Slain by a Prussian bullet, leading the men who loved him,

Dying, cheered them on.'

Charles Bentley was one of the first officers in the B.E.F. to suffer from what nowadays would be termed severe combat stress. A few months later, future double V.C. winner and surgeon Noel Chavasse acknowledged the effect of warfare in France on officers: 'It is wearing out their nerves… the bravest fellows after six months feel themselves getting jumpy and constantly have to keep a hold on themselves. I am very sorry for them.'

Gregarious, popular, charming and well regarded as a soldier by his superiors, to relieve his battle fatigue and depression, Charles Bentley's escalating drink problem meant that he would become an increasing liability in the six week period from 11 September until his death on 23 October 1914. He received little if any official medical support for his condition but on several occasions was given another chance to redeem himself; despite the difficulties, he never shirked his responsibilities on the battlefield and was Mentioned in Despatches by Sir John French on 14 January 'for gallant and distinguished service in the field.'

There was a systemic failure to deal with Charles Bentley's illness which placed an extra burden on fellow officers so his death conveniently solved a problem that the Battalion commanders were only just beginning to confront.

When one scans row upon row of Great War gravestones, the extent of trauma and stress suffered before a soldier's death will in general never be known. In the case of one 36 year old British officer, married with three children, we are fortunate to have an insight into his inner turmoil when his life was brought to a tragic and abrupt end by an enemy shell.

Standing in front of his grave, one is consumed with sadness for 'Poor Bentley'.

CHARLES BENTLEY:

Born:	11 February 1878 at Kirkliston, near Edinburgh, eldest son of Dr. George and Anna Bentley of Loanhead House, Kirkliston. Husband of Geraldine Sadleir Stoney and father of Charles, Sybil and Hester
Education:	Callander School, Perthshire and Edinburgh University
Occupation:	Professional soldier
Unit/ Regiment:	Royal Scots Greys and 'A' Company, 1/ Royal Warwicks
Rank:	Captain
Died:	23 October 1914 at Houplines, near Armentières
Age:	36
Buried:	Cité Bonjean Military Cemetery, IX.A.50.

The cemetery is on the edge of Armentières and was designed by Sir Herbert Baker. There are over 2,100 casualties and the cemetery was used by Field Ambulances and New Zealand, Australian and British fighting units. There is a New Zealand Memorial and more than 500 German graves

Charles Bentley's grave at Cité Bonjean Military Cemetery near Armentières
A Hamilton

MANTA SINGH

One of 160,000 Indian soldiers who fought on the Western Front

Manta Singh was a professional soldier in the Indian Army. He died in a military hospital for Indian soldiers in Brighton after gunshot wounds sustained on 10 March 1915 at Neuve Chapelle had become infected with gangrene. Surgeons amputated the Indian soldier's legs and not long afterwards he died of septicaemia.

He was brought up in a village near the Punjabi city of Jalandhar and after leaving school, chose a career in the Army. He joined the 15/ Ludhiana Sikhs Infantry Battalion which in 1914 was incorporated into the 3rd Lahore Division. He had reached the rank of *subadar*, the equivalent of a lieutenant in the British Army and was expected, therefore, to speak English and liaise with the British officers in the Battalion.

After a long voyage he disembarked in Marseilles in late September 1914, one of 160,000 Indian soldiers to fight for the 'mother country' on the Western Front.

Subadar Manta Singh

The Indian contingent played a vital role in the first major British offensive of the War at Neuve Chapelle on 10 March 1915. General Sir John French, the Commander-in-Chief of the British Expeditionary Force, planned to capture the small village of Neuve Chapelle and then Aubers Ridge. The Ludhiana Sikhs found themselves on the right flank as part of Sir Douglas Haig's First Army. The attack was preceded by a massive bombardment of the German front line. The village was taken at dusk but at great cost with over 13,000 casualties. The Battalion War Diary recorded: 'The stretcher-bearers were at work all night picking up the wounded. We had Subadar Gattajans killed and Subadar Manta Singh wounded.' It transpired that the Sikh officer was shot in both legs when rescuing Captain Henderson, a wounded colleague. When Manta was hit, he was, apparently, lifting him into a barrow and wheeling him to safety.

The Indian Corps lost more than 4,000 men during the three day offensive. The wounded were transported by ship to Brighton where they received treatment in hospitals adapted to cater for the Indians' differing social and religious needs.

A workhouse was converted into a hospital grandly named the Kitchener Indian Hospital where Manta was treated. It was no surprise that Brighton's

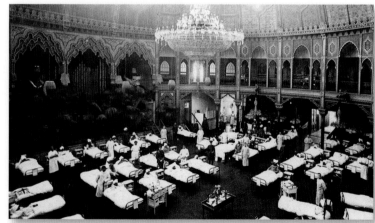

The Royal Pavilion hospital ward

Royal Pavilion and Museums, Brighton and Hove

Royal Pavilion was utilised in the same way. An architectural masterpiece, the building works started in 1787 under the auspices of John Nash and inspired by King George IV, its startling Indian architectural style offered an oriental welcome to ill, homesick soldiers thousands of miles from their homeland. In a letter home, one patient wrote: 'Do not be anxious about me. We're very well looked after. Our hospital is the place where the King used to have a throne. Men in hospital are tended like flowers, and the King and Queen sometimes come to visit them.'

The hospital network in and around Brighton was a triumph of planning and organisation. The hospitals treated 12,000 Indian soldiers and the sensitivity shown to the various religious, cultural and social differences was remarkable. Hindus, Sikhs and Muslims were provided for in designated wards. Toileting arrangements were kept separate and kitchens catered for the differing dietary requirements.

Unlike the other subjects covered in this book whose bodies were recovered from the battlefields, there was no burial for Manta Singh: a Sikh, he was cremated in April 1915 on the Sussex Downs and his ashes were scattered in the English Channel in line with Sikh customs. This was another example of the authorities' sensitivity and compassion as outdoor cremations in Britain were illegal.

The Indian *Chattri* (domed umbrella-type pavilion) Memorial to the Indians who died in the War, was unveiled by the Prince of Wales in 1921 at Patcham on the Sussex Downs. It was designed by E.C. Henriques of Mumbai and built with white Sicilian marble. The edifice rests on three large granite slabs over the crematorium site. The inscription on the *Chattri* is 'to the memory of all the Indian soldiers who gave their lives for their King-Emperor in the Great War, this monument, erected on the site of the funeral pyre where the Hindus and Sikhs who died in hospital at Brighton, passed through the fire, is in grateful admiration and brotherly affection dedicated.'

The Memorial is positioned in sight of the sea in beautiful rolling English countryside of the kind used in recruitment posters.

The Commonwealth War Graves Commission restored it and added another memorial in 2010 to commemorate Manta Singh and 52 other Hindus and Sikhs who died in the Brighton hospitals. The *Chattri* is a much recommended visit for a fine day, a gentle half mile walk from Braypool Lane, off the London Road and

Top: Ambulance at the Royal Pavilion   Royal Pavilion and Museums Brighton and Hove
Bottom: The Royal Pavilion, Brighton   A Hamilton

The Chattri *Memorial at Patcham on the Sussex Downs*   A Hamilton

The Muslim burial ground and Chattri *at Horsell Common, Surrey*
English Heritage

A27. A Memorial service is held at the Chattri every second Sunday in June at 2.30. p.m.

During the War 19 Muslims were buried in the Mohammedan burial ground at Horsell Common near Woking in Surrey. Its *chattri* and surrounds were designed by the India Office Surveyor, T. Herbert Winney. Works were completed in 1917. The cemetery fell into disrepair and due to vandalism all the burials were moved to the nearby Brookwood Cemetery.

In 1914 and 1915 the British Expeditionary Force might not have stemmed German advances without the Indian reinforcements. The Indian soldiers suffered from the atrocious winter and battlefield conditions more than most but still stayed loyal to the cause and fought with vigour and courage, receiving between them over 13,000 medals and 12 V.C.s. The roll call of dead and missing on the Western Front was over 7,000 and for all fronts over 74,000.

Prime Minister Lloyd George conversing with Indian soldiers near Fricourt on the Somme in September 1916   IWM Q1186

Prime Minister Lloyd George recognised their contribution to the war effort when he visited them at King George's Hill near Fricourt in the Somme in September 1916.

The story of Manta Singh's rescue of Captain Henderson still has a resonance for their sons who fought side by side in the Second World War and their grandsons who attended the *Chattri* ceremony on the Sussex Downs in 2010.

MANTA SINGH:

Born:	1870 at Masandan near Jalandhar, Punjab, India, son of Khem Singh
Occupation:	Professional soldier
Unit/ Regiment:	15/ Ludhiana Sikhs of 3rd Lahore Division
Rank:	Subadar (equivalent to a lieutenant)

Died:	10 March 1915 in the Kitchener Indian Hospital, Brighton
Age:	45
Commemorated:	He was cremated on the South Downs near Brighton and his name is to be found on the 2010 Memorial next to the *Chattri* monument on the South Downs. He is also commemorated on the Neuve Chapelle Indian Memorial in northern France, one of over 4,700 soldiers and officers, some of whom were British. The Memorial was designed in the form of an Indian shrine by Sir Herbert Baker and unveiled in 1927. A 15 feet high column holds up the Imperial British Crown and the Star of India. Inscribed on the lower part of the column in English, Hindi, Arabic and Gurmukhi are the words:

'God is One, He is the Victory.'

Manta Singh is commemorated on the Neuve Chapelle Indian Memorial
J Kerr

The grave of a Muslim Indian soldier was originally at Horsell Common but was transferred from the Muslim burial ground to Brookwood Cemetery, near Woking, Surrey *A Hamilton*

The Indian Memorial at Neuve Chapelle *J Kerr*

ANTHONY WILDING

'No finer athlete, no man better equipped physically for the fray, no man inspired with such a consuming desire to do his best, has ever heard the cheers ring from the stands'

Among the crowd of 7,000 at Wimbledon in July 1914, there was an air of anticipation and excitement. The dashing New Zealander, Tony Wilding, was aiming to win his fifth consecutive Men's All Comers' Singles title against Norman Brookes, his Australian friend and great rival.

The 1914 Final scarcely bears comparison with any 21st century counterpart. The protagonists wore tailored long white trousers, used small wooden racquets and hit white rather than yellow balls at each other. Not a trainer, coach, nutritionist nor psychotherapist was to be seen. Nowadays the players arrive for the championships in top of the range chauffeur driven cars: in contrast, Tony Wilding made his way to Worple Road, the original Wimbledon venue before it moved to Church Road in 1922, on a four horsepower BAT motor cycle.

In his 1912 autobiography *On the Court and Off*, Wilding encapsulated the warmth of his feelings towards the south London tennis complex: 'There is no place so hallowed as the Centre Court of the All England Club and no championship so worth striving for or so highly prized, as the World's Championship at Wimbledon.' From 1907 the Centre Court at Wimbledon became a second summer home for Tony Wilding- in 1907 and 1908 he won the Men's Doubles Championship, in 1910 he triumphed in Singles and Doubles and in 1911, 1912 and 1913, he was crowned Singles Champion. His record of four consecutive Singles titles remained intact until the Swede, Björn Borg, surpassed it with his fifth consecutive Championship win in 1980.

The Wimbledon crowd was disappointed that Wilding was not at his fluent best, struggling against the dogged consistency of his Australian opponent. He succumbed in three sets, 4/6, 4/6, 5/7. Brookes won the match with a miss-hit off the frame, a fluke that Wilding shrugged off with a resigned smile. It is possible that on this occasion, he had been disadvantaged by having not played matches in the Challenge competition. Until 1922 the holder of the men's title was not required to 'play through' the tournament until 'challenged' in the Final.

He partnered the French Women's champion, Marguerite Broquedis, in the Mixed Doubles Final which they lost but he did not leave Wimbledon empty handed. In the Men's Doubles Final he and Norman Brookes overcame the British pair H. Roper-Barrett and C.P. Dixon 6/1, 6/1, 5/7, 8/6 to clinch what proved to be his final Wimbledon title.

Julia Wilding's 'Little Hercules'
A. Wallis Myers Captain Anthony Wilding *Hodder and Stoughton 1916*

Wilding's practice when a young boy against a wall at the family home near Christchurch in New Zealand was, he recalled, 'a splendid education'. He was raised in a family for whom sport was a fundamental part of growing up physically and mentally. His lawyer father Frederick had been a fine all-round sportsman in Herefordshire before he and his wife Julia decided to move to New Zealand. *The Daily Telegraph's* tennis correspondent, A. Wallis Myers in his biography of Anthony Wilding, commented that Frederick was 'an all-round sportsman of the type who has done much to mould the strength and character of our Empire.'

Frederick Wilding's law practice in Christchurch, Wilding and Acland, was successful enough to provide his five children with a wonderful sporting environment at 'Fownhope', named after a village on the river Wye in Herefordshire. The Wildings' property boasted a swimming pool, cricket pitch, **173** croquet and lawn tennis court. Anthony was encouraged to concentrate on cricket as a young boy but he was already showing signs of a precocious talent for tennis. When her son was a toddler, Julia wrote in a scrap book: 'Darling sonny is so well, I really believe he will do something great some day… he is so splendid in physique, so sturdy and yet so sweet and affectionate.' He frightened her to death when at the age of four, he climbed to the top of a 60 ft. high pine tree!

By the time Julia Wilding's 'Little Hercules', as she called him, had left Mr. Wilson's School in Christchurch to go to Canterbury College, he was living up to her description. He was a sportsman of distinction- swimmer, athlete, rugby player, rower, marksman, cricketer and tennis player! Wallis Myers maintained he was not an ardent student and Wilding admitted: 'My irregularity at lectures was in a measure compensated for by my zest on behalf of the University at lawn tennis and rugby football.'

Not that he was in the academic slow lane; after only six months at Canterbury College, encouraged by his English parents, he decided to travel to England to take the Cambridge University entrance examination. He and three other passengers allegedly shared a cargo ship in 1902 with 100,000 carcasses of frozen lamb! Much of the six week journey was spent preparing for the examination particularly for the Greek unit which he found tiresomely dull. After a few weeks at a 'crammer' at Hunstanton in Norfolk, he was accepted by Trinity College, Cambridge in October 1902 to read Law.

His main objective at Cambridge was to win a cricket 'Blue' but he found the cricket fraternity arrogant and aristocratic; he wrote that 'they talk lardy da don't you know.' By the end of his first year he was gravitating towards lawn tennis.

Wilding was astonished by the stuffiness of students at Cambridge and the 'ludicrous formality between undergraduates.' Despite being a plain speaking Antipodean, he was, nonetheless, elected Honorary Secretary of the Cambridge University Lawn Tennis Club which was, in effect, the start of his journey to Wimbledon stardom.

Wilding developed his tennis career in his second year at Cambridge at the expense of his academic studies. He took part in tournaments nationwide. Although tennis was an amateur sport, his tournament wins were being rewarded by not insubstantial 'vouchers'.

Anthony Wilding in action   *A. Wallis Myers* Captain Anthony Wilding

Frederick and Julia Wilding were so concerned by their son's difficulty in concentrating on his studies that they sent their eldest daughter Gladys to keep a watchful eye on him which, if not hugely welcome, did have the desired effect, as he completed his third year at Cambridge with a degree.

Wilding decided to dedicate himself to tennis on completion of his studies. Finding enough money to subsidize his life choice would be a constant problem for the next eight years. His 'winnings', endorsements for the F.H. Ayres 'Wilding racquet', articles written for newspapers and magazines, tutoring for the Prince of Bohemia's children and some parental help, covered his main outgoings until necessity dictated that he take on a real job. He found that, for a highly prized sportsman, doors opened to an opulent lifestyle that was gratefully received and was, importantly, free!

The New Zealander was one of the first sportsmen to understand the importance of fitness and diet; he did not smoke and drank in moderation. He dedicated himself to practice, training and analysis and maintained that a great player becomes 'a good general' after laborious practice and many defeats; he set himself a rigorous training programme and personal fitness regime, much of it based on conversations with the world title-holding boxer Bob Fitzsimmons. Wilding would analyse his game with cerebral incisiveness and dissected his opponents' game, seeking out, then mercilessly attacking their 'most vulnerable points'. 'Little Hercules' was in the process of, as Len and Shelley Richardson assert in their fascinating biography *Anthony Wilding*, transforming tennis 'from a garden pastime to a competitive sport'.

Wimbledon became Wilding's annual hunting ground after honing his game in tournaments throughout Europe where, handsome and dashing, the 'young Viking' became a darling of the 'chattering classes' who attended the tournaments.

He invested in his first motor cycle in 1907, a Belgian FN 4 cylinder 4.5 horsepower machine which transported him to tournaments all over Europe at speeds touching 60 m.p.h. He travelled in 1908 by motor cycle from Bohemia to San Remo, to Cannes, Paris and finally to Queen's Club in west London. Imagine his next tennis playing trip from London to a tournament in Wiesbaden via Huntingdon, Cambridge, Ipswich, Harwich, Utrecht, Rotterdam, Cologne and Coblenz at a time when roads did not offer motor cyclists a particularly comfortable ride! In the early days of manufacture, motor cycles were unreliable but a puncture on the rutted roads of Europe or a leaking petrol tank were challenges that Wilding would tackle with relish.

Long days on his motor bike were, unsurprisingly, not the ideal preparation for a tennis tournament but for Wilding, 'wheels meant motion and motion meant life'. He was, in modern parlance, a genuine 'petrol head'... he exchanged his FN machine for a BAT and in July 1909 rode it from Land's End to John O'Groats.

He spent 1909 in New Zealand attempting to concentrate on his Bar exams; his heart, however, was in a motor cycle agency he set up to import cycle parts from the U.K. There was a decline in his tournament activity. He opted out of Wimbledon but contributed to a Davis Cup whitewash of the U.S.A. at Sydney when he won his three matches.

Wilding enjoyed the thrill of motor cycling...
A. *Wallis Myers* Captain Anthony Wilding

Wilding's first Wimbledon Singles title was achieved in 1910. His pre-match preparation was unusual as he was charged in the West London Magistrates' Court with riding a motor cycle without a licence! Despite the distraction the stamina and strength of the 27 year old proved too strong for the 42 year old British player Arthur Gore; the new tennis star won the Challenge round 6/4, 7/5, 4/6, 6/2. Wallis Myers

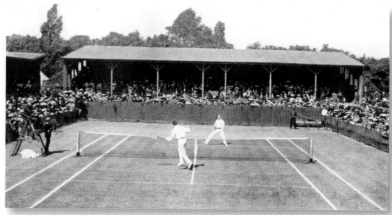

In action: Wilding's first Wimbledon All Comers' Singles Title in 1910. He is at the far end Anthony F. Wilding On the Court and Off Methuen 1912

considered that 'more brilliant players, greater artists and more subtle tacticians have appeared on the Centre Court but no finer athlete, no man better equipped physically for the fray, no man inspired with such a consuming desire to do his best, has ever heard the cheers ring from the stands.' For the tennis-watching public and the female element in particular, the New Zealander was in the process of being considered an 'honorary Englishman'.

Wilding's mother could scarcely contain her excitement that in 1911 her 'Hercules' appeared to be on the cusp of marriage: 'Tony is in love at last with a Miss Davis Joel… and very much in love too.' Her son was beginning to realize that he needed the security of full time employment and thanks to contacts made through a Queen's Club member, joined a wood and pulp business which allowed him some latitude for tournament play and the opportunity to play with the star struck King Gustav of Sweden whose quality of play impressed the Wimbledon champion. Tony was not enamoured with work in the wood and pulp business and his mother's assessment of the depth of his love for Miss Joel proved to be wide of the mark.

Maxine Elliott, 'the Candid Friend' of Tony Wilding
National Portrait Gallery, X16487 Ernest Walter Histed

Tennis was opening doors to the 'great and the good' that Tony Wilding could never otherwise have unlocked. He was invited to play some 'mild tennis' with Mrs. Winston Churchill and Maxine Elliott, a tall, dark and smoulderingly beautiful star of New York's theatre land.

Wilding's blonde good looks and 'manly brand of tennis' had captivated the hearts of the female tennis audience. Like the air ace Albert Ball (see p.182) Wilding was much sought after by admirers and found their interest an unwelcome intrusion. Early in his career he wrote to his sister Gladys: 'If a girl, be she pretty or ugly, comes up and asks one to be photographed, what can a poor fellow do?'

Tony Wilding was lawn tennis's first matinée 'idol', so it was no surprise that he captivated the heart of one. Born Jessie C. Dermott, Maxine Elliott became such a successful actress that she set up, none too modestly, the 'Maxine Elliott Theatre' in Times Square, New York. She was also in great demand in London's West End, and caught the eye of King Edward VII, one suspects more for her beauty than her acting skills!

She invited Wilding to Hartsbourne Manor, her newly-purchased mansion in Hertfordshire in 1911. Her intention was that he would, as it were, 'give her some advice on her courts.' Their 'courtship' blossomed and Maxine's niece, Diana Forbes-Robertson, wrote in her biography, *My Aunt Maxine*, that it seems 'he loved her dearly… Whatever existed between Maxine 42 and Tony 27, it was the best she had during her lifetime.'

Before they met she had been married to an attorney and an actor. She also had a number of liaisons with, among others, a heavyweight boxer, a baseball star, the financier J.P. Morgan who is thought to have helped finance her theatre and no surprises- King Edward VII.

Wilding was devoted to Maxine; he rushed back from a business trip in Sweden and arrived in London just in time to see some of the first night of *Joseph and his Brethren* in which she starred as Potiphar. Wilding wrote that he was invited to watch her 'dress' but was at pains to point out that this entailed only make-up and hair styling!

On one occasion, the taxi taken by the actors Gerald and Muriel du Maurier (parents of novelist Daphne) broke down- Maxine Elliott's car drew up driven by Tony Wilding who 'bundled my wife into Miss Elliott's car and the ladies went off. Then he remained behind and after a grimy overhauling of the taxi's works, detected the fault and repaired the damage.' On occasions when Maxine's car broke down, he would enthusiastically roll up his sleeves and lie on his back under the car and return it to working order for her.

Hours were spent coaching Maxine's nieces in the skills of tennis but her approach to the game frustrated the Wimbledon champion: 'Max you must run.'! Languidly smoking from a cigarette holder, one can imagine her response.

Their relationship was conducted with discretion but its exact nature was clear to Diana Forbes-Robertson: whereas her many guests stayed in another wing of the house, 'Mr. Wilding's room' was on the floor immediately above Maxine's suite. It had also been, in her words, 'The King's Suite'!

Such was her love for Wilding that Maxine would support him not only at Wimbledon but further afield in European tournaments in Nice, Cannes and Paris. Her niece recalled that 'fat tears of despair rolled down Maxine's face as she saw Tony beaten for the first time in the Men's Singles at Wimbledon in 1914.'

Tony Wilding had reached the pinnacle of his career by 1913. For many critics he was one of the greatest players the game had produced. He won the French Championships in Paris and, by all accounts, played 'the very best game of his life' in Wallis Myers's opinion, to defeat the talented 23 year old American, Maurice McLoughlin in the Wimbledon Challenge match 8/6, 6/3, 10/8. The game was now, thanks in great part to Wilding, enjoying a surge in popularity. Thousands of hopeful fans failed to get a seat for the Final to support a player whom they regarded as 'one of their own'.

Wilding had tired of wood and pulping. He was pleased to accept a directorship of the Victor Tyre Company through a contact at Queen's Club. Working with motor cars was eminently preferable and in 1914 he eschewed travel to tournaments by motor cycle, choosing instead the comfort and safety of his brand new Alda motor car.

Maxine partnered him in mixed competitions on the Riviera and in men's doubles tournaments his partner was the 66 year old former Conservative Prime Minister A.J. Balfour. It was an odd combination. Wilding considered that 'Bloody' Balfour, scourge of the Irish Nationalists when Chief Secretary for Ireland, 'plays a good game... he can hold an end up in a good men's four' and that 'he was a dear man and I have the profoundest admiration for him.' Even so, why he should have sought solace after his 1914 Wimbledon defeat with the intellectual politician is difficult to explain. The pair of them chewed over his defeat on a grassy knoll near the outside courts.

WIMBLEDON, 1914: TEA WITH MR. BALFOUR.

Wilding and former Conservative Prime Minister, A.J. Balfour   *A. Wallis Myers* Captain Anthony Wilding

Tony Wilding was satisfied with his preparation for the championships and his attempt at a 5th consecutive title shrugging it off as 'one of those days' suffered occasionally by all the greatest sportsmen.

He could now concentrate on the Davis Cup due to be held in the U.S. in July. He was only too aware from the fevered atmosphere of parties at Hartsbourne that the European situation was in free fall. Unsure as to whether the Davis Cup would take place, he was advised to travel to New York: personal advice from none other than the British Foreign Minister, Sir Edward Grey and Winston Churchill, First Lord of the

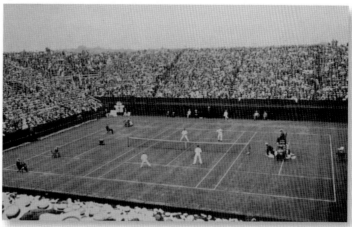

Tony Wilding's last Final in 1914 when he and Norman Brookes won the Davis Cup in New York   *A. Wallis Myers* Captain Anthony Wilding

Admiralty. The Australasian pairing of Wilding and Brookes duly sailed from Liverpool on 11 July.

To a background of gloomy news from Europe the Australasians were pitted, in their second round tie, against the Germans Otto Froitzheim and Oscar Kreuzer, both of whom were in the German Army Reserve, the former as an officer. Their match was in Pittsburgh where there was a sizeable German population. The crowd's fervent support for the Germans was passionate and verged on the hostile. Brookes and Wilding, whom the crowd perceived as 'British', were so incensed by the attitude of the partisan crowd that they were spurred on to annihilate their opponents 5/0. Brookes won his   177 singles matches, Wilding defeated Kreuzer 6/2, 6/2, 6/4 and Froitzheim 6/3, 6/4, 6/2 and he and Brookes destroyed the German doubles pair 6/1, 6/1, 6/2.

News was filtering through that the Kaiser's Army was marching relentlessly westwards. The German pair beat a hasty retreat to join up in the Fatherland.

Wilding and Brookes brushed aside the British team and won the Davis Cup against the U.S.A. with a 3/2 victory in the Challenge Round. Wilding beat R.N. Williams but, not for the first time, found McLoughlin too hot to handle but he and Brookes won the doubles tie.

The colonials returned to Liverpool, according to Diana Forbes-Robertson, 'hilarious when they learned that their German opponents had been intercepted by a British destroyer' when on their way to Genoa in an Italian liner. Their first 'port of call' was a camp in Gibraltar and it is known that Froitzheim was later interned in Lofthouse Park Prison, Wakefield. There was a rumpus over his status there- the German Government, using the U.S. Embassy as an intermediary, requested that Froitzheim and two others be treated as 'officer prisoners of war' and the case was important enough for the involvement of Sir Edward Grey, the Foreign Secretary. In correspondence on the subject, a War Office official wrote that 'Froitzheim is the German lawn tennis champion and an objectionable person,' a view that probably did not help his cause! At least he was safer in a British prison than on the Western Front and thus survived to become the Chief of Police in Wiesbaden in 1927.

The German pair defeated in the Davis Cup by Wilding and Brookes, at Pittsburgh in July 1914 *A. Wallis Myers* Captain Anthony Wilding

On his return to Britain, Wilding chose to bide his time and during a stay at Hartsbourne with Maxine, sought advice from contacts made in the tennis world. He was guided by the Duke of Westminster, commander of a squadron of armoured cars, who suggested Wilding join a car division which, given his love of cars and engines, was most appealing. Winston Churchill proved a useful contact in pointing him in the direction of the Royal Naval Air Service. Wilding joined a unit of car owners engaged in reconnaissance and he and his Alda crossed the Channel from Dover on 6 October. From the outset he found his role the 'most intensely interesting he had undertaken' as the unit drove into Belgium and was active during the First Battle of Ypres. He was proud to be playing a role as 'a Motor Bandit' and to be gazetted a 2nd lieutenant. He wrote a letter home on 16 October: 'I go out about 5.30 a.m. and motor as near to the German lines and outposts as possible and report all the information to HQ. I motor the senior intelligence officer, an awfully nice chap.'

Wilding's letters reflected a growing concern about the nature of the conflict and fear for his unit's safety. He acknowledged to his mother that as it got colder, it was 'too awful to think of the poor devils in the trenches.' At least he had a roof over his head and 'some degree of comfort'. His thoughts were on the next defence of the Davis Cup but as the War became increasingly trench-bound and static, he realised that his tennis racquet was unlikely to hit a ball in anger for some time.

His morale was boosted in early 1915 by a visit from Maxine who stayed at the Grand Hotel in Calais. She was determined 'to do her bit' for the war effort and donated an ambulance- a converted car which was large enough to take four wounded soldiers and a nurse. She and her friend Millicent, Duchess of Sutherland, joined the Red Cross and tended the sick and wounded in Boulogne.

Tony Wilding was a man of action but life was unexciting until an upturn in activity in the Ypres area. He was now attached to the Lahore Division of the Indian Army Corps and in command of 30 men, three armoured cars and a number of machine-guns. He enjoyed designing and building trailers to house 3-pounder guns which were towed by the armoured vehicles. He and the Duke of

Westminster were out together on 31 March in a lorry 'loosing off about 50 rounds of high explosives at the enemy's parapets' and successfully demolishing several small cottages from which a battery of machine-guns was operating.

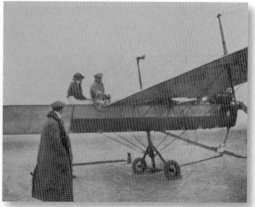

Wilding and armoured car   A. Wallis Myers Captain Anthony Wilding

Not content with motor bikes and armoured cars, the tennis star tried his hand at flying
A. Wallis Myers Captain Anthony Wilding

Wilding was involved in the Second Battle of Ypres when the Germans used chlorine gas for the first time on 22 April. Many of the men under his command were lost on 25 April in the most gruesome fighting he had yet encountered. Balmy days at Wimbledon were distant and pleasant memories; in his letters home Wilding was unable to contain his hatred of the warfare and its effects, wishing with all his heart that 'the damned thing would end.'

Tony Wilding celebrated his promotion to captain on 2 May with a cup of tea in Méteren. The following day he was driving lorries loaded with 3-pounder guns to the front line to take out German machine-guns which was dangerous but exciting work- he was candid about his chances once formal orders came through on 4 May for the offensive to take Aubers Ridge and the German salient at Neuve Chapelle. He predicted his demise in a letter written on 8 May, the day before his death: 'For really the first time in 7 ½ months I have a job in hand which is likely to end in gun, I and the whole outfit being blown to hell. However, it's a sporting chance and we will help our infantry no end.'

Green pea soup, roast lamb, potatoes and fruit served with a glass of chilled white wine: the menu for Tony Wilding's last supper in a small ruined cottage may have fallen short of those enjoyed at Hartsbourne Manor or the Duke of Westminster's Eaton Hall, but he declared it was the best he had enjoyed at the Front and was glad to have done so in the company of Lieutenants Milburn and Barnes of the 1/4 Suffolks, both of whom were tennis players.

At 5.00 a.m. on 9 May there was a deafening and thunderous dawn chorus of 600 guns firing at the German lines. Seaforth Highlanders were the first to attack but were pinned back and scythed down by machine-gun fire. The Royal Sussex and Northamptonshire Battalions fared no better. Wilding throughout was cool and calm, his men firing with hardly a break.

Tony Wilding's marker and grave in 1915
A. Wallis Myers Captain Anthony Wilding

By 4.30 p.m. Wilding was in need of a cat nap. He was advised against going into a nearby dug out which was at the back of the trench and open to shell fire. He took no notice. A large shell landed on the dugout killing two privates and severely wounding 23 year **179** old Lieutenant Donald Petty, another tennis player from Suffolk who died of wounds two days later. The record breaking Wimbledon tennis star's body was discovered under 'a mass of iron, earth and sandbags', barely recognizable as the handsome athlete who had entertained tennis crowds world-wide.

Captain Anthony Wilding's body was wrapped in a blanket and buried quickly and silently in the corner of a nearby small orchard without a chaplain-led ceremony. Only a few were present to witness the burial of the world's finest tennis player. Fittingly, it was the kind of warm, sunny day that Wilding had enjoyed so much during tournaments on the Riviera. He now rests in the Rue-des-Berceaux Military Cemetery.

He loathed the War but wholeheartedly threw himself into it. Julia Wilding received heart-warming eulogies from two of her son's superior officers- the Duke of Westminster informed her that her son was 'one of my best officers and had just done such very vital work... I saw him not long before he left and now he is among the band of heroes who have made the great sacrifice.' Lieutenant Commander Chilcott of the Royal Naval Air Service had 'learnt to love him as few men love each other. My admiration for him was unbounded... I always felt he was an example to his fellow men in everything. God rest his great soul.'

Maxine Elliott directing operations on her barge 'Julia'
Diana Forbes-Robertson My Aunt Maxine *Viking Press 1964*

Maxine Elliott was distraught when she received the news of his death which her niece believed 'took from her the one, simple, trusty, devoted man of her life, the knight who served and admired her without demand.' There was no element in Tony Wilding's character she believed that 'could possibly be twisted into the attitude of a *gigolo*; he was a "pure man"... he looked straight through her veneer. He never used her, he never abused her or turned on her.' Apparently they did, however, have a blazing row during their final rendezvous.

She was inspired to continue her good works at the Front and to use her fortune to provide humanitarian aid. She found that the Belgian authorities were more prepared to accept the offers of help from an enthusiastic and charming American lady than the British. They accepted use of a large barge she bought and refurbished called the 'Julia' which was used for Hartsbourne-type socializing and for transporting supplies to aid starving Belgians from February 1915 to May 1916. 'Our Lady of the Boats', as she was known to the Belgians, helped feed and clothe 35,000 Belgian refugees for which she was awarded the Belgian Order of the Crown in person by King Albert of Belgium.

The American actress experienced the dangers of the War first hand: '... the barge is shaking with the fury of a bombardment not far away'; she was shocked by the nature and effects of the conflict: 'We see nothing but sad sights' and 'the pity of it clutches at the throat. I know that war killed and maimed men and broke the hearts of women, but I never realized before how its chill hand laid icy on a nation's soul, arresting all life, slaying poor women and little children as surely and inexorably as the screaming shells rend the bodies of their husbands and fathers.'

Maxine also contributed to the war effort in England- *The Times History of the War* reported that 'a very fine operating theatre' in the Red Cross Hospital at Netley near Southampton was the generous gift of the 'well known American actress' and that 'it was replete with every modern appliance, and a fully equipped pathological laboratory and a dispensary on the same complete scale.'

When she returned to London tired and exhausted but content that the situation of the local Belgians had been ameliorated, Maxine turned to spiritualism as a way to contact Tony in an attempt to atone for their heated argument on the barge during their last moments together.

Tony Wilding had raised the playing standards of tennis with a muscular and athletic brand of power play and introduced a new audience to a game that win or lose, he played with great style and physical and moral grace. Norman Brookes believed that 'tennis followers the world over will mourn his loss and more especially in Australasia. I shed a tear in memory of the many happy days we spent in the struggle for the Davis Cup.'

Anthony Wilding was a proud New Zealander, determined to give his life to his 'mother country' for what contemporaries claimed, was 'the greater game.'

ANTHONY WILDING:

Born:	31 October 1883 at Opawa, New Zealand, son of Frederick and Julia Wilding
Education:	Wilson's School, Christchurch, New Zealand University of Canterbury and Trinity College, Cambridge
Occupation:	Tennis player, businessman and barrister
Unit/ Regiment:	Armoured Car Division, Royal Naval Air Service
Rank:	Captain
Died:	9 May 1915, Battle of Aubers Ridge
Age:	31
Buried:	Rue-des-Berceaux Military Cemetery, Richebourg-L'Avoué, II.D.37. The cemetery was established in January 1915 and was expanded from smaller cemeteries in the surrounding area. There are 450 graves including 241 of identified soldiers. It is located 17 kms south west of Armentières and was designed by Charles Holden

Anthony Wilding's grave at Rue-des-Berceaux Military Cemetery   *A Hamilton*

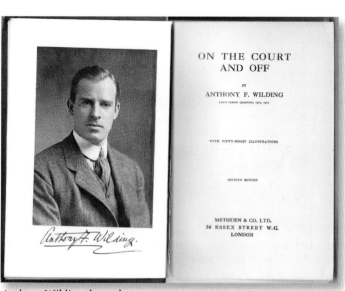

Anthony Wilding the author
Anthony F. Wilding On the Court and Off *Methuen 1912*

ALBERT BALL V.C.

'O I do get tired of always living to kill, and am really beginning to feel like a murderer'

On Good Friday 1917 a dinner was held for pilots of the Royal Flying Corps before they returned to the Front. Captain Albert Ball D.S.O., M.C. sneaked away early and met 18 year old Flora Young at her home and proposed to her. It had been a whirlwind romance and moments after they had first met, he kitted her out in flying gear and took her on a plane ride above the London Colney air base where he was being trained. She could scarcely turn down the offer of marriage from a 20 year old national hero, an 'air ace' who had captured the imagination of the British public for his courage and heroism in bringing down record numbers of German aircraft and pilots. He gave her his gold identification disc and a silver brooch, shaped like the R.F.C. wings; in return she handed him a small bound copy of Robert Louis Stevenson's *Prayers Written at Vailima* and at his request, sang in her beautiful opera-trained voice his favourite song *Thank God for a Garden*.

Albert Ball after he had been awarded his flying certificate in late January 1915
From *Captain Ball V.C. by Briscoe and Stannard 1918*

Sadly for Flora, Albert had unfinished business to attend to in the skies above the war zone and on the following morning, he departed to France for the final time: 'I am simply full of joy to have met you' was his unequivocal message in the letter he wrote to her on his arrival.

Flora had won the heart of a young man who had achieved remarkable fame in a very short time- he had been a member of the Royal Flying Corps for little more than a year but had been awarded a Distinguished Service Order with two Bars, the Military Cross and the Russian Order of St. George. His achievements were acknowledged by the city of his birth when Nottingham City Council invited him to be an Honorary Freeman on 19 February 1917. Diffident by nature, his exploits had thrust him into the public eye. He was one of the first 'celebrities' to suffer from intrusive journalism which he disliked intensely; on many occasions he resorted to wearing civilian clothes to avoid recognition.

Albert was born on 16 August 1896. His father, also called Albert, was a prosperous and ambitious businessman who had successfully developed the family plumbing business in Lenton, a suburb of Nottingham. In the 1890s he branched into estate agency and by the outbreak of war was a pillar of the community and was elected Mayor of Nottingham in 1909 and 1910.

Albert, his brother Cyril and sister Lois were brought up in a happy and safe environment, firstly in Lenton and later at Sedgeley House, 43 Lenton Road in the genteel Park District of the city. He and his siblings were lively and adventurous and from an early age, Albert displayed signs of a determined independence and an inquiring and inventive mind. He and his father built a hut in the garden where he tinkered with engines and electrical gadgets and, encouraged by his father, developed into an accurate rifle and pistol shot. The audacity and courage which he displayed during the War were evident in his youth- on one occasion he climbed a tall industrial chimney stack with a steeplejack and walked around the top of it without a hint of fear…

Albert attended the local church school in Lenton, moved on to Grantham Grammar School and then Nottingham High School where it was mutually agreed between the school and the Ball family that it would be best if he continued his education elsewhere. Roy Henderson C.B.E. was a fellow pupil who gave an interview in 1989 to Simon Williams, the school's Head of History, in which he remembered that Albert and his brother Cyril could be quite badly behaved! The Ball brothers were not great fans of Music nor Mr. Dunhill the Music master. He would point from the piano at a boy he wanted to stand up and sing. Unfortunately he had one eye that looked one way and one another so when he stared at a boy and told him to stand up, usually four boys would stand up. Mr Dunhill would become exasperated, tell them to sit down and then demand that the boy he had wanted to stand up do so, at which point four boys would stand up in another part of the room. The Ball brothers were 'notable exponents of this tactic!' A story, which may be apocryphal, could explain why Albert was 'withdrawn' from the school. He brought a big paper bag of aniseed balls into assembly one day which burst, spewing them all over the floor and creating a riotous scene as boys scrambled after them…

Albert was not academic by nature and Trent College at Long Eaton offered him the opportunity to pursue his practical interests. He enjoyed the Officer Training Corps and excelled at carpentry, metal work, photography and was an accomplished violin player. He wrote to his parents that 'I have a great love for my school.'

Albert Ball's interest in shooting began at an early age and would prove invaluable in the skies over France

He understood the importance of duty to his God, King and above all his family from an early age. He was a keen church goer and welcomed the peace and tranquillity that a church offered: 'I like it very much for it is quite a change to think quietly for a short time.' His family were never far from his thoughts and wherever he was posted after August 1914, he wrote a prodigious amount of loving and respectful letters to them.

On leaving Trent College he joined the University Engineering Works in Lenton, in which his father had a financial interest but Albert junior was keen to work his way up and wrote that 'I shall try my level best to be a good straightforward business man and follow to the best of my ability in my father's footsteps.'

Albert enlisted with the Sherwood Foresters (Robin Hoods) when war was declared in August 1914. His experience in the Trent College Officer Training Corps, combined with his enthusiasm and determination, resulted in rapid promotion on 28 October to 2nd lieutenant. He was desperate to join the action in France and believed that his passport to the Front could be achieved by transferring to the North Midland Divisional Cyclist Company. In June 1915 he was posted to Perivale in Middlesex for Officer Training but found the goings-on at the nearby Hendon aerodrome far more glamorous and alluring. He informed his father that 'I go to Hendon every morning at 4 o'clock… in the first place you have to pay £75… I love flying and as

Albert Ball like Werner Voss and Tony Wilding enjoyed the thrill of motor cycling, here on a Campion

they are very short of pilots, I may do a little good.' He decided to join the Ruffy Baumann Flying School and paid his fees, probably with a paternal subsidy.

He obtained his Royal Aero Club Certificate on 15 October and was transferred to the Royal Flying Corps. He was trained at Norwich and Upavon in Wiltshire; his letters home emphasised the dangers he faced. His mother Harriett would have been concerned to receive news of a 120 m.p.h. crash: 'It was a rum feeling coming down, for I had time to see that my number was up; however, it's not' he

Albert Ball leaving for France on 7 April 1917

From Captain Ball V.C. *by Briscoe and Stannard 1918*

added with bravado. In another missive he described a crash he walked away from, despite his machine being 'smashed into matchwood.'

He was posted in February 1916 to No.13 Squadron which was based at Marieux in France and initially he flew BE2c aircraft for reconnaissance and intelligence gathering over enemy trenches. For an impetuous young man the BE2c was too cumbersome and slow and not a fighting machine. Albert Ball hankered after a more stimulating flying experience without having to be accompanied by an 'observer' who sat at the front of the aircraft.

Ball's letters capture the excitement of his escapades; he was sent to do some reconnaissance over German lines on 21 February: 'Oh it was sport!' and on 1 March he was sent on a patrol to report movements in and around a train station. He recorded with idiosyncratic spelling: 'On the way back I had a rotten time… We had nearly got back over our lines when a Hun Focker attacked us. My observer let fly with the gun but after two shots the beastly thing went whonkey. I also pulled out my revolver but this also stuck. However, by this time we were over our own lines and the Focker did a bunk.'

Ten days later when flying through thick cloud, he lost his bearings and came through it at only 500 feet. He was reprimanded by his commanding officer Major Marsh for exposing himself to such risk when, procedurally, 7,000 feet was considered a safe height. Ball accepted he had been foolish 'but it was sport.' In similar circumstances over a year later he was not so fortunate.

By the end of April he was allowed to engage with the enemy on his own: 'I like this job' he wrote to his father 'but nerves do not last long and you soon want a rest.' He vividly recalled a close encounter with the enemy on 29 April: 'the interesting thing about it was that we could see the Huns' faces and they could see ours, we were so near.' But he 'didn't think them devils. I only scrap because it is my duty, but I do not think anything bad about the Hun. He is just a good chap with very little guts, trying to do his best. Nothing makes me feel more rotten than to see them go down, but I see it is either them or me, so I must do my best to make it a case of them!'

He was posted in early May to 11 Squadron and entrusted with a single seater aircraft- the Bristol Scout. He wrote on 16 May: 'Now for a bit of cheerful news. I was on patrol in a Bristol Scout. I was at 12,000 feet and saw a Hun at 5,000… I went after it, catching it up when 20 miles over its own lines. It took 120 shots to do it in, but in the end it went down upside down. I got back but it was archied (hit by anti-aircraft fire) badly.'

There was no respite from the stress and excitement- he received orders in the afternoon to fly a new French machine, a Nieuport which was powered by a 110 h.p. engine and could fly at over 100 m.p.h. He was delighted to be given aircraft number 5173; no longer would he be held back by an 'observer'. He was now alone on missions, master of his own destiny and indeed his path to fame and glory had begun. His reputation as a fearless pilot and excellent marksman was burgeoning by the day and he had accounted for a 'catch' of three Albatros Cs, four LVGs, a Roland, a Fokker and an observation balloon by the end of June.

He received the Military Cross, gazetted on 27 July 'for conspicuous skill and gallantry on many occasions, notably when, after failing to destroy an enemy kite balloon with bombs, he returned for a fresh supply, went back and brought it down in flames. He has done great execution among enemy aeroplanes. On one occasion he attacked six in one flight, forced down two and drove the others off. This occurred several times over the enemy's lines.'

The young Ball must have often cut a solitary figure. Reliving his past in Nottingham, he built a shed next to 11 Squadron's air hangar where his aeroplane was housed. Now on site he could quickly take the controls of his fighter, on occasions when, he once wrote, still in his pyjamas! In a little plot alongside his shed, he cultivated a small vegetable patch from seeds sent over from Nottingham which a local tended when he was moved temporarily to another squadron.

Still in his teens, diplomacy was not Albert's strongest card and he would often speak his mind. The stress of his aerial combat was taking its toll: 'Although my nerves are quite good, I really do want a rest from all this work… I always feel tired.' Brigadier General Higgins may not have been too impressed when the 19 year old pilot demanded some time off to rest. To his chagrin, Ball's 'reward' was to be downgraded to 8 Squadron which was involved with reconnaissance and bombing which meant he could no longer work in isolation as a 'lone wolf' and now had to work again with an observer- it was 'a rotten job' as far as he was concerned and 'I am feeling in the dumps.' For those closer to him like Major Hubbard, Commander of 11 Squadron, it was a case of managing Ball in the right way: 'He is young, so naturally wants a little more rope than the older pilots.'

Albert building his hut in France
From Captain Ball V.C. by Briscoe and Stannard 1918

His stock rose in a hair-raising 'spy drop' when he landed a plane in German territory after dodging attacks by three enemy aircraft. The French spy 'Monsieur Victor' refused to leave the plane, as he considered that Ball had probably attracted too much attention. He landed three more times but the spy still refused to move!

Higgins and the R.F.C.'s overall Commander, Sir Hugh Trenchard, were impressed by his doggedness and Ball was recalled to 11 Squadron- it was the perfect 20th birthday present and in a letter home his relief at linking up again with his old squadron was palpable: 'Hello, I am back again in my dear old hut… my garden is fine. I went up again and attacked five Hun machines… I have got one of the latest Nieuports and, oh, it is nice to be without a passenger again.' It was a special birthday as he also received news of his promotion to temporary captain.

By the end of August he had accounted for 19 enemy aircraft and had achieved the first 'hat trick' by an R.F.C. pilot of German aeroplanes- Roland C IIs. He celebrated by buying a gramophone and played along on his violin to Schubert's *Unfinished Symphony*.

He was granted two weeks leave in September and on his return to Nottingham was fêted as a national hero. Heroic deeds of courage and gallantry were officially recognised. He was awarded a Distinguished Service Order on 26 September 'for conspicuous gallantry and skill. Observing seven enemy machines in formation, he immediately attacked one of them and shot it down at 15 yards range. The remaining machines

Trappings of fame- a weary-looking Albert Ball had become a household name by Argent Archer National Portrait Gallery P657

retired. Immediately afterwards, seeing five more hostile machines, he attacked one at about 10 yards range and shot it down, flames coming out of the fuselage. He then attacked another of the machines, which had been firing at him, and shot it down into a village, when it landed on top of a house. He then went to the nearest aerodrome for more ammunition, and, returning, attacked three more machines, causing them to dive under control. Being then short of petrol he came home. His machine was badly shot about in these fights.'

Two 'Bars' were added to his D.S.O. for diving in amongst 12 enemy machines in formation and firing a drum of ammunition into the nearest, repelling 'more hostile machines' and for bringing down eight aircraft in a short period, and forcing many others to land. The impression is of a maverick at work- Ball was acting on instinct and in isolation rather than as part of a cohesive unit.

A letter written to his mother on his return from leave reveals Albert's belief in his family, God and duty to his King and Country: 'Really dear, my leave has been so very happy. It is hard to leave such dear people, but you are brave as well as dear and it makes it less hard. It is an honour to be able to 185 fight and do one's best for such a country and such dear people. Mother, I shall fight for you and come home for you and God always looks after me and makes me strong.'

The level of mental strain for R.F.C. pilots continued to concern their superiors and Albert was given a break from the action. He spent the winter months of 1916 to 1917 training new pilots for the fray. The young hopefuls were keen to accept advice the famous 'air ace' imparted. The best method of attack, he taught them, was to fly under opposing aircraft and fire the Lewis machine-gun upwards into the fuselage: 'Manoeuvre for the other man's blind spot, hold your fire until you are on the point of colliding and then hose him.'

Albert, his parents and sister Lois at Buckingham Palace to receive his D.S.O. from King George V on 19 November 1916 From Captain Ball V.C. *by Briscoe and Stannard 1918*

Ball also acted as a consultant to the Lewis gun factory, working to improve the effectiveness of machine-guns used in aircraft. A German counterpart, Werner Voss also engaged in similar consultancy work. Life as a consultant and flight instructor, however, was dull and unrewarding- Albert was desperate to return to the action in the skies over France. At least his exploits were acknowledged by the highest authority in the armed forces. On 18 November Albert Ball, accompanied by his parents, was presented his triple D.S.O. (the first ever received by a serviceman) and M.C. by King George V at Buckingham Palace.

Albert was delighted to join No. 56 Squadron in February 1917 as a Flight Commander. 'God bless you dear' was his parting message to Flora before he and 12 SE5s flew out of London Colney to France at Easter. On the back of a photograph of the machine which he flew to France for the last time, he wrote to his parents: 'Dearest People, This is my machine all ready for France. I will do my best. Your loving boy, Albert.'

He was not a great fan of the new SE5 which he believed had 'turned out to be a dud. Its speed is only about Nieuport speed and it is not so fast in getting up. It is a great shame, for everyone thinks they are so good, and expects such a lot from them. Well, I'm making the best of a bad job!' Nonetheless, he managed to bring down five Albatros DIIIs.

The SE5 machine in which Albert Ball left England for the final time From Captain Ball V.C. *by Briscoe and Stannard 1918*

He was involved during the first week of May in several 'dog fights'. He wrote to his family on 3 May: 'Dearest People, am so sorry that I am not sending you all the letters you so well deserve, but my dear people it is quite impossible but I am doing all I can. My total up to last night was 38. I got two last night. Oh! It was a topping flight. About twenty of the Huns and fifteen of ours.' He explained why he found it difficult to find time to write due to damage to his old SE5 and teething problems with the replacement. The strain was beginning to tell: 'It is all trouble, and is so getting on my mind, am feeling so old now.'

On the same day Albert apologised to Flora for taking so long to respond to her letter: 'I have been having such a poo poo time' he declared with a quaint phrase he used on many occasions.

Like all those serving at the Front he was buoyed by letters from home and on the eve of his death he wrote to his sister Lois: 'Received your topping letter and cake. It is good of you to think of me so much. Well I made my 42nd Hun yesterday, so am now four in front of the French.' He was referring to Frenchman Georges Guynemer in whose tally he took a keen interest. Albert was eager to be the first of any air force to record 50 'victories', ahead of his 'rivals' Guynemer and the German air aces Oswald Boelcke and Werner Voss.

He expressed disappointment that his name had not been drawn out of a hat for leave which he considered 'a bit hard' as the new intake of pilots had not seen much action nor had they 'got any Huns.'

He was dreaming of a settled and idyllic future with Flora: 'O won't it be nice when all this beastly killing is over and we can just enjoy ourselves and not hurt anyone.' He admitted to his father that he was being looked after by God but 'O I do get tired of always living to kill, and am really beginning to feel like a murderer. I shall be so pleased when I've finished.'

While the Battle of Arras was raging on the ground below on 7 May, 56 Squadron was ordered to provide air cover for troops in the Cambrai and Douai sectors. Captain Ball commanded an eleven strong patrol against a group of Albatros DIIIs. Mystery surrounds the exact nature of his death. It was a propaganda coup for the Germans and Lothar von Richthofen, the brother of the infamous 'Red Baron', claimed that he personally brought down Ball's plane. The weight of evidence, however, points to the likelihood that the young British flying ace became disorientated when flying through a bank of low dark cloud, lost control and crashed. Von Richthofen was on leave at the time and his claim to have shot down a 'triplane' has been invalidated because Ball was flying a biplane. As there were no bullet holes on Ball's SE5, the cause of death was in all probability caused by pilot error; tiredness may have been a factor. Another possibility is that he ran out of fuel- a full tank would last little more than two hours and he had in the past gambled on the contents of his fuel tank.

Albert Ball died of wounds associated with a crash: a broken back and crushing of the chest. In keeping with his reputation as a dashing 'young Romeo', he died in the arms of a young French girl, Cécile Deloffre, who ran to his aid on hearing the crash. He was buried by the German authorities with full military honours and unusually, in a wooden coffin, on 9 May 1917 in the German extension of the communal cemetery at Annoeullin. Albert Ball's grave is the only one of an allied serviceman in the cemetery and still the family of Cécile Deloffre place flowers on his grave every year on 7 May.

Newspapers like *The Nottinghamshire Weekly Dispatch* clung to the hope that Ball had been taken prisoner. Hopes were dashed when news of 'the brilliant young airman's' death was disseminated in messages dropped over British lines and 56 Squadron's airfield by German aircraft.

Albert Ball was awarded a posthumous V.C. for 'conspicuous bravery' between 25 April and 6 May 1917. It entailed another visit to Buckingham Palace for his parents who received their son's medal from the King. He was officially promoted posthumously to captain on 7 June and awarded the French Légion d'Honneur. They would have been comforted by the words of Field Marshal Sir Douglas Haig's eulogy: 'The record of his deeds will ever stir the pride and admiration of his countrymen and act as an example and incentive to those who have taken up his work.' **187**

Albert Ball's grave in the German Cemetery at Annoeullin   *J Kerr*

Albert Ball's death was headline news- the bottom photo shows Albert with a casket containing the Freedom of the City of Nottingham   *British Library Board (Daily Sketch)*

Albert and Harriett Ball on 22 July 1917 receive their son's posthumously awarded V.C. From Captain Ball V.C. by Briscoe and Stannard 1918

Albert Ball Senior was knighted in 1924 for his work for charity and local industry. He served two further terms as Mayor of Nottingham in 1920 and 1935 and dedicated himself to the honouring of his son's name. He purchased land at the exact spot where his son crashed, near the cemetery at Annoeullin and erected a simple stone monument in his memory. In Church Street, Lenton, he built eight 'Albert Ball Memorial homes for widows of servicemen'. Albert's mother was so affected by losing her son that she reputedly never mentioned him by name up to her death in 1931. Flora Young married in 1925.

Nottingham City Council set up a subscription fund in 1920 which raised enough to commission a fine statue of the young air ace by Henry Poole which stands in the grounds of Nottingham Castle.

In a letter of condolence to Albert's parents written on 19 May 1917, a Lieutenant Wood declared that their son 'put up a glorious fight, a fight that should be written in red letters when the history of the war is published. He was only a little chap, and the jolliest and most modest little fellow imaginable. But he could not go on for ever.'

Albert Ball was one of the great swashbuckling heroes of the Great War, a kind young man of integrity and honour, whose courage and fearlessness were even acknowledged by his German enemies.

The 'Albert Ball Memorial Homes' in Nottingham paid for by Albert Ball senior A Hamilton

The procession through Nottingham to St. Mary's Church, where a Memorial Service was held on 10 June 1917
From Captain Ball V.C. by Briscoe and Stannard 1918

ALBERT BALL V.C.:

Born:	16 August 1896, 301 Lenton Boulevard, Lenton, Nottingham, son of Albert and Harriett Ball
Education:	Lenton Church School, Grantham Grammar School, Nottingham High School and Trent College
Occupation:	Trainee electrical engineer, Universal Engineering Works, Nottingham
Unit/ Regiment:	2/7 (Robin Hood) Sherwood Foresters (Notts and Derby) then North Midland Division Cyclist Company and finally the Royal Flying Corps
Rank:	Captain
Died:	7 May 1917
Age:	20
Decorations:	V.C., D.S.O. and two Bars, M.C., Légion d'Honneur (France), Order of St. George (Russia)
Buried:	Annoeullin Communal Cemetery, German extension, grave 643. The cemetery was started in October 1915 and contains 1,600 German burials. Albert Ball's grave is the only British one

German Cemetery at Annoeullin, the field in the background is where Albert Ball crashed J Kerr

JOHN KIPLING

'This will be my last letter most likely for some time...
Well so long old dears'

On 27 September 1915 2nd Lieutenant John Kipling was a member of a small group of Irish Guards who advanced with a unit of Scots Guards at 6.30 pm on Puits 14, a German position near the mining village of Loos. They were met by a hail of machine-gun bullets. The last recorded sighting of the young subaltern and his batman was near a red-brick house. Both men were never seen again.

Like hundreds of other young officers killed on the Western Front, John had attended a Public School and after leaving, was caught up in the prevailing mood of euphoria and enlisted enthusiastically.

He attended Wellington College in Berkshire, founded in 1859 in memory of the great military Duke and dedicated to preparing its pupils for a career in the Army. His two years at Wellington between 1912 and 1913 were unspectacular. Academically he achieved little and displayed limited talent on the College's sports fields. He suffered from regular bouts of ill-health and was chronically myopic. His final school report baldly stated that he had been 'in the middle school and reached no position of responsibility.' Family members, however, considered he was witty and 'quick on the uptake'.

When only 17 years old he received his preliminary training at Warley in Essex with the Irish Guards and reported to his parents that: 'This is the life' and despite his tender years and lack of leadership experience, he wrote that the men in his platoon were 'behaving splendidly and the weather is top hole.'

John Kipling would have been just another statistic, another casualty in a war that wiped out thousands of young men cut off in the prime of their lives: each a gut-wrenching tragedy for their families to face. What set him apart from most members of the British Expeditionary Force who were killed was the overbearing fame of his father Rudyard Kipling: novelist, poet, staunch supporter of the British Empire and pro-war propagandist. Kipling's son would suffer from a huge burden of expectation placed on his slender shoulders.

2nd Lieutenant John Kipling

Kipling and his wife Carrie had lost their first-born, Josephine, in 1899 which may explain his obsessive and suffocating relationship with John. Before the outbreak of hostilities Rudyard Kipling had exhorted 'every fit young man to come forward and enlist and every young man that chooses to remain at home should be shunned by his community.' Imagine Kipling's dismay when John's attempt to enlist in the Army was thwarted because of his poor eyesight.

Kipling the imperialist and nationalist could not risk the personal humiliation of his own son watching the War from the sidelines. He proceeded to pull every string available to him to secure a commission for his son. The celebrity accorded to the author of the *Just So Stories*, *Jungle Books* and poems like *If* had the desired effect- there was cause for optimism when Sir Edward Ward, Under Secretary for War, agreed to write a letter on young Kipling's behalf to the Head of the Physical Examining Board but John proceeded to fail his medical for a second time. Undaunted, Kipling senior took the case to his friend Lord Roberts, a Victorian military hero and Colonel of the Irish Guards who offered to nominate John for a commission in the Regiment. Father and son were delighted with the outcome and in September 1914 John began his military training.

His excitement at being sent to the Front in August 1915 was tempered by the news that his good friend Oscar Hornung had died in the Ypres Salient on 6 July (he is commemorated on the Menin Gate). It was a death that rang alarm bells with his mother who feared the same could happen to her son.

John's letters home reflect a growing self-confidence. He chided his father for his views on the campaign and made the point that his commanding officer in the Irish Guards was a greater expert on trench warfare than his father!

Suffering from the appalling state of the flooded trenches, John made it clear that he wished to receive a parcel from his parents that contained an oilskin coat rather than another one of underwear. His final request was for a 'really good pair of slippers'.

The letter he wrote home on the eve of the Battle of Loos on 25 September is confident and bullish: 'This is the great effort to break through and end the war... We have to push through at all costs, so we won't have much time in the trenches, which is great luck. They are staking a tremendous lot on this great advancing movement as if it succeeds the war won't go on for long. You have no idea what enormous issues depend on the next few days! This will be my last letter most likely for some time... Well so long old dears. Dear Love, John.'

His prediction, or more likely that of his superiors, about the swift outcome of the War was, of course, to prove wide of the mark. Ironically his death spared him further time in the trenches. Enemy fire ensured it was his last letter to the 'old dears'.

The news of John's death may have been passed on to Kipling by his friend the Conservative Party leader Andrew Bonar Law who is reputed to have reported that, on hearing the news, Rudyard Kipling uttered 'a curse like the cry of a dying man'.

The Kiplings never recovered from their tragic loss and spent the rest of the War clinging to the forlorn hope that John might have been captured by the Germans. Carrie Kipling wrote: 'I cry for some confirmation, some real proof that John is dead.' Rudyard was more realistic; he knew what effect an exploding shell could have on a body lying in the open and admitted to himself in 1919 that John was 'probably wiped out by the shell fire'.

The Kiplings received copious messages of sympathy from the 'great and the good'- their journalist friend H.T. Gwynne reported in the *Morning Post* that John Kipling was 'missing, believed killed. He was the child for whom his father wrote the *Just So Stories*... was barely eighteen, a boy of delicate health but indomitable zeal and resolution... the sympathy of the whole Empire will go out to Mr and Mrs Rudyard Kipling in their sorrow.' Gwynne's insinuation that John Kipling's death could have been avoided if his father had not pushed so hard for a commission, nagged at Kipling's conscience for the rest of his life.

The following year, his poem *My Boy Jack* was a painful *cri de coeur*, addressed to his son:

My Boy Jack

"Have you news of my boy Jack?"
Not this tide.
"When do you think that he'll come back?"
Not with this wind blowing, and this tide.

"Has anyone else had word of him?"
Not this tide.
For what is sunk will hardly swim,
Not with this wind blowing, and this tide.

"Oh dear, what comfort can I find?"
None this tide,
Nor any tide, except he did not shame his kind-
Not even with that wind blowing, and that tide.

Then hold your head up all the more,
This tide and every tide;
Because he was the son you bore,
And gave to that wind blowing and that tide.

The Kiplings received some comfort from their interviews with John's regimental colleagues who told them he was keen and stoical in the face of adversity and had behaved in his final hours of life with great gallantry and had 'handled his men splendidly'. Kipling would have derived some consolation from the gazetting of his son's promotion to lieutenant on 11 November 1915.

By 1919 both parents had accepted the inevitable. Rudyard Kipling now concentrated on two projects in John's memory; he was asked to write a history of the Irish Guards and was invited to play a role with the Imperial War Graves Commission which had received a Royal Charter in April 1917.

Sadly for the Kiplings they were unable to locate their son's body for, like all parents in a similar situation at the time, they were desperate for a tangible memorial to what Rudyard 'treasured most'. It was a poor substitute but in August 1930 Kipling unveiled the carving of John Kipling's name on the Loos Memorial at Dud Corner Cemetery.

During the 1920s Kipling made a significant contribution to the Imperial War Graves Commission with inscriptions like 'Their name liveth for evermore' on Stones of Remembrance in cemeteries with more than 400 burials and 'A Soldier of the Great War Known unto God' for gravestones of unidentified soldiers.

Rudyard Kipling of the Imperial War Graves Commission accompanies King George V on a visit to a cemetery in 1922
Daily Sketch National Portrait Gallery x36220

John Kipling's name on the Loos Memorial   J Kerr

Obsessive and exhaustive efforts were made to find the location of their son's body but to no avail. It was a surprise, therefore, when the Commonwealth War Graves Commission announced in 1992, that the grave for an unknown 'lieutenant of the Irish Guards' in St. Mary's A.D.S. Cemetery near Loos was in fact that of John Kipling. The headstone was altered to 'Lieutenant John Kipling, Irish Guards'.

The Commission's decision has been questioned by Great War historians Tonie and Valmai Holt in *My Boy Jack?* in which they documented the Kiplings' search for their son and have made a cogent case against the 'discovery' of John Kipling's grave in 1992. They argue that their study of letters, military records and maps point to the grave being the final resting place of Lieutenant Arthur Jacob of the London Irish Rifles who went missing on 25 September 1915. The original burial search party in 1919, the Holts believe, found the body of a lieutenant of the London Irish Rifles and not the Irish Guards. They also make the point that John Kipling would have been considered a 2nd lieutenant when he died as it was not until 11 November 1915 that he received a posthumous promotion to the rank of a full lieutenant.

A grave originally of an unknown lieutenant of the Irish Guards: it was established in 1992 by the C.W.G.C. to be John Kipling's   J Kerr

It is doubtful that we will ever know whether the grave at St. Mary's A.D.S. was John Kipling's or if his name on the Loos memorial at the Dud Corner Cemetery is the correct form of commemoration. What cannot be disputed is that the story of John's relationship with his father, the manner of his death and its effect on his father are heart-rending.

JOHN KIPLING:

Born: 17 August 1897, son of Rudyard and Carrie Kipling of Bateman's, Sussex

Education: Wellington College, Berkshire

Career: School leaver

Unit/ Regiment: 2/ Irish Guards

Rank: Lieutenant

Died: 27 September 1915, Battle of Loos

Age: 18

Buried: St. Mary's A.D.S. Military Cemetery north of Loos, although there is uncertainty as to whether his grave is VII.D.2.
The cemetery started because the Advanced Dressing Station was set up to deal with casualties during the Battle of Loos. There are nearly 2,000 graves, two thirds of which are unidentified. He is also commemorated on the Loos Memorial Panel 9 at Dud Corner Cemetery. The walls of the Loos Memorial surround the cemetery and commemorate over 20,000 officers and men who died in the surrounding area with no known grave. The Memorial was designed by Sir Herbert Baker

Also commemorated: The poet Captain Charles Sorley 7/ Suffolk, died on 13 October 1915, aged 20, Panel 37. One of his most famous poems is 'To Germany'.
A similar case to John Kipling's surrounds Captain the Hon. Fergus Bowes-Lyon of the 8/ Black Watch (Royal Highlanders), the older brother of Queen Elizabeth, mother of Queen Elizabeth II. He died on 27 September 1915 (same day as Kipling) aged 26 and his name appears on Panel 78. When details of his death were provided by his grandson, the C.W.G.C. erected a headstone, A.15, in the nearby Quarry Cemetery at Vermelles with an inscription stating that Bowes-Lyon is buried 'near this spot'

View from St. Mary's A.D.S. Cemetery with Ninth Avenue Cemetery in the foreground and the two slag heaps (double crassier) at Loos in the background   *J Kerr*

ISAAC ROSENBERG

'Artist and Poet'

Private Isaac Rosenberg was killed on 1 April 1918. His remains lay in No Man's Land for over a fortnight until buried, initially, in Northumberland Cemetery near Arras. To his fellow soldiers, he had often cut a forlorn and distant figure; only 5' 2" tall, he was painfully introverted and unsoldierly. His strong cockney accent set him apart from most of the northern-based King's Own (Royal Lancaster Regiment) and his stammer and Jewishness made him a target for bullying. Throughout his 27 years of life Isaac Rosenberg was an outsider and loner, but behind a diffident exterior there lurked a steely determination to overcome the obstacles and hardships he faced throughout his life.

In quiet moments Isaac scribbled poems on any piece of paper he could lay his hands on. Apart from one or two of his commanding officers, most found his poems impenetrable and complex. Fellow soldiers who survived the War would have been surprised to learn that they had been in the company of one of the most highly regarded of Great War poets.

His poems drew on the experiences of the ordinary Tommy at the Front. Officer poets like Brooke, Graves, Hodgson, Owen and Sassoon were less likely to have been tortured in the same way by lice infested uniforms- the problem would have been solved for them by their batmen... In *Louse Hunting*, Rosenberg portrays the feverish efforts of members

Isaac Rosenberg Self-Portrait   *National Portrait Gallery 4129*

of a Highland regiment to kill lice as yet another struggle to be faced; his powerful use of language and imagery bring the 'demon's pantomime' scene to life- the Scottish soldiers remove their uniforms and take them to candles to burn the 'verminously busy' lice to death:

Louse Hunting

Nudes- stark and glistening,
Yelling in lurid glee. Grinning faces
And raging limbs
Whirl over the floor one fire.
For a shirt verminously busy
Yon soldier tore from his throat with oaths
Godhead might shrink at, but not the lice.
And soon the shirt was aflare
Over the candle he'd lit while we lay.

Then we sprang up and stript
To hunt the verminous brood.
Soon like a demon's pantomime
The place was raging.

See the silhouettes agape,
See the gibbering shadows
Mixed with the battled arms on the wall.
See gargantuan hooked fingers
Pluck in supreme flesh
To smutch supreme littleness.
See the merry limbs in hot Highland fling
Because some wizard vermin
Charmed from the quiet this revel
When our ears were half lulled
By the dark music
Blown from Sleep's trumpet.

Rosenberg was also an accomplished artist; when war broke out, he was engaged in a desperate struggle to make a living from his paintings and portraits. However, at the Front, the logistics of writing were easier than painting for which there was need for an easel, paints, brushes and a pot of water: an old envelope and a pencil were all he required for writing poetry. Portrait commissions were available to official war artists like William Orpen and as Rosenberg's reticence and unsociability precluded impromptu portraiture, he was reduced to production of the occasional self-portrait.

The painter's eye for colour is evident in his poetry. The page becomes a canvas and his words paint vivid pictures as in the first verse of *Marching* which includes a 'splash' of four colours. He also successfully conveys the 'sound' of marching feet:

Marching

Marching- as seen from the left file
My eyes catch ruddy necks
Sturdily pressed back,
All a red brick moving glint.
Like flaming pendulums, hands
Swinging across the khaki-
Mustard-coloured khaki-
To the automatic feet.

It was remarkable that Isaac Rosenberg should have become such an accomplished painter and poet in view of his upbringing. His father Dovber was a Lithuanian Jew and pacifist who fled from persecution and conscription into the Russian Army. He planned a new life in America but funds ran out and he and his wife Hacha put down roots in Leeds and more permanently in Bristol where Isaac was born on 25 November 1890 but his twin brother died at birth which may explain some of Isaac's psychological difficulties later in life. The family lived in the city's poor Jewish quarter; Barnett, as Dovber now called himself, was a pedlar who eked out a meagre living, often away on the road for months at a time.

Isaac was a sickly child whose artistic talents surfaced when he spent many hours drawing with chalks on the pavements near his home. In Jewish culture the education of the oldest son was paramount and Barnett and Hacha (who anglicised her name to Annie) were confident that the appropriate schooling for Isaac could be found in London. They moved there in 1897 but life in the East End in the overcrowded Jewish Quarter was a great disappointment. Their accommodation was cramped and insanitary and later Isaac described the area as a 'monstrous mass that seethed and flowed.'

Barnett hoped that his son would become a *rabbi* and was disheartened when his tireless efforts failed to secure a place for Isaac at the Jewish Free School in Spitalfields. He had to make do with the Baker Street Board School which offered classes in Hebrew for the Jewish boys. Isaac's first language was Yiddish but he was beginning to rebel against it and refused to attend after-school Hebrew classes. It was fortunate that the Headmaster, Mr. Usherwood, recognised Isaac's potential and offered him a haven in his study to paint in peace, a welcome break from the depressing 'Gradgrind'- type learning in huge classes that stifled individuality. Usherwood remarked on young Rosenberg's difficulty with forming friendships, a problem that he would never overcome.

Isaac left school in 1904 at the age of 14 to start an apprenticeship at Henschel's, a firm of Fleet Street engravers- a job he found suffocatingly dull. He wrote that 'I am bound, chained to this fiendish mangling machine without hope and almost desire of deliverance.' He craved the freedom of expression that Art provided and in 1907 enrolled for evening classes at Birkbeck College where he won a number of prizes including one for a nude study in oils.

He divided his time between Birkbeck and Whitechapel Library where he immersed himself in the works of Keats, Shelley, Byron and Blake. He found the light and bright library building the perfect antidote to the squalor of the surrounding area. The librarian, Morley Dainow, was a Jew who made a point of satisfying Isaac's insatiable appetite for reading. Despite his social awkwardness, Rosenberg was gradually accepted by a coterie of Jewish intellectuals known as the 'Whitechapel Group' who based themselves at the library. It included the writers Stephen Winsten, Joseph Leftwich, John Rodker and the painters John Amschewitz and David Bomberg. There was a free exchange of political ideas with socialism a popular topic of debate. They were intrigued by Rosenberg- bemused by his

awkwardness but in broad agreement that he was a painter and poet with great potential. Joseph Leftwich acknowledged Rosenberg's influence on their circle: 'His strange, awkward earnestness and single mindedness have had their effect on us.'

Rosenberg was sacked by Henschel's in 1911: a merciful release as far as he was concerned. He could now concentrate on his art and in September commenced studies at the Slade School of Fine Art. Entry to such a prestigious establishment was only possible thanks to the financial support of the wealthy Mrs. Herbert Cohen.

Rosenberg was a conscientious student and moved in the same circles as artists who would later make their mark like the Jewish Mark Gertler and David Bomberg, Stanley Spencer, Dora Carrington and the war artists Paul Nash and Richard Nevinson. Gertler described

Students' picnic at the Slade 1912- Rosenberg is kneeling away from the main group on the left. Professor Brown is back row third from right, David Bomberg in the white shirt, is to his right, Dora Carrington is extreme left on front row, to her left is Richard Nevinson with bow tie and black hat, Mark Gertler is to his left wearing a tie and Stanley Spencer is second from right on the front row
College Collection of Photographs, UCL Library Services, Special Collections

Rosenberg as 'a funny little man' but the Slade students were impressed by his independence of thought and willingness to argue with the redoubtable Professor Brown. David Bomberg believed that during their days at the Slade 'not Augustus John, William Orpen or Sir William Rothenstein would ever presume to argue with Professor Brown.'

A photograph of a Slade students' picnic taken in 1912 highlights Rosenberg's social isolation. He is kneeling a marked distance away from the rest of the middle row. He was at a defining moment in his life; he was questioning his painting ability and his true passion for poetry was now coming to the fore.

He self-published a collection of poems *Night and Day* in 1912 and was introduced to Edward Marsh, a wealthy civil servant who worked for Winston Churchill, the First Lord of the Admiralty. Marsh supported and encouraged 'poor little Isaac Rosenberg', buying some of his paintings and acting as a sounding board for his poetry. For Rosenberg, his patronage was a double-edged sword as Marsh was never comfortable with the unorthodox form and structure of his poetry which he found 'obscure and puzzling'.

Rosenberg's upbringing in poor housing in Bristol and the East End adversely affected his health for the rest of his life; he was rarely free from bronchial and lung problems and in June 1914, hoping to improve his health, he decided to visit his sister Minnie who had settled in South Africa. It was no surprise that his first trip abroad left him 'isolated and lost' but he was enchanted by the brightness of the light which was ideal for painting. Perversely, he appears not to have produced many paintings of note apart from a self-portrait that now hangs in the National Portrait Gallery. He lectured on the development of modern art but considered the colonial backwater 'a barbarous land' and in a letter to Edward Marsh described Cape Town as 'an infernal city by the sea.' He missed the intellectual and artistic challenges of the Arts' world at home and decided to return in October 1915 to London well aware of the progress of the War in Europe.

Private Isaac Rosenberg in uniform
National Portrait Gallery P230

His enlistment in late October 1915 caused a raised eyebrow or two amongst the Whitechapel Group, several of whom were pacifists. It was ironic that Isaac should join up given that his pacifist father had fled from conscription in Russia. The reason for his voluntary enlistment was pragmatic- the War had ended any chance he had of making a living from painting and poetry so it was shortage of cash rather than a sense of duty to his country that explains his acceptance of the 'King's Shilling'. He had always been closer to his mother than his itinerant father and it was his intention that she should receive half his pay.

He hoped to join the Royal Army Medical Corps but was too short- like the Souls brothers (see p.147) Rosenberg was below the Army's 5' 3" minimum height limit but 'Bantam' battalions had been created to increase manpower by recruiting able-bodied men who were below the height limit. He joined the 'Bantam' 12/ Suffolks and training began at the Bury St. Edmunds Army camp. He was unimpressed. Letters to family and friends were a litany of grumbles, particularly about the food. Nor was he impressed by his fellow recruits whom he described as 'a horrible rabble'. The mind-numbing training was, as for so many others, a trial. The route marches and drills drove him to distraction. It would appear though, that the Army's food and exercise regime did improve his health and there was talk of a promotion to the rank of lance corporal but he decided not to join a system he despised: 'Believe me', he wrote in early 1916, 'the army is the most detestable invention on this earth and nobody but a private in the army knows what it is like to be a slave.' Isaac's sense of isolation was heightened by regular instances of anti-semitism.

As the War progressed and losses mounted, measures taken to bolster under strength units meant that many soldiers like Rosenberg were never sure of which regiment they would be attached to. During his 2 ½ years in the Army, he received training with the 12/ Suffolks followed by the 12/ South Lancs and his first posting to the Front was with the 11/ King's Own (Royal Lancaster Regiment) in June 1916. Thanks to Edward Marsh's contacts, Rosenberg temporarily escaped action in the front line when he was attached in May 1917 to the 40th Division's Works Battalion and with the Royal Engineers.

Rosenberg's thoughts invariably turned to his poetry. When in the war zone, he welcomed quiet moments when he could weave his ideas and images into poems. One of his most powerful pieces

Break of Day in the Trenches uses a 'sardonic rat', a symbol of darkness, to grin mockingly at the human cruelty being perpetrated on 'the torn fields of France' where bloody death is symbolised by the poppy. The rat is free to travel between English and German trenches, an impartial and 'cosmopolitan' observer:

Break of Day in the Trenches

The darkness crumbles away
It is the same old druid time as ever,
Only a live thing leaps my hand,
A queer sardonic rat,
As I pull the parapet's poppy
To stick behind my ear.
Droll rat, they would shoot you if they knew
Your cosmopolitan sympathies.
Now you have touched this English hand
You will do the same to a German
Soon, no doubt, if it be your pleasure
To cross the sleeping green between.
It seems you inwardly grin as you pass
Strong eyes, fine limbs, haughty athletes,
Less chanced than you for life
Bonds to the whims of murder,
Sprawled in the bowels of the earth,
The torn fields of France.
What do you see in our eyes
At the shrieking iron and flame
Hurled through still heavens?
What quaver- what heart aghast?
Poppies whose roots are in man's veins
Drop, and are ever dropping;
But mine in my ear is safe-
Just a little white with the dust.

More romantic inhabitants of the natural world were Rosenberg's larks. In *Returning, We Hear the Larks*, the larks shower music on 'soldiers' upturned listening faces.' They provide a beautiful interlude, a break from the sinister threat of deathly shells that 'drop from the dark.'

Returning We Hear the Larks

Sombre the night is:
And, though we have our lives, we know,
What sinister threat lurks there.

Dragging these anguished limbs, we only know
This poison-blasted track opens up on our camp-
On a little safe sleep.
But hark! Joy- joy- strange joy.
Lo! Heights of night ringing with unseen larks:
Music showering on our upturned listening faces.

Death could drop from the dark
As easily as song-
But song only dropped,
Like a blind man's dreams on the sand
By dangerous tides;
Like a girl's dark hair, for she dreams no ruin lies there,
Or her kisses where a serpent hides.

In *Dead Man's Dump* written in 1917, the author visits Death as a limber driver for the Royal Engineers. The limber cart is loaded high with barbed wire which Rosenberg uses as a symbol of the 'crown of thorns'. It lurches over the dead, crunching their bones. The stretcher-bearer, possibly Rosenberg himself, similarly meets Death when he has 'a man's brains splattered on his face.' Rosenberg's use of language powerfully evokes the effects of Man's cruelty in one of the Great War's most doom-laden poems:

Dead Man's Dump

The plunging limbers over the shattered track
Racketed with their rusty freight,
Stuck out like many crowns of thorns,
And the rusty stakes like sceptres old
To stay the flood of brutish men
Upon our brothers dear.

The wheels lurched over sprawled dead
But pained them not, though their bones crunched,
Their shut mouths made no moan,
They lie there huddled, friend and foeman,
Man born of man, and born of woman,
And shells go crying over them
From night till night and now.

A man's brains splattered on
A stretcher-bearer's face;
His shook shoulders slipped their load,
But when they bent to look again
The drowning soul was sunk too deep
For human tenderness…

Isaac Rosenberg's self-portrait in pencil 1917
Imperial War Museum

Rosenberg received scarcely a fortnight's leave in 18 months at the Front. When he did return to the East End to visit his family in September 1917, he found that they could not relate to him and his experiences at the Front. In that, he was little different to thousands of other soldiers and he was, in a bizarre way, keen to return to the battlefields. The last time they saw him was on 28 September 1917.

Soon after his return to France, he was struck down by bronchial problems and was hospitalised; as a result he missed the Bourlon Wood massacre when the 11/ King's Own suffered heavy losses. As he lay in hospital, he turned his talents to writing poetry and started an ambitious project: *Moses*, a play written in verse.

He recovered but physically frail since birth, his struggle with the demands of war and the challenges of survival and hard work were taking their toll. His creative powers were also on the wane and in a letter to Miss Winifreda Seaton, a middle-aged school mistress from Highgate in North London, with whom he corresponded regularly, he confessed that 'I seem powerless to compel my will to any direction and all I do is without energy and interest.' He was tired of dragging himself through the all-pervasive mud and it was ironic that in view of his Jewish upbringing, he should write that 'Christ never endured what I endure.' He tried without success to transfer to a Jewish battalion heading to the Middle East.

His survival so long was due to good fortune but his luck ran out when in February 1918 the 11/King's Own was disbanded due to heavy losses and was merged with the 1st Battalion which was engaged in front line action. It is unclear as to whether he was out on patrol or defending his trench.

Isaac Rosenberg's body lay silent like those lurched over by the limber driver. At least he received a burial of sorts, one of six out of 11 members of the King's Own killed on 1 April 1918. His and other graves were exhumed and moved from the Northumberland Cemetery to Bailleul Road East in 1926. His family asked that the inscription on his gravestone should describe him as 'Artist and Poet'.

The Great War brought Isaac Rosenberg posthumous fame. His poetry and painting were noteworthy before 1914 but in both genres he would probably have been of peripheral importance. The War gave his poetry an impetus and focus- its darkness and edginess were generated from his experiences at the Front. Jean Moorcroft Wilson, a recent biographer, believes that his success can be explained by his deprived background, lack of formal education and a lifetime spent as an outsider. If he had been Public School educated like Graves and Sassoon, his poetry would, in all probability, have lost its jangling, harsh realism.

Isaac Rosenberg deserves to be hailed as the finest of the British Great War poets- a remarkable feat for a self-educated man from the humblest of beginnings. He may well have been frail in body but in mind and spirit, he was a Judean and English lion.

Isaac Rosenberg's grave in Bailleul Road East Cemetery   *A Hamilton*

ISAAC ROSENBERG:

Born:	25 November 1890, son of Barnett and Annie Rosenberg of 87 Dempsey Street, Stepney, East London
Education:	Baker St. Board School, London, Birkbeck College, Slade School of Fine Art
Occupation:	Artist and Poet
Unit/ Regiment:	12/ Suffolks, 12/ South Lancs, Royal Engineers, 11 and 1/ King's Own (Royal Lancaster Regiment)
Rank:	Private
Died:	1 April 1918
Age:	27
Buried:	Bailleul Road East Cemetery, V.C.12. The grave is a Special Memorial- it has an inscription BURIED NEAR THIS SPOT at the top of the stone
Inscription:	ARTIST & POET
	The cemetery is located near St Laurent-Blangy, north east of Arras and it was begun by the British 34th Division in April 1917. It was designed by Sir Reginald Blomfield and there are over 1,000 burials, half of which are unidentified

WALTER TULL

'Tull is so clear in mind and method as to be a model for all white men who play football whether they be professional or amateur'

One of the book's most remarkable personalities is the professional footballer Walter Tull who played for Tottenham Hotspur and Northampton Town. His father Daniel was the son of a West Indian slave who emigrated to England and settled in Folkestone where he met and married a young Kentish girl Alice Palmer. Walter was only seven years old when she tragically died of cancer and thanks to support from the local Methodist community, he and his brother Edward were raised in a Children's Home and Orphanage in Bethnal Green, London.

Widower Daniel Tull and his family- Walter is seated next to his father and older sister Cecilia. Edward is standing on the left　　*Finlayson Collection*

Walter remained at the orphanage after his brother Edward was adopted by a Glasgow dentist James Warnock and his wife Jean. He trained as a printer but displayed such talent as a footballer that he was signed by Tottenham from 2nd Division Clapton Orient (now Leyton Orient) in 1909, making his home début against Manchester United in a 2-2 draw when he won a penalty. Later in the season, during a game at Bristol City, he was subjected to a shocking level of racism by the home fans. The *Football Star*'s correspondent reported that a 'section of the spectators made a cowardly attack on him in language lower than Billingsgate... Let me tell those Bristol hooligans that Tull is so clear in mind and method as to be a model for all white men who play football whether they be professional or amateur. In point of ability, if not actual achievement, Tull was the best forward on the field.'

Walter was unceremoniously dropped after the game. Phil Vaseli who has told Walter's life story in *Walter Tull, 1888-1918 Officer, Footballer* maintains that 'it is hard to find a football reason for Tull's virtually permanent demotion from the first team.' He speculates that 'the Spurs board, after the Bristol match, felt they should exile the target of the abuse for the sake of team spirit, form and, most importantly, the gate. A loss of form would mean lower crowds would mean less money.'

It was convenient for the north London club that Tull was signed by Northampton Town for whom he played 111 times as a midfielder, scoring nine goals. His football career was interrupted by the onset of war.

Walter Tull in the Clapton Orient team of 1909, seated second from the right
Finlayson Collection

In December 1914 he volunteered his services in response to Lord Kitchener's recruitment campaign and joined the 17/ Middlesex which by 1916 had attracted 122 footballers.

He started his training as a private but adapted to army life successfully enough to be promoted to corporal by the time the 'Footballers' Battalion sailed for France on 18 November 1915. He was based in the war-torn northern area of the Pas-de-Calais. He and his footballer 'pals' were typical in their dislike of the monotony of life 'in reserve' and craved for front line action. The reality of the warfare, however, was rather different. Walter was one of thousands of men worn down by life in the trenches; he suffered from shell shock for which he was treated in an Anglo-American hospital in April 1916 before being transferred to England. In his absence the 'Footballers' suffered huge losses during the Battle of the Somme.

Walter's recuperation lasted until August 1916. By now a lance serjeant, he was assigned to the 23/ Middlesex (2nd Football). His return to France in September was with foreboding and not the enthusiasm of the previous November.

Walter visited his brother Edward's foster mother Jean Warnock in Glasgow   *Finlayson Collection*

The 1914 Manual of Military Law clearly stated that 'a candidate for a commission must be of pure European descent and a British born or naturalised subject.' Walter had impressed his enlightened battalion commander, Lieutenant-Colonel Alan Haig-Brown D.S.O. who recommended him for a commission. They were polar opposites in terms of background, one educated in an orphanage, the other a teacher at Lancing College who had attended Charterhouse in Surrey where his father was the Headmaster.

Walter applied for a commission on 25 November 1917. He was British born but was not of 'pure European descent'; however, by this stage of the War, there was a grave need for more officers. A huge percentage of the predominantly Public School educated 2nd lieutenants, lieutenants and captains had perished in trench warfare. It was they who had led their men when the whistle was blown to 'go over the top'. He was accepted for an officer training course at Gailes in Ayrshire from 6 February to 29 May 1917 and took the opportunity to make contact with his brother Edward. The mixed-heritage orphans, one a professional footballer and army officer in the making, the other a dentist practising in Aberdeen, had plenty of catching up to do.

Walter and fellow trainee officers on the course in Gailes, Scotland   *Finlayson Collection*

Walter graduated as an officer on 29 May 1917, an extraordinary achievement at the time, given prevailing prejudice and his background which was in stark contrast to that of another officer of mixed heritage, George Bemand, whose mother was West Indian. He was educated at Dulwich College and studied Engineering at University College, London. Commissioned as a 2nd lieutenant with the Royal Field Artillery in May 1915, he was killed by a shell on Boxing Day 1916 and buried in Le Touret Military Cemetery, Richebourg-L'Avoué near Béthune.

Walter Tull was immediately commissioned to the Special Reserve of Officers as a 2nd lieutenant. He returned to action with the 23/ Middlesex and took part in the Battle of Messines on the Ypres

Walter's final family visit- he is standing behind sister Cecilia and Edward is behind Jean Warnock
Finlayson Collection

2nd Lieutenant Walter Tull   *Finlayson Collection*

Salient in early June and the Passchendaele Offensive in the third week of September when the 23/ Middlesex played a major role at a cost- 15 men were killed in action, 23 went missing presumed dead and 121 were wounded. Leading from the front, he was lucky to survive.

Walter and the Battalion were sent to the Italian Front in November 1917 where his actions over Christmas and the New Year resulted in a recommendation for the award of an M.C. To his dismay the 23/ Middlesex were recalled to the Somme front line on 8 March 1918. During the Second Battle of the Somme on 25 March at Beugny, the Battalion suffered severe shelling and was forced to retreat. Tull and Lieutenant Colonel Haig-Brown were killed. Walter's body was never recovered but his commanding officer is buried in Achiet-le-Grand Communal Cemetery.

Walter was never awarded the M.C. for which he had been recommended although Northampton South M.P. Brian Binley and Phil Vasili have campaigned for him to receive it posthumously.

Behind Walter Tull's name on the Arras Memorial, there is a history of extraordinary achievement by a footballer and soldier who rightfully takes his place as an icon of black culture and the struggle for recognition and equality. The Memorial records that when Walter Tull was killed, he was an officer in the British Army. Against all the odds, that was his greatest achievement.

WALTER TULL:

Born:	28 April 1888, son of Daniel and Alice Tull of Folkestone, Kent
Education:	Orphanage at Bethnal Green, East London
Occupation:	Professional footballer
Unit/ Regiment:	17 (1st Football) then 23 (2nd Football) / Duke of Cambridge's Own (Middlesex Regiment)
Rank:	2nd Lieutenant
Died:	25 March 1918
Age:	29
Commemorated:	Arras Memorial, Bay 7 The Memorial, designed by Sir Edwin Lutyens, commemorates nearly 35,000 soldiers with no known grave. The sculpture is by Sir William Reid Dick. There is also a cemetery with over 2,650 graves
Also commemorated:	13 V.C.s, the most of any of the major memorials, including the Hull Rugby League player 2nd Lieutenant John (Jack) Harrison, V.C., M.C., 11/ East Yorks, aged 26, died 3 May 1917, Bay 4 Two R.F.C. pilots are to be found on the Flying Services Memorial, Major Lanoe Hawker V.C., D.S.O., aged 25 died 23 November 1916 and Major Edward (Mick) Mannock, V.C., D.S.O. and two Bars, M.C. and Bar, aged 31, died 26 July 1918

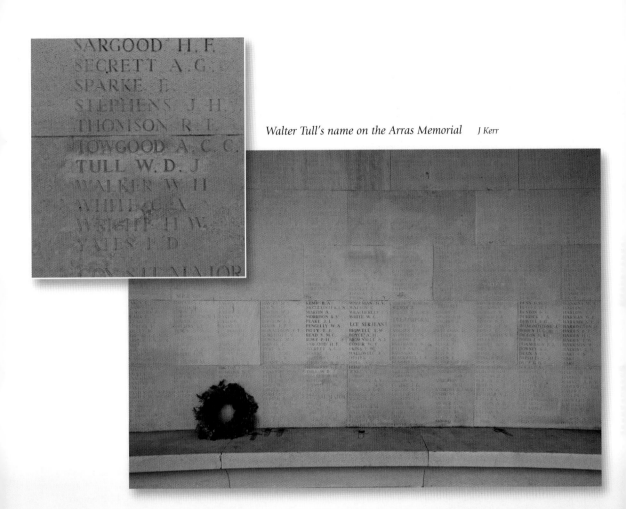

Walter Tull's name on the Arras Memorial   J Kerr

The Arras Memorial designed by Sir Edwin Lutyens
J Kerr

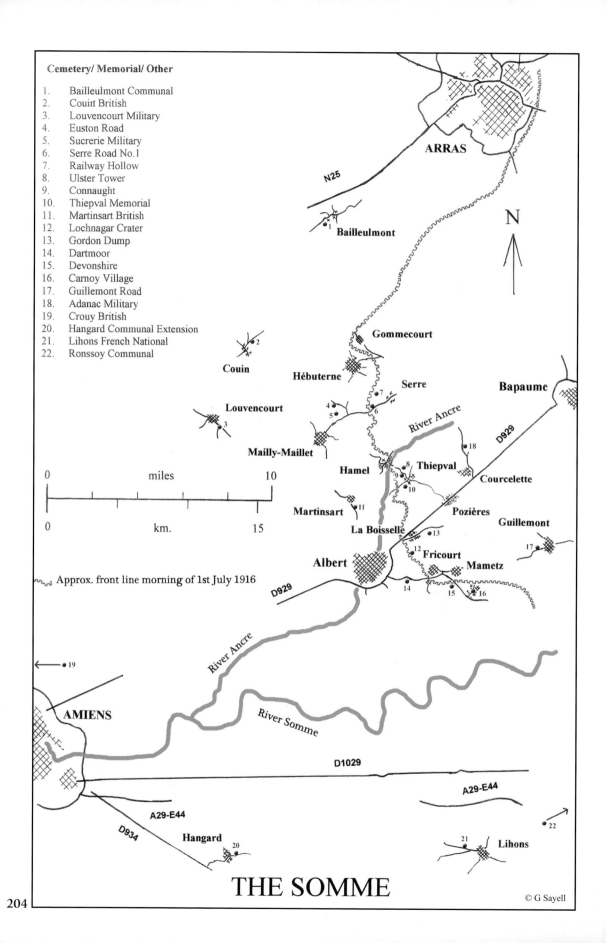

Cemetery/ Memorial/ Other

1. Bailleulmont Communal
2. Couin British
3. Louvencourt Military
4. Euston Road
5. Sucrerie Military
6. Serre Road No.1
7. Railway Hollow
8. Ulster Tower
9. Connaught
10. Thiepval Memorial
11. Martinsart British
12. Lochnagar Crater
13. Gordon Dump
14. Dartmoor
15. Devonshire
16. Carnoy Village
17. Guillemont Road
18. Adanac Military
19. Crouy British
20. Hangard Communal Extension
21. Lihons French National
22. Ronssoy Communal

ARRAS

N25

Bailleulmont

N

Gommecourt

Couin

Hébuterne

Serre

Bapaume

Louvencourt

River Ancre

D929

Mailly-Maillet

Hamel

Thiepval

Courcelette

0 miles 10

Martinsart

Pozières

Guillemont

0 km. 15

La Boisselle

Albert

Fricourt

Mametz

Approx. front line morning of 1st July 1916

D929

River Ancre

River Somme

AMIENS

D1029

A29-E44

A29-E44

D934

Hangard

Lihons

THE SOMME

© G Sayell

204

THE SOMME
Day 4 Itinerary

Thiepval Memorial   A Hamilton

THE SOMME

Day 4 Itinerary

The first stop is the interesting Bailleulmont Communal Cemetery: there are only 34 graves which include as many as three soldiers who were Shot at Dawn. The graves are of the experimental Locharbriggs red sandstone rather than the white Portland stone.

At Couin lies the body of one of the most famous of pre-war actors who suffered one of the more unusual deaths when his parachute failed to open after he jumped out of an observation balloon. Louvencourt is one of the first cemeteries to be designed for the Imperial War Graves Commission by Sir Reginald Blomfield. It includes 76 French graves pleasing to the eye but discontinued due to expense. The central figure of one the most widely read Great War books, *Testament of Youth* by Vera Brittain, is also buried here with a brigadier general, a 'red tab' who was often seen on the front line and died in a forward trench. A miner and poet's final resting place is Euston Road Cemetery. One of the many heart-rending stories in the book was the execution of a shell shocked private sanctioned by a future brigadier general. The young Irishman's grave is to be found at Sucrerie Cemetery. A 16 year old who died on 1st July 1916, the fateful first day of the Battle of the Somme, is buried in Serre Road No.1.

We recommend a visit to a cemetery where a number of Pals were buried: Railway Hollow contains graves of Sheffield and Accrington Pals who fell on 1st July 1916. Close by is the Ulster Tower, a fine monument to members of the 36th (Ulster) Division who were also killed during the Battle of the Somme.

And so to Sir Edwin Lutyens's masterpiece, the Memorial at Thiepval that commemorates over 72,000 soldiers with no known grave. On the never-ending lists of casualties are a musician, a county cricketer who was the inspiration for the name of P.G. Wodehouse's valet and a famous novelist and satirist.

In need of lunch now? We recommend 'Le Tommy' Café which is on the main Bapaume to Albert Road at Pozières where there are realistic and interesting reconstructions of British and German trenches in the back garden.

One of the most fascinating characters covered in the book, an Australian composer, concert pianist and Olympic rowing gold medallist, was buried in Martinsart Cemetery which, like Bailleulmont Communal, introduced red sandstone graves which were later discontinued. A breathtaking experience is to walk round the Lochnagar Crater, the largest British mine crater on the Western Front. A footballer and teacher V.C. can be found at the Gordon Dump Cemetery and the nearby Dartmoor Cemetery contains a number of significant graves- those of a father and son, a New Zealander Shot at Dawn, a V.C. and the oldest British soldier killed in action at the age of 67.

The Somme tour concludes with visits to the Devonshire Cemetery where a poet rests and one of the most visited of graves in the Somme is in the Guillemont Road Cemetery where the war-time Prime Minister H.H. Asquith's son lies. On your way to Guillemont you may wish to pay your respects to Jack the pet dog who was 'billeted' in Carnoy village. One of the unusual V.C. winners, a young Scottish/Canadian piper who played his pipes to encourage men of his battalion during an offensive, is buried in Adanac Cemetery which is 'Canada' spelled backwards.

If you plan to stay at Albert, you will have the chance to see the Basilica and the statue of the Virgin Mary and Child which was hit by a German shell but miraculously remained aloft until 1918 although at an angle. It was known to British soldiers as 'the Leaning Virgin of Albert'.

Cemetery/ Memorial/ Other	Address/Post code/ Google map ref.	Name	Page
1 BAILLEULMONT COMMUNAL	D1, 62123 Bailleulmont, France 50.21275,2.60895	🌺 William Hunt	15
		🌺 Albert Ingham	14
		🌺 Alfred Longshaw	14
2 COUIN BRITISH	Rue de Souastre, 62760 Couin, France 50.13941,2.53346	🌺 Basil Hallam Radford	210
3 LOUVENCOURT MILITARY	2-4 Rue de L'Eglise, 80560 Louvencourt, France 50.08929,2.5037	🌺 Roland Leighton	218
		🌺 Charles Bertie Prowse	225
4 EUSTON ROAD	D4129, 80560 Colincamps, France 50.10181,2.61972	🌺 Will Streets	228
5 SUCRERIE MILITARY	D919, 80560 Mailly-Maillet, France 50.09581,2.6232	🌺 James Crozier	235
6 SERRE ROAD No. 1	D919, 62116 Hébuterne, France 50.09996,2.65718	🌺 Major Booth	244
		🌺 Horace Iles	240
7 RAILWAY HOLLOW	14 Rue de Mailly-Maillet, 62116 Puisieux,France 50.10607,2.65546	✝ 1st July 1916 Pals	233
8 ULSTER TOWER	D73, 80300 Thiepval, France 50.061548,2.680374	✝ Monument to 36th (Ulster) Division	209
9 CONNAUGHT	D73, 80300 Thiepval, France 50.059,2.68065	🌺 James Sayell	42

10 THIEPVAL MEMORIAL	Mémorial Britannique, 80300 Authuille, France 50.05081,2.68569	🌺 George Butterworth	245
		🌺 Percy Jeeves	253
		🌺 Hector Munro ('Saki')	256
		🌺 Frederick Souls	151
11 MARTINSART BRITISH	Les Treize, 80300 Mesnil-Martinsart, France 50.03773,2.63487	🌺 Frederick S. Kelly	260
12 LOCHNAGAR CRATER	Route de la Grande Mine, 80300 Ovillers-la-Boisselle, France 50.01553,2.697226	● 1st July 1916 British mine crater	209
13 GORDON DUMP	Les Champs Malpart, 80300 Ovillers-La Boisselle, France 50.02104,2.70672	🌺 Donald Bell V.C.	271
14 DARTMOOR	4-6 Rue de Bécourt, 80300 Bécordel-Bécourt, France 49.99169,2.68813	🌺 G. and R. Lee	277
		🌺 James Miller V.C.	277
		🌺 John Sweeney	278
		🌺 'Harry' Webber	275
15 DEVONSHIRE	D938, 80300 Mametz, France 49.9883,2.73597	🌺 William Noel Hodgson	279
16 CARNOY VILLAGE	80300, Carnoy, France 49.98578,2.75601	🌺 Jack the pet dog	284
17 GUILLEMONT ROAD	D64, 80360 Guillemont, France 50.01047,2.81579	🌺 Raymond Asquith	287
18 ADANAC MILITARY	D107, 80300 Miraumont, France 50.07415,2.74349	🌺 James Richardson V.C.	295

'The Leaning Virgin' of the Basilica at Albert

Ulster Tower and keeper

Lochnagar Crater   J Kerr

Basil Hallam and 'troop'

MISS ELSIE JANIS.

Elsie Janis, the American actress who played
opposite Basil Hallam in The Passing Show
National Portrait Gallery AX160283

Performing Rights reserved for Theatres, Music Halls and Picture Theatres.

GILBERT THE FILBERT.

SUNG BY
BASIL HALLAM.

IN
ALFRED BUTT'S
Successful Production

THE PASSING SHOW.
(PALACE THEATRE, LONDON.)

Book and Lyrics by
ARTHUR WIMPERIS.

Music Composed and Arranged by

Photo by MOFFETT STUDIO, CHICAGO.

PRICE 2/- NET.

Basil Hallam, actor and star of
The Passing Show in 1914-15

MISS GABY DESLYS AND MR. BASIL HALLAM
IN 'THE RAJAH'S RUBY'

Basil Hallam and Gaby Deslys in 1911
National Portrait Gallery AX160275

MR. BASIL HALLAM

Basil Hallam at the height of
his fame in 1915
National Portrait Gallery AX160184

Basil Hallam Radford

(stage name Basil Hallam)

'Gilbert the Filbert, the Knut with a K'

Basil Hallam took his bow to rapturous applause for his performance in *The Passing Show* revue at the Palace Theatre in London's West End. When he left later by the stage door, he was handed some white feathers, the guilt-provoking symbols of cowardice. It was a tiresome contrast to the reaction of another packed audience and he wearied of the sneered comments about his failure to respond to Lord Kitchener's call to arms. His door-stepping detractors were probably ignorant of the fact that eight months earlier, when war had been declared, he had attempted to enlist but was rejected, due to having had an instep smashed in his foot when only nine years of age which had necessitated the use of a steel plate in his right boot. As only the physically fit were recruited at that early stage of the War, Basil Hallam had little choice but to continue his work on the stage.

He first appeared in *The Passing Show* in April 1914 opposite the beautiful 25 year old American star, Elsie Janis. She had been entranced by him at their first meeting in New York in 1910 when he was playing the Hon. Archie Graham in Cosmo Hamilton's *Blindness of Virtue*. He and a friend, John Ogilvie Davis, were invited to her apartment for tea and in her autobiography she professed her love of their cut-glass English accents and Davis's spats! She considered herself pro-British but 'Basil and Jack put the final strengthening touch on my intention to play England before I married.' Hallam was definitely eligible for the role of marriage despite her disappointment that he was not, as she had hoped, the second son of a Duke, but 'O… an actor.' In her opinion he was 'not only one of the best looking men anyone ever saw, but sartorially he looked like an "illustration of what the well-dressed man will wear."'

When rehearsals for *The Passing Show* began in London, Elsie was unhappy that her leading man, Clay Smith, was too short: 'I liked looking up to men, at least on the stage.' She complained to impresario Alfred Butt who replied that if she could find someone better suited for her taste and dimensions, he would be delighted!

Over lunch at the Carlton, between the *hors d'oeuvre* and cold lamb, she was 'inundated by a brain wave'. She asked Basil Hallam if he would like to play in revue. His expression of horror was such that she realised she might have asked 'would you like to go swimming with a school of man-eating sharks?' Hallam was a classical actor playing at the time in a 'heavy' drama, *The Grand Seigneur*, and the concept of revue filled him with fear and trepidation: 'But, darling, I can't sing or dance!' His concerns were brushed aside and he reluctantly agreed to join a rehearsal and run-through of various numbers, the lyrics written by Arthur Wimperis and the music by Herman Finck. Basil looked at her antagonistically and walked to the piano… he cleared his throat and began:

> *'I'm known about town as a fearful blood,*
> *For I come straight from the dear old flood,*
> *And I know who's who and what's what,*
> *And between the two I'm a trifle hot.'*

He stopped and glared at Elsie: 'I say, I can't do this sort of thing' he complained but Elsie refused to be beaten and urged him to try the chorus:

> *'I'm Gilbert the Filbert, the Knut with a K,*
> *The Pride of Piccadilly, the blasé roué,*
> *Oh Hades, the ladies who leave their wooden huts*
> *For Gilbert the Filbert, the Kernel of the Knuts.'*

Within four weeks Basil Hallam was 'the talk of London' playing 'himself'- the typical Mayfair 'dandy' or 'nut'. Gilbert the Filbert's title song became a favourite, whistled and sung throughout the land and later at the Front. The reviews were ecstatic. Elsie wrote on 21 April that 'the papers are wonderful! They say I have the biggest hit in years… he has made a big hit too.'

Elsie and Basil were both stars and in love: 'And so night after night he came back with us, I cannot find many nights in my diary during the six months we played at the Palace Theatre when Basil did not bring us home and have a bite of supper.' A compulsive socialiser he would then go on 'to Lady "Whatnot's" dance, making a late but interesting entrance at about 1.00 a.m. … I can feel Basil's arm round me as we "browsed" in the moonlit garden.' On one occasion when they returned to a houseboat Elsie had hired at Datchet on the Thames, her mother remarked when they were in a nearby rose garden, 'Come in, you two! Don't you see enough of each other all evening?'

Basil Hallam Radford (Hallam was his stage name) was an unlikely star of the stage. His father, Walter Hallam Radford, a merchant and master of the Ironmongers Company, sent his son to Charterhouse, the Public School in Surrey with a view to him going into the City. In his report on leaving in 1907, he was graded 50th in Mathematics and 36th in French out of a year group of 53 boys. His sporting exploits were more impressive. He played football for his house team and was a semi-finalist in a rackets competition (a much faster version of squash played in a court three or four times the size and played with bullet-hard balls.) He was a member of the School Fire Brigade which was an elected and much respected group.

Despite the weakness of his Maths and French, obituaries suggested he went to Oxford University. The University Archives, however, have no record of him having matriculated there! He might have attended a 'crammer' of some sort in the city.

His heart was set on becoming an actor and, according to E.B. Osborn in *The New Elizabethans*, after a dentist's appointment in London, he visited Her Majesty's Theatre and managed to secure an audition with the theatre manager who, unbeknown to him, was the famous actor and theatre manager, Sir Herbert Beerbohm Tree. He was asked to recite some passages from *Hamlet* which he performed well enough to be offered some minor Shakespearean parts in 1908, including Pistol in *The Merry Wives of Windsor* at the Palace Theatre. His father was underwhelmed by his son's choice of career. Elsie Janis wrote that 'Basil took his dramatic acting very seriously; however, his family took his being on the stage as something that should be locked away with the family skeleton!'

Elsie Janis left *The Passing Show* on 14 September to return to America. Her role was taken by the French actress Gaby Deslys alongside whom Basil did not wish to play: she was 'a little French so-and-so and I shall loathe playing love scenes with anyone but you, darling…' Elsie once remarked that 'Ladies not only left their wooden huts for him, but were willing to leave their husbands!' so it did not come as a surprise to her when Gaby, 'one of the most attractive women I have ever met' should have cast a spell over 'Bazzeel' as she would huskily call him and that they would become more than 'just good friends' during Elsie's absence in America.

Basil Hallam's appeal was such that he was never short of female admirers like Diana Manners, the young socialite daughter of the Duke of Rutland, who described him as 'her little stick of barley sugar'. According to Philip Ziegler, she fell for his 'dreamy charm' and after parties, he 'would linger and take Diana home in the early hours professing his love.' In her autobiography, she admitted that 'I should have liked to have danced all night with Basil Hallam, being a little in love with him.'

Elsie returned to the second edition of *The Passing Show* in January 1915. Remarkably, she was prepared to forgive Basil for his *peccadillo* with Gaby; she exonerated him by saying: 'After all, the Gabys of the world play a very definite and important role in life, and if I don't care to compete in that line, then it is up to me to sit firmly on my pedestal and not be too observant!' She decided, however, that she would not 'send him to too many parties alone!'

The pressure on Basil to enlist was mounting. Diana Manners received a letter asking: 'Is it you or your sister who is most responsible for keeping shirkers and cowards like Basil Hallam from fighting for his country? You are no better than a traitress!' Elsie observed that 'practically every man I knew was in uniform and I saw at once that Basil felt that he should be.' His dressing room was often full of his friends on leave from the Front who argued that the theatre was such a treat and relaxation for them and someone had to 'carry on' entertaining. They comforted him with the thought that his bad foot would not stand up to the training he would have to undertake. He would be mollified momentarily but every time the Germans 'turned a new trick' like the use of poison gas, the sense of guilt overwhelmed him.

The sinking of the *Lusitania* on 7 May 1915 certainly hardened Elsie's attitude towards the Germans. She had sailed on the liner on many occasions and was horrified by the loss of crew and friends, like the multi-millionaire industrial magnate and banker Alfred Vanderbilt who, she noted, had chivalrously handed his lifebelt to an old lady. Hallam was talked out of resignation on a number of occasions but on 10 May he finally handed in his notice. His final curtain call was an emotional affair for Elsie: 'They loved him for going and they loved me for refusing to play with anyone else… They knew our love scenes in the theatre were continued in the home! Basil recited "Where are you, God" holding my hand, and I never want to hear cheers and tears mingle again as they did that last night.'

Similar to so many who answered the call, Basil Hallam Radford was not cut out to be a soldier: 'He didn't want to fight, poor boy! He was "Peace personified."' Basil told Elsie that 'I don't mind being killed but I don't want to be maimed. Darling, I couldn't face life if I couldn't be on the stage.' Elsie was proud of her Basil in uniform and as his departure became imminent, they were now seriously discussing marriage. After many long and 'loving' talks they decided to wait until the following spring when they predicted the War would be over and 'we would have our own theatre.'

Elsie and her mother left Basil standing on the platform of Euston Station on 24 July 1915, 'chin up, blue eyes clear and fearless.' In her hand she held a photograph he had posed for in his uniform and on the back he had written: 'If we still love those we lose, can we ever quite lose those we love?'

Basil Hallam Radford was a celebrity and according to E.B. Osborn 'at the outbreak of war, Gilbert the Filbert was the most popular character on the English stage.' His decision to enlist was a great fillip to the recruiting authorities. Initially he joined Motor Transport but was considered fit enough to join the Royal Flying Corps Kite Balloon Section; his training started on 23 August at Roehampton and he was commissioned on 20 September as a 2nd lieutenant.

Elsie left for America to play vaudeville at the Palace Theatre in New York. The show *Miss Information* opened on 3 January 1916 and broke a house record. She returned to England in April and played a number of benefits for soldiers in hospitals and camps. Her presence would have been a much needed tonic for Basil who had been on sick leave, staying at his parents' home in Park Crescent, Regent's Park, for several weeks under treatment by a Dr. Swan for colitis. He returned to the Front before she arrived and she was excited to hear that he was due home on leave in July so she rented the houseboat at Datchet again and made plans for 'doing a bit of "forgetting" under those willows on the Thames.' Her hopes were dashed when he informed her that all leave had been cancelled. He assured her in August that 'I'm not deaded yet, darling, and as soon as the present "show" quietens down a bit, I will come over.'

Basil may not have been 'deaded' yet but he and his parents had suffered the tragic death of his older brother Maurice, an Army regular and captain in the Royal Berkshire Regiment who was killed on 29 September 1915 at the age of 31. He had been awarded a D.S.O. three months earlier 'for conspicuous gallantry and devotion to duty at Cuinchy on the night of 21 June, 1915, when the Germans pumped gas into a mine in which four of our men were on listening-post. Under direction of Capt. Radford, who displayed great gallantry and resource, the efforts of two N.C.O.s and two men, who bravely went down the mine, were successful in getting the men out. At about 4.15 a.m., on 22 June, following their gas attack, the Germans exploded a mine in front of our own, in which were a serjeant and about eight of our men, but owing to the gallant efforts of Capt. Radford, another officer and a few men, who repeatedly went down among the fumes, all the men were rescued, although the rescuers suffered considerably.' Radford was buried at the Vermelles British Cemetery.

Kite Balloons of the kind Basil was being trained to operate were used by German armies from the outset of the War; the first British ones were not utilised until May 1915 above the Aubers Ridge. Their main functions were to take photographs for mapping where enemy shell and gunfire were concentrated and to plot trench positions. They were flown at 3,000 feet with a crew of two observers. They were soon found to be more reliable than aeroplanes for such work and their worth was acknowledged in 1915; General Munro of the Third Army noted that 'the balloon is an essential adjunct to the aeroplane, providing a permanent observing station from which it is very difficult for guns to remain long concealed' and General Haig of the First Army on 22 October was adamant that 'the experience of this Army shows that the value of the Kite Balloon Sections is such as to justify a continuance of their use.'

'... ugly sausage-like contraptions'   IWM Q011873

Moored to the ground, the ugly sausage-like contraptions were usually flown about three miles behind the lines and in clear conditions their observers would have up to 10,000 yards of vision. They were tethered to a steel cable which was attached to a winch that reeled out the balloon to the required height and they were kept flying by 30,000 cubic metres of hydrogen gas. They were between 50 and 60 metres in length and 15 metres in diameter. In the basket the two observers' equipment included a telephone, binoculars, cameras, a barometer, maps and a parachute each.

Each balloon required an operational crew of over 70 personnel and they were notoriously unreliable; for example in May 1916, there were problems with the winches supplied to one of the Kite Balloon sections. A balloon's unreliability and susceptibility to enemy aircraft meant the life expectancy of the craft was little more than two weeks- they were in effect 'sitting ducks'. German observation balloons were the target of a number of Captain Albert Ball's flying missions in 1916-17 (see p.184) and he was awarded a D.S.O. for bringing one down in the summer of 1916.

An R.F.C. SE5 flying over a British Caquot Kite Balloon above Boyelles on 3 February 1918   IWM Q011906

As an officer Radford would have received a missive from General Headquarters: 'It has been decided that in future each British Kite Balloon employed with the Expeditionary Force will carry in the basket a Union Jack. In the event of the balloon breaking loose, the flag will be flown from one of the after-balancing guys. The flag will be flown when the balloon breaks loose and while it is drifting over the allied area.' In a mind-numbing display of stating the obvious, commanding officers were asked: 'Will you please warn all concerned that a drifting balloon displaying the Union Jack is probably a British Balloon'!

By now a captain, Basil Hallam Radford and 2nd Lieutenant Moxon, were winched up in a stiff wind west of the Ancre Valley on 20 August 1916. There are several contemporary descriptions of the incident. Rudyard Kipling described the incident in his *History of the Irish Guards in the Great War*: 'On a windy Sunday evening at Couin in the valley north of Bus-les-Artois, the men saw an observation balloon, tethered near their bivouacs break loose while being hauled down. It drifted towards the enemy line. First they watched maps and books being heaved overboard, then a man in a parachute jumping for his life, who landed safely. Soon after, something black, which had been hanging below the basket, detached itself and fell some three thousand feet. We heard later that it was Captain Radford (Basil Hallam). His parachute apparently caught in the rigging and in some way he slipped out of the belt which attached him to it. He fell near Brigade Headquarters. Of those who watched, there was not one who had not seen him at the "Halls" in the immensely remote days of "Gilbert the Filbert, the Colonel of the Nuts."'

Major T.D. McCarthy, a serjeant at the time in the 2/ Irish Guards but a major when he recorded the event, adds that 'a man (i.e. Lieutenant Moxon) jumped out at 1,500 feet' and that it had been 'a very exciting incident to watch.'

Moxon landed safely and later wrote Elsie 'a most beautiful letter giving me the details. "I never thought", he said "it would be Gilbert the Filbert who would give me the courage to face death!"' John Davis (he of spats fame) informed her that 'although practically every bone was broken from the impact, his face was untouched and he was almost smiling.'

Kipling's and Moxon's versions were confirmed by a letter written on 22 August by Grenadier Guard Raymond Asquith, the Prime Minister's son, to Diana Manners. 'I cannot end without telling you that the day before yesterday Basil Hallam was killed before my eyes by falling 6,000 feet or so from an escaped balloon. He came to earth in a village half a mile from where I stood... shockingly foreshortened, but recognisable by his cigarette case. His companion descended more gradually by parachute. I saw Edgy Knollys today who had come from burying him. A frightening death even to look at.' It would appear that Davis's account hid from his friend Elsie Janis the true state of Basil's body.

The Rev. W.P.G. McCormick D.S.O. who would bury Raymond Asquith only a month later on 16 September, describes the balloon as being shaped like a sausage and 'as the balloon was drifting over German lines, our guns turned on it and it came down over the enemy lines'. It was presumably brought down in case any sensitive information was on board although it would appear that Hallam and Moxon had conscientiously thrown out anything that might have been of use to the Germans. McCormick recalled that the incident created quite a gloom in the 2/ Irish Guards Mess as 'Baden-Powell had actually been up in that balloon with Basil Hallam the day before.' He was referring to the famous Scout leader who may have been working in Intelligence at the Front.

Captain A. Gibbs M.C. of 1/ Welsh Guards wrote two letters to his mother. In the first, on 20 August, he expressed the hope that the occupants got down safely and confirms that British anti-aircraft guns fired at it. He described the event as 'quite a little excitement and one that is quite unusual.' Two days later, like all the other witnesses, news had reached him that it was Basil Hallam who had fallen to his death. He concluded that it was very bad luck that he should have been killed as he claimed that 'the Ballooning section of the R.F.C. is one of the safest jobs that there are.'

Brigadier General W. Evans C.M.G. D.S.O. of the Guards Division reported that the day before, a German had parachuted to safety after his observation balloon had been 'bombed' and in a letter drew a picture of British Kite Balloons: 'It was a curious sight seeing the balloon crumple up. I suppose it was either hit by an Archie (anti-aircraft gun or gunfire, from a music-hall song with the words 'Archibald- certainly not!') or they slit the bag.'

The type of Kite Balloon manned by Captain Basil Hallam and Lieutenant Moxon on 20 August 1916 with parachutes attached
The Times History of the War 1916

The scenario that would have been observed from the ground on 20 August 1916- in this case a German is jumping to safety   Alex Imrie Collection

In an interview with the Imperial War Museum, V.R.D. Hutting, a wireless operator of 9 Squadron R.F.C., spoke of enjoying a performance by Basil Hallam of 'Gilbert the Filbert' at a Christmas Party in 1915 but his recollections of Hallam's death were hazy.

For the troops on the front line in the Somme, Basil Hallam Radford's death was a major talking point, noteworthy because of his fame and the appalling nature of his death.

Elsie Janis recorded that 'he got his endless "leave" on the 22nd August!' It was an odd farewell in an autobiography entitled *So Far So Good* to the man she had planned to marry and who merited scarcely another mention other than a reference to a visit to Basil's grave at the Couin British Cemetery south west of Arras. Nonetheless it was reported that when she died in 1956, aged 76, the photo of Basil Hallam was still on her bedside table.

Elsie threw herself into entertaining troops at the Front after his death, performing wherever large numbers could be accommodated. Her comedic impersonations and song and dance routines at first boosted the morale of British troops but she was delighted when 'America slipped in to take her share of the burden and glory of the world… From that time on I had but one idea, and that was to get to France and do for our boys what I had done for the others- for I thought, if the Tommies liked me in their own land and were surrounded by their families, what would our boys feel, three thousand miles away from home?'

In true vaudeville style she would start her act posing the question to her assembled audience: 'Are we downhearted?' which received in unison a raucous 'No!' Her effect on morale was such that an American officer was moved to write that 'the British gave their men rum before a battle, the French cognac and we gave ours Janis.' The War was the defining moment for her: 'There is no doubt that with the end of the war came the death of something inside me. I've been pleased with work that I've done and grateful for the success I've had, but the war was my high spot and I think there is only one real peak in each life.'

A Memorial Service was held for Basil Hallam Radford in London attended by Gaby Deslys British Library Board (The Daily Sketch)

It is hard for us to comprehend one hundred years after the event, that a 'celeb' played his part in the war effort alongside his fans who would have been whistling or playing his latest hits. Raymond Asquith in curmudgeonly mood wrote: 'Our band has just arrived and is playing out in the square. It is extraordinary what a difference it seems to make to the men and to all of the officers except me. They stand in the cold for hours listening to it playing "Gilbert the Filbert" or any other nonsense, and talk about it afterwards too as if it were an important event.'

The death of the much loved and famous actor Basil Hallam Radford was appropriately dramatic. His final curtain call was before a disbelieving and horrified audience, not admiring a star performance by an established star but stunned by the hopeless and tragic fall of an unknown observation balloonist to a shocking and instant death.

Basil Hallam Radford's grave in Couin British Cemetery A Hamilton

BASIL HALLAM RADFORD:

Born:	3 April 1889, son of Walter T. H. and A. L. M. Radford, of 25 Park Crescent, Portland Place, London
Education:	St. Andrew's Eastbourne and Charterhouse
Occupation:	Actor
Unit/ Regiment:	Motor Transport and No. 1 Army Kite Balloon Section, Royal Flying Corps
Rank:	Captain
Died:	20 August 1916, Battle of the Somme
Age:	27
Buried:	Couin British Cemetery II.C.15.
Inscription:	THE LORD GAVE

THE LORD HATH TAKEN AWAY
BLESSED BE
THE NAME OF THE LORD

The cemetery, designed by Sir Reginald Blomfield, is 15 kms east of Doullens and was begun by Field Ambulances of the 48th (South Midland) Division in May 1916 and was used during the Battle of the Somme. There are over 400 burials

Couin British Cemetery in the Somme   *A Hamilton*   217

ROLAND LEIGHTON

'It is my duty to be there. I should hate myself if I were not there'

The sun shone on parents and their families as they filed into the chapel at Uppingham School for the end of year Chapel Service in July 1914. When the choir made their way up the aisle, one onlooker, Vera Brittain, recalled many years later that 'there was a thrilling, a poignant quality in those boys' voices, as if they were singing their own requiem, as indeed they were.' There was a dissonant contrast to the ethereal beauty of the choral music- 'a shocking jingoism' pervaded the school at the time according to old boy and war artist C.R.W. Nevinson. It was embodied in the address given by the Headmaster the Reverend Harry Ward Mackenzie before the prize giving in the Memorial Hall, in which he highlighted the words of a Japanese general: 'Be a man- useful to your country; whoever cannot be that, is better dead.'

Within four years, 447 of the school's former pupils had succumbed to 'the Great War that darkens the whole world' and of those, Roland Leighton would attract the greatest attention due to his friendship with the celebrated author Vera Brittain. In *Testament of Youth*, published in 1933, she related the horrifying inevitability of the deaths of three of the boys who left Uppingham after the Speech Day in 1914- her brother Edward, his friend Victor Richardson and Roland Leighton. Her tranquil pre-war world was turned upside down, an experience shared by hundreds of thousands who were forced to face an uncertain future without their loved ones.

Roland had first come to Vera's attention at the school's speech day in 1913 when she had been impressed with several accolades for his academic achievements but in 1914, he swept the board. He was awarded prizes for English Essay, Latin Prose, Greek Prose Composition, Latin Hexameters, Greek

The 'Three Musketeers' in their final term at Uppingham in 1914. Roland Leighton is seated third from the left, Vera Brittain's brother Edward is on his right and Victor Richardson is next to Mrs. Puckle, the Housemaster's wife
Uppingham School Archives

Epigram and Classics. His mother Marie wrote that a bookcase at their home in Lowestoft was 'gloriously rich' with his prizes from the school. He was also captain of Lodge House and colour serjeant in the school's O.T.C.

Roland was invited in 1913 by his school friend Edward Brittain to the family's large house in Buxton, Derbyshire where Vera and Roland's love for each other gently developed. Roland later sent her a copy of Olive Schreiner's *The Story of an African Farm*, as the main character Lyndall reminded him of her. Vera was struck by how Roland 'seems to share both my faults and my talents and my ideas in a way that I've never found in anyone else yet.' By the time war broke out, it was clear that Vera and Roland were in love.

She was excited that he had enlisted but irritated that fate meant that 'women get all the dreariness of war and none of its exhilaration.' 'The Three Musketeers', as the author Marie Leighton called them- Roland, Edward and Victor, were rushed back from their Officers Training Corps camp to concentrate on 'real war'. Marie had been keen to grant her son permission to join the O.T.C.: 'Of course he must join it. It will do him all the good in the world both in body and character' but she wrongly predicted that he was unlikely to 'have to practise what he will learn there.'

Roland Leighton's award-laden schooldays were likely to be replicated thereafter with more glittering prizes. He had been offered the Senior Open Classics Postmastership at Merton College, Oxford but he opted to defer his studies, perhaps with the words of his Headmaster ringing in his ears. He was encouraged by the enthusiasm of his girlfriend who did not know how students at Oxford 'could endure not to be in khaki' and mindful of his mother's exhortation that it would be better for him to have his name on the walls of Uppingham's chapel than 'to live a long, smooth life at home'. He embarked on strenuous efforts to gain an army commission; his mother was 'glad you are where your duty of honour and manhood demand that you should be.' He in turn, told her that a 'life of scholarly vegetation at such a time as this' would be at odds with his sense of duty... 'It is my duty to be there. I should hate myself if I were not there.'

The 'Three Musketeers'- Edward, Roland and Victor in Army uniform in 1915
William Ready Division of Archives and Research Collections, McMaster University Library

Failure was alien to Roland Leighton's nature, so it was a grave blow when he found himself in the same position as Rudyard Kipling's son John, who was initially rejected from active service because of poor eyesight. He wrote to his mother on 21 August explaining that he 'could not see more than the first line of large letters' on a board and he grumbled to Vera that the 'regimental doctor declares that I am practically certain to be rejected on account of this confounded eyesight of mine.' His only chance would be 'to get the special intercession of some influential person.' That influential person was the family doctor, whose report made no mention of his myopia. Now declared fit for service, Roland was commissioned into the 4/ Norfolks but was transferred to the 7/ Worcesters in September 1914.

Vera went up to Somerville College, Oxford in late September to read English Literature. Roland corresponded with enthusiasm and humour- he was, after all, at the start of a great adventure in pursuit of glory. They managed to meet in London for two days over Christmas. Any intimacy was thwarted by the presence of Vera's aunt. They did manage a chaperone-free tryst in Oxford on 18 March 1915, after which he sent her an amethyst brooch as a memento of the occasion which heightened her sense of loss when he was at the Front: symbolic of love and faithfulness, violets would become a recurring theme in their relationship.

Roland left for the Front on 31 March when the Worcesters sailed from Folkestone to Boulogne. Marching via Béthune in the coalmining area of northern France and Armentières near the Belgian border, Leighton and the 7/ Worcesters arrived at Plugstreet Wood. The reality of war soon hit him. He wrote on 15 April to Vera about three German graves located not far from his trench: 'There is no name on them, but merely a piece of board with "German grave- R.I.P." scrawled on it. And yet somebody loved the man lying there' he concluded, with the air of someone not consumed with hatred of the 'Hun'. There was, for him, nothing glorious about trench warfare- it was 'all a waiting and a waiting and taking of petty advantages- and those who can wait longest win. And it is all for nothing...'

A defining moment for Leighton was his first sight of a dead British soldier, hidden in the undergrowth a few yards from the path as he walked up to the fire trench through a sun-drenched Plugstreet Wood: 'He must have been shot there during the wood-fighting in the early part of the war and lain forgotten all the time. The ground was slightly marshy and the body sunk down into it so that only the toes of his boots stuck up above the soil. His cap and equipment were just by his side, half buried and rotting away.' Leighton decided to have a mound of earth thrown over him 'to add one more to the other little graves in the wood.' The sight inspired the poem *Villanelle*. In April he sent Vera four violets that he had picked in Plugstreet Wood:

Villanelle

Violets from Plugstreet Wood,
Sweet I send you oversea.
(It is strange they should be blue,
Blue when his soaked blood was red,
For they grew around his head;
It is strange they should be blue.)

Violets from Plugstreet Wood,
Think what they have meant to me-
Life and Hope and Love and You
(And you did not see them grow
Where his mangled body lay
Hiding horror from the day
Sweetest it was better so.)

Violets from oversea,
To your dear, far, forgetting land
These I send in memory,
Knowing you will understand.

Vera Brittain in her V.A.D. nurse's uniform   *Roland Leighton in uniform*

It was an officer's duty to care for the men under his command. Lieutenant Leighton was popular with his men and was deeply affected by his first loss on 9 May: 'I have been taking things out of his pockets and tying them round in his handkerchief to be sent back somewhere to someone who will see more than a torn letter, and a pencil, and a knife and a piece of shell. He was shot through the left temple while firing over the parapet. I did not see it- thank heaven. I only found him lying very still at the bottom of the trench with a tiny stream of red trickling down his cheek onto his coat.'

Roland was then confronted with another death, of his school friend, co-editor of the school magazine and Cambridge scholar, Roland Garrod, who was killed on 22 May. Vera remembered him playing the 'cello at the Uppingham speech day. She expected he 'little dreamed of his own fate' when he heard the tub-thumping words of the Reverend Mackenzie. Roland was adamant that 'one could not find anyone less of a born soldier than he. A scholar, and a musician and above all a peace lover.' When her term finished, Vera abandoned her studies in Oxford and returned home to Buxton where she volunteered for service in the town's Devonshire Hospital as a V.A.D. nurse.

Vera received a postcard from Marie Leighton on 19 August informing her that Roland was due home on leave. She managed to take time away from her hospital duties in Buxton and met him the following day at St. Pancras station in London; she also managed to schedule a visit to the 1st London General Hospital in Camberwell for an interview which proved successful.

Much of Roland's leave was spent on trains- they took the train to Buxton and during the journey Roland proposed to Vera. She was cautious in her response but eventually agreed to their engagement which was now official- the couple's next journey was to break their happy news to the Leightons in Lowestoft where, on the cliffs, they were able at last, to snatch a few moments to themselves.

It was not long before Roland had to return to the Front and the painfully sad departure was evocatively described by Vera in *Testament of Youth*: 'Too angry and miserable to be shy any more, we clung together and kissed in forlorn desperation.' To her amazement she saw him 'hastily mop his eyes with his handkerchief, and in that moment, when it was too late to respond or to show that I understood, I realised how much more he cared for me than I had supposed or he had ever shown.' A despairing last kiss and as the train started, he turned and walked rapidly down the platform. She watched him move through the crowd... 'He never turned again.' It was the last time she would see him.

The Worcesters were on the Somme near Hébuterne by September. Roland's letter to Vera of 11 September was an angry rejection of his pre-August 1914 view of 'The Beauty of War'; he was now earnestly questioning the reasons for it and the deathly and pervasive shadow that it cast. 'Let him who thinks that war is a glorious golden thing ... look at a little pile of sodden grey rags that cover half a skull and a shin bone and what might have been its ribs... let him realise how grand and glorious a thing it is to have distilled all Youth and Joy and Life into a foetid heap of hideous putrescence.' He concluded by asking if anyone could convincingly argue that 'Victory is worth the death of even one of these.' For her part, Vera conceded that 'this war will only justify itself if it puts an end to all the horror and barbarism and retrogression of war for ever.'

Roland was seconded to the Somerset Light Infantry as an Adjutant in November. When Vera learned of this she wrote: 'Does it mean that they have been clever enough to discover how intelligent you are?' How splendid it would be, she hoped, if he could be more involved with 'the theory of war' rather than 'the dirty work'... but he had returned to the dangers and discomforts of the Worcesters' trenches by 26 November. He painted a picture for Vera of how he could see small mounds of snow through the door of his dugout, glistening under the light of a full moon. Unable to sleep, he wondered what Vera was doing. Asleep perhaps or sitting in front of the fire? He yearned to see her in her blue and white striped pyjamas: 'You are always very correctly dressed when I see you'... There was indeed an aching desire for his fiancée, whom he once saw in a dressing gown with her hair down her back as she played an accompaniment for her brother Edward in the drawing room in Buxton...

Vera's spirits were boosted when Roland wrote to tell her that he would be home for Christmas. Her parents booked a room at the Grand Hotel in Brighton and Roland's parents were by now renting a cottage in Keymer, Sussex having sold their house in Lowestoft.

Vera had to work in the hospital on Christmas Eve but in a whirl of excitement and anticipation, travelled down to Brighton on Christmas Day morning. She was unperturbed when there was no news of Roland's time of arrival. There was a telephone call for her on Boxing Day... 'I dashed joyously in the corridor! But the message was not from Roland but from his sister Clare.' Vera learned that her fiancé had died of his wounds on 23 December 1915.

To help overcome her grief, Vera dedicated herself to piecing together a picture of Roland's final hours. The 7/ Worcesters had taken over new trenches which they found had been poorly maintained by their predecessors the 1/4 Ox and Bucks Light Infantry. The barbed wire entanglements were deemed to be in need of repair and before work proceeded, in the clear moonlight of 22 December, Roland Leighton and a fellow officer left the safety of the trench to inspect them. As a communication trench was flooded, they made their way unwittingly through a gap in a hedge but the 7/ Worcesters had not been informed that the Germans often fired volleys at the gap. Roland was hit by a sniper's bullet. He was hit in the stomach and rescued by his company commander and a serjeant. He was taken by 1/2 South Midland Field Ambulance ten miles to a Casualty Clearing Station at Louvencourt where his dying moments were eased by a large dose of morphine.

The surgeons were unable to cope with the severity of his wounds caused, according to the official record of his death, when 'the bullet exploded inside him and literally blew out his back.' To the surprise of Vera and Marie Leighton, Roland received the last rites from a Roman Catholic priest, Father A.B. Purdie. He had, apparently, converted to Roman Catholicism in the summer of 1915.

Lieutenant Roland Leighton's funeral was held at Louvencourt Church and he was buried in the nearby cemetery. The family and Vera were told by the Lieutenant Colonel that when his body was brought out of the church, 'the sun came out and shone brilliantly.' Leighton's final act had been, in his servant's opinion, foolhardy and Vera Brittain asked in *Testament of Youth* whether it was a case of 'heroism or folly'. She lamented 'Why did you go so boldly, so heedlessly, into No Man's Land when you knew that your leave was so near?'

Officers' belongings were, when identifiable, returned to their families. Vera described the scene at the Keymer cottage when Roland's personal effects were laid out in the sitting room. His mother and sister were 'in helpless distress... Everything was damp and worn and simply caked in mud... The smell of those clothes was the smell of graveyards and the Dead.' Vera now understood only too well what her fiancé had meant when he referred to 'this refuse heap of a country' or 'a trench that is nothing but a charnel house.' Marie Leighton ordered her husband to remove the feotid clothes which she never wished to see again.

Vera was, however, pleased to find amongst the returned kit Roland's leather cigarette case and a photograph of her which had been kept dry by the warmth of his body. She also found his exercise book in which he had written the poem *Hédauville* in November 1915:

Hédauville: November 1915

The sunshine on the long white road
That ribboned down the hill,
The velvet clematis that clung
Around your window sill,
Are waiting for you still.

Again the shadowed pool shall break
In dimples round your feet,
And when the thrush sings in your wood,
Unknowingly you may meet
Another stranger, Sweet.

And if he is not quite so old
As the boy you used to know,
And less proud, too, and worthier,
You may not let him go-
(And daisies are truer than passion flowers)
It will be better so.

The poem came as a great shock. Vera read and re-read it, trying to figure out what he had meant. Was he being realistic about his chances of survival or did he see no future in their relationship even if he did come through unscathed? Had there been a cooling of their relationship evidenced by Vera's letter of 8 November 1915? 'I sometimes feel that little by little the individuality of you is being as surely buried as the bodies of those who lie beneath the trenches of Flanders and France.' Had the horrors of war and the long periods of Roland's absence extinguished their passion which, because of convention, may never have been consummated? Why had Roland converted to Roman Catholicism and why without a word to his mother and fiancée?

Whatever the answers, Vera's loss is plain to see in her tribute to Roland, written in August 1916:

Perhaps
(To R.A.L. Died of wounds in France, December 1915)

Perhaps some day the sun will shine again,
And I shall see that still the skies are blue,
And feel once more I do not live in vain,
Although bereft of you.

Perhaps the golden meadows at my feet
Will make the sunny hours of spring seem gay,
And I shall find the white May blossoms sweet,
Though you have passed away.

Perhaps the summer woods will shimmer bright,
And crimson roses once again be fair,
And autumn harvest fields a rich delight,
Although you are not there.

Perhaps some day I shall not shrink in pain
To watch the passing of the dying year,
And listen to the Christmas songs again,
Although you cannot hear.

But though kind time may many joys renew,
There is one greatest joy I shall not know
Again, because my heart for loss of you
Was broken long ago.

Vera believed that Roland's mother suffered a nervous breakdown. Marie Leighton was desperate to complete her book about Roland, *Boy of My Heart*, as quickly as possible. It was published in 1916 in the form of a conversation between herself, 'Big Yeogh Wough', and Roland, when he was her much loved son, 'Little Yeogh Wough'. 'As soon as the war is over I will come and see you in your bed under French grass. And I will say good night to you there kneeling by your side as I've always done.'

Vera was struck down with measles and confined to a bed in Stockwell Hospital in April 1916. She was too weak to write, 'so I lie here and think about Roland and picture to myself the details of his death over and over again.' She received a letter from her brother Edward about her fiancé's grave: 'I walked up along the path and stood in front of the grave… And I took off my cap and prayed to whatever God there may be that I might live to be worthy of the friendship of the man whose grave was

The Memorial in Uppingham School's Chapel to the 447 ex-pupils who fell in the Great War   *A Hamilton*

before me.' Within three years, the 'three musketeers' were dead; Victor Richardson died on 9 June 1917 of wounds and the following year Edward was killed by an Austrian sniper on the Italian Front, and buried in the small cemetery of Granezza.

Roland Leighton was supremely talented and intelligent. He would have succeeded in whatever happened to be his chosen field, possibly in academe. Thousands of officers died with little recognition of their lives and achievements: his posthumous fame and our knowledge of him are due in the main to Vera Brittain's moving account of the effect of the War on their relationship and of his death.

Vera Brittain married Sir George Caitlin and between the World Wars became an acclaimed pacifist and feminist. Roland Leighton was central to her poignant exposition of how a generation of brilliant young men was slaughtered and buried with their hopes and loves in the 'blood stained mud' of France and Belgium. Her daughter Baroness Shirley Williams wrote that her mother was haunted by the men she had lost and in a preface to her mother's *Testament of Youth* maintained that 'it was hard for her to laugh unrestrainedly; at the back of her mind, the row upon row of wooden crosses were planted too deeply'.

ROLAND LEIGHTON:

Born:	27 March 1895 at 40 Abbey Road, St. John's Wood, London, son of writers Robert and Marie Leighton
Education:	Uppingham School, Classics Postmastership of Merton College, Oxford, deferred due to the outbreak of war
Occupation:	Enlisted August 1914 on leaving school
Unit/ Regiment:	4/ Norfolk and 1/7 Worcestershire
Rank:	Lieutenant
Died:	23 December 1915
Age:	20
Buried:	Louvencourt Cemetery, I.B.20.
Inscription:	GOOD NIGHT THOUGH LIFE AND ALL TAKE FLIGHT NEVER GOODBYE

(from *A Wink from Hester* by the English poet William Ernest Henley 1849-1903)

Field Ambulances were set up at Louvencourt, 10 kms behind the front line. It was one of the first cemeteries to be built after the War and was designed by Sir Reginald Blomfield. There are 151 burials and 76 French graves from 1915

Roland Leighton's gravestone in Louvencourt Cemetery which incorrectly records his age as 19- he was 20.
A Reed

Louvencourt Cemetery contains French graves of a design that was discontinued due to expense
A Hamilton

CHARLES BERTIE PROWSE

'He showed great gallantry in his efforts… exposing himself to great danger'

Brigadier General Charles Bertie Prowse was one of 73 Great War generals who were either killed in action or died of their wounds; a further 146 were wounded. The figures, collated by Frank Davies and Graham Maddocks in *Bloody Red Tabs*, do much to debunk the myth that the 'châteaux generals' rarely experienced front line action. Other documentary evidence supports their findings- the War Diary of the 1/ Royal Warwicks recorded three visits to the front line in the Aisne area by General Rawlinson in late September and early October of 1914; Captain Robert Hamilton of the same Battalion recorded a visit by the General at 6.30 a.m. on 2 October and in 1917, Private George Hewins of the Warwicks recalled that 'you could smell the "Top Brass" when they came to the trenches.'

When war broke out Prowse had reached the rank of major and fought with the 1/ Somerset Light Infantry which was part of the 11th Brigade in the 4th Division. Like the Warwicks of the 10th Brigade, the Somersets in November and December were located near Plugstreet Wood.

Trench maps show that it was common practice for points of interest in the area to be named after noteworthy officers or regiments: 'Poole's Cottage' was named after the popular Major Poole, later the lieutenant colonel in command of 1/ Royal Warwicks and 'Hull's Burnt Farm' after Brigadier General Charles Hull. 'Seaforth Farm' was named after the Seaforth Highlanders who held the line there. 'Prowse Point' was named after an heroic stand on the farm land by the then Major Prowse who was leading the 1/ Somerset Light Infantry in October 1914, an action for which he received the D.S.O.

Brigadier General Charles Bertie Prowse

Prowse Point Cemetery was set up on 14 November 1914 by the 2/ Royal Dublin Fusiliers and 1/ Royal Warwicks and was named after Charles Prowse in recognition of his deeds. 'Prowse Point' remained in use until April 1918 when fighting moved away from the Plugstreet Wood

Prowse Point Cemetery south of Ypres- Mud Lane Cemetery is in the background
A Hamilton

sector. It is unique in the Ypres Salient for being the only cemetery named after an individual. It is 11.5 kilometres south of Ypres and contains 225 burials and was designed by W.H. Cowlishaw.

Charles Prowse was a career soldier. He joined the 2/ Somerset Light Infantry in 1892 with whom he served in the Boer War from 1899 to 1902 after he left Marlborough College. He did so with great distinction, being Mentioned in Despatches three times. He took part in the operations in Natal, Cape Colony, Orange River and Transvaal and was involved in the actions at Ladysmith and Spion Kop.

He was awarded the Queen's Medal with five clasps and the King's Medal with two clasps. His performance on the battlefield merited his appointment as an Adjutant with the responsibility of assisting the commander of the 1/ Somerset Light Infantry- Lieutenant Colonel E.H. Swain.

He fought in the early battles in northern France- at Le Cateau on 26 August when the British Expeditionary Force was forced into retreat and in the Marne and Aisne offensives. He was mentioned in Sir John French's first despatch for saving the British lines at St. Yvon and was promoted to brevet lieutenant colonel, the first brevet of the War. He took on the leadership of the 1/ Leinsters on 19 January 1915 but was swiftly promoted on 29 April to G.O.C. the 11th Brigade of which the 1/ Somerset Light Infantry was part. He commanded the Brigade at the Second Battle of Ypres in late April 1915 and during the battle was placed in command of 15 battalions, three of which were French.

Prowse's rise to brigadier general had been meteoric and as Dr. John Bourne of the University of Birmingham Centre for First World War Studies points out, he had risen from 'a 45 year old junior major to brigadier general in nine months'. Before the War, promotion prospects were limited but as the War unfolded, opportunities suddenly improved dramatically.

The British Army suffered the blackest day in its history on 1st July 1916 in the Somme. There were almost 58,000 casualties including 19,000 deaths. Prowse was in command of the 11th Brigade, entrenched north of Beaumont. Captain G.A. Prideaux in *The Regimental History of the Somerset Light Infantry* recorded that 'at about 9.45 a.m. the General decided to move his H.Q. into the German front line, thinking that it was cleared of all Germans. Just as he was getting out of our front line trench, near "Brett Street", he was shot in the back by a machine-gun in the "Ridge Redoubt" and died in the afternoon.' Prowse had been assembling men of the Seaforth Highlanders and Lieutenant G.A. Robinson of the 1/ Rifle Brigade commended the brigadier general for showing 'great gallantry in his efforts, ignoring the great breaches in our parapets and exposing himself to great danger.'

Brigadier General Prowse's body was recovered thanks to the brave efforts of a Seaforth Highlander, Private W.R. Bailey, who wrote to Mrs. Violet Prowse detailing her husband's final moments. He described how a fellow Seaforth Highlander rushed off to find a doctor or stretcher-bearers and to inform Headquarters: 'I myself did all in my power for my beloved master holding my hand over his wound for quite some half an hour or so to keep the blood in… We then started on a journey back, after we had procured a stretcher, which took a considerable time. It was a terrible journey moving up these small trenches… He was conscious and happy until we reached Divisional Headquarters when he grew weaker. We got to the hospital as soon as possible. He practically died in my arms, breathing his last at the hospital.' Bailey may not have survived the War himself- a Private W. Bailey of the 2/ Seaforth Highlanders died on 4 October 1917 and is commemorated on the Tyne Cot Memorial.

The brigadier general who was awarded a D.S.O. during his time on the Western Front was buried at Louvencourt Military Cemetery amongst other ranks and fate would have it that he happened to be buried near Private Harry MacDonald, a soldier Shot at Dawn for desertion. A regular soldier, MacDonald had, like Prowse, served in the Boer War and in 1915 with the Duke of Wellington's Regiment at Gallipoli. He returned home on sick leave suffering from frostbite. When his pregnant wife fell ill, he requested an extension on compassionate grounds but was refused. He was arrested and sent to France to join the 12/ West Yorkshire Regiment but went absent without leave from trenches near Loos, suffering in all probability from shell shock. The 34 year old father of three was executed by firing squad on 4 November 1916 'for the sake of example'. He was condemned by the Division's Commander, Major General Deverell as 'worthless and a soldier of no fighting use'.

Brigadier General Charles Bertie Prowse was the epitome of the type of tough and audacious officer who led his men with fearless courage in the Great War. He was one of the hands-on 'Red Tabs' who directed operations from the trenches and not a nearby château.

His family suffered a double tragedy as his brother Cecil Irby Prowse of the Royal Navy died aboard H.M.S. *Queen Mary* which was hit in May 1916 at the Battle of Jutland.

Brigadier General Charles Prowse's war record would suggest that he was a 'lion' rather than a 'donkey'- a daring soldier, often in the thick of the action who deserved the accolade of a cemetery being named after him.

CHARLES BERTIE PROWSE:

Born:	1869 at West Monkton, Taunton, son of George Prowse J.P. and Emmeline and husband of Violet of Devizes, Wiltshire
Education:	Marlborough College, Wiltshire
Occupation:	Professional soldier
Unit/ Regiment:	2 then 1/ Somerset Light Infantry (Prince Albert's), 1/ Leinster (Prince of Wales's) and G.O.C.11th Brigade
Rank:	Brigadier General
Decoration:	D.S.O.
Died:	1st July 1916, first day of the Battle of the Somme
Age:	47
Buried:	Louvencourt Military Cemetery I.E.9.
Inscription:	BE THOU FAITHFUL UNTO DEATH AND I WILL GIVE THEE A CROWN OF LIFE

(King James Bible Revelation 2:10)

Brigadier General Charles Bertie Prowse's grave in Louvencourt Cemetery   *A Reed*

Prowse Point Cemetery from Plugstreet Wood   *J Kerr*

WILL STREETS

'We go to meet death grim-lipped, clear-eyed and resolute-hearted'

During his army training, a son wrote home to prepare his parents for the possibility that he might not return from the War: 'Death that some people seem to fear, is but part of life. Why should we sorrow if one goes out in the morning instead of the evening? I know this, that any man, born of a true mother, ought to count it a privilege to die for his country… As Kipling so truly put it "Who dies if England live?" I did not intend to write in this strain. I do not think I have ever done so before. Yet I do it because I know that after the first trial, Mother, you have learned to bear the facts of this phase with stoicism… You have faced life in its merciless demands up to now, and now you must learn to face it in its extreme bitterness… It is the fact that those at home are agonising that makes the soldiers' lot harder. Knowing that the fact (or the possibility) is accepted by you, believe me, I could go to face death as calmly as I used to face the morning's existence. And there is always the chance that one may

William and Clare Streets and their twelve children, Will is in the middle row far right

Victor Piuk

return. But never to go to this crisis would be bitterness indeed.' These moving words were written by Will Streets, a Derbyshire miner, who in September 1914, had answered Lord Kitchener's call to fight for King and Country.

Will Streets was born on 24 March 1885, the oldest of 12 children. His parents, William and Clare, worked hard to ensure that they were all well fed and clothed, demonstrated by a photograph in which Will stands out as the chief sibling.

His father had moved from Lincolnshire to Whitwell in Derbyshire looking for work in the coal mines. He worked a 12 hour day, walking 15 miles in total to and from work. He was a union official keen to secure a fair deal for his fellow exploited miners. Will's parents were staunch Methodists and Sunday chapel played a vital role in developing Will's intellectual skills; he helped with the Sunday School and took children on nature walks.

Had he been offered the chance to further his education, Will Streets would have been an able and conscientious student, but at the age of 14, filial duty meant that he had no option but to work down the pit at the Whitwell Colliery. In May 1916 he reflected in a letter that 'I had dreams, I had ambitions. Because I strove, even in boyhood, after learning, after expression. But because I had love (I am proud to say this) I drowned all my ambitions of a brilliant career and gave my life for my family… I lost what I deserved, a good education, but life gave me something out of her store of experience that many men might envy- character.' True to the contemporary Victorian ideal of self-help, he believed he could better himself through his own endeavours: 'Yet even in that environment, my soul craved for learning, and with limbs aching with physical weariness and pain, I have sat up until the hours of midnight devouring the books that I had been able to buy after many weeks saving my spending pittance.'

Will read the Classics and enrolled on correspondence courses. He obtained a 97% mark in conversational French- all achieved after exhausting shifts underground and in a three-bedroom terraced house with large numbers of children around. It is, therefore, astonishing that he found time to draw, write essays and submit poems for publication; his creative side was encouraged by a local school master. *The Poetry Review* published in 1912 *Truth, an Allegory* about his experiences down the mine. One of the judges was struck by 'the realism with which it dramatically described the frustration of an intellect trapped in a literally inescapable pit.'

His sketch books are full of horses and flowers. Nature is a recurring theme in his poetry. *Sky Lark* written in 1907, strikes a premonitory note of the dreadful events of the Battle of the Somme when soldiers heard the song of sky larks in quiet moments in between the fury of bombardments:

Why seek the blue sky's solitude
To trill the sweetest note?
Where nought of discord can intrude,
And swan-white cloud forms float.
O why not sing where cares abound,
About thy nest upon the ground?'

When war broke out, encouraged by the success of recruitment in Liverpool, two students from the University of Sheffield approached the Vice-Chancellor with the idea of forming a fighting unit. Permission was granted by the War Office and the unit was called 'The Sheffield University and City Special Battalion' and later 'The Sheffield City Battalion'. An advert in *The Sheffield Daily Telegraph* stated that this Battalion was 'intended primarily for Professionals and Business Men and their Office Staff'. Engineers, ex-Public School boys, students and schoolmasters joined but those from other walks of life, such as shop assistants, secretaries and miners, also enlisted. It is tempting to surmise that Will joined the Battalion because of its university and academic connections; in a letter written in October 1914, he mentions three reasons for enlisting- the civilians killed in Louvain the Belgian university town, their pillaged houses and the burning of one of the great European libraries. For Will, 'the fire of freedom and patriotism burns strongly within the British soldier's breast.'

The Battalion was fully subscribed within just two days. Three of his brothers also joined up- Joe in the Sherwood Foresters (Nottinghamshire and Derbyshire Regiment) and the twins, Arthur and Harry, signed up to the Royal Army Medical Corps. All three would survive the War.

Will enlisted at the Sheffield Corn Exchange and was designated to 'B' Company. The first drill session for the 12th (Service) Battalion of the York and Lancaster Regiment, i.e. the Sheffield Pals, took place at Bramhall Lane. It was the home of Sheffield United Football Club and in summer a cricket ground that hosted an England v Australia Ashes Test match in 1902 and regular Yorkshire county matches. At first the recruits drilled in civilian clothing with broom handles and in November, blue serge uniforms were issued which made the men look like postmen! They would not be fully kitted out until mid-1915. Their first camp in December 1914 was at Redmires, on a moor where during a harsh winter two men died of pneumonia.

Lance Corporal Will Streets
A. St. John Adcock For Remembrance

Will made an instant impression on his superiors and was promoted to lance corporal which was quite an achievement in view of the quality of the men in the unit. His officers probably recognised in him the qualities of mutual support and discipline which he had acquired when working in the mine.

He found time to write more poetry and achieved a breakthrough when his poem *Gallipoli* was accepted by *The Times* in April 1915:

Upon the margin of a rugged shore
There is a spot now barren, desolate,
A place of graves, sodden with human gore
That time will hallow, Memory consecrate.

229

The Pals moved in May to Cannock Chase in Staffordshire to link up with the other three battalions, all Pals units that made up the 94th Brigade: The Accringtons (11/ East Lancashire), and the first and second Barnsley Pals (13 and 14/ York and Lancaster). There was banter between them; the Sheffields were dubbed 'the coffee and bun boys' as they received numerous parcels full of supplies from home. All the Pals troops enjoyed singing when on the march and it was with some irony that Will wrote: 'Sometimes you cannot persuade them to sing when going through the village when people are waiting to hear them, but as soon as they reach the lanes, they fill them with lusty songs'!

Streets was promoted to full corporal. It was at this time that he fell in love with a local girl who may have inspired him to write *To…*

> *Tho' hope be dim, tho' fade Youth's rosy flush;*
> *Tho' Death may come, tho' Life my spirit crush;*
> *Two haunting eyes will never cease to shine;*
> *Two magic lips will ever press on mine.*

The Brigade joined the 31st Division in Ripon during July. In a letter home, Will referred again to the possibility of his death: 'Now mother, I am going to be frank. I hate to be cruel, but one has to be so in order to be kind… We all know the struggle you and father have had to bring us up, yet you accomplished it in a rare and supreme manner… Your letters show that you are not yet facing the real possibility that this war may bring- I must encourage you both to face it. As you will never regret, four of your sons have volunteered. For what? Not because they looked to the army for their career (I hate it from the bottom of my soul.) Rather because they wished to save civilisation from being destroyed by one of the most sinister fates.'

The Division moved to Salisbury Plain in September while, in France, the Battle of Loos raged which inspired Will to predict: 'Out of this bloody war, believe me, there will blossom an enduring and fruitful peace. I hope to see it, but if I do not, I am content to know that I have helped to produce it.'

On 21 December the Division sailed from Devonport for Egypt and arrived at Alexandria on 1 January 1916. They were sent to Port Said to guard the Suez Canal where they remained untroubled until early March. As part of the build-up to the Somme Offensive in France, the Division sailed to Marseilles and after a long train journey, they arrived in the Somme. After staying in several billets en route they reached the village of Bertrancourt by the end of the month.

Will's letters home reflect the contrasts of war that he experienced and a veneration of his fellow soldiers: 'There are moments in the trenches when you can sit down and imagine that you are in some quarry or cutting. There is a blue sky above. Larks are singing… then there is the rat-a-tat machine-guns… you realise that you are at war, that you are part of a great game, that you are only 50 or 80 yards away from men like you and wrestling for something… It is the agony of suspense which tugs the nerves. The monotony of trench life is varied with moments of high excitement and intense fear, so there is no fear of stagnancy… Life in a wet, flooded trench is inconceivable. I will wager that thousands there now are praying for a bullet or piece of shrapnel to give them forgetfulness… The English Tommy in spite of his faults, which are legion, is a splendid fellow, to prove which I could narrate to you many a tale. But he needs not any praise, for what he does is natural and free, and wherever there is freedom of action, there is freedom of spirit.'

The Sheffield Pals were subjected to their baptism of fire on 15 May when they helped to repel a German raid at a cost of 15 men killed and 45 wounded. Their stand earned them seven Military Medals and recognition and respect from their sister battalions. Will wrote to his brother Ben: 'Our battalion, though perhaps over intellectual for a soldier-battalion, is made of fighting stuff. The Barnsleys, who being miners, used to chaff us at first, are first in our praise. One man, echoing sentiments of his mates, said "Well, we used to call you the bun and coffee men, but by God you can fight."'

Streets was promoted to lance serjeant and moved to 'D' Company. In spite of his duties, he was still finding time to write poetry and was working on a collection of sonnets *The Undying Splendour* which he described as 'youth, full of love, hope and aspiration, leaving it all for an idea- liberty-scorning death, proud, true to his race.'

Will Streets was aching to be recognised: 'If I get through, I shall win through some day as a poet.' He foretold on 14 June that 'the next month or two will see me in a position to endeavour to have a book printed or see me beneath the sweet soil of France.' On 24 June his mood was doom laden: 'I look death squarely in the face, but I hope to come through if only to feel the pulse of the world when the present fever has passed and to give my message to the saddened hearts and to inspire growing youth with the great things in life.'

The 'Big Push' in the Somme was only days away. The Sheffield Pals had grown accustomed to the front line from which they would 'go over the top' on the fateful first day of July. It lay west of the village of Serre, incorporating four copses which were named by the British after the Apostles-Matthew, Mark, Luke and John. One of his poems was entitled *Matthew Copse*:

> There by the fallen youth, where heroes lie,
> Close by each simple cross the flowers will spring,
> The bonnes enfants *will wander in the Spring,*
> And lovers dream those dreams that never die.

Serre was the most northern objective of the British line of attack, the 'job' of the 31st Division. Their strategy was to form a blocking flank to prevent German reinforcements breaking through from the north. The Division consisted of Pals battalions from the north of England: Accrington, Barnsley, Bradford, Leeds, Hull, Sheffield and Durham- men who had enlisted together, trained together, would 'go over the top together' and, for many, die together.

The Sheffields were on the left flank of their brigade, the most northerly in the line. The Battalion was in place by 4.00 a.m. - they were to attack in waves. By now a full serjeant, Will Streets and 'D' Company were in the second wave. The first, 'A' and 'C' Companies, moved into No Man's Land just before Zero Hour at 7.30 a.m. The Germans were not taken by surprise and were ready; six machine-guns covered the ground in front of Serre and their guns, placed on the higher ground, would shell the attackers. The fate of the Sheffield Pals was graphically described by R.A. Sparling in his *History of the 12th (Service) Battalion York and Lancaster Regiment*: 'They had to pass through a terrible curtain of shell fire, and German machine-guns were rattling death from the sides. But the lines growing even thinner, went on unwavering… Whole sections were destroyed… The 3rd and 4th waves suffered so heavily that by the time they reached No Man's Land they had lost at least half their strength.'

No Man's Land at Serre- the Sheffield Pals attacked towards the right from the wood on the left. Serre Road No.3 Cemetery is in the foreground and behind is Queens Cemetery   J Kerr

The Germans were amazed by the tactic employed by the British High Command. Musketier Karl Blenk was in 169th Regiment which was opposite the Sheffield and Accrington Pals: 'When the English started advancing we were very worried... We were surprised to see them walking... The officers were in front. I noticed one of them walking calmly, carrying a walking stick... They went down in their hundreds. You didn't have to aim, we just fired into them. If only they had run, they would have overwhelmed us... Normally, after 5,000 rounds had been fired we changed the barrel of the machine-gun. We changed it five times that morning.'

A few reached the German front line but more than half the Battalion were casualties: 18 officers and 495 other ranks including three sets of brothers. Among the dead was Corporal Alexander Robertson, aged 34, a lecturer in History at the University of Sheffield and a poet who was in the first wave; he is commemorated on the Thiepval Memorial (Pier 14 Face B).

A Leeds Pal, Private A.V. Pearson survived the day's slaughter when his battalion the 15/ West Yorks lost 15 officers and 233 other ranks. His chilling conclusion was that the Pals had been 'Two years in the making. Ten minutes in the destroying'. 'So ends the golden age' concluded the author of *The History of the 9/ York and Lancaster*, a battalion which lost 423 men.

Will Streets was one of the missing Sheffield Pals. According to some accounts, he had returned to the British line wounded but, on being informed that one of his men was in need of help, he went back into No Man's Land to look for him and was not seen alive again. Victor Piuk in his informative *A Dream within the Dark- a Derbyshire Poet in the Trenches* records that, after the War, one of Will's brothers, Walter, met a man who had been with Will on 1st July and his last sight of him was 'in a shell hole in No Man's Land with his arm blown off.' Captain R. Moore was in no doubt as to Serjeant Streets's qualities: 'It is given to few men to win the confidence of their comrades as completely as did Srgt. Streets... he was always to be counted on both by his officers and the men under him... he gave the impression of coolness even under extreme tension. He was not of those who ignore danger; rather, he faced it and found the cause more than sufficient compensation.' Like so many other mothers, Clare Streets refused to accept the reality of her son's death and clung onto the hope that he had survived.

The Germans moved east to the strongly defended Hindenburg line in February 1917. The British entered Serre and the grim task of burying the remaining bodies could start. Will was officially recorded as dead in May 1917. His body was buried at John Copse and then moved to Euston Road Cemetery. The inscription on his grave was chosen by his family from his poem *An English Soldier*, substituting the first person instead of the third:

> *I fell but yielded not my English soul;*
> *That lives out here beneath the battle's roll*

In a bitter twist of fate, *The Undying Splendour*, a volume of 30 poems including 13 sonnets, was published posthumously in May 1917. One of Will's letters home was prominent in the preface: 'I may not see the end of the poems, but hope to live to do so. We soldiers have our views of life to express, though the boom of death is in our ears... in the midst of our keenest sadness for the joy of life we leave behind, we go to meet death grim-lipped, clear-eyed and resolute-hearted.'

Will received the recognition he craved when his work was appraised in A. St. John Adcock's *Remembrance* (1920): 'No militarism is here... no strut of the goose-step, no taste for slaughter nor lust of conquest for its own sake, nor any of the cheap, dazzling blatancies that belong to the militaristic spirit. These men were too sanely human to cherish hatred except of war and the folly or mad ambition of those who had plunged the world into it.'

When Will's diary and belongings arrived home, the family discovered that he had fallen in love. Dorrie Streets who had married Will's brother Walter, believed the love of his life was Nora Riley who lived in the Cannock area. Brother Ben met her and described her as 'a noble woman, beautiful in character, most spiritual in temperament and very literary strung'. It appears that the family kept in contact with her after the War.

What of the survivors of the Sheffield Pals? After the losses in July, the Battalion was returned to strength numerically but during the harsh winter of 1916 to 1917, a staggering 887 men were evacuated to hospital.

The area where the 31st Division attacked on the first day of the Battle of the Somme has long been returned to agriculture but four cemeteries are a permanent reminder of that fateful day: Luke Copse British, Queens, Railway Hollow and Serre Road No. 3. Three of the copses now form a small wood; at its southern end is the Sheffield Memorial Park where various memorials to the northern Pals can be seen and the remnants of the trench from which the Accringtons jumped. One of their platoons was led by 2nd Lieutenant Reginald St. John Battersby who was a mere 16 years old. He at least survived the War but one of his legs was amputated in 1917.

One of the most emotive cemeteries in the Somme can be accessed down a cratered slope through the Park: Railway Hollow Cemetery where there are 109 burials, some for the first day of the Battle of the Somme and some for the last day on 13 November 1916. It is the final resting place of several Sheffield Pals like Alfred Goodlad, aged 23, whose parents made an unusual choice for the inscription on their son's grave (A.22.), a sentiment from his last letter home: 'The French are a grand nation worth fighting for.' It is a statement that exemplifies the spirit of the men who fought in the Somme on 1st July 1916, a spirit that would evaporate during the ensuing autumnal months of conflict in increasingly muddy conditions.

Alf Goodlad's grave in Railway Hollow Cemetery with its unusual inscription   *A Reed*

The commanding officer of the Sheffield Pals, Major Plackett, who was wounded on 1st July, commended Will for being 'conspicuous amongst a battalion of brave men' and his prediction for *Undying Splendour* was 'if his verses are as good as his reputation as a soldier, you may rest assured that the book will be a great success.' A fitting memorial to Will Streets is his most famous poem:

A Soldier's Cemetery

Behind that long and lonely trenched line
To which men come and go, where brave men die,
There is a yet unmarked and unknown shrine,
A broken plot, a soldier's cemetery.

There lie the flower of youth, the men who scorn'd
To live (so died) when languished Liberty:
Across their graves flowerless and unadorned
Still scream the shells of each artillery.

When war shall cease this lonely unknown spot
Of many a pilgrimage will be the end,
And flowers will shine in this new barren plot
And fame upon it through the years descend:
But many a heart upon each simple cross
Will hang the grief, the memory of its loss.

He foresees here the development of stark and 'unmarked' front line burial plots into today's places of 'pilgrimage', beautifully tended cemeteries that one hundred years later commemorate the fallen, the 'flower of youth', the Pals who like Streets would never return.

It is hard to dispute the assessment of Will Streets's boyhood friend John Millnes that 'condemned as he was, to toil from boyhood in the mine, and also to an environment that wounded his sensitive nature, his was yet ever the search after the beautiful and the true.'

Will Streets's grave in Euston Road Cemetery
A Reed

Railway Hollow Cemetery (designed by W.C. Von Berg)
viewed from Sheffield Memorial Park   *A Reed*

WILL STREETS:

Born:	24 March 1885, eldest son of William and Clare Streets of 16, Portland St., Whitwell, Derbyshire
Education:	St. Lawrence's Elementary School, Whitwell
Occupation:	Miner
Unit/ Regiment:	12/ York and Lancaster Regiment (Sheffield Pals)
Rank:	Serjeant
Died:	1st July 1916, first day of the Battle of the Somme
Age:	31
Buried:	Euston Road Cemetery, A.6. His grave is a Special Memorial as there is an inscription at the top of the stone which states that Will is BELIEVED TO BE BURIED IN THIS CEMETERY
Inscription:	I FELL: BUT YIELDED NOT MY ENGLISH SOUL THAT LIVES OUT HERE BENEATH THE BATTLE'S ROLL

(from *An English Soldier* by Will Streets)

The cemetery is located near Colincamps, 11 kms north of Albert. It started as a front line burial ground after the unsuccessful attacks on Serre on 1st July 1916. There are 1,293 burials, 170 of which are unidentified. The cemetery was designed by Sir Reginald Blomfield

JAMES CROZIER

'He was no rotter deserving to die like that. He was merely fragile'

This is the story of two unrelated men from different backgrounds who shared the same surname. James Crozier was a young apprentice in a shipyard near the home he shared with his mother Elisabeth off the Shankill Road in a poor Protestant area of West Belfast. His namesake, Frank Crozier, was from a well-heeled Anglo-Irish family- his father was an army officer in India and wealthy enough to send Frank to Wellington College for a military-based education. After he left Wellington Frank Crozier's life lacked direction but no shortage of desire for adventure. He worked on a tea plantation in Ceylon and then as a cook on a ship bound for South Africa where in 1899 he joined the Mounted Infantry in the British campaign against the Boers. It was here that Crozier first witnessed the dark reality of war and crimes perpetrated by the British Army against enemy soldiers and civilians. When serving in Nigeria a few years later, he himself was responsible for assaults against African workers for which he was fortunate to escape punishment. In 1909 he moved on to Canada where he was involved in a number of entrepreneurial pursuits and his time there was blighted by severe bouts of drunkenness which, on one occasion, resulted in police custody. He also attracted a reputation for failing to honour his debts.

An avowed Orangeman, he was involved in gun running in 1914 for the Protestant Ulster Volunteer Force. The onset of war halted the deteriorating situation between the U.V.F. and the Roman Catholic Nationalist Volunteers at which point the maverick Crozier joined the 9/ Royal Irish Rifles in August as a private. Amazingly, given his chequered career, he rose to the rank of major by the end of September, as second in command of the Battalion. His meteoric rise was such that by the end of 1916, he had become a brigadier general.

In contrast, young James Crozier's record in the British Expeditionary Force from September 1914 to February 1916 was a failure- that his final days should be so well chronicled, is due to his inclusion in two books written by Frank Crozier after the War: *A Brass Hat in No Man's Land* and *The Men I Killed*, published in 1930 and 1937 respectively.

James Crozier visited the recruiting station near his home in Battenberg Street, West Belfast on 11 September 1914. It is likely that he was below the legal age of recruitment (18 years) when he volunteered for Kitchener's Army. War with Germany offered him an exciting alternative to his monotonous daily routine. His mother Elizabeth accompanied him but was concerned about his safety at a time when reports of heavy losses suffered by the B.E.F. were beginning to filter home from the Front. She attempted to dissuade him from enlisting but the officer in attendance, Major Frank Crozier, was most reassuring and put her mind at rest. He promised to keep an avuncular eye on her son and comforted by this assurance, Elizabeth Crozier acceded to her son's desire to volunteer for the British Army.

Private James Crozier joined the 9/ Royal Irish Rifles, known locally as the 'Shankill Road Boys'. Training lasted for over a year until 3 October 1915 when the Battalion was sent to the Front.

In January 1916 Private Crozier was based in the front line trenches at Redan Ridge in the Somme where weather conditions had been appalling; constant rain had turned the area into a muddy morass. He was scheduled for sentry duty at 9.00 p.m. on 31 January but failed to turn up. Four days later he was apprehended 25 miles away by a Corporal Taylor 'strolling along our Mechanical Transport lines.' He had no items of identification like a cap badge or pay book. He did not have a rifle and when challenged, admitted that he had deserted his post.

He was committed to trial by a Field General Court Martial which first sat on 13 February. There were two witnesses for the prosecution but there was no one to speak on his behalf. When asked why he had failed to turn up for sentry duty, Crozier's defence was that 'I was feeling very ill with pains all over me. I do not remember what I did. I was dazed. I do not remember being warned for any duty. I cannot remember leaving the trenches even.' In his defence he claimed that 'there were some rifle grenades bursting about ten yards from me' and that he was ill before going into the trenches and that 'it had got worse with the cold.'

The officer in charge of proceedings stated in the Court Martial Report of 15 February that 'from a fighting point of view this soldier is of no value. His behaviour has been that of a "shirker" for the past three months. I am firmly of the opinion that the crime was deliberately committed with the intention of avoiding duty in the Redan.'

Frank Crozier had risen from the rank of private in 1914 to brigadier general by 1916 From A Brass Hat in No Man's Land *by Brigadier General F.P. Crozier*

James Crozier's mother would have been surprised to learn that such damning words about her son were penned by none other than the 'kind' Major Crozier who had by this stage of the War been promoted to the rank of lieutenant colonel and was the commanding officer of the 9/ Royal Irish Rifles.

Lieutenant Colonel Crozier decided not to commute the death sentence although he could have reduced it to a lesser punishment of imprisonment with hard labour as had been the case for another soldier who had deserted before Crozier. The file was passed to brigade level and on 16 February, the commanding officer of the 107th Brigade, Brigadier General Withycombe, recommended that 'the extreme penalty in the case of Rifleman Crozier be carried out' and that the young soldier should face death by firing squad 'for deliberately avoiding duty in the trenches' and 'as a deterrent to a repetition of offences of this nature.' Commanding officers were fearful of insubordination and this was a clear message to men of the Battalion that such a breach of discipline would not be tolerated.

Unfortunately for James Crozier his record sheet counted against him. His character had been assessed as 'bad' due to two previous charges of absence from his post- for absenting himself from a working party and on another occasion from his billet. When the report made its way to the Divisional level of the process, Major General Nugent of the 36th (Ulster) Division concurred that 'the sentence should be carried out'. It was noted that medical evidence had not been considered by the Court Martial. A medical officer, Lieutenant Colonel Fawcett of the 108th Field Ambulance, examined Crozier and certified on 18 February that 'there is no evidence to show that he has recently been other than sound in mind and body' and when questioned Crozier had admitted that he had not reported sick previously.

Major General Edward Montagu-Stuart-Wortley, commander of XVIIth Corps confirmed that 'in the interests of discipline the sentence, as awarded, should be carried out.' The death penalty was confirmed at the next stage by General Allenby Commander of the Third Army on 21 February 1916 and at the very highest level by the Commander-in-Chief of the British Army, General Haig, on 23 February 1916.

Private James Crozier was found guilty of 'deserting His Majesty's Service' and sentenced, as written in the schedule, to DEATH.

It may not have passed unnoticed by other ranks that when one of their officers, 2nd Lieutenant Annandale deserted during shelling in full view of other ranks, he virtually received a free pardon on health grounds as recommended by Lieutenant Colonel Crozier: he had been receiving treatment for venereal disease.

Before dark on 26 February 1916 a wooden execution post was driven into the frozen ground of the walled garden of a villa at Mailly-Maillet, a village behind the Somme front line. Later in the evening Lieutenant Colonel Crozier was concerned that the young officer in charge of the firing squad might over indulge and be incapable of commanding it next morning. To keep an eye on his alcoholic intake, he was invited by Crozier to dine with him that evening.

Private James Crozier, meanwhile, received a visit in his cell from the Battalion's chaplain and during the night, on the orders of Crozier the commanding officer, was plied with copious amounts of rum.

At dawn on 27 February snow lay on the ground. Soldiers of the 9/ Royal Irish Rifles were marched to within a few yards of the wall that surrounded the villa. They drew to attention. In the quiet of the garden Private James Crozier was carried to the wooden post, virtually unconscious due to the 'generosity' of his rum issue.

According to Frank Crozier, there were hooks on the post and that he was 'hooked on like dead meat in a butcher'shop.' A firing squad stood just ten yards from the target, their fingers on triggers.

The men on the other side of the wall were standing to attention. They were frozen mentally and physically to the spot. The order was given by the lowering of a handkerchief. At 7.05 a.m. a 'nervous, ragged volley was fired'. The medical officer on duty checked the body and confirmed that the young rifleman was still alive. Had his orders been ignored? Was the firing squad guilty of a subtle but pointed protest? After the War Frank Crozier suggested that 'death, despite all the precautions, was not instantaneous owing to nervousness.'

The thoughts of the soldiers on the other side of the wall were interrupted by a single pistol shot, according to Brigadier General Crozier's account, to Private James Crozier's heart. Despite his earlier promises to the victim's mother, Frank Crozier had presided over her son's death.

It is thought that James Crozier was executed on the other side of this wall in Mailly-Maillet in the Somme on 27 February 1916   J Kerr

Judged from a 21st century perspective it was a callous travesty of justice. Young Crozier was poorly educated and could not draw on a so-called 'prisoner's friend' who would have supported and represented him at the court martial. His age was not taken into account and it was rare for medical officers to offer any mitigating circumstances for alleged desertion or cowardice and importantly, there was no right of appeal. The Court consisted of a small number of officers who not only acted as prosecutors but also sat in judgement.

For the authorities in 1916 it was a justifiable sentence 'for the sake of example'. Unlike two other privates in the 9/ Royal Irish Rifles, James Crozier was the unlucky one whose sentence was not downgraded. He was unfortunate that his commanding officer was one of the most hard line in the British Army. In *The Men I Killed*, Frank Crozier's attitude to the performance of military 'duty' is clear- if for the sake of success in the field, he had to kill a panic-stricken officer in retreat or a deserting private, then he had no option but to do so. Fear of punishment and especially court martial leading to execution was essential for units 'sticking it out'. Crozier ordered fleeing Portuguese soldiers to be killed by machine-gun fire in 1918, by which time he had been promoted to brigadier general.

He admitted in *A Brass Hat in No Man's Land* that some thought of him as young Crozier's 'butcher'. There is evidence that even the 'butcher' may have been uncomfortable with the sentence of execution. His woeful attempts to add the executed man's name to the list of casualties who had been killed in action were blocked by higher authority. James Crozier's mother was duly informed of the exact manner of her son's brutal death.

There are flickers of humanity in Frank Percy Crozier's assessment of young Private Crozier whom he named as 'Crocker' in 1930 and 'Crockett' in 1937: 'He was no rotter deserving to die like that. He was merely fragile. He had volunteered to fight for his country… at the dictates of his own young heart. He failed. And for that failure he was condemned to die- and he did at the hands of his friends, his brothers, with the approval of his Church. To us, what was he? He was poor Crockett. And we never made up our minds for whom we were sorrier- him, or ourselves. Such is war.'

Private James Crozier was one of 306 soldiers executed by the British authorities on the Western Front- 264 were for cowardice and desertion, seven for quitting post, five disobedience, 19 murder, four striking a superior officer, two casting away arms, surprisingly only three for mutiny and two for sleeping while on duty.

A soldier in the British Army who had been executed in the Great War was issued an official posthumous pardon by Act of Parliament on 8 November 2006 which stated that 'the pardon stands as recognition that he was one of many victims of the First World War and that execution was not a fate he deserved.' The sentences, however, remain unaltered.

Private James Crozier was initially buried in the village of Mailly-Maillet but was later re-interred after the War at Sucrerie Military Cemetery near Colincamps. He is now 'Remembered with Honour' like all the other soldiers buried there, a rather different sentiment to that expressed by the authorities at the time. The treatment of his mother by the War Office, however, is tainted with dishonour. She was not entitled to have a pension paid to her because her son had been executed for 'gross misconduct'.

It is fair to surmise that in January 1916 James Crozier was suffering from shell shock; he was home sick, and in poor health. He had been frightened by his experience of warfare on the Western Front; it had all been a desperate disappointment for him after the excitement of enlisting for King and Country in September 1914.

His death left an indelible mark on Frank Crozier. The young apprentice shipyard worker looms large in his writings. The brigadier general argued that he could not show any mercy to deserters and cowards who retreated: 'When unchained, funk, (either by word, deed or suggestion) becomes a military menace' and he would think nothing of 'throwing away a thousand men an hour providing a position is held or gained.' When he visited the battlefields in 1919, he thought of 'the wasters who avoided military service for "conscience sake"'.

Brigadier General Frank Crozier was virtually a lone voice as a high ranking commander to reject the concept of war. One of the most callous and hard hearted of generals, in a marked *volte-face*, after 1920, he came out keenly opposed to war and in 1937 he dedicated *The Men I Killed* to 'the genuine fighters of all nations who stuck it to the end in the front lines, and to the genuine conscientious objectors of all nations who stuck it to the end in jail...'

James Crozier's grave in Sucrerie Cemetery   A Reed

What prompted Crozier's change of heart? Why 20 years after hostilities ended, did he admit to being a 'war resister' and to promulgate trenchant views that 'war is useless' and 'war is murder'?

His behaviour was hardly typical of a retired general; he joined the Labour Party in 1923 in sympathy with the Army's rank and file whom he believed had been badly let down in the immediate post-war years. In the 1920s he immersed himself in the foundation of a League of Nations Union- 'Peace' was his new mantra and reminded of the lady he met who zealously handed out white feathers of cowardice early in the War, he hoped that 'this patriotic lady will work as hard in the cause of peace as she did in the cause of war.'

A major reason for his iconoclasm was the frantic rearmament of the European powers in the 1930s: 'What men sow, so shall they reap: in other words, we are sowing armaments in order that we may reap war.'

Crozier found it difficult to come to terms with the collective European failure to prevent another war: 'The Great War was the S.O.S. danger signal to civilisation- if we ignore that S.O.S. and the lessons of war, civilisation is doomed.' As far as he was concerned: 'The fate of Belgium was not really worth the life of a single British soldier.'

Desertion was one of the greatest threats to all the armies on the Western Front. The life of one sad young volunteer was brutally ended 'for the sake of example' by Brigadier General Frank Crozier because he had little option but to follow the rules of war at a time when no thought was given to 'Human Rights'. Conversely, he would argue from 1930 onwards: 'Those who wish to abolish the death sentence for cowardice and desertion in war, should aim at a higher mark and strive to abolish war itself.'

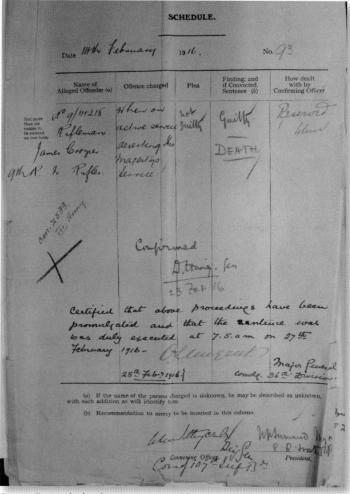

James Crozier's death warrant signed by General Haig
National Archives WO71/450

JAMES CROZIER:

Born:	Date unknown. Elisabeth Crozier, his mother, lived in Battenberg Street, West Belfast
Occupation:	Apprentice shipyard worker
Unit/ Regiment:	9/ Royal Irish Rifles
Rank:	Private
Died:	Shot at Dawn on 27 February 1916 at Mailly-Maillet
Age:	Possibly 18
Buried:	Sucrerie Military Cemetery, Colincamps, Somme, I.A.5.

The cemetery was designed by Sir Reginald Blomfield. It was originally started by the French but their burials were removed after 1918. There are 1,103 graves of which 219 are unidentified

HORACE ILES

'A soldier's son and a soldier born'

Horace Iles was a strapping young Yorkshire lad. On leaving school in 1913 he worked as an apprentice blacksmith and boasted a physique to prove it.

Leeds was buzzing with war fever in August 1914 and young men were bombarded with anti-German propaganda and exhortations and pressure to volunteer for Kitchener's Army. Horace enlisted on a recruitment tram in Leeds and his interview was a formality. He was welcomed into the British Army with open arms. There should, however, have been a problem for the recruitment officer. Young Horace Iles was only 14 years old and was, therefore, four years below the legal age for enlistment. He had no doubt been economical with the truth if asked about his age, but Iles was one of an estimated 250,000 under age soldiers who were allowed to join up. A massive 'blind eye' was turned to the issue and for a good reason- unlike Germany, Britain did not have a conscripted army but one consisting of regulars, territorials and volunteers. The British Expeditionary Force would have struggled without such a body of men and 'boys'.

Serre Road No. 1 Cemetery with French military chapel in background   *A Hamilton*

Horace would have seen the 'God Save the King' recruitment tram in the Woodhouse area of Leeds and might have witnessed young men not wearing uniform being handed a white feather, a symbol of cowardice. He may have been a recipient of one himself. It is more likely, though, that his decision to enlist was inspired by the memory of his father William Iles, a professional soldier who had fought under Lord Roberts in the Second Afghan War between 1878 and 1880. His father's reminiscences and army talk must have left their mark on his young son.

Horace's widowed mother Elizabeth and his sister Florrie were unhappy with his decision to join up and took him to task. His retort to Florrie's pleadings for him not to volunteer reflected his confidence and determination to take the 'King's Shilling'. 'I may be only 14 but I am a man' and he propounded the myth that 'the war will be over by Christmas' and registered happiness that he had been so 'quick off the mark' to enlist.

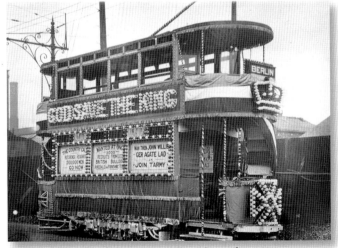

Leeds Pals 2nd Battalion Recruiting Tram September 1914
David Atkinson Archive - Leeds City Council Library and Information Service

Horace had joined the Leeds Pals and was now in the company of men from all walks of life. Teachers, professional sportsmen and factory workers all rubbed shoulders together in an exciting adventure to halt the 'Hun'. The Leeds Pals were the 15/ West Yorkshire Regiment and went by train to Colsterdale Camp in North Yorkshire.

Life at Colsterdale was a monotonous diet of drill, route marches and weapon training. A teacher, P.A. Margetts, wrote on 21 March 1915 that 'the battalion is tired of the place. They are eager to be up and doing and I am convinced that if they are called upon to go to the Front, each man will give a good account of himself.'

The Battalion was sent to Egypt on 22 December 1915 to defend the Suez Canal, a posting that lacked the excitement and adventure that the majority craved. However, the 15/ West Yorks were transferred to France by March 1916. Horace was hospitalised by a leg wound on 22 May and returned home on a short period of leave before returning, with the pleas of his mother and sister not to, ringing in his ears.

The true horrors of the conflict now loomed large in households nationwide. Florrie attempted again to persuade her brother to give himself up and return to his family in Leeds and wrote to him at the Front:

Horace Iles, under-age recruit

'My Dear Horace,

I am so glad you are alright so far but I need not tell you what an anxious time I am having on your account, you have dropped in for the thick of it and no mistake. I only hope you have the good luck to come back safely like your father did and my dear boy I don't care how soon. I should be more than pleased to see you, I can tell you. You have no need to feel ashamed that you joined the "Pals" now for by all accounts they have rendered a good account of themselves, no one can call them "Featherbed Soldiers" now.

We did hear that they were fetching all back from France under 19. For goodness sake Horace tell them how old you are. I am sure they will send you back if they know you are only 16, you have seen quite enough now, just chuck it up and try to get back you won't fare no worse for it. If you don't do it now you will come back in bits and we want the whole of you. I don't suppose you can do any letter writing now but just remember that I am always thinking of you and hoping for your safe return.

Your loving sister,

Florrie'

She alludes in her letter to efforts being made in Parliament to return 'boy' soldiers to their families. A strenuous campaign was being pursued by the M.P. for Mansfield, Sir Arthur Markham whose attempts were thwarted at every turn by a Government desperate for manpower and fully prepared to block and ignore his efforts. He did not mince his words on the floor of the House of Commons in November 1915: 'There has been fraud, deceit and lying practised by the War Office. You have taken boys of the ages of fourteen, fifteen and sixteen rather than face the issue of conscription… You have taken these boys knowing that they were boys, and then the War Office have said that they did not think they were under age. You have said that you would not send them to the Front until they have reached the official age, but you have time after time broken this promise and sent little lads to the front.'

Harold Tennant, the Under Secretary for War, agreed that 'over-zealous recruiting officers were responsible for recruitment of under-age soldiers and that commanding officers should send the boys back to their homes.' He did admit that 'in some cases they are not returned, because not only have these boys cost the country a certain amount of money, but they have been given training and uniforms, and in some cases these boys of sixteen, seventeen and even fifteen years are very efficient soldiers.' So despite not condoning the deployment of under-age soldiers, if they were physically strong enough and wanted to continue fighting, the official line was that they could remain at the Front.

Events overtook the parliamentary debate- losses had been so heavy that the Coalition Government decided to introduce conscription in January 1916 which resulted in tighter controls and more rigorous age checks.

Florrie's letter to her brother was returned

Horace Iles's physical strength was such that he was allowed to remain at the Front. He and many other 'boys' were about to participate in one of the bloodiest moments in British military history.

The 15/ West Yorks were aware on 30 June 1916 that they were about to 'go over the top' as part of a major offensive the next day. At about 7.30 a.m. Horace Iles and his fellow Leeds Pals, on the sound of a whistle, made their way across No Man's Land towards the German trenches. It was the day from hell. On this, the first day of the Battle of the Somme, 1st July 1916, the British Army lost 19,000 men and 39,000 were wounded. Richard van Emden in his *Boy Soldiers of the Great War* has calculated from the Commonwealth War Graves Commission records that 118 boys aged 17 or less died during the disastrous attack on 1st July. Horace Iles was one of the youngest. Others to die alongside him included the Yorkshire and England cricketer 2nd Lieutenant Major Booth and the England footballer Evelyn Lintott.

Florrie Iles's letter imploring Horace to return home was written on 9 July over a week after her brother died. The envelope was returned with a stark message stamped on it: Killed in Action.

Horace's body remained for several months on the battlefield until it was removed in April 1917 to Serre Road No. 1 Cemetery. He was one of 528 casualties suffered by the Leeds Pals.

Horace Iles had attended the local church choir and Sunday school in Woodhouse Lane, Leeds, a stone's throw from his family home. An obituary in the Emanuel Church magazine stated that Horace 'joined the Army over a year ago though he was but 16 years of age in January last but his build and strength would easily pass him for a lad of 18. Eager to join, he refused to be dissuaded and his letters showed how congenial his preparation was to him. He was a soldier's son and evidently was a soldier born.'

HORACE ILES:

Born:	1900, son of William (died 1913) and Elizabeth Iles of 7 Spenceley St, Woodhouse Lane, Leeds
Education:	Unknown
Occupation:	Apprentice blacksmith
Unit/ Regiment:	'B' Company, 15/ West Yorkshire (Prince of Wales's Own) known as the 'Leeds Pals'
Rank:	Private
Died:	1st July 1916, first day of the Battle of the Somme
Age:	16
Buried:	Serre Road No.1 Cemetery, I.E.39.
Inscription:	EVER IN OUR THOUGHTS

The cemetery was started in May 1917 and was added to from seven neighbouring, smaller cemeteries after the Armistice. It now contains 2,426 casualties buried or commemorated. 1,728 of the graves are unidentified. It was designed by N.A. Rew.

The grave of Horace Iles, aged 16, buried in Serre Road No. 1 Cemetery   A Reed

According to the Commonwealth War Graves Commission **PRIVATE JOHN CONDON** of the 2/ Royal Irish Regiment is 'thought to be the youngest battle casualty of the War commemorated by the Commission.' His gravestone (LVI.F.8.) in Poelcapelle British Cemetery in Belgium, states that he was 14 at the time of his death but research has cast doubt on whether Condon's body is interred

there and whether he was actually 14. An intense debate on the Western Front Association Forum about his age does lead to the conclusion that Condon was unlikely to have been the youngest to die and Richard van Emden acknowledges that 'there is currently some dispute about this.' Regardless of the much-visited grave's authenticity, it is at least a focus and memorial to the many young boys whose lives were brought to an appalling end on the Western Front.

One of the youngest 'boy soldiers' to have died in the Great War was **RIFLEMAN VALENTINE JOE STRUDWICK** of the 8/ Rifle Brigade from Dorking in Surrey. He is thought to have been 15 when he died on 14 January 1916 near Ypres. He is buried alongside six other soldiers in the 8/ Rifle Brigade, all killed on the same day possibly by the same shell. His grave in Essex Farm Cemetery is of particular interest to visiting school parties. The inscription on his grave (I.U.8.) is:

NOT GONE FROM MEMORY

OR FROM LOVE

Strudwick may not be the youngest British Army casualty as the C.W.G.C. has a record of a 14 year old from Johannesburg, Private David Ross of the 2/ South African Regiment having been killed on 25 March 1918 during the German Spring Offensives. He is buried at Heudicourt Communal Cemetery north east of Péronne but his age is not recorded on his grave at present.

The grave of 15 year old Valentine Joe Strudwick in Essex Farm Cemetery   *J Kerr*

On 6 June 1915 a German soldier was badly hit in the forearm by a bullet which also set fire to ammunition in his pocket. His wounds were appalling. He was one of thousands of casualties during the three month long Battle of Lorette near Arras. What was unusual was the age of the wounded German- he was only 14 years old.

KRIEGSFREIWILLIGER (Wartime volunteer) **PAUL MAUK** was born on 19 July 1900 in Waldkirch, a small German village in the Black Forest, 15 kilometres north of Freiburg. His father was a book-keeper with a local firm and Paul's upbringing in a family of eight children was a happy one. He attended Waldkirch Secondary School and when the family moved to Freiburg in 1911, he and his brother Walther, who was two years older, attended Freiburg Grammar School. Paul was kind and generous by nature and his aim was to be a doctor. When Germany went to war in August 1914, Paul and Walther were keen to sign up and enrolled at the Freiburg recruiting office. They were tall and well-built which made them look more mature looking, as can be seen in the photograph of Paul.

Paul Mauk is thought to be the youngest soldier to die in the Great War at the age of 14

The brothers performed well as marksmen and received the certificate of 'Aptitude for all types of Firearms'- they were now fully fledged soldiers. They trained as reservists and Paul was noted for his enthusiasm and humour. At Christmas he and Walther were responsible for decorating the regimental Christmas tree and arranging the presents surrounding it- Paul was, after all, still virtually a child...   243

Young German recruits possibly in 1917
www.greatwar.nl (Rob Ruggenberg)

*Paul Mauk's grave in the German
Cemetery at Lens-Sallaumines*
A Hamilton

The brothers were determined to make it to the Front and overcame the efforts of an officer concerned by their age who tried to post them on a bugling course! They were assigned on 1 March 1915 to the 5th Baden Infantry Regiment No. 113, 4th Company in which their older brothers Karl and Fritz were already drafted. Karl warned his younger siblings of the ferocity of trench warfare but undaunted, they took part in the Battle of Lorette near Arras and the defensive action against the French advance.

Paul was hit in the head on 9 May by a shell fragment when crawling under barbed wire. He was desperate to return to the action and discharged himself from hospital after a week and rejoined his comrades of 4th Company in the trenches. A month later his luck had run out. He died on the morning of 7 June. The German writer Ernst Jünger included the young German in his *Die Unvergessenen* (The Unforgotten) and recorded that 'this boy soldier remained dignified in the face of death… his lips were set in a smile for eternity.'

Paul Mauk was buried in the Lens-Sallaumines German Cemetery alongside over 15,600 German comrades, and is thought to be the youngest soldier to die in the Great War.

His brother Karl was gravely affected by his young brother's death and wrote a poem in his memory:

> *My brother, my beloved brother,*
> *Let me see once more the brightness of your eyes,*
> *More alive and happy, I will embark on the next combat,*
> *With the true courage of the German soldier.*

Karl did embark on further combat but met the same fate as 14 year old Paul- he was killed exactly three years later on 7 April 1918.

Also buried in Serre Road No. 1 Cemetery is **2nd LIEUTENANT MAJOR WILLIAM BOOTH** (Major was his Christian name). He died at the age of 29 on the first day of the Somme offensive, fighting with the Leeds Pals (15/ West Yorks). He was born in Pudsey in 1886 and took 167 championship wickets for Yorkshire in 1913 and scored 1,228 runs. He was selected for the M.C.C. tour to South Africa and in the 4-0 victory, played in the first Test Match at Durban and in the fifth at Port Elizabeth taking a total of 7 wickets and making 46 runs. In the 1914 edition of *Wisden Cricketers' Almanack*, Booth was chosen as one of the five cricketers of the 1913 season. Lord Hawke, the President of Yorkshire C.C.C. mourned the death of his county's leading all rounder: 'England lost one of the most promising and charming young cricketers it was ever my lot to meet.'

The inscription on his grave (I.G.14.) reads:

IN PROUD & LOVING MEMORY
OF OUR DEAR BROTHER

*Major William Booth's grave in Serre
Road No.1 Cemetery*   *A Hamilton*

GEORGE BUTTERWORTH

'Great in what he achieved, greater still in what he promised'

When war was declared on 4 August 1914 George Butterworth was attending a folk dance school in Stratford-on-Avon. He was one of the finest folk dancers in the country and an esteemed member of the English Folk Dance Society's demonstration morris dance team. He claimed that 'I am not a musician. I am a professional dancer'- he was, indeed, paid as a member of the team. He was an eminent collector of folk songs and dances and was also, despite his protestations, a musician of note whose work was highly regarded by distinguished contemporaries like the composer Ralph Vaughan Williams and the conductor Adrian Boult.

Butterworth took his leave of the dance school and travelled to Oxford to visit the University O.T.C. to ascertain what the chances were of him enlisting but receiving little encouragement, he returned to Stratford, noting in his diary that 'there will be plenty of time to think about volunteering after the first enthusiasms have died down.' He left on 29 August to visit Vaughan Williams and his diary entry is indicative of the febrile atmosphere that had engulfed the country. Vaughan Williams 'had taken his family for a holiday to Margate where he was arrested by a boy-scout (for spying) while writing a lecture on Purcell'!

Within just four days Butterworth and seven friends, mostly musicians, including Geoffrey Toye and R.O. Morris, had enlisted with the Duke of Cornwall's Light Infantry.

George Sainton Kaye Butterworth was born in London on 12 July 1885. Music was in his blood. His mother Julia was a professional soprano and composer of songs and she chose his second name, Sainton, after her much loved singing teacher. George's father, Sir Alexander Butterworth, was solicitor to the North Eastern Railway Company and held high hopes that his son would follow him into the Law.

Butterworth in the foreground performing a folk dance at Stratford-on-Avon in July 1914   English Folk Dance and Song Society

The family divided their time between London and York where the Headquarters of the N.E.R. were located. George was sent to Aysgarth Preparatory School in Yorkshire where from 1896 to 1899 he impressed with his independence of thought and leadership qualities. He was academically gifted enough to be awarded a King's Scholarship to Eton College where he enjoyed a variety of sports, especially cricket.

He was an accomplished pianist from an early age but was not in the same league as F.S. Kelly (see p.260) who left the College in the year Butterworth first attended. When very young, George surprised his father by playing a simple piece, *Rousseau's Dream* in twelve keys. The day before, his father had promised him five shillings as soon as he could master this and was taken aback that the money was claimed so quickly. George merely remarked with disarming modesty that the reward seemed too much for so simple a task.

In a 1901 concert at Eton 'a dainty *Humoresque* neatly played by Kaye-Butterworth and Hugesson, was scarcely appreciated as much as it deserved to be' and the following year Butterworth apparently 'played well'. He was a sufficiently talented musician to be appointed Keeper of the College Harmonium from 1902-04. He must have made an impression with his musical performances as it was reported that, at the College Concert in April 1903, 'Butterworth's appearance was the signal for a torrent of applause, which was again continued after the Orchestra had played his own *Barcarolle*' 245 which was described as 'a delicately scored orchestral piece.' Butterworth was elected to the College's Music Society Committee in May 1903 but although an enthusiastic musician, it could be argued that there was limited evidence at Eton of his future musical fame.

He accepted a place at Trinity College, Oxford in 1904 to study *Literae Humaniores* or 'Greats', a course which failed to enthuse him, turning his attention instead to music. He was elected President of the University Music Society which would bring him into contact with Vaughan Williams and Boult.

After leaving Oxford Butterworth failed to find a career that suited him. He spent a year as a music critic for *The Times*, which he found 'irksome', followed by a year's teaching at Radley College. He was a popular member of staff and contributed much to the College's musical and sporting life but according to the author of *The Butterworth Memorial Book*, 'the cloistered aloofness of school life bored him and its ecclesiasticism jarred.' He was keen to develop his music skills and enrolled at the Royal College of Music in 1910; he failed to complete the course, critical of its lack of professionalism and dismissive of the kind of music he was expected to study.

Butterworth no longer felt shackled and was able to concentrate on his main musical interests of composing, collecting and recording English folk song and dance. He met Cecil Sharp, the great collector of folk music and dance in 1906, when an undergraduate and member of the English Folk Dance and Song Society; he worked with him and Vaughan Williams scouring the country for traditional songs. Among the counties Butterworth visited were Sussex, Kent, Oxfordshire, Yorkshire and Shropshire.

Pursuit of the English folk song was not always plain sailing- Vaughan Williams's widow Ursula recorded an incident in 1911: 'In December Ralph went with George Butterworth on a short trip to collect songs in Norfolk. One night, in a pub where they had found several singers, one of them suggested it would be much quicker if he rowed them across the water than that they should bicycle round the Broad by road. It was a brilliantly starry night, frosty and still. They piled their bicycles into the boat and started. Their ferryman rowed with uncertain strokes, raising his oar now and then to point at distant lights, saying "Lowestoft" or "Southwold". Before long they realised they were always the same lights and that he was taking them round and round in circles. The night air after the frowsty bar parlour and beer had been fatal and he was thoroughly drunk. Eventually they persuaded him to let them row. Luck guided them to a jetty in the reeds. By this time their singer was sound asleep and did not wake even when they extricated their bicycles from under him. So they tied the boat up and left him there while they bicycled down an unknown track and found their way back to Southwold. The singer survived and was found in the same pub the following evening. But this time they did not accept his offer of a short cut by water.'

Butterworth worked with Cecil Sharp in 1912 and 1913 and concentrated on Oxfordshire where he found that the town of Bicester had a particularly rich tradition of folk song. He collected a total of 300 folk songs and 134 dances which was significantly less than his mentors' achievements. Vaughan Williams recorded over 800 songs and Sharp in excess of 3,000.

George Butterworth dancing in 1913- he is on the far left
English Folk Dance and Song Society

Richard Osborne asserts in *Till I End My Song* that folk song and dance collection was regarded at the time as anti-establishment. The New College organist and future Professor of Music at Oxford University, Hugh Allen, on seeing Butterworth and Reginald O. Morris, a fellow collector and later a contributor to *The Butterworth Memorial Book*, caustically commented: 'There goes more red revolution than in the whole of Russia.'

Before the onset of war George Butterworth received critical acclaim for his own compositions which created a genuinely English, pastoral sound. He, Vaughan Williams and Sharp were keen to create an intrinsically English style to outdo the popularity of the Germanic or 'Teutonic' sound of Brahms, Schubert and Schumann. They were responsible for creating an English style with its roots in their collections of rural music. Butterworth composed two *Rural Idylls* in 1911 and his orchestral rhapsody, *A Shropshire Lad* inspired by A.E. Housman's poetry, was premiered on 2 October 1913 by the London Symphony Orchestra at the Leeds Festival which, for one critic, heralded a 'new voice in English music.' The writer of his obituary in *The Eton College Chronicle* described it as an ambitious work 'which made a deep impression on those who heard it performed.' It was ironic that Butterworth, who died in the Great War, should choose to orchestrate the work of A.E. Housman who had been a vocal pacifist during and after the Boer War.

George Butterworth in typical pose
English Folk Dance and Song Society

Butterworth was a perfectionist and like F.S. Kelly was angered by any musician's failure to play his music as requested. When on one occasion his piece was ecstatically received 'amid all the clapping of hands, his predominant feeling was one of indignation with a harpist who had, he asserted, played her part precisely as he had told her not to'!

Vaughan Williams was 13 years older than Butterworth, but was, nonetheless, indebted to him for encouraging him to write his *London Symphony*. No doubt puffing on his pipe, and in his typically abrupt tone, Butterworth goaded him: 'You know, you ought to write a symphony' which he duly did with Butterworth's help in developing the piece. Vaughan Williams conceded that Butterworth had 'a wonderful power of criticism of other men's work and insight into their ideas and motives.'

With remarkable foresight Butterworth was concerned that in 1914 the score for Vaughan Williams's *London Symphony* was in the hands of the German publishers Breitkopf and Hartel and might never be returned. He proceeded to organise the piecing together of the score from the separate orchestral parts which were still in London and in recognition of George's salvage operation, Vaughan Williams dedicated the score to him when it was published in 1920.

There was a limit to how long Butterworth could scrape a living together on his earnings from music. The War offered, as it did to many others, the prospect of a job and regular income. It seemed to give him a new focus: 'Life, hitherto a somewhat perplexing riddle, took on a strange and captivating simplicity.' He entered a completely different world in which he could find no room for music- he went so far as to destroy some of his early compositions the worth of which he questioned. Music played very little part during his time in the Army; it hardly merited a mention in his letters and diary entries, although he may have collected some songs and sword dances from Durham miners under his command at the Front.

He started training with the Duke of Cornwall's Light Infantry at Aldershot in early September and later moved to Bodmin. For the Eton and Oxford educated Butterworth, regimental life was an eye opener: a large number of recruits were from Handsworth in Birmingham, 'a district I believe notorious… These worthies kept us supplied with a constant stream of lewdness… one real humourist made some excellent jokes but scarcely repeatable.' At least there were 'two splendid Birmingham chaps, young, married working men' but he was unconvinced about 'two or three less desirable Londoners of the shopkeeper class'!

Butterworth believed in attention to detail. He was impressed by the success of Kitchener's national recruitment campaign but was disappointed by the initial failure to supply the volunteers with sufficient equipment and food. He was appalled that 1,500 volunteers were crammed into accommodation for 500 and supervised by a handful of N.C.O.s. The conditions were 'disgraceful' and he pointed out that 'if the Government say they require half a million men, they must be 247 prepared to receive them in large numbers.' It was absurd, he felt, that men were exhorted to bring as little luggage as possible with them, but received no military clothing nor equipment for days.

The D.C.L.I. returned to Aldershot. Butterworth and friends steadfastly refused commissions, wishing to stay together, and George decided not to pull any strings to secure one. He was, however, not averse to using his comparative wealth to purchase articles that were in short supply, 'luxuries which are denied our comrades', like much needed wet weather gear.

After a few weeks at Aldershot Butterworth and two friends decided after all that they were better suited to the life of an officer: 'Seeing crowds of beardless youths, shipped down here as officers, has made us rather less satisfied with our position as privates.' They accepted commissions in the 13/ Durham Light Infantry. He was pleased to be in a northern regiment as during his time in York, he had come to respect northern plain speaking and determination. He complimented them on their strength and enthusiasm and considered them 'very good fellows'.

The Battalion remained in England until August 1915 by which time George Butterworth had been promoted to lieutenant. It had been a long period of preparation and the majority were desperate to cross the Channel and play their part. Once in France Butterworth was unimpressed that further training was inflicted on the men as 'we quickly relapsed into our dull and monotonous habits.'

For the rest of 1915 and the first three months of 1916, the 13/ Durham Light Infantry were fortunate to avoid the most dangerous zones but had to contend with worsening weather conditions. Butterworth wrote in November that 'I am billeted with two other officers in a nice farmhouse- with beds! And our only discomfort is the MUD. This word may be said pretty well to describe our existence- it is bad enough here and everywhere, but in the trenches there is nothing else (even the water is really liquid mud.) My trench coat now has an extra thickness from top to bottom. In short we are getting some idea of what a winter campaign really is… one wades to one's bed and eats one's dinner with water over the ankles, but with waders and four changes of socks, I keep fairly dry.'

Butterworth tells a delightful story of his induction to life in the trenches in the Armentières sector. He and other officers were given a guided tour: 'We filed into the fire trench and immediately opposite the entrance, I found to my astonishment a little wooden shanty, and the officers of the company having dinner; so just at the moment when I felt braced up for a vigorous onslaught on the Hun, I was hauled off to roast beef and beer while a sergeant posted my men.' Typically British!

He was grateful to be sent on an instruction course on 'bombs' (hand grenades) at the end of November. He was rather pleased with his 'bomb chucking'- no doubt aided by his cricketing skills. Christmas was fairly peaceful and in February, Butterworth went on a signalling course which 'is the first time I have ever taken the slightest interest in anything scientific.'

Butterworth wrote in letters home that they had been fortunate with good spring weather and not too much danger in the trenches- when in reserve they had been in a remote village as yet unspoiled by warfare. He calculated that 'there must be few battalions with seven months' trench experience whose total killed amount to less than fifty.'

The first week of June 1916 was spent on home leave. When he returned to France, the 13/ Durham Light Infantry were moving south to the front line in the Somme. They were spared action on the fateful 1st July and five days later they were about four miles from the Front. His letters reveal that: 'We still get very little news.' He was now commanding his own company due to his superior officer being hit by a shell when he was standing next to him. George escaped with no more than 'slight deafness in one ear' which soon passed off. The Durhams took part in the capture of Bailiff Wood to the west of the village of Contalmaison on 9 July for which Butterworth was commended for his actions between 7 and 10 July.

From 15 July the Battalion's objective was the village of Pozières on the Albert to Bapaume Road. On the night of 17 July, 1,600 yards of trench were consolidated only 250 yards from the enemy; heavy casualties were suffered including the loss of every officer in one company. For his role in the action, Lieutenant George Kaye-Butterworth, as he was known in the Army, was recommended for the award of an M.C. and his citation was for his command of the company after assuming responsibility 'with great ability and coolness. By his energy and total disregard of personal safety, he got his men to accomplish a good piece of work in linking up the front line.'

The Battalion joined the 2nd Australian Division east of Pozières on 26 July to attack 'Munster Alley' which ran from the British forward trenches into the German lines. Butterworth was not involved in the capture of 70 yards but was wounded in the back by shrapnel, not seriously enough to prevent him from front line action on 1 August. His company dug a deep trench under the cover of fog from the start of 'Munster Alley' to a distance of 200 yards from the Germans prior to attack. The trench was later named 'Butterworth Trench' in his memory.

Butterworth led a bombing raid on 'Munster Alley' on 4 August which gained 100 yards after what was described as 'an exceedingly bloody and brilliant attack.' However, the small gain was offset by George Butterworth's death on 5 August when he carelessly allowed a sniper too much of a target. Brigadier General Page Croft (at 34 the youngest brigade commander during the War, as well as being a businessman and the sitting M.P. for Christchurch) described Butterworth's last moments: 'I went up to the farthest point reached with Lieutenant Kaye-Butterworth. The trench was very low and broken, and he kept urging me to keep low down. I had only reached the Battalion Headquarters on my return when I heard poor Butterworth, a brilliant musician in times of peace and an equally brilliant soldier in times of stress, was shot in the head by a bullet. So he, who had been so thoughtful for my safety, had suffered the same fate he warned me against only minutes before.'

He was buried near 'Munster Alley'. His grave was destroyed by the ensuing bombardment and no trace of his remains was found. As a result, his name is one of over 72,000 on the Thiepval Memorial, dedicated to soldiers killed on the Somme without a known grave. It is possible that Butterworth never received official confirmation of his M.C., news of which was gazetted on 25 August.

George Butterworth was renowned for his modesty so it comes as no surprise to learn of General Ovens's admission in a letter of condolence to George's father that 'I did not know he was so very distinguished in music.' It was no doubt a surprise to many that George should have taken to soldiering so positively and that he was so successful at it.

The works that survived his cull in 1915 include at least 20 vocal compositions, a number of song and morris dance arrangements and six orchestral pieces, three of which were idylls with a folk music influence and a rhapsody for A.E. Housman's *Shropshire Lad* which, according to the music critic George Hall, are viewed 'as a musical epitaph not just for Butterworth himself but for an entire generation and way of life.' *The Daily Telegraph*'s reviewer of the work played in a concert at the Queen's Hall on 6 September 1917 enthused: 'The haze and heat of a spring day, the fragrance of the bloom, the beauty of life on such a day, all seem in this music, a most worthy example of the great talent of a musical son of this land, now "gone west" ere his prime.'

The most famous of his pieces and most associated with the aftermath of the Great War, is the rhapsody *The Banks of Green Willow* composed in 1913. It had its origins in two folk song melodies that he heard sung in 1907 by David Clements who was an inmate of the Basingstoke workhouse. It was the jolly tale of a farmer's young daughter who eloped to sea with a sea-captain who stole her parents' money and made her pregnant. She suffers a desperately difficult and painful labour and aware that she will die, asks her lover to throw herself and her baby overboard. In her dying moments, he sings a lament to 'his true love' whom he once 'loved so dearly' and whose burial he hopes will be on *The Banks of Green Willow*. The work was first performed on 27 February when 24 year old Adrian Boult conducted a forty-strong orchestra in West Kirby and its first London performance was shortly after in March.

Hugh Allen became Director of the Royal College of Music as well as Professor of Music at Oxford. He had known Butterworth as an undergraduate and colourfully lamented his loss as a musician 'and especially as a friend. His dear wayward manner, that friendly scowl, that tenderly gruff voice-all gone to pay a rotten debt to a bloody-minded lot of miscreants. And George I'm sure looking peacefully on, somewhere.' Ralph Vaughan Williams dreaded the post-war world 'with so many gaps-especially of course, George Butterworth.' It had been his privilege to 'hear him improvise harmonies to the tunes which he had collected, bringing out in them a beauty and character which I had not realised when simply looking at them... he could no more help composing in his own national idiom than he could help speaking in his own mother tongue.' Butterworth's theory was that music 249 should be national and that German music should be 'an alien thing to the English musician. He was greatly inspired by English folk music which was well suited to his skills and talents.'

According to *The Eton Chronicle* Butterworth had 'obtained a wide recognition as a composer of unusual promise who combined classical economy and firmness of texture with modern resourcefulness in harmony and a mastery of instrumental technique. There is little doubt that the publication of his latest works will justify the conviction of his friends that English music has suffered an incalculable loss by his untimely death.'

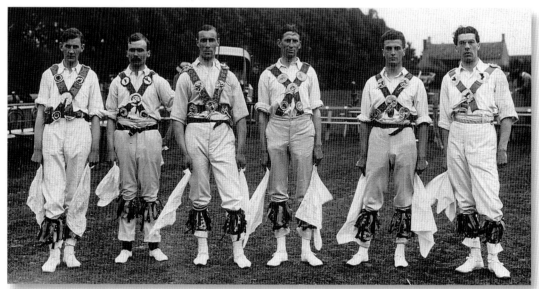

'So many gaps…' Of the 1912 English Folk Dance Society first morris 'side', three fell in the Great War-Butterworth (second from left), Perceval Lucas (fourth from left), and G.J.Wilkinson (far right), were all killed on the Somme. Also to fall was Reginald J. Tiddy, lecturer in English at Oxford University, who was first reserve for the demonstration team.
English Folk Dance and Song Society

How influential in the world of music would Butterworth have been if he had survived? In a B.B.C. Radio programme in 1942, the view was propounded that he was 'great in what he achieved, greater still in what he promised.' Butterworth may have continued to collect songs and dances and to play an important role in the post-war introspection when English music reflected a desire to escape the horrors and realities of the War; he yearned nostalgically for a return to the pre-1914 life of 'Merrie England'. He might have been converted to the modernist, dissonant and atonal work of the Austrians- Berg, Schoenberg and Webern, and the Hungarian Bartok who, like Butterworth, had been influenced by folk music and dance. There are echoes of the lush harmonies of French Impressionists like Debussy in his work but whichever route he might have taken- the English introspective phase, modernism or impressionism, his talent and drive would have guaranteed success and acclaim of the kind he would receive for his contribution to English Song.

George Butterworth M.C. commemorated on the Thiepval Memorial in the Somme
J Kerr

George Butterworth was 31 years of age when he died. Both Elgar and Vaughan Williams struggled to make a living early in their careers. The former had to wait until he was 42 before lasting success with *Enigma Variations* and the latter was 38 when his *Fantasia on a Theme of Thomas Tallis* and *Sea Symphony* made his name.

He was a recorder and upholder of England's rural traditions. He was, like A.E. Housman, wedded to the English countryside and his life revolved around the quintessentially English pastimes of song and dance. It was for the defence of England and its traditions that he laid down his life in the mud-filled trenches of the Somme. He was a gentleman- modest and thoughtful, whose loss was deeply felt by musicians and fellow soldiers.

GEORGE BUTTERWORTH:

Born:	12 July 1885 at 16, Westbourne Grove, London, son of Sir Alexander and Lady Julia Butterworth
Education:	Aysgarth Preparatory School, Eton College and Trinity College, Oxford
Occupation:	Teacher, music critic, collector of English folk song and dance, and composer
Unit/ Regiment:	Duke of Cornwall's Light Infantry and 13/ Durham Light Infantry
Rank:	Lieutenant
Died:	5 August 1916, Battle of the Somme
Age:	31
Decoration:	M.C.
Commemorated:	Thiepval Memorial, Pier 14 Face A

The Thiepval Memorial to the Missing of the Somme commemorates more than 72,000 officers and men who died in the Somme sector before 20 March 1918 and have no known grave. The majority died between July and November 1916. It is an Anglo-French Battle Memorial in recognition of the joint nature of the 1916 offensive. The only Imperial Forces remembered here are the South Africans. The Memorial was designed by Sir Edwin Lutyens and was built between 1928 and 1932. It reflects his philosophy that 'all that is done of structure should be for all and for equality of honour.' The largest British memorial in the world, it was unveiled by the Prince of Wales in the presence of the President of France, Albert Lebrun, on 1 August 1932

Also commemorated:	Author's grandson:	Major Cedric Charles Dickens, 13/ London Regiment (Kensington), grandson of the famous 19th century novelist, died on 9 September 1916, aged 27, Addenda Panel on Pier 4 Face C
	Footballer:	Lieutenant Evelyn Henry Lintott died on 1st July 1916 at the age of 33. Born in Farncombe near Godalming in Surrey, he was a teacher who like Donald Bell (see p.271) played football professionally for Plymouth Argyle, Q.P.R., Bradford City and Leeds City. He was one of the first footballers to receive a commission, with the 15/ West Yorks (Leeds Pals), Pier 2 Face A
	Poets:	Lieutenant Thomas Kettle, 8/ Royal Dublin Fusiliers died 9 September 1916, at the age of 36, famed for his poem dedicated *To my Daughter Betty, the Gift of God*, Pier 16 Face C
		Corporal Alexander Robertson 12/ Yorks and Lancs (Sheffield Pals) author of a collection of poems *Comrades*, died on 1st July 1916, age 34, Pier 14 Face B
	Shot at Dawn:	Three including Private Harry Farr, 1/ West Yorks (Prince of Wales's Own) executed on 18 October 1916 for cowardice, aged 25, Pier 2 Face D. His daughter Gertrude Harris, who was only three when he was shot, unveiled a statue at the Shot at Dawn plot at the National Memorial Arboretum, Alrewas, in 2001
	Under age:	Five 15 year olds including Private Henry Woodward, 1/6 Royal Warwicks who died on 1st July 1916, Pier 9 Face A
	V.C.s:	There are seven, including Rifleman William McFadzean, 14/ Royal Irish Rifles who died on 1st July 1916, Pier 15 Face A. He was awarded the V.C. posthumously for an act of 'most conspicuous bravery… he gave his life for his comrades.' He had thrown himself onto the top of a box of grenades which had slipped, dislodging two of the 'safety pins'. His was the first V.C. awarded on that fateful day

Author Alan Reed with Rifleman William McFadzean's V.C.

Thiepval Memorial   J Kerr, A Reed

SOMME
1916

PERCY JEEVES

'I remember admiring his action very much'

On 14 August 1913 Percy Jeeves bowled first change for Warwickshire against Gloucestershire at Cheltenham College's cricket ground. Well-built and athletic, his approach to the wicket was smooth and fluent. The return for his efforts was disappointingly modest. He bowled 17 overs and failed to take a wicket at a cost of 43 runs. Nor did his batting exploits raise many eyebrows: a duck in the first innings and a mere single in the second.

Immaculately turned out in spotless white trousers and shirt, his performance, however, left an indelible mark on the celebrated author P.G. Wodehouse. He was visiting his parents in Cheltenham and had decided to spend a day at the cricket. Three years later when casting around for a name for 'Bertie' Wooster's personal valet, the cricketer's surname sprung to mind. Jeeves, the fictional character, inimitable and imperturbable, was born, making his first appearance

The Warwickshire all-rounder Percy Jeeves   *Warwickshire C.C.C*

during the war years in the short story *Extricating Young Gussie*. The start of a permanent starring role was in the 1919 novel *My Man Jeeves*.

The surnames of two other cricketers, Derbyshire's Mordecai Sherwin and Frank Shacklock, are thought to have inspired the first name of Sherlock Holmes, the creation of Sir Arthur Conan Doyle, an M.C.C. member good enough to have taken the wicket of the cricketing colossus, Dr. W.G. Grace.

In response to a request from Warwickshire County Cricket Club, P.G. Wodehouse confirmed that their all-rounder had indeed been the inspiration for the name of the famous valet: 'I suppose Jeeves's bowling must have impressed me for I remembered him in 1916 when I was in New York and starting the Jeeves and Bertie saga and it was just the name I wanted.'

Percy Jeeves was a Yorkshireman, born on 5 March 1888, at Earlsheaton near Dewsbury. He made his mark at Goole Cricket Club at all levels despite his family having no interest in cricket. He was a hard hitting middle-order batsman and a dangerous bowler who could swing the ball in the air both ways. He was only 5 feet 8 inches tall

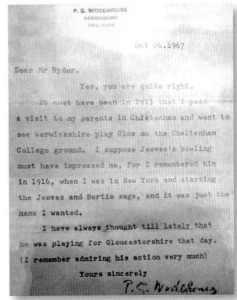

P.G. Wodehouse's response to Rowland Ryder's request for confirmation of the inspiration for the surname of Bertie Wooster's valet
Warwickshire C.C.C.

and weighed little over 10 stone: variation rather than raw pace was his hallmark. He was employed as a professional for Hawes Cricket Club and became proficient enough to be invited for a trial by Yorkshire but failed to impress and was not asked to further his career at the county.

Fortunately for Jeeves his talents were fortuitously unearthed by R.V. Ryder, Warwickshire's secretary from 1895 to 1944, who saw him in action when on a walking holiday in the Yorkshire Dales in 1910. During a round of golf he met Arden Crallan, captain of the Hawes Club, who Jeeves remembered 'recommended me as a likely man for Warwickshire.' He had to qualify for two years before playing Championship cricket. He honed his skills on the ground staff in 1911 when Warwickshire won their first County Championship and performed well enough to receive a letter of engagement from the Club in September offering him a year's contract for £62, which he gladly accepted.

His début for Warwickshire in 1912 in front of a crowd of 10,000 against the touring Australians at Edgbaston was inauspicious. He amassed a total of one run in his two innings and took 2 wickets for 35 runs.

Now qualified, he announced his arrival in county cricket in 1913 with several eye-catching exploits not least in his first championship game at Edgbaston against Leicestershire when he made 46 and 23 and took 3 for 24 and 5 for 37 which prompted *Wisden Cricketers' Almanack* to record: 'A particularly gratifying feature of the match was the fine work with bat and ball of Jeeves, one of the most promising of the younger generation of cricketers.' Jeeves was gaining himself a reputation as a prodigious hitter; on two occasions he hit the ball over the Edgbaston pavilion. His bowling performances were of a consistently high standard- against Kent at Tunbridge Wells he took 4 for 32 but was out-bowled by England left-arm spinner Colin Blythe, who took 5 for 8 in Warwickshire's paltry total of 26. Blythe would also lose his life in action during the Great War (see p.112).

No one was more surprised than Jeeves at taking 106 wickets at an average of 20.88 runs per wicket in his first full season. He recalled with endearing modesty that 'I never dreamed of getting anywhere near my 100 wickets. In fact, at the commencement of the season, I bet one of my colleagues a sovereign that I did not play in more than a dozen county matches. I quite enjoyed handing over that quid!' He also scored a creditable total of 765 runs at an average of 20.13 per innings. At the end of the season he was awarded his county cap.

As storm clouds gathered over Europe during the summer of 1914, Percy Jeeves took 85 wickets and scored 403 runs. He was by now on the fringe of selection for England and was chosen for the Players to take on the Gentlemen at the Oval in early July. Wealthy, often Oxbridge-educated amateurs would play a team of county professionals three times a year, fixtures that highlighted the idiosyncrasies of the Edwardian class system. The 26 year old Jeeves spent three days rubbing shoulders with some of the greatest names in cricket, playing against among others, the swashbuckling amateurs C.B. Fry, Gilbert Jessop, Percy Fender and Pelham 'Plum' Warner.

He listened to the wisdom imparted by his own team members, hardened professionals like Jack Hobbs, Frank Woolley, George Gunn and Herbert Strudwick. He advanced his claim to an England cap with 4 wickets for 44 in the Gentlemen's 2nd innings and as he led the Players off the field with the applause ringing in his ears, *cognoscenti* like the England captain 'Plum' Warner predicted a bright future for the Warwickshire all-rounder. Michael Falcon played for the Gentlemen in the match and was impressed with what he saw: 'Hello, here's Someone!' In the view of Frank R. Foster, the Warwickshire and England fast bowler who was Jeeves's county new ball partner, he was 'the greatest all-rounder in the game in 1914.'

The editor of *Cricket: A Weekly Record of the Game* had predicted in November 1913 that 'given good health, Jeeves may well gain the highest honours on the cricket field.' During the 1914 season he was living up to the billing and in his last game of the season he destroyed the strong Surrey batting line-up, clean bowling Jack Hobbs who was still one of the greatest of English batsmen. Tragically, it was the last game of first-class cricket that Percy Jeeves would ever play.

Within two months Jeeves joined a Pals battalion, the 15/ Royal Warwicks (2nd Birmingham) alongside two of his county team mates, brothers Harold and Len Bates. The enlistment of famous cricketers was a powerful propaganda tool for Army recruitment as fit and athletic heroes led the way in playing their part for King and Country. Gentlemen and Players answered the call to play in the same team together against the advancing 'Hun'. Captain Gilbert Jessop fought in the Manchester Regiment, Privates Jeeves and Harold Bates joined the Royal Warwicks and Serjeant Blythe enlisted initially with the Kent Royal Fortress Engineers and later joined the King's Own Yorkshire Light Infantry.

Jeeves survived the slaughter in the Somme on 1st July 1916. Orders were received on 21 July by the Devons and the Gordon Highlanders to attack the Germans at High Wood, a forested hill near the village of Bazentin-le-Petit, a crucial part of the German line and heavily defended with machine-guns covering every approach. The ground between the British trenches and the hill top was open and bodies from previously unsuccessful offensives littered the area. Despite suffering heavy losses, the 14/ Royal Warwicks and 1/ Royal West Kents were ordered 'over the top' for an assault but their artillery back-up was woefully off target and the Germans were able to pick off their attackers- there were 906 casualties for both battalions. At 11.50 p.m. it was the turn of Private Jeeves and the 15/ Royal Warwicks. Two companies went over the top and were met with a hail of bullets. The Battalion suffered 143 casualties. No trace was found of one of England's most promising cricketers. Percy Jeeves was listed in the 1917 *Wisden* as one of 461 cricketers killed in action, 'England losing a cricketer of whom high hopes had been entertained.' He was one of over 72,000 British soldiers who fell on the Somme before March 1918 whose names are to be found on the Thiepval Memorial.

Jeeves in his Royal Warwicks' uniform with the regimental badge of an antelope on his cap
Warwickshire C.C.C.

Whatever a cricketer's background and however adroit he might have been at avoiding a round red leather missile, no amount of skill would save him from a shell, machine-gun fire or a sniper's bullet. Gilbert Jessop was fortunate to survive the dangers, invalided back to 'Blighty' in 1918. Serjeant Blythe and Privates Jeeves and Harold Bates were not so lucky. Bates died on 19 July 1916 and is commemorated on the Loos Memorial.

Percy Jeeves would probably have been selected to play for England. He never had the opportunity to make his way through the Long Room at Lord's onto the hallowed turf. His fame was due not to his exploits on the cricket fields of England but to his indirect contribution to P.G. Wodehouse's literary success which, tragically, he did not survive to appreciate.

PERCY JEEVES:

Born:	5 March 1888 in Earlsheaton, Yorkshire, son of Edwin Jeeves of 72, Manuel Street, Goole
Education:	Alexandra Street Board School, Goole
Occupation:	Professional cricketer
Unit/ Regiment:	15/ Royal Warwicks (2nd Birmingham)
Rank:	Private
Died:	22 July 1916, Battle of the Somme
Age:	28
Commemorated:	Thiepval Memorial, Pier 9 Face A

Percy Jeeves, one of over 72,000 men killed in the Somme with no known grave, commemorated on the Thiepval Memorial J Kerr

HECTOR MUNRO ('SAKI')

'Waldo is one of those people who would be enormously improved by death'

'Put that bloody cigarette out' were Lance Serjeant Hector Munro's final words in No Man's Land near Beaumont in the Somme. Fearful that cigarette smoke might alert the enemy, his cautionary order to one of the soldiers sheltering with him in a muddy and flooded shell crater, merely drew attention to himself. One German sniper's bullet to the head ended his life.

Munro enlisted in the 2/ King Edward's Horse during the euphoric atmosphere of August 1914. For a not particularly robust 43 year old, the training was too challenging physically and in September he secured a transfer to 22/ Royal Fusiliers. His new battalion's recruiting poster would have appealed to him- it depicted a Tommy killing several German soldiers and the caption underlined the conscripted German Army's numerical superiority over the British Expeditionary Force: 'It's 4 to 1, come and help us lads, quick!'

Munro was keen to become one of the 'lads' and eschewed a commission which would have been a formality in view of his background and celebrity. He took pride in announcing that he was volunteering as a 'trooper'. When a general inspected the Battalion in 1916 and found Munro mundanely preparing potatoes in the kitchens, he asked 'What on earth are you doing here Munro?' It was an understandable reaction from an establishment figure but many of Munro's fellow 'Tommies' were unaware of their promoted lance serjeant's pre-war exploits as an author and journalist.

Munro followed his father Colonel Charles Augustus Munro into the Burma Military Police Force in 1894. After six years of service he contracted malaria so severely that he was forced to return home. After recovery at his father's home in Westward Ho! Devon, he embarked on a writing career. He based himself in London and subsidised by his father, somewhat ambitiously produced a Gibbons-type history of the rise of the Roman Empire. His *magnum opus* was damned with faint praise and had it not been for a chance meeting in 1900 with the eminent cartoonist Francis Carruthers Gould, his writing career might have faltered at the first hurdle. Gould worked as a political cartoonist for *The Westminster Gazette*, a daily paper patronised by the politically influential. It was to prove a fruitful collaboration. Munro complemented Gould's cartoons with biting parodies and satire. Their targets included the Prime Minister, A.J. Balfour, for his handling of the Boer War and Rudyard Kipling whose gung ho imperialism was parodied in *The Political Jungle Book* and the *Not-So Stories*. The poet laureate Alfred Austen's work was witheringly attacked in the *Gazette's Alice in Wonderland* series: 'What have you got there?' asked the Cheshire Cat as Alice picked up the paper and opened it: 'It seems to be a kind of poetry' said Alice doubtfully. 'At least' she added 'some of the words rhyme and none of them appear to have any particular meaning.'

Munro penned most of his satirical contributions under the *nom de plume* of 'Saki'. Much of his work was suffused with an undercurrent of homoeroticism and homosexuality; his choice of pseudonym was no coincidence- poems by the 14th century Persian poet Hafiz refer to the 'Saki' or cupbearer who was portrayed as a beautiful boy and the object of male desire. The extent of Hector Munro's male relationships can only be guessed at- his sister Ethel destroyed the majority of his papers after using them first for her *Biography of Saki*. She may have considered his papers harboured secrets that should remain outside the public domain at a time when homosexuality was illegal.

Hector's early years were blighted by the death of his mother Mary Frances who was killed, improbably, by a rampaging cow. As their father was stationed in Burma, he, his brother Charles and sister Ethel were brought up by their two spinster aunts Charlotte and Augusta near Barnstaple in Devon. The children were deeply resentful of their aunts' despotic régime and some of Munro's most vitriolic pieces were aimed at Aunt Charlotte during her lifetime. Hector was sent to board at Bedford Grammar School, an unhappy time that lasted only four terms.

Cynics at *The Morning Post*, the forerunner of *The Daily Telegraph*, for which Munro wrote between 1902 and 1914, scornfully suggested that he had opted to be a 'trooper' because of the potentially rich pickings amongst the 'men'. In the only major biography of 'Saki' other than Ethel Munro's, Professor A.J. Langguth maintains that there was little evidence to support such a stance and that Munro was highly regarded by his fellow soldiers. He was a colleague who never shirked his responsibilities and was remembered as witty and thoughtful.

There are parallels with Oscar Wilde- both were open about their sexuality and 'Saki' was also revered for a fine collection of entertaining witticisms. One of his characters, the effete and elegant Reginald, observed that 'beauty is only sin deep' and 'the cook was a good cook, as cooks go; and as cooks go, she went.' Another, Clovis, maintained that 'Waldo is one of those people who would be enormously improved by death.' Possibly referring to Prime Minister A.J. Balfour, 'Saki' strikes a chord with his political truism: 'We all know that Prime Ministers are wedded to the truth, but like other wedded couples they sometimes live apart.' In a wonderful example of his craft, Munro wrote 'the wine lists had been consulted with the blank embarrassment of a schoolboy suddenly called upon to locate a minor prophet in the tangled hinterland of the Old Testament.'

Hector Munro was a keen ornithologist and animal lover from an early age. When in Burma he tamed a tiger cub which on one occasion he took to a hotel. An old lady in the next door bedroom was, unsurprisingly, somewhat concerned by the proximity of the lively beast that kept banging into the wall and in a letter to Ethel he recalled that 'I met the old lady at dinner and was greeted with an icy stare which was refreshing in such a climate'!

Hector Munro aged 10 and in his youth

Hector's Christmas missive to his sister in 1915 from the Front included a reworking of the popular carol which was brutally apposite:

> *'While shepherds watched their flocks by night*
> *All seated on the ground*
> *A high explosive shell came down*
> *And mutton rained around.'*

Munro was *The Morning Post*'s special correspondent in the Balkans in 1902 and two years later was moved to St. Petersburg where he spent three happy years, apart from when he and Ethel, who was visiting at the time, witnessed the massacre of demonstrators by Tsar Nicholas II's Cossacks in 1905. A staunch supporter of monarchy, Munro was nonetheless highly critical of this oppression of political views: 'I do not believe that the best way to fight revolution is by lawless and arbitrary repression.' He correctly predicted that 'Russia is unmistakeably on the eve of a very acute period of disorder'. Twelve years later in 1917, mounting turbulence was the result of the Tsar's personal handling of the Russian war effort, the catalyst for revolution and the removal of his régime.

Munro could also take credit for his constant warnings in *The Morning Post* of the economic military and naval growth of Kaiser Wilhelm II's Germany. He argued vigorously that war was inevitable and so certain was he of such a scenario that the subject of his second novel *When William Came* was of life in a Britain subjugated by the Kaiser. *The Times Literary Supplement* congratulated Munro on a 'remarkable *tour de force*'. If the German advance on Paris in 1914 had not been halted by the French and British in the conflict around the rivers Aisne and Marne, another of Munro's predictions would have been correct. In view of his dire warnings about the German threat, it was inevitable that Hector Munro would enlist with enthusiasm. He had, after all, played a considerable role in raising awareness of Germany's intentions.

A common theme in many soldiers' accounts of the first months of the War, is impatience with an endless wait for the order to join the action at the Front. He could continue to write for a number of publications during his period of military inactivity including *The Morning Post* and *The Bystander*.

Hector complained to his sister Ethel in February 1915 after six months of training that 'it is a poor game to be waiting when others are bearing the brunt and tasting the excitement of real warfare.' It was not until November that he was able to exclaim to Ethel that 'it seems almost too good to be true that I am going to take an active part in a big European War.'

On 18 November the 22/ Royal Fusiliers arrived by train at St. Omer. His first taste of warfare was when he volunteered to mend barbed wire entanglements in front of trenches near Fromelles. He refused to allow the hardships of war to depress him. In a romanticised account of the trenches for his niece Felicia, he wrote that 'it is nice being out here' but complained about all the marching: 'I think you would enjoy going out at night to mine the wire entanglements in front of our lines. You have to creep like a prowling cat, and when the enemy sends a flare light every few minutes, you have to press yourself flat on the ground and pretend to be a lump of earth.'

Munro family photo- Hector is on the right, sister Ethel is second from the right and his niece Felicia   National Portrait Gallery X134930

Munro survived the carnage of the Somme but in October 1916 he succumbed for a second time in his life to malaria. He admitted to disappointment that he was letting his 'boys' down whom he kept thinking of 'all the time'. When palpably unfit for combat, he insisted on leaving his sickbed to join 'A' Company for the attack on 14 November in the area of the Redan Ridge, south west of Serre. They were given the order to go 'over the top' at dawn. It was a forlorn exercise as little progress could be made as men sank to the waist in mud. Lance Serjeant Munro

Munro in uniform and performing military duties

and members of 'A' Company found themselves marooned in No Man's Land. It was ironic that he had admitted in August 1914 that 'it is only fitting that the author of "When William came" should go to meet William half way.'

Hector Munro spent much of his life enjoying the comforts of European hotels and embassies but his death in the muddy wastes of the Somme was the way he would have wanted it- fighting for his country against an aggressor that he had known for longer than most, threatened the British way of life that he held so dear. His body was never recovered.

HECTOR MUNRO ('SAKI'):

Born:	18 December 1870, son of Charles and Mary Munro
Education:	Bedford Grammar School
Occupation:	Journalist, political satirist and author
Unit/ Regiment:	2/ King Edward Horse then 22/ Royal Fusiliers (Kensington)
Rank:	Lance Serjeant
Died:	14 November 1916, Battle of the Somme
Age:	45
Commemorated:	Thiepval Memorial, Pier 16 Face A

Hector Munro's name on the Thiepval Memorial   *J. Kerr*

The Thiepval Memorial from the Anglo-French Cemetery   *J Kerr*

FREDERICK S. KELLY

'He had a wonderful enjoyment of life and communicated his electricity to those he was with'

One of the finest rowers of the Edwardian era, Frederick Septimus Kelly, received a letter in January 1908 from the Committee of Selection and Control for the Olympic Regatta expressing the hope that he would be 'able and willing to assist us… by placing your services at our disposal.' He was to be available for practice and training in the months of May, June and July. Appreciation was shown that 'considerable expenditure of time and energy would be required' but importantly the Committee wished to point out that 'well tried oarsmen should be available at the present time to regain much of the rowing prestige of the country as has been lately lost, and to defend that which remains.'

Preparation for the Rowing Olympians in 1908 was rather more relaxed than for their 2012 'Team G.B.' counterparts. Kelly must have been slow to respond for on 18 June, just six weeks before the Olympics, he received a telegram from Dr. Raymond Etherington-Smith, the captain of the Leander Club of Henley-on-Thames, seeking confirmation that he intended to row for the Club which, with Cambridge University, would represent Great Britain. His reply was, according to Thérèse Radic, editor of his diary, strangely indecisive. He claimed he had 'a great deal to do' but would participate if they 'were really in a hole'. In reality, there was never any doubt as to his intentions, having admitted in his diary in May that he was leaving Frankfurt where he was studying musical composition to concentrate on his rowing.

Oxford Rowing 'Blue' F.S. Kelly

The line-up of the Leander crew could now be finalised and the chosen eight rowers and their cox, Gilchrist Maclagan, (see p.65) could take to their 'home waters' at Henley to train in earnest for the greatest challenge of their sporting careers.

Kelly's rowing talents were nurtured at Eton College between 1893 and 1899. He was 'stroke' of the eight that won the Ladies' Challenge Plate at the 1899 Henley Regatta- the stroke was positioned at the stern of the boat opposite the cox and set the tempo for the rest of the crew. Surprisingly he was awarded only one Oxford 'Blue' in 1903 when Cambridge were victorious. His best discipline was sculling- at Oxford in 1902, he beat Etherington-Smith in the final of the Diamond Challenge for Sculling at Henley which he won again in 1903 and in 1905, his time of eight minutes and 10 seconds setting a record which remained intact until 1938.

The Henley Regatta was a happy hunting ground for F.S. Kelly in the way that Wimbledon was for the New Zealander Anthony Wilding (see p.173). He won the Wingfield Amateur Championship for sculling on the Thames and rowed in the Leander eights which won the Grand Challenge Cup in 1903, 1904 and 1905. He won the Stewards' Challenge Cup in 1906 to seal his place as one of the best rowers of his generation. Such was his mastery of the art of sculling, that he was asked by Rudie C. Lehmann, a Liberal M.P. and rowing devotee, to contribute a chapter for *The Complete Oarsman*, a coaching manual which was published in May 1908, two months before the Olympics started.

Frederick Septimus Kelly was, as his second name suggests, the seventh child of Thomas and Anne Kelly. Despite his slightly pretentious name and Eton and Oxford education, F.S. Kelly was an Australian, born in Sydney and educated at Sydney Grammar School. His father's ancestry was Irish; he made his wealth in the wool trade and later became a Director of the Union Bank of Australia. He was a major shareholder in the Australian Kerosene, Oil and Mineral Company and by 1900 had significant holdings in 20 gold and copper mining companies. An Eton College education for Frederick and his older brothers Thomas and William (who later sat in the Australian House of

Representatives from 1903 to 1919) was, therefore, well within his means. The length of sea journeys to and from Australia meant that Frederick was virtually tied to the 'mother country' for his time at school and university; his love of England was such that he rarely returned. With the sizeable inheritance left by his father on his death in 1901, Frederick and his sister Maisie were able to rent Bisham Grange, a large house on the banks of the Thames near Marlow. For Kelly it was the perfect location: a good scull away from Eton and Windsor downstream and Henley upstream!

Frederick Septimus spent many happy hours as a child in Sydney harbour in a variety of water craft. But he had a more important string to his bow… he was a musical child prodigy. By the age of five, he had memorised several Mozart piano sonatas (which Mozart may well have written at the same age!) and his piano-playing developed well enough for him to be tutored at Eton by the eminent Dr. Charles Harford Lloyd.

By 1895 the 13 year old Kelly had made his mark on the College's musical life as a musician of great talent and skill. His performance at the Concert in January 1895 caught the attention of the reviewer: 'Kelly has now become an institution in our concert, and he seems quite at home on the platform; his playing is crisp and clear, and he only lacks a little more delicacy to make him a really first rate performer.' On the second night the audience called him back for an encore, 'a rare distinction for an instrumental soloist.' Frederick would soon outshine his violin-playing brother Thomas.

F.S. Kelly 'surpassed himself' for Mendelssohn's *Capriccio Brilliant* in the December Concert and in March 1896 'he played splendidly.' In the Michaelmas Concert, 'Kelly was wonderful as usual, Weber's Konzertstück suited him exactly and he did it full justice.' He also turned his hands to the glockenspiel during another piece.

The following year he proved himself to be something of a virtuoso in a 'showy piece by Godard'. Reviews for his performances in 1898 and 1899 wax lyrically about his standard of playing and the reviewer grumbled that he would 'gladly have heard more of Kelly' without the accompanying orchestra! In his final concert at Eton, not only did he play a Beethoven Piano Concerto with *élan* but his own composition, a song entitled *Eton and Winchester*, was sung by the choir.

Kelly concentrated on music and rowing at Oxford to the detriment of his academic studies- he achieved a 4th class degree in History. He was elected President of the prestigious Oxford University Music Society, a post held a few years later by George Butterworth, the composer and English folk and dance collector (see p.245). Kelly decided to concentrate on pursuing a musical career after leaving Oxford. He studied piano under Ernst Engesser and composition and counterpoint with Iwan Knorr at the Hoch Conservatoire in Frankfurt from 1903 to 1905 but returned at regular intervals for further tuition and practice. His ambition was to be 'a great player and a great composer' like another Australian graduate of the Hoch- Percy Grainger. Kelly's performance in his graduation piece, the Brahms 2nd piano concerto, was of a sufficiently high standard to suggest that he could realise his ambition.

In the May of Olympics year F.S. Kelly was in Frankfurt practising Brahms piano concertos and receiving lessons from Engesser. He was keeping fit with early morning runs and doing exercises in the evenings to strengthen his stomach muscles, in fact following the advice he imparted in his chapter of *The Complete Oarsman* in which he declared: 'The commonest form of strain is that of the abdominal muscles, which is a serious matter' and that his readers should do regular exercises to prevent it.

By July he had returned to Bisham. His diary entry for 14 July records that after dinner he read 'most of E. Smith's chapter on training in the "Complete Oarsman"'. His pre-Olympics schedule on 16 July was busy and idiosyncratic: he read some books on Christian Science which he was interested in but not converted to, practised the piano, read R.L. Stevenson's *Prince Otto* and after dinner had two glasses of wine and a game of bridge.

Three days before Leander's first race at Henley, Kelly was caught in a speed trap when driving to an organ recital in St. George's Chapel, Windsor Castle, travelling at an eye watering 25 m.p.h.! Was his extreme speed a portent for the upcoming competition?

For the 1908 Olympics, competition for crews of eight was on a knock-out basis. Only five countries were represented in the draw- Great Britain (Leander and Cambridge), Belgium (Royal Club Nautique

The Leander Olympic gold medal-winning eight and officials. F.S. Kelly is standing behind a balustrade post and to the left is the cox Gilchrist Maclagan wearing a cap and cravat
River and Rowing Museum, Henley-on-Thames

de Gand), Norway (Norge), Canada (Toronto Argonauts) and Hungary (Pannonia) (see p.66). Hopes were high that the highly regarded Leander crew would triumph. Raymond Etherington-Smith was the 'stroke' and the diminutive 'Cocky' Maclagan the cox, described by R.C. Lehmann as a 'trusted guide and counsellor of his crews'. Kelly rowed at No. 2 and in the first race on 29 July, Leander overcame the Hungarian crew. The following day, the Canadians were pipped to the post to earn Leander a place in the final against the powerful and much respected Belgians. It was an eagerly anticipated battle of differing methods and style but on the day, the British crew eased to a two length victory.

F.S. Kelly may have originated from a far flung dominion of the British Empire but he was proud to be selected for a quintessentially English rowing club. He and the Leander crew, commonly agreed at the time to be the best ever seen at Henley, were presented individually with a gold medal and a diploma and collectively a statue of Pallas Athena (the ancient Greek goddess of strength, strategy and skill) by Lady Desborough, wife of Lord Desborough who was the driving force behind the 1908 Olympics. The statue was presented to the International Olympic Committee by Comte Brunetta D'Usseaux: it was made of bronze and Lady Ettie Desborough would have needed several helping hands to present it to the captain of the victorious Leander crew!

The statue of Athena presented to the Leander medal-winning eight
River and Rowing Museum, Henley-on-Thames

Her husband, Lord Desborough, was the equivalent of Lord Coe of the 2012 London Olympics who faced a huge challenge of organisation but at least, unlike Desborough, he did not have a mere 18 months to organise the Olympics. Naples was to have been the Olympic venue but in 1906, Mount Vesuvius erupted destroying the city. Lord Desborough, Chairman of the British Olympic Council, stepped in and offered London as the substitute venue.

The Olympic gold medal signalled the end of Kelly's competitive rowing career. His involvement would now be limited to umpiring and stewarding.

Lord Desborough speaking at the 1908 Olympics awards' ceremony- the statue of Athena is in front of Lady Desborough
From The Official Report by the British Olympic Council of the London 1908 Olympic Games

The main years of F.S. Kelly's musical activity were 1911 and 1912. He went on a concert tour of his homeland where he played Beethoven's G Major Piano Concerto with the Sydney Symphony Orchestra in June 1911 and gave three solo recitals which included works by Bach, Beethoven and Mozart. He also played his own *Cycle of Lyrics* composition. The Australian press were appreciative and enthusiastic- *The Sydney Morning Herald* lauded an Australian artist 'of the highest rank'.

He played a series of recitals with the Hungarian violinist Jelly d'Aranyi in the spring of 1912 which elicited critical praise for his 'crisp, clear enunciation, melodious touch and intelligent grasp of the music'. Reputedly Jelly was in love with Frederick Septimus and played his compositions until her death in 1960- whether her love was reciprocated or not is uncertain but had they married, she might have been advised to keep her maiden name.

Kelly played a series of concerts with the London Symphony Orchestra under the baton of George Henschel playing pieces by Beethoven, Schumann, Mozart and Brahms. In his diary he recorded on 21 February that 'I got about a dozen papers in the morning and at teatime to see the criticisms of my concert yesterday and with the exception of about three (including *The Times*) they were all rather bad.' His rather sad conclusion was that 'most of the critics seem to be on their guard against being taken in by a sculler who has turned to music.' He also expressed disappointment at the size of the audiences which were generally 'meagre' and a 'good' audience was in the region of 200.

It may be that at this stage Kelly was accepting that his progress to musical greatness was on hold- *The Times* on 28 September 1912 was of the opinion that 'Mr. F.S. Kelly's playing of Mozart's Concerto in D (K.537) failed where the orchestral playing succeeded.' That he should have been still playing at such a level was remarkable as he had experienced every soloist's nightmare: memory loss when playing in a Queen's Hall Promenade Concert. He also suffered from a nervous complaint in his hands.

His major appearances were limited after 1912 but he continued to be involved in music- he succeeded Sir Edgar Speyer, a generous sponsor of the Arts, as Chairman of the Classical Concert Society of London which he had been advising on concert programmes since 1909. He performed small-scale recitals and played informally with Edward Elgar and professionally with the 'cellist Pablo Casals with whom he also played friendly games of tennis. He was not a prolific composer; by the outbreak of war his portfolio of compositions numbered little more than a dozen.

The friendships Kelly made at Oxford, with in particular Raymond and Herbert 'Beb' Asquith, sons of H.H. Asquith the future war time Prime Minister, coupled with his fame as an oarsman, offered him an *entrée* into the world of Edwardian high society which he moved in with consummate ease. He was a naturally gregarious and popular character whose great trump card was that he could entertain fellow guests at house and dinner parties with piano playing of a standard not usually experienced at such social gatherings. Affectionately known as 'Sep' or 'Cleg', after S.R. Crockett's adventurer in *Cleg Kelly: Arab of the City*, he enjoyed rubbing shoulders with the 'great and good'. During a visit to Brownsea Island off Dorset on 10 September 1909, he recalled that it 'rained all morning but cleared up sufficiently for a foursome of golf at about 3.30 p.m. in which Prince Maurice and I beat Mrs. Van Raalte and Prince Alphonso.' The house guests played 'hide and seek' in the morning, a game that the British royal princes, Leopold and Maurice of Battenberg played 'ardently'. They then played 'Rabbits and Ferrets' in the billiard room... After his afternoon game of golf 'Cleg' played Chopin to the Princess and he happily averred it was 'one of the jolliest days I have ever experienced.'

A less jolly day was when someone must have confided to the Prime Minister's daughter, Violet Asquith, that 'Cleg' had been mimicking her. 'It was true, but I can't imagine who could have told her. At all events, she became extremely sarcastic and a regular little spitfire in manner.' He did manage to charm his way back into her favour, enough for her to ask him to perform a recital at her home in early August 1914.

In the weeks before the declaration of war, music was uppermost in F.S. Kelly's mind. He played recitals with Jelly d'Aranyi and one of his final public appearances was as a conductor at the Aeolian Hall in London- he was unimpressed that much of the orchestra failed to attend the afternoon rehearsal and that the 'fixer' had brought in a 'minute female drummer from one of the theatre orchestras who began the Beethoven Concerto making a noise like someone beating a tambourine with an old shoe'! He was grateful she had not been engaged for the evening performance and that the missing players did turn up on cue. It was, in Kelly the conductor's words, 'a miracle of a performance.'

On Saturday 18 July Eddie Marsh, a well-known patron of artists and musicians, joined W. Denis Browne, music critic and composer, for a weekend at Bisham. After dinner Browne played Percy

Grainger's arrangement of *Londonderry Air*, a Couperin *Rondeau*, and provided the accompaniment for some Fauré songs. He also played his ballet, *The Comic Spirit* which the conservative-minded Kelly considered a little too influenced by Stravinsky. In only a few months' time Browne and Kelly would be music-making in less auspicious and comfortable circumstances.

F.S. Kelly was a man of action and on Tuesday 4 August he was wondering whether he should join up with the Territorials. The following day he travelled to London to investigate how he could enlist and used his political 'strings' to good effect. After lunching at the Union Club, he visited Hugh Godley, a contemporary of his at Balliol, who worked at the Treasury. From there contact was made with 10 Downing Street: the Olympic gold medallist met Maurice 'Bongie' Bonham-Carter, now married to Violet Asquith, who advised him to apply to a Public School battalion to receive initial training.

Born in Australia and educated in England- Kelly saw himself as a 'British Australian', which was typical of the general attitude of those in the 'colonies' at the time and as Thérèse Radic asserts, England was still being referred to in Australia as 'Home' even if someone had been born in Australia.

'Cleg' described the kind of scenario at the end of August that must have been played out throughout the land: 'There were not many people on the river and below Marlow lock a fisherman shouted out to us in rather a bitter tone that we'd make four good recruits!' Kelly underlines the pressures on young and able men to enlist: 'There is a considerable rat hunt going on in the press for those who ought to serve and don't!'

Technically too old for combat, 'Cleg' had hoped to join the prestigious Grenadier Guards Regiment but there was no place there for an Eton and Oxford-educated Australian.

When dining on 16 September with the poet Rupert Brooke, Eddie Marsh and W. Denis Browne, Kelly learnt that he had received a commission with the Royal Naval Division Volunteer Force as a sub lieutenant in the Drake Battalion. He was delighted to be with a number of friends who styled themselves as the 'Latin Club'- Rupert Brooke, W. Denis Browne, Arthur 'Oc' Asquith, Charles Lister the scholar son of Lord Ribblesdale, Patrick Shaw-Stewart, at 25 a Director of Barings Bank, and Bernard Freyberg, a New Zealander and later a General, V.C. holder and Governor-General of New Zealand.

Jelly d'Aranyi to whom Kelly dedicated a violin sonata written at Gallipoli   National Portrait Gallery 5735

'Cleg' was in his element- at the Walmer Naval camp near Deal he wrote on 25 September: 'After dinner I was prevailed upon to play on a wretched little upright piano in the Officers' Anteroom.' His programme choice of Brahms, Rachmaninov, Chopin, Grieg and Mendelssohn created 'somewhat of a severe atmosphere.' But his musical ability was such that he could adapt to the prevailing mood and when at sea, he entertained those on board with a selection of sea shanties and music hall songs.

F.S. Kelly had displayed great self-discipline and attention to detail in his music and rowing. He found it difficult to accept the inevitable organisational changes required as the War progressed. 'Interference with the composition of the force' he complained 'makes it a disheartening business to try and work it up into efficiency and there is the wearisome prospect of joining up with other units.' Music offered him an escape from such irritations: he played the organ at church services for his platoon, once being unable to use the bass pedals due to an attack of cramp! Having rowed against Belgian eights, he was, understandably, happy to play to a hospital ward of wounded Belgian soldiers. He played Mozart's E Minor violin sonata with Jelly d'Aranyi on 5 January 1915 'which gave me great pleasure.' He spent many off duty hours composing and

arranging folk songs- the current fashion, driven by Ralph Vaughan Williams and George Butterworth.

He transcribed the words of several songs from Cecil Sharp's *Collection of Folk Songs for Schools* and had them printed for the Drake Battalion.

Kelly and the 'Latin Club' were transferrred to the Hood Battalion of the Royal Naval Division that sailed from Avonmouth in the *Grantully Castle* on 15 February 1915 for the Dardanelles to perform military rather than naval operations. It was the First Lord of the Admiralty Winston Churchill's ill-fated scheme to take pressure off the Western Front by opening a supply route to Russia by taking the Ottoman capital of Constantinople, modern-day Istanbul.

Before Kelly left for the Dardanelles, he sat for a charcoal drawing by John Singer Sargent on the insistence of Maisie who may well have had fears for her brother's life and a desire, therefore, to commission a worthy pictorial record of him.

'Cleg' was often in touch with Rupert Brooke before the War. They would meet at the Union Club in Trafalgar Square but their friendship developed on the journey to the Dardanelles. On 16 April he had 'a delightful talk about literature and poetry... He strikes me as being made of really fine stuff, both physically and mentally' and on another occasion 'we had a talk about literary matters. I asked him to read his five sonnets... I enjoyed the sound of his voice and the way he read them a great deal.' Kelly was unaware that the poet, whose patriotic *The Soldier* and other poems would become best sellers, was dangerously ill. He was suffering from septicaemia as a result of a mosquito bite. Kelly feared the worst: 'I have had a foreboding that he is one of those like Keats, Shelley and Schubert, who are not suffered to deliver their full message.'

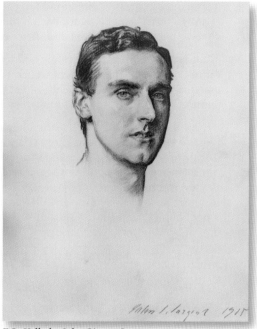

F.S. Kelly by John Singer Sargent
National Portrait Gallery D36773

Rupert Brooke died on a French hospital ship on 23 April 1915. The 'Latin Club' was devastated. They buried their friend on the Greek island of Skyros, reputedly the birthplace of Achilles, with full military honours at a spot chosen by W. Denis Browne. The ceremony was, for F.S. Kelly, 'a most moving experience... The small olive grove in the narrow valley and the scent of the wild sage gave a strong classical tone which was so in harmony with the poet we were burying, that to some of us the Christian ceremony seemed out of keeping.' The mourners covered the grave with stones and as many pieces of marble as they could find. There was 'no more fitting resting place for a poet' in such a beautiful 'foreign field'. With admirable prescience, Kelly copied the contents of Brooke's notebook before going to bed, 'as a precaution against loss.' He expected the Battalion to be in action the following day; consumed with thoughts of his departed friend, he played Scarlatti's C Minor Sonata, Chopin's F Minor Ballade and two of his own Studies.

Rupert Brooke's grave on the island of Skyros
Archive Centre, King's College, Cambridge

The Hood Battalion took part in attacks against the Turks in the Gallipoli Peninsula on 2 May and between 6 and 8 May when 'Oc' Asquith was shot in the leg. The remnants of the Battalion were supported on 4 June by the Collingwood Battalion and in an attack on the Turks, Kelly was shot in the heel and was taken for treatment to a hospital in Alexandria. While recuperating he was informed of his award of a Distinguished Service Cross for his gallantry. It was a time for spiritual and physical healing- *hors de combat*, he dedicated himself to composing a musical tribute to his fallen friend: his *Elegy for Strings 'In Memoriam Rupert Brooke'* to which he would add the harp part later. The author of Kelly's obituary in *The Eton Chronicle*, 'Oc' Asquith, recalled that 'he told me he had tried to introduce the atmosphere of Greek temples and the movement of the leaves of the olive trees, excluding Christian sentiment, with which he did not associate Rupert.'

On his return to Gallipoli, in quiet moments away from the trenches at Cape Helles, he composed a violin sonata for Jelly d'Aranyi- he wrote it in his head initially and in a letter to her he confided: 'It is all there in my head but not yet on paper. You must not expect shell and rifle fire in it! It is rather a contrast to all that, being somewhat idyllic.' He managed to score the music in manuscript form when he returned to England and they were able to play the piece he had dedicated to her.

Kelly returned to Gallipoli in July and was now in charge of a company 'which under him became a model company in matters of trench routine and discipline and smartness of appearance.' His attention to detail reflected the 'true artist's desire to perfect his company.' The Battalion would spend alternate weeks in the trenches and apart from two days 'Cleg' was with his men at all times.

He took leave in January 1916 after the Battalion had been withdrawn from Gallipoli. To celebrate her step-son Arthur's return, Margot Asquith held a dinner party at 10 Downing Street on 1 March. This provided 'Cleg' with a wonderful opportunity to showcase *The Elegy*. After dinner the Prime Minister retired to play bridge. 'Cleg' played his piece and when the British Premier noisily interrupted him, he was told in no uncertain terms by his daughter Violet to be quiet and listen! She was so impressed with Kelly's musicianship that she overcame her antipathy to him and asked him to play at her house. Rupert Brooke's death had caused such a stir that he was in great demand to play *The Elegy* at London society gatherings.

The first public performance of his piece was at Rugby School, Brooke's *alma mater*. In *The Rugby Meteor* the reviewer considered that '*The Elegy* recaptured something of that wistful pagan burial on Skyros with a fair breeze beginning to stir the olive leaves under a beclouded half moon.'

A second Hood Battalion was formed in May 1916, commanded by 'Oc' Asquith with Kelly as his second-in-command. Their return to the Eastern Mediterranean was short lived- having reached Malta via Marseilles, the Battalion was recalled for the planned offensive on the Somme. The Dardanelles campaign had been an expensive and misconceived strategy that claimed the lives of 21,000 British and over 10,000 Australian and New Zealand soldiers.

The Royal Naval Division spent several weeks training in France. Kelly was based in the Abbeville area where he and two other officers were responsible for finding billets. The Mayor of Citerne provided accommodation for them in the *Mairie* but insisted they dine first with his wife and two 'pretty daughters'!

The Division was ready for front line duties by early July but escaped the 'hot zones'. Although they were in the Royal Naval Division, Kelly and his men were trained as infantrymen and wore khaki uniforms but retained naval ranks and habits. They were commanded by senior army officers and it seems that there was plenty of scope for friction. Feisty as ever Kelly refused to shave off his beard during instruction for trench warfare- a beard was as much part of naval uniform as moustaches were for the military. They had a new commanding officer in October 1916, Major General Shute, who had a great dislike for naval traditions and became very unpopular in trying to stamp them out. He made the men wear army rank badges so in quiet protest they wore them on one arm but naval ones on the other.

Shute had also been complaining about the poor management of the latrines and potential risk to health and after one of his particularly critical inspections of trenches that the sailors had only just taken over, Sub Lieutenant A. P. Herbert, of later fame, was moved to write the following ditty apparently sung to the tune of the *Eton Boating Song* which summed up the feelings of the men!

The general inspecting the trenches
Exclaimed with a horrified shout
I refuse to command a division
Which leaves its excreta about.

But nobody took any notice
No one was prepared to refute,
That the presence of shit was congenial
Compared to the presence of Shute.

And certain responsible critics
Made haste to reply to his words
Observing that his staff advisors
Consisted entirely of turds.

For shit may be shot at odd corners
And paper supplied there to suit,
But a shit would be shot without mourners
If somebody shot that shit Shute.

Kelly was unimpressed with the trenches in the Somme which he compared unfavourably with those in the Gallipoli Peninsula. He considered that deep dugouts were death traps (he had not yet seen the impressively constructed, deep German dugouts) and he expressed concern that some sections of trenches were so shallow that they were a sniper's delight. He was shocked by how easily the trenches flooded and felt the mosquitos they attracted were more of a problem than the ubiquitous rats which at least served 'a very useful purpose as scavengers.'

His sector was relatively quiet but dangerous missions had to be performed nonetheless and he and Arthur 'Oc' Asquith never shirked them. They would go out into No Man's Land under cover of darkness to inspect German listening posts which involved an arduous and painful crawl along the edge of a river through long grass and nettles and they 'frequently encountered barbed wire.'

As ever 'Cleg' Kelly and his 'hyena-like' laugh, was the life and soul of the Battalion and 'Oc' Asquith claimed that he conducted the regimental band in a performance of Tchaikovsky's *1812 Overture* in a wood full of batteries to the accompaniment of a Somme bombardment which provided the 'percussion'. It was certainly his intention, as he outlined in a letter to Sir Edgar Speyer in September and although it seems barely credible that the bombardment supplied the part of the guns, knowing Kelly's eccentricity, it may well have been the case.

F.S. Kelly was a natural leader and was promoted to the rank of lieutenant commander; he overbearingly insisted on the strictest of discipline but was respected by those under his command for his fairness and generosity. When training in England before sailing to the Dardanelles, he had paid for all the men of his platoon to visit a dentist at Blandford in Dorset and when the *Grantully Castle* docked in Malta, he treated all his men to a pair of sunglasses.

His personality did not appeal to everyone- Asquith's obituary of Kelly, one whole page of *The Eton Chronicle*, pointed out that 'the exuberance and directness, and his passion for argument, brought him critics as well as friends, as did his habit of violent and uncontrolled merriment at inconvenient and even inappropriate moments.' The hyena laugh…

He was killed during the last week of the Battle of the Somme on 13 November 1916. He was shot in the head when leading an attack on a machine-gun emplacement at Beaucourt-sur-Ancre (when Bernard Freyberg won his V.C.) in a 'gallant and successful attack' on the machine-gun which 'threatened to enfilade' the advance. A fellow officer wrote: 'Poor Cleg was killed right at the beginning. He was so enthusiastic about the whole thing and told me the night before he was really glad to be in it.'

He was buried in Martinsart Cemetery. It is worth a visit- the gravestones were not of the usual white Portland stone but of an experimental ochre-red Corzehill or Locharbriggs stone. The photograph (see p.270) shows why the experiment was discontinued.

The musical friends and colleagues of 'Cleg' Kelly arranged a Memorial Concert in his memory on 2 May 1919 at the Wigmore Hall in London. The celebrated pianist and friend Leonard Borwick played a number of Kelly's compositions and a *Prelude for Organ* which was composed on the *Grantully Castle* when moored off Rhodes in 1915. A selection of his songs was sung by the contralto Muriel Foster. Not surprisingly it was *The Elegy to Rupert Brooke* that provoked the greatest reaction. It was odd that Jelly d'Aranyi did not appear to take part but she did at least play a leading role in a Memorial Tribute held in the Balliol College Hall when she played three Hungarian dances and Maisie Kelly sang three of his songs. Jelly had kept her copy of the violin sonata dedicated to her by Kelly.

Arthur 'Oc' Asquith survived the last week of the Somme; he lost a leg in 1917 but became a brigadier general in December. He knew 'Cleg' better than most and their friendship grew during the war years to the extent that he admitted to Violet: 'I have grown fond of Cleg, laugh and all.' His death left Asquith severely angered: 'Cleg had a wonderful enjoyment of life and communicated his electricity to those he was with.' Asquith was happy to accede to Maisie's wish that he write the tribute to her brother in *The Eton Chronicle*: 'He was not, and I think never would have made an enthusiastic soldier. He spent most of his leisure time composing music and reading books... but he had a true artist's desire to perfect his company. He was an uncompromising

Frederick Septimus Kelly's grave in Martinsart Cemetery　　*J Kerr*

disciplinarian, spared neither others nor himself and rarely turned a blind eye. Highly strung and brave as a lion, aware and utterly contemptuous of all risks, he commanded the confidence and respect of all under his command. He was contentious, always happiest in argument. He was interested in the psychology of his friends, highly critical of them, and warm heartedly loyal to them and violently intolerant of anything that bore the faintest tinge of cheapness, insincerity, pretentiousness and bad manners.'

Not one of Kelly's cats! A regimental cat in the front line at Cambrai 6 February 1918　　*IWM Q008463*

The Balliol College War Memorial Book considered his disciplinary régime was at first 'too austere to be generally palatable to his subordinates but service in the field bred in them a healthy respect for his unfailing fearlessness and scrupulous justice.' The author commented on his vitality and physique and referred to his bluntness and disregard for the conventions of polite society. Kelly was complimented on his honesty, transparency, lack of pretension and his enjoyment of 'stripping humbug' but if anyone appeared to him as boring, pompous, complacent, affected or insincere, they were treated with undisguised contempt. At least he felt at ease in the company of cats! He collected a number of kittens from deserted French villages and when the Battalion was on the move, each of his officers had to carry a kitten in a sandbag slung over his shoulder!

F.S. Kelly's record as a champion oarsman speaks for itself and he deserves the accolade in Hylton Cleaver's 1956 *History of Rowing*: 'Many think Kelly the greatest amateur stylist of all time' and Rudie C. Lehmann enthused in *The Field* that: 'There never was a sculler who had achieved a more perfect counterpoise between the two sides of his body, and the consequence was that not an ounce of his strength was wasted... In music he had shown high promise of brilliant success as a pianist and composer. He seemed to exercise over the piano something of the same mastery with which he controlled a sculling boat... His natural sense of poise and rhythm made his boat a living thing under him.'

Kelly's fellow Leander crew member Guy Nickalls wrote in *Life's a Pudding*: 'I thought that F.S. Kelly was most likely the fastest sculler of all time- quick, neat and polished' but grumbled, as was his wont, that he was 'a poor waterman on the tideway and a difficult man to train.' His younger brother, Major Vivian Nickalls, who also wrote a book- *Oars, Wars and Horses*, believed Kelly was 'an extraordinary fellow as he hated training and spent his whole time playing the violin, on which he was a wonderful performer. He was one of the many good men who fell in the war.' His view of Kelly's training is questionable and talented as Kelly was musically, his main instrument was the piano.

He would, though, have wanted to be remembered for his musicianship. Like Keats, Shelley, Schubert and Rupert Brooke, he did not have the opportunity to 'deliver his full message'- at the early age of 35, his composing would have developed and with the stamp of his own style. *The Grove Dictionary of Music and Musicians* describes Kelly's music as 'essentially conformist' but his greatest work, *The Elegy for Strings and Harp 'In Memoriam Rupert Brooke'*, did break the mould and his works composed during the War were influenced by the poet whom the author of *The Balliol College War Book* claims, encouraged in Kelly a greater freedom of play, vitality and freshness in his ideas for composition. His friend Leonard Borwick, in a flowery tribute, felt that 'in music... the needs of his spirit were fully answered and satisfied and to that end, he served his beloved art as something holy, with a devotion, a faith, a steadfastness that did but grow with the years.'

He was a superb solo performer, if not truly 'great', who failed to live up to his early promise but was good enough to perform with the very best of the time. The centenary of the Great War should generate more interest in his compositions and focus the debate on his place in English music's hall of fame. Kelly was, Asquith noted, 'entering on a period of great fertility and promise as a composer.'

The Memorial to F.S.Kelly and the lost villagers of Bisham in Buckinghamshire, designed by Eric Gill and commissioned by Maisie Kelly   *A Hamilton*

There has been an upsurge in interest in the hero the Australians 'have yet to discover,' thanks to the efforts of the leading Australian violinist and musicologist Chris Latham who has tracked down the lost copy of Jelly d'Aranyi's *Lost Gallipoli Sonata* which he found in Florence. He will be publishing the version of Kelly's diary that was transcribed by 'Oc' Asquith and arranging concerts in 2015 to celebrate his works in England, Turkey, Australia and New Zealand.

Frederick Septimus 'Cleg' Kelly was a talented eccentric, a marvellous character who inspired loyalty and friendship. Above all he was an entertainer with a rich zest for life. He brought happiness to people's lives, inspiring those in his company with the brilliance of his musicianship at dinner parties, concert halls, aboard ship and behind the front line. He was one of the greatest rowers of his generation- he entertained the crowds at the Henley regatta with his skills and style. His many talents, his energy, vitality, interest in others and general *joie de vivre*, were extinguished by a single bullet during the dying days of the Battle of the Somme.

FREDERICK S. KELLY:

Born:	29 May 1881, son of Thomas and Mary Kelly of Sydney, Australia
Education:	Sydney Grammar School, Eton College, Balliol College, Oxford and Hoch Conservatoire, Frankfurt
Occupation:	Musician: soloist, composer and conductor. Olympic oarsman and gold medallist in 1908
Unit/ Regiment:	Drake and Hood Battalions, Royal Naval Division
Rank:	Lieutenant Commander
Decoration:	D.S.C.
Died:	13 November 1916, Battle of the Somme
Age:	35
Buried:	Martinsart Military Cemetery I.H.25.
	The cemetery was first used at the end of June 1916 and was a front line cemetery until October 1916 and again in October 1918. Designed by Sir Reginald Blomfield, there are nearly 500 burials. The graves are marked by experimental red sand stone rather than the commonly used white Portland stone

Experimental cemetery at Martinsart- the red sandstone is not as easy on the eye as the white Portland stone

J Kerr

DONALD BELL V.C.

'We have lost the best officer and gentleman that ever was with this battalion'

After his death on 10 July 1916, professional footballer Donald Bell's estate was valued at £40 5s 0d which is equivalent to a few thousand pounds in 2014. The amount is a far cry from the wealth that can be accumulated by a Premier League footballer nearly 100 years later. A Manchester United star can earn in just a few minutes on the training ground the equivalent of the paltry amount saved by Donald Simpson Bell, the pre-war Bradford Park Avenue left back.

Donald Bell was born on 3 December 1890, one of seven children. His father was a successful butcher in Harrogate and the children were raised in a strict Methodist household.

He displayed academic ability at St. Peter's School in the town and won a scholarship to the secondary school where he distinguished himself as an all-round sportsman. His physique was ideal for the sports he played and his strength would prove invaluable on the battlefield; by the age of 16, he was over 6 feet tall and weighed nearly 14 stone.

Smith Bell was keen for his son to continue his academic studies so Donald enrolled in 1909 at Westminster College, a Methodist teacher training establishment in London. For three years he excelled at athletics, cricket, rugby and was talented enough to play football as an amateur for Crystal Palace of the Southern League. It was recorded that he could accomplish the 100 yards sprint in 10.35 seconds.

Once he had qualified as a teacher Donald returned to Harrogate as an assistant master at Starbeck School. 'Street cred' amongst his pupils must have soared when he moved in 1911 from Bishop Auckland to the most powerful football club in England- First Division Newcastle United, FA Cup winners in 1910, Division 1 winners in 1905, 1907 and 1908 and not surprisingly nicknamed 'The Edwardian Masters'. The boot money he received after each match was a welcome supplement to his teacher's salary. His first appearance was for the club's 2nd XI in the local Infirmary Charity Cup 1-0 win at High Spen against the Spen Black and Whites in front of a few hundred fans. The closest Bell got to first team football was a White versus Stripes trial match which never took place because of a waterlogged pitch. His chances of selection were hampered by the talented full backs Bill McCracken, Tony Whitson and Frank Hudspeth.

Donald Bell, left back for 2nd Division Club Bradford Park Avenue
The Green Howards Museum, Richmond, Yorkshire

His chances of a first team place were limited in 1912, so Bell took the dramatic decision to sign professional forms with the 2nd Division club Bradford Park Avenue who had lost in the previous year's F.A. Cup final to Newcastle United. 'Donnie' as he was known by his team mates, made his league début in the 3-2 win against Leicester Fosse on 3 November and impressed in the following week's match against Wolverhampton Wanderers at Molineux when he put in a 'sterling' performance. Unfortunately an injury sustained in the crucial promotion clash against Notts County sidelined him for the rest of the season and in his absence, Bradford Park Avenue were promoted to the First Division.

In the summer of 1914 Bell could look forward to playing against the major clubs in the land like Blackburn Rovers, Aston Villa and his former club Newcastle United .

Any dreams he may have harboured were dashed by the declaration of war on 4 August 1914. Most footballers' written requests to the Board of Directors nowadays are for a transfer. Donald Bell's request, however, was to be released from his contract to enlist with Kitchener's Army. 'I have given

2nd Lieutenant Donald Bell
The Green Howards Museum, Richmond, Yorkshire

the subject some very serious consideration and have now come to the conclusion I am duty bound to join the ranks. Will you kindly ask the directors to release me from my engagement?' The directors acceded to his request 'with the utmost pleasure' and wished him a safe return and 'an honourable career'. They were sure that his 'estimable character and strong personality will gain you all that a soldier desires.' He was one of the first professional footballers to enlist: an important catch for the recruiting authorities.

He joined the 9/ Yorkshire Regiment or 'Green Howards' as they were more commonly known, as a private but was soon promoted to lance corporal, a rank considered by an old school friend Archie White, an officer in the Green Howards, to be too low for Bell. A word in the ear of the commanding officer, Lieutenant Colonel Chapman, was enough to ensure that Bell was commissioned as a 2nd lieutenant by June 1915.

Many months were spent at Wisley in Surrey training monotonously for the action in France, a time that many soldiers like Bell found acutely tedious, their enthusiasm compromised as they kicked their heels waiting to 'mix it' with the 'Hun'.

2nd Lieutenant Bell and the Green Howards crossed over to France in August 1915. They were based in the Armentières sector where life was relatively quiet. In June 1916 he returned on leave to Yorkshire for 10 days and married Rhoda Bonson on 5 June in the Wesleyan Methodist chapel in her family's home town of Kirkby Stephen. There was no time for a honeymoon. Donald was due back at the Front.

The Green Howards were by now in reserve south east of the village of La Boisselle. During the Battle of the Somme on 5 July, the Green Howards, in the 69th Brigade of the 23rd Division, were ordered to capture 'Horseshoe Trench' that ran about 1,500 yards from Lincoln Redoubt to Scots Redoubt. At 16.00 hours on 5 July, the 8 and 9/ Yorkshires attacked 'Horseshoe Trench'. During the action Bell's company suffered heavy fire from two machine-guns which Bell decided had to be 'taken out' and he, his batman and a corporal attacked the machine-gun post. In his last letter home to his mother, written two days later on 7 July, he described the action and his own contribution with great modesty and with an overriding belief that he was being watched over by God: 'When the battalion went over, I, with my team crawled up a communication trench and attacked the gun and trench and I hit the gun first shot from about 20 yards and knocked it over. The G.O.C. has been over to congratulate the battalion and he personally thanked me. I must confess it was the biggest fluke alive and I did nothing. I only chucked one bomb but it did the trick. The C.O. says I saved the situation for this gun was doing all the damage. I am glad I have been so fortunate for Pa's sake; for I know he likes his lads to be at the top of the tree. He used to be always on about too much play and too little work, but my athletics came in handy this trip. The only thing is I am sore at the elbow and knees with crawling over limestone flints. Please don't worry about me, I believe that God is watching over me and it rests with him whether I pull through or not. I will write again as soon as I get another chance and will send Field P. C.s every day if possible.'

Behind the lines Bell heard that he might receive an award and wrote to a friend that 'there is talk of me getting a military cross or something of the sort, talk about luck! Fancy, just chucking one's bomb even if it was a bull's eye.' There was little opportunity for idle chatter- although as it happened, he was awarded the V.C. Duty to the cause was more important to him and only five days later he was part of a mission to capture the village of Contalmaison. For a second time the young officer decided that a machine-gun post had to be silenced and he led an attack on it with his pockets filled with grenades. The chances of him surviving a second frontal foray towards a machine-gun were minimal and, not surprisingly, his former good fortune eluded him on this occasion.

A fellow officer recorded the footballer's final moments on 10 July: 'Bell dashed forward with an armful of bombs and started to clear out a hornet's nest of Huns who were ready to take toll of our advancing troops. He advanced with great courage right up to where the enemy was posted. He took careful aim, and bowled out several of the Germans. Unfortunately he was hit… for a while he fought on, but was hit again. He got weaker and weaker and had to relax his efforts. He collapsed suddenly and when we reached him he was dead.'

Once again Bell had acted with immense courage. Had he survived, he might well have received a second V.C. (Bar) to add to the one for his earlier actions which were described in his citation: 'On July 5th 1916, at Horseshoe Trench, Somme, France, a very heavy enfilade fire was opened on the attacking company by an enemy gun. 2nd Lieutenant Bell immediately, on his own initiative, crept upon a communication trench, and then, followed by a Corporal Colwill and Private Batey, rushed across the open under heavy fire and attacked the machine gun, shooting the firer and destroying the gun and the personnel with bombs.'

The former footballer and teacher did not live to receive his award. He was buried on the battlefield at a spot dubbed by the regiment as 'Bell's Redoubt'. His grave was marked by a wooden cross and the inscription 'He gave his life for others.' His grave was relocated in 1920 to the Gordon Dump Cemetery where he was buried alongside 11 other Green Howards who fell during the action on 10 July near Contalmaison. A memorial to Donald Bell V.C. was

Donald Bell's grave in Gordon Dump Cemetery   *A Hamilton*

unveiled on 9 July 2000 by the Professional Footballers' Association and The Green Howards.

A mere six weeks after her wedding Rhoda Bell received the unwelcome news of her husband's death. She would have found some solace in the many eulogies of her husband. The Principal of Westminster College, the Rev. Dr. H.B. Workman, wrote of his recently qualified student that 'Lieutenant Bell possessed a wide circle of friends, whose sympathies go out today to his young bride to whom he was married on his last leave only a few weeks ago, and to his sorrowing parents, who are closely and honourably associated with the Church in Harrogate. "Don" was surely one of the finest representatives of Westminster.'

Lieutenant Colonel H.G. Holmes, the Green Howards' commanding officer, considered that Bell was 'a great example, given at a time it was most needed, and in his honour, the spot where he lies and which is now a redoubt, has been officially named: Bell's Redoubt. He is a great loss to the Battalion and also to me personally and I consider him one of the finest officers I have ever seen.'

Donald Bell's batman, Private John Byers, answered Rhoda's request for first hand information about Donald's death: 'I would to God that my late master and friend had still been with us, or better still, been at home with you… the men worshipped him in their simple wholehearted way and so they ought, he saved the lot of us from being completely wiped out by his heroic act… We have lost the best officer and gentleman that ever was with this battalion and we have lost some good ones. He was called to go to the 8th Battalion of this regiment that was just on our right, so that we heard nothing of his death until the next day. The last time we were on the Somme, some of the lads came across Mr. Bell's grave and they told me that it was being well cared for and that there is a cross erected over it… I am very pleased his valise arrived to you and that you think it was alright. You would find in the souvenirs that we got on 5th July in the first great attack, a Prussian helmet, bayonet and pair of boots. I packed them all in it but I cannot remember whether his little toilet bag was packed or he carried it with him at the time of his death … You ask me if I smoke, yes but not cigarettes, only a pipe and tobacco so if you will send some, I will be very grateful to you. Believe me, wishing you the best of health and wishes, Yours in Sympathy, John W. Byers.'

Bell's Redoubt, near Contalmaison, Somme   *J Kerr*

Donald Bell's school friend Colonel A.C.T. White V.C., M.C. penned a fitting tribute in the regimental magazine: 'At Contalmaison the problem was to cross No Man's Land, badly cut up by

V.C. Who Taught His Boys To Play The Game.

Newspaper report after Bell's death- left to right: Rhoda Bell reading a letter from her husband to his pupils; two boys saluting his portrait; and Lieutenant Bell (back left) with his class. British Library Board (Daily Sketch)

shell fire. Probably no one else on the Front could have done what he did. Laden by helmet, haversack, revolver, ammunitions and Mills bombs in their pouches, he was able to hurl himself at the German trench at such speed that the enemy would hardly believe what their eyes saw. Well knowing the risk, he made a similar attempt a few days later, and died. He was a magnificent soldier, and had he lived, with his high intelligence, superb physique and firm religious principles, he would have risen high in the teaching profession.'

Sapper T. Endenby was based in a dugout about 50 yards from Bell's grave which was 'the highest spot in the vicinity. Over it is erected a cross and around it are neat railings. Within these is smoothly laid turf, which is even now quite green and fresh. His helmet rests on the grave… Don Bell was a great friend of mine when I used to play football... Poor old Don! Everybody liked him... it will be comforting to Don's friends to know with what loving care his grave has been tended.'

Donald's father generously decided that Rhoda should receive her husband's V.C. She travelled to London and was presented with her husband's medal by King George V on 13 December 1916. She received an annual pension of £100 and a similar one-off sum from *The Daily Mail*. She never remarried.

Donald Bell's V.C. was bought at auction on 25 November 2010 by the Professional Footballers' Association for £250,000, the amount allegedly negotiated for a high profile player's weekly wage in 2013.

Whether charging across No Man's Land towards enemy fire or making a last ditch defensive tackle, Donald Simpson Bell V.C. was a team man. He fought selflessly to win for his King and Country and his fellow soldiers. He paid the ultimate price.

DONALD BELL V.C.:

Born:	3 December 1890, Queen's Road, Harrogate, Yorkshire
Education:	St. Peter's School and Harrogate Municipal Secondary Day School (in 1931 Harrogate Grammar School), Westminster Teacher Training College, London
Occupation:	Teacher and professional footballer
Unit/ Regiment:	'A' Company, 9/ Yorkshire (Alexandra, Princess of Wales's Own) known as the 'Green Howards'
Rank:	2nd Lieutenant
Died:	10 July 1916, Battle of the Somme
Age:	25
Decoration:	V.C.
Buried:	Gordon Dump Cemetery IV.A.8.
Inscription:	HE GAVE HIS LIFE FOR OTHERS

The cemetery (see p.323) is two miles north east of Albert in 'Sausage Valley'. It was begun on 10 July 1916 and was closed soon after in September with 95 burials. Numbers increased after 1918 when graves were relocated from the surrounding Somme battlefields. There are over 1,600 British and Empire burials or commemorations, over half of which are unidentified. It was designed by Sir Herbert Baker

'HARRY' WEBBER

The Oldest Killed in Action

In 1915 many men in their 60s would have been quietly grateful that they were too old for active combat at the Front. For 66 year old Henry Webber, the War Office's age limit at the time of 38 was a challenge to circumvent. He was determined 'to do his bit' for the war effort and taking an enthusiastic part in the recruitment campaign was not enough for the energetic and vivacious stockbroker and Master of the Old Surrey and Burstow Hunt. He offered to serve 'in any capacity'

Inscription on 'Harry' Webber's grave   A Hamilton

but was rejected. Like the rugby international Edgar Mobbs, Webber decided to raise his own company of 'rough riders' from the hunting fraternity, an offer that, unlike Mobbs's, was rejected. Not wishing to be outdone he persisted so doggedly that the War Office, probably keen for a quiet life, relented and on 1 May 1916, he received a commission with the 7/ South Lancashire Regiment as a lieutenant. After his battles with authority he wrote of being 'victorious after a strenuous fight with the War Office.' He was deployed in the Horse Transport Section due to his equestrian skills and knowledge and was appointed officer-in-charge of taking supplies to the front line.

He had lived since 1875 in the small east Surrey town of Horley where he threw himself into serving the community. *The Surrey Mirror and County Post*'s obituary, in the edition published on 4 August 1916 exactly two years after the War started, stated that Horley had 'rarely been so stirred' when news of his death became known.

He was the first chairman of the Parish Council in 1894, a member of the newly-formed Surrey County Council, Honorary Treasurer of the Cottage Hospital, Chairman of the Directors of the Horley Gas Company and a County Magistrate. His 'wonderful business instincts' and 'ready grasp of facts' made him a formidable committee man and a 'doughty opponent in debate' with 'the capacity to arrive at a prompt decision.' He was 'the finest chairman of a public meeting that Horley has ever known.'

'Harry' Webber, at 67, the oldest British soldier killed on active service
Tonbridge and the Great War
Tonbridge School Archives

'Harry' Webber was an ardent churchwarden of the parish church of St. Bartholomew and was prime mover for its restoration in 1882. He was a member of the committee set up to build a new church room and he insisted that a boiler be provided to ensure the establishment of a soup kitchen for the poor. He had been a successful businessman but, in tune with the times, he considered it his duty and responsibility to provide care for the less advantaged of the community. On his retirement as churchwarden he was presented with a silver fruit dish for his efforts. A plaque in his memory can be found to the right of the main door. To conclude the copious list of the positions he held, he was also the first commissioner of the Horley scout troop.

Webber was a fine sportsman. He was a member of Tonbridge School's cricket XI from 1865 to 1867 and was still a good enough batsman to score 200 for Horley Cricket Club in his mid fifties! He often returned to play against his old school for M.C.C. or the 'wandering' side, Incogniti, which was founded in 1861 and for whom he played 18 matches in 1871. He batted 25 times scoring 402 runs at an average of 17.11. According to *The Surrey Mirror* 'he never believed in letting the ball hit the bat: mid-on and mid-off knew it was not a tennis ball when they had to field to him'! He also bowled in eight matches and took 14 wickets at an average of 12.4, a record that compared favourably with the County players who represented the Incogniti during that season. He was a determined battler who enjoyed a challenge and his undefeated 47 in a low scoring two innings match at Mitcham on a difficult pitch was significantly better than the next highest score of 21. If sport mirrors the man, then it certainly did so in 'Harry' Webber's case.

He was also an accomplished shot and the first captain of Gatwick Golf Club when a round of golf would have been a considerably quieter experience than nowadays!

Amazingly Webber had time for a day job. He joined the Stock Exchange in 1872 after graduating from Pembroke College, Oxford. He worked for Norman Morris and Co. for 42 years and married the owner's daughter Emily, with whom he raised a family of three sons and six daughters at their house in Horley.

The Junior Common Room, Pembroke College, Oxford- 'Harry' Webber is in the back row sixth from the right   *Archives, Pembroke College, Oxford*

It was no surprise, therefore, that someone as deeply involved in his local community as 'Harry' Webber should wish to defend the area he loved so dearly and volunteer for service at the Front. A public meeting in Horley was convened when war broke out. Webber's primary aim was 'to bring home to the minds of the people the urgent necessity for recruiting.'

Nearly two years later in May 1916, after a short period of training, Webber sailed to France to join the 7/ South Lancs which was involved later in the capture of La Boisselle on the third day of the Battle of the Somme. In a letter to his school dated 17 July 1916, he described his experiences which were published in the July edition of *The Tonbridgian*: 'Fifty one years ago I got my colours in the XI and last year 51 years ago I was bowling v. the Old Boys and looking upon some of them as "sitters" and in the "sere and yellow leaf," and here I am a Lieut. in H.M. Army, having to salute three sons if I meet them out here- a Colonel and two Majors. I am 1st Line Transport Officer to this battalion, and we have been plumb in the centre of the picture during the last ten days and gained no end of kudos and also a very severe mauling. We have been resting for a week and refitting, and are at them again tomorrow. I am so far extraordinarily fit and well, though, when I tell you that for four consecutive days I was either on my feet or in the saddle for twenty one hours out of twenty four, you will see, that there is a bit of work attached to the job. There was an obstinate obstacle that resisted three efforts by others, and our boys eventually took it. They were simply splendid, and now after a rest they are as keen as- well, as a schoolboy to be put on to bowl.'

'Harry' Webber who had achieved so much in a life dedicated to the service of his community, died on 21 July of a serious head wound. During the afternoon he had, as usual, organised the transport of rations to the Battalion's front line trenches in Mametz Wood. He left his men to unload the horses and went to join a group of officers and their commanding officer Lieutenant Colonel C.R.P. Winser D.S.O. whose father, Webber discovered, rowed with him 50 years earlier in 1867 for Pembroke College, Oxford in the Christ Church 'scratch fours'.

At 19.10 an 18 inch shell exploded 15 yards from Webber, killing him, 10 others and three horses. He was taken to the Advanced Dressing Station and then transferred to a Field Hospital and, never regaining consciousness, he died not long after. *The Tonbridgian* recorded: 'There can be no doubt that it was the death he would have chosen, a painless death in battle in the service of his country, a fitting end for one who had, by his determination to serve in spite of his years, set so inspiring an example to the manhood and youth of our country.'

His commanding officer was struck by his energy: 'We all had the greatest respect for him.' His widow Emily received the news with messages of sympathy from King George V and Queen Mary but never recovered from the shock. She died in 1918. Her husband's exploits did not escape the attention of Sir Douglas Haig who mentioned him in his despatches of 4 January 1917.

'Harry' Webber, at the age of 67, was the oldest British soldier to have been killed in action during the Great War. He was buried in Dartmoor Cemetery which lies to the north east of the village of Bécordel in the Somme. He was survived by his three sons: Brigadier General N.W. Webber C.M.G., D.S.O., Major H. Webber and Major L. Webber of the Royal Field Artillery. They may not have had the chance to be saluted by their 'mere' subaltern father but on the news of his death there must have been mixed emotions: pride at his courage and determination but despair at his apparent foolhardiness. He was 'young in everything but years' and even at his advanced age, he still had much to offer his family and the townspeople of Horley.

He crowned a full and active life as *The Surrey Mirror* asserted 'by making the supreme sacrifice on behalf of the country he knew so well.'

'HARRY' WEBBER:

Born:	3 June 1849, youngest son of Dr. William and Eliza Webber of Tunbridge Wells. Husband of Emily (née Morris), father of six daughters and three sons
Education:	Tonbridge School and Pembroke College, Oxford
Occupation:	Stockbroker with Norman Morris and Co.
Unit/ Regiment:	7/ South Lancashire (Prince of Wales's Volunteers) known as 'The Excellers'
Rank:	Lieutenant
Died:	21 July 1916, Battle of the Somme
Age:	67
Buried:	Dartmoor Cemetery, Bécordel-Bécourt I.E.54.
Inscription:	OF HORLEY, SURREY
	DULCE ET DECORUM EST
	PRO PATRIA MORI

The cemetery started as Bécordel-Bécourt Military Cemetery in August 1915 and was used by the battalions holding that part of the line; its name was changed in May 1916 at the request of the 8th and 9th Battalions of the Devonshire Regiment. In September 1916 the XV Corps Main Dressing Station was established in the neighbourhood but throughout 1917, the cemetery was scarcely used and it came under German control on 26 March 1918. It was recaptured on 24 August by the British. The cemetery contains 762 Great War burials and was designed by Sir Edwin Lutyens

Private James Miller V.C. was featured in the Gallaher V.C. series of cigarette cards
Museum of the King's Own (Royal Lancaster Regiment)

Also buried in Dartmoor Cemetery are a father and son from Peckham in South London- 44 year old **SERJEANT GEORGE LEE** and 19 year old **CORPORAL ROBERT LEE** who were both in 'A' Battery of the 156th Brigade of the R.F.A. They were probably killed by the same shell on 5 September 1916. Fittingly, they were buried side by side in Row 1.A.35. and 36. The inscription on both graves is: THY WILL BE DONE

The grave of 26 year old **PRIVATE JAMES MILLER V.C.** from Withnell in Lancashire of the 7/ King's Own (Royal Lancaster Regiment), who was awarded a posthumous V.C., can be found in I.C.64. *The London Gazette* of 16 September records the citation of his award for his bravery at Bazentin-le-Petit Wood on the Somme on 30 July 1916: 'For most conspicuous bravery. His battalion was consolidating a position after its capture by assault. Private Miller was

The graves of George and Robert Lee- some regiments commemorated their Christian casualties with the badge in the centre of a broad cross   A Hamilton

277

ordered to take an important message under heavy shell and rifle fire and to bring back a reply at all costs. He was compelled to cross the open ground, and on leaving the trench was shot almost immediately in the back, the bullet coming out through his abdomen. In spite of this, with heroic courage and self-sacrifice, he compressed with his hand the gaping wound in his abdomen, delivered his message, staggered back with the answer and fell at the feet of the officer to whom he delivered it. He gave his life with a supreme devotion to duty.'

His father George Miller was presented with James's medal by King George V at Buckingham Palace on 29 November 1916. Memorials were raised by public subscription at the church of St. Paul's, Withnell and the Wiggins Teape Paper mill where James worked.

The inscription on his grave is:

GREATER LOVE

HATH NO MAN THAN THIS

(King James Bible John 15:13)

Not so celebrated after his death was the 37 year old Tasmanian-born **PRIVATE JOHN SWEENEY** of the 1/ Otago Regiment of the New Zealand Expeditionary Force. His grave (II.B.1.) simply records that he died on 2 October 1916. No mention is made of the fact that he was executed at dawn at 5.44 a.m. for desertion from his battalion on 24 July 1916 at Armentières. He was arrested there five weeks later and immediately brought to a court martial. In *Shot at Dawn*, Julian Putkowski and Julian Sykes note that a creek in the Haurangi Forest Park where he worked as a feller before he volunteered in October 1914, was named after him. They also record that Sweeney's father Bernard committed suicide 'prior to the public announcement of the New Zealand wartime executions'.

James Miller's grave   A Reed

John Sweeney's grave   A Hamilton

WILLIAM NOEL HODGSON

'By all delights that I shall miss,
Help me to die, O Lord'

Early in 1916 a series of articles in *The Spectator* was written from the front line by Edward Melbourne. The subject of one of them was his batman Private Pearson of whom he wrote: 'If he were Commander-in-Chief, the war would be over in a week. But I should get no baths, so I'm glad he isn't.' By all accounts Pearson was a most resourceful fellow- on one occasion when they were on front line duty, Melbourne declared that he was 'lousy' to which his batman replied: 'You must have a bath, sir, and a change of clothes.' The officer smiled and gave the matter no further thought. Early next day, Pearson informed his officer that 'your bath is ready in your dugout, sir.' Momentarily speechless, Melbourne discovered that with the help of a cook, his batman had found an iron boiler in a bombed factory and had dragged it to the dugout and set it on a pile of bricks! The promised change of clothes had been 'borrowed' from the M.O.

A bath being moved from a German dugout at Ovillers in September 1916

IWM Q004125

Edward Melbourne was, in fact, the *nom de plume* for the poet William Noel Hodgson, a junior officer in the 9/ Devonshire Regiment.

Hodgson was born in 1893, the same year as Wilfred Owen, in Thornbury, Gloucestershire where his father Henry was the vicar. William was the youngest of four children and when only four, the family moved to Northumberland where his father's career took him to appointments at Berwick-on-Tweed, Newcastle as a Canon at the cathedral and then to Lindisfarne where in 1904 he was ordained as an Archdeacon. His hope was that Noel would follow him into the Church.

Henry was a good family man and Noel's childhood was happy and idyllic with regular trips to the Lake District where the family had its roots. Noel was academically gifted enough to be awarded a King's Scholarship to Durham School in September 1905. His sporting talents also thrived there; he coxed the 2nd eight in 1907, was in the cricket 1st XI in 1910 and 1911, was awarded his rugby colours in 1910 and won the Open Steeplechase in 1909 and 1911. Like many other young men from a similar background and schooling, Noel Hodgson's qualities were nurtured at a Public School and they would prove invaluable when he became an officer in 1914. He left Durham School in July 1911 along with his friend and poet Nowell Oxland, a fine rugby player who was commissioned as a lieutenant in the Border Regiment and was killed at Suvla Bay in Gallipoli on 9 August 1915.

Noel won an Exhibition to Christ Church, Oxford which was a continuation of the happy days of his school life, succeeding academically with a First in Classical Moderations in 1913. He found time to play rugby, cricket and hockey for his college and to join the Officers Training Corps which fostered his qualities of leadership. The War brought a halt to further study of 'Greats'.

He started to write poems in earnest during 1913 including *The Hills* written in the English pastoral tradition:

For in the hills a man may go
Forever as he list
And see a network of distant worlds
Where streams and valleys twist
A league below, and seem to hold
The whole earth in his fist…

To while away time during months of training in 1914, Hodgson immersed himself in poetry writing and found solace in returning to the halcyon days of his youth. He cannot be categorised in any particular school of poets. Although deceptively simple at times, his verse is elegant in style with melancholic undertones. His gentle nature pervades his poetry which is touching in its youthful sincerity. Described by John Ruskin as 'one of the wonders of the world for the majestic views of its cathedral and castle', Durham would always hold a special place in Noel's affections, offering him comfort and assistance for him to rationalise his experiences of horror and chaos on the Western Front. *Durham Cathedral* was written in June 1916, three weeks before his death:

Long years we learned and grew, and in this place
Put on the harness of our manhood's state,
And then with fearless heart and forward face
Went strongly forth to try a fall with fate.

Like many thousands of young men who volunteered in 1914, Noel Hodgson did not question the concept of war. For some, enlisting with Kitchener's Army would mean adventure, camaraderie and escape from drudgery and for others like Hodgson it was accepted that the duty of youth was to display loyalty and patriotism. In his *England to her Sons* his exhortation is to:

Go, and may the God of battles
You in his good guidance keep:
And if He in wisdom giveth
Unto his beloved sleep,
I accept it nothing asking,
Save a little space to weep.

He enlisted in September and was posted to the 9/ Devonshire Regiment which consisted mainly of Kitchener volunteers. It was part of the 7th Division, known as the 'Immortal' in which Siegfried Sassoon and Robert Graves were officers. The Battalion was a mixture of recruits from Birmingham, Lancashire, London, Wales and the West Country but Noel's affable nature and cheerful smile ensured acceptance and the endearing nickname of 'Smiler'.

The 9/ Devons sailed for France on 28 July 1915 after months of training and found themselves at Festubert between Neuve Chapelle and Béthune. They were chosen to support the 8/ Devons for a major offensive at Loos, east of the mining town of Lens, which was held by the Germans. The attack started on 25 September with, for the first time, use of poison gas by the British five months after the Germans' first released it in April near Ypres.

Uncut barbed wire, drifting gas and machine-gun fire caused chaos in the first wave when the 8/ Devons lost their commanding officer Major Henry Carden D.S.O. aged 60. The 9/ Devons, however, achieved their objectives and dug defensive trenches. Without reserve support, Noel with three other officers and about 100 men managed to defend their position for 36 hours in spite of enemy fire and counter attacks. For Noel, this was a baptism of fire but he worked with efficient calm for which he was awarded the Military Cross. The 9/ Devons lost seven officers and half of the men.

During the Battle of Loos the British sustained over 50,000 casualties and the Germans 26,000. In
his *Memoirs* David Lloyd-George, the Prime Minister between 1916 and 1922, described the battle as

'futile carnage'. Amongst the British dead were the Queen Mother's elder brother Fergus Bowes-Lyon from the Black Watch, John, the 18 year old only son of Rudyard Kipling (see p.189) and the 20 year old poet Charles Sorley of the Suffolk Regiment who contrary to perceived wisdom at the time, had foreseen that the young of Europe were going to be sacrificed as cannon fodder: 'You are blind like us' were the stark opening words of his poem *To Germany*. Three other old Durham School boys fell at Loos. There is disagreement as to whether 97 or 98 old Dunelmians died in the War but, in their memory, 97 steps were built up to the chapel.

After the fighting at Loos, Hodgson penned *Back to Rest*:

> We that have seen the strongest
> Cry like a beaten child,
> The sanest eyes unholy,
> The cleanest hands defiled,
> We that have known the heart blood
> Less than the lees of wine,
> We that have seen men broken,
> We know man is divine.

Noel Hodgson in his officer's uniform with the Devonshire Regiment badge and his M.C. ribbon   Durham School

Even after his experiences of war, Hodgson's poetry, unlike most of his contemporaries', did not concentrate on the darker side of man's behaviour. He neither glorified nor idealised death but considered it as something to be accepted which was in keeping with his Christian beliefs.

The 9/ Devons were fortunate to survive the Battle of Loos and early in 1916, were located near Fricourt in the Somme. It was at this time that Noel wrote articles under the pseudonym of Edward Melbourne for *The Spectator*, *The Yorkshire Post* and the *Saturday Review*. Like many who wrote about the War, he did not pass comment on the generals or the horrors experienced but relied on readers to draw their own conclusions. *The Affair of the Mess Carpet* featured his batman, whose real name was Ogden, in an event behind the lines. The officer had a bet with the Mess President that the batman could not find a carpet for the stone floor of the Headquarter Mess by the following day. Although he was not able to obtain a pass to go to a ruined town which the Germans continued to shell, the batman still went to it to find a carpet: 'I could not let you lose a bet, sir, for the sake of a little trouble.' A pre-requisite for being a successful officer was to provide for the well-being of his men and to stay cool and collected. The trouble taken by Hodgson's batman highlights how Noel had won the respect of his men to the extent that Ogden was prepared to take a major risk on behalf of his officer.

By June 1916 more than 200,000 soldiers in General Rawlinson's Fourth Army were on alert for the 'Big Push' in the Somme. The attack started on 1st July: the worst day in the history of the British Army when 39,000 were wounded or missing and 19,000 killed. The 9/ Devons, with the 8th Battalion in support, were in the first wave to go 'over the top' opposite the German-held village of Mametz.

Captain Martin of 'A' Company had built a plasticine model of the valley which the Devons were to advance across, a distance of about 400 yards. He was aware that by the crucifix in the civilian cemetery, a position known as 'The Shrine', the Germans had set up a machine-gun which, as he expected, would wreak havoc among the advancing British troops.

Lieutenant Hodgson was the bombing officer and while bringing grenades forward, he was shot through the neck and killed within an hour of the attack. In his absence, Mametz was captured by the 7th Division, one of only two first day objectives achieved that day. The 9/ Devons suffered heavily: 18 out of 19 officers were casualties, 8 of whom died including Captain Martin; 141 other ranks were killed, 267 wounded and 55 were missing. The 8/ Devons suffered 207 casualties.

The padre of the Devons, Reverend E.C. Crosse, buried all the regimental dead that could be recovered. Among them was Noel Hodgson who was found next to his batman who held a bandage in his hand. They were laid to rest in the trench from which they attacked, now known as the Devonshire Cemetery. At the far end is a mass grave where Captain Martin is buried with nine others. Lieutenant Noel Hodgson lies next to his 'faithful servant', Private Samuel Ogden, aged 21 from Heywood in Lancashire.

The survivors erected a wooden marker by the entrance to the cemetery, now made of stone, which reads: 'The Devonshires held this trench. The Devonshires hold it still.' On 4 July they attended a ceremony for their fallen comrades.

Noel's last poem, *Before Action* was published two days before he fell. In it, he foresees his death, with a quiet acceptance of what was to follow. It is emotionally charged and prayer-like. He encourages us to think about simple things that are all too easily taken for granted- hills, sunsets and glorious sunny days. He realises the attack will be costly and that a sacrifice will have to be made:

Officer and batman- Lieutenant Noel Hodgson buried alongside Private Samuel Ogden   *A Reed*

The stone marker to the left of the Devonshire Cemetery entrance   *A Hamilton*

Before Action

By all the glories of the day
And the cool evening's benison,
By that last sunset touch that lay
Upon the hills when day was done,
By beauty lavishly outpoured
And blessings carelessly received,
By all the days that I have lived
Make me a soldier, Lord.

By all of all man's hopes and fears
And all the wonders poets sing,
The laughter of unclouded years,
And every sad and lovely thing;
By the romantic ages stored
With high endeavour that was his,
By all his mad catastrophes
Make me a man, O Lord.

I, that on my unfamiliar hill
Saw with uncomprehending eyes
A hundred of thy sunsets spill
Their fresh and sanguine sacrifice,
Ere the sun swings his noonday sword
Must say good-bye to all of this;
By all delights that I shall miss,
Help me to die, O Lord.

In *For Remembrance* published in 1918, A. St. John Adcock, the English author and critic commented: 'There is strength and spiritual and emotional beauty in his verse and that air of plain sincerity which distinguishes all these poets who were soldiers.' A senior officer described Lieutenant Hodgson as 'a particularly fine officer, a most inspiring personality with a great hold on his men and nearly as much liked and respected by the 8th as his own Battalion. His loss was severely felt.'

After his death, Noel's father, by now Bishop of St. Edmundsbury and Ipswich, a new bishopric created in 1914, arranged the publication of his son's poems. A window in Durham School's chapel was dedicated to his memory.

Noel Hodgson's obituary appeared in *The Dunelmian* magazine published in August 1916 and included a poem written in mid-1913:

Dunelmia Mater Nostra

Time is the stronger destroyer
Of much that heaven sends,
And cherished treasures daily
Draw to their destined ends;
But youth shall live for ever
In the trusty grip of friends.

Similar to thousands of young men from comparable backgrounds, William Noel Hodgson had approached his duties with great resilience and a quiet acceptance of constantly stressful situations and above all with a determination not to give up: all humbling qualities when seen through the eyes of a modern day student of the War. His was just one of thousands of tragic lives cut short, a man with talent and great potential destroyed by a hail of machine-gun fire.

The Devonshire Cemetery entrance　　　　　　　*A Hamilton*

WILLIAM NOEL HODGSON:

Born:	3 January 1893 at Thornbury Vicarage, Gloucestershire, son of the Rt. Reverend Henry Hodgson, first Bishop of St. Edmundsbury and Ipswich and Mrs. Penelope Hodgson
Education:	Durham School and Christ Church, Oxford
Occupation:	Student studies halted by the War. He was a poet and author of the posthumous *Verse and Prose in Peace and War*
Unit/ Regiment:	'A' Company, 9/ Devonshire
Rank:	Lieutenant
Died:	1st July 1916, first day of the Battle of the Somme
Age:	23
Decoration:	M.C.
Buried:	Devonshire Cemetery, Mametz A.3.
	The cemetery is south of the village of Mametz about 6 kms east of Albert. All 163 burials are Devonshires apart from two. It was designed by W.H. Cowlishaw

JACK THE PET DOG

'He truly did his bit'

A fox terrier photographed in 1916

When he exactly arrived, or from where, nobody seemed to know. We were all agreed, however, that he was a very smart-looking little fox-terrier- well bred and well marked. He had probably belonged to some officer and had got lost. The battalion first made his acquaintance one morning as the men were drawn up in column of fours waiting to march off to the next village to new billets. Jack- as he was promptly christened- trotted out of an estaminet, and, seeing the battalion being drawn up, sat on his tail and calmly surveyed what was going on in the street.

The men took a fancy to Jack at once, and whistled and shouted at him. The dog got up and gravely strolled along as though he had made up his mind to inspect the men. He went to the front of the column and made the acquaintance of the second-in-command, and then, as if he had thoroughly made up his mind, he attached himself to B Company. This choice he probably made because company sergeant-major of B Company had stooped down, and, patting him, cheerfully said, "Hello Jack, and how are *you* today?" Of course nobody really knew the little dog's name, but when Sergeant Brady called him Jack, Jack he remained until he finally disappeared in the mist and smoke of one terrible day on the Somme.

From the date of his arrival Jack never left the battalion, nor, indeed, B Company. After a while he was provided with a collar, bright green in colour. If ever there was a pure-bred English fox-terrier, Jack undoubtedly was one; but having joined, so to speak, an Irish battalion, he graciously submitted to the green collar, though, indeed, it was as often as not covered with the mud through which he cheerfully trotted as his company marched along. The company sergeant-major and the little dog became friends; though Jack, being probably an old soldier, thoroughly understood the advantage of being on good terms with the company quartermaster, whose store he promptly made the acquaintance of in every village where the battalion found billets.

It was extraordinary how the presence of this little animal cheered up the men. He never missed a parade and even early on the cold and bitter mornings, Jack was always present, always cheery and 'merry and bright' as the men used to remark. Wherever Jack was, it might be assumed that the company sergeant-major was not far off. Just as we read in the *Cricket on the Hearth*, that whenever people met the carrier's dog, Boxer, on the road, they always looked out for John Pereybingle himself; so, whenever any one saw Jack trotting round the street of a village, somewhere in France, it became a certainty that Sergeant Brady was close at hand. Just too as Boxer used to drop into houses along the road, so Jack did the same, always with an air, however, of friendly politeness, as of one who should say to the inmates, "There are a lot of Irish soldiers coming along, but you need not mind them; they are good fellows all, and you should come out and hear the pipes!"

Sometimes the battalion returned to the same villages, and then Jack was hailed as an old friend by lots of the inhabitants. In marching through the streets of some considerable town, Jack and his green collar gained quite as much attention as the stately regimental sergeant-major, or even the colonel himself at the head of the battalion, and many were the exclamations of interest and admiration showered upon him, particularly by the children, as he trotted along. The little chap never seemed to tire, even on the longest march, and he always found time to get off the road and scamper through the fields at each side with a business-like air, as much as to say "If there *is* a rabbit to be had, it might come in handy."

Once, when the battalion was drawn up ready to march out of the village, Jack was not to be found, and it is no exaggeration to say that there was consternation in the company. When the captain came out to inspect his men prior to marching off, it was with a real knot of trouble in his voice, that the sergeant, after announcing "all present", declared that Jack was not to be discovered. Then the captain exhibited signs of trouble too, and ordered a search to be made in the billets. Later on, after he had been released from an old stable, the door of which had been inadvertently closed upon him, Master Jack was received with acclamation, and, having jumped upon the sergeant by way of explaining his absence and apologising for it, he scampered off according to custom to have a word with the colonel, see the band, and then back, so that the second-in-command in the rear might know, that as far as he, Jack, was concerned, everything was alright!

The battalion's days of billeting in French villages and walking along country roads soon came to an end, and the grim life in the trenches commenced. Jack went to the trenches too and always with B Company and, though clearly puzzled by the absence of landscape, the little dog still kept 'merry and bright' and followed the sergeant everywhere. Once he got- how, nobody could tell exactly- over the top, and was discovered sitting on a sandbag calmly surveying No Man's Land. He was hurriedly pulled down, and not a moment too soon, for several rifle bullets came thudding unpleasantly close to where he had been.

The rats were his special and particular interest, and from one end of the trench to the other he declared war on them, and many a one he brought in triumph to lay at the feet

Carnoy today in the Somme where 'Jack was billeted'   *J Kerr*

of his friend the sergeant. The writer of these lines (for, be it understood, this is true narrative) once asked the sergeant whether he kept Jack with him in his dugout at night. "Lord bless you, sir! No, sir! Jack has a dugout of his own! I'll show you, sir." With a smile the sergeant walked along the trench till he came to a great niche or indentation in the side, where rifle ammunition was stored. Two of the boxes had been removed in the centre, and in the hole thus made, with some sandbags underneath, Jack was discovered comfortably curled up: a quaint and curious picture, making one long for a Kodak; the little dog, with his brown eyes peering out from a bed banked all round with boxes of cartridges! This was his sleeping place by night.

When the sergeant went for a little rest, Jack, so to speak, bid him good night and trotted along to his own little nest amidst the explosives! Every morning, however, at 'stand-to' Jack was on duty, and usually accompanied the officer who superintended the serving out of tots of rum to the men.

As to meals, Jack bestowed his company impartially. One day he had breakfast with one platoon and the next day with another, but wherever he went he never lacked offers of hospitality, and the men laughed as they noticed that life in the trenches made their little pet fat. The day finally arrived when the battalion marched to the Somme and took part in an advance. Jack was with them to the end; but, like so many of his friends amongst the men, he never returned out of the smoke and turmoil of that terrible day. He was after all, it is true only a wee little animal, but nevertheless he truly did his bit, and cheered the men many a day in the trench and along the weary road of march. Jack is gone, but there are some men still left who remember him, and any of them would think little or nothing of settling a Hun; but not a single one of them would ever agree that a pet dog should be put to death. That is their tribute to the memory of little Jack!

Known to have been written anonymously by Major William Redmond M.P. in *The Daily Chronicle*   **285**

JACK THE PET DOG:

Born:	Unknown but approximately between 1906 and 1914
Education:	A dog's life
Occupation:	Rat catcher
Unit/ Regiment:	'B' Company, 6 /Royal Irish Regiment
Rank:	Private and mascot
Died:	9 September 1916, Battle of the Somme
Buried:	No known grave- possibly in a shell hole in No Man's Land near Ginchy

For animal lovers here is another charming canine tale of **'Prince'** whose exploits are hard to believe but the R.S.P.C.A. investigated his story and confidently established its authenticity shortly after the War. 'Prince' was a fine upstanding half-Irish terrier, half-collie who was devoted to his master, Private James Brown of the 1/ North Staffs. He was heart-broken when his master left for France in September 1914. He disappeared one dismal day in November with little sensitivity to the feelings of a distraught Mrs. Brown who searched high and low for him but to no avail. She dreaded having to break the news to her husband that his dog had gone 'awol' and the day after she sent her deeply apologetic letter, she was astounded to learn that 'Prince' had followed his master's trail to the Front near Armentières. The news of this astonishing reunion reverberated round the Battalion. He was paraded and adopted as a mascot for the remainder of the War. As a fighter he could hold his own anywhere but his real delight was ratting and he was known to have killed 137 rats in one day, the corpses having been collected and counted. Such activity was, naturally, much appreciated by the men in the trenches. He was taught the word 'Allemand' and on 'hearing it he would rush around looking for a pair of legs not clad in the familiar British khaki.' The R.S.P.C.A. took charge of him in 1919 and arranged his return to England and his required period of quarantine. Once back home he was fêted by well-wishers who sent him letters and presents including a large iced Christmas cake. Two years after being discharged from active service, he died of a heart attack after giving chase to a mouse. Contrary to what you might think, this story was not written on 1 April nor in a column in *The Wipers Times* but appeared as the first chapter in *Animal War Heroes* by Peter Shaw Baker in 1933.

'Prince' who made his own way to the Front!
Staffordshire Regimental Museum

RAYMOND ASQUITH

'And well we know that his father, then bearing the supreme burden of the State, would proudly have marched at his side'

Disaster struck at all levels of society during the Great War. Few families were fortunate enough to escape the loss or wounding of loved ones and when H.H. Asquith, the Prime Minister and most powerful man in the land, took the decision to declare war on Germany, he would spend his time as Premier fearing for the safety of his four sons who had enlisted. His eldest son Raymond's wife Katharine predicted that 'if Raymond and Cys (Cyril) go into fighting lines as well as Oc (Arthur) and Beb (Herbert), the strain will be terrible for us' and indeed the Prime Minister openly admitted that he could not face the prospect of losing any one of his sons.

H.H. Asquith was not a warmonger by nature- as a Liberal he had opposed the Boer War and had hopes that Britain would not be drawn into hostilities. While Kaiser Wilhelm's Armies were invading Belgium, Asquith was guilty of wishful thinking when he announced on 22 July 1914 that 'happily there seems to be no reason why we should be anything other than spectators'. A fortnight later Britain was embroiled in a war that would prove the toughest assignment Asquith had yet faced and which, within two years, would signal his downfall.

Herbert H. Asquith, 1st Earl of Oxford and Asquith- Prime Minister 1908-16, by Walton Adams   National Portrait Gallery P140

Asquith was one of the first Prime Ministers to depend on his Government salary rather than private means. He came from a middle-class background; his father was a nonconformist Leeds wool manufacturer, which prompted King George V to consider him 'not quite a gentleman.' He was educated at the City of London School and won a Classics scholarship to Balliol College, Oxford being awarded a first class degree in 1874. He trained and practised as a barrister but in 1886 turned his attention to politics. He was elected Liberal M.P. for the East Fife constituency in 1886 which he represented for 32 years. His inexorable rise to 10 Downing Street was confirmed and a boyhood dream realised when he was appointed Home Secretary by the 85 year old William Gladstone in 1892, an office he retained under the Earl of Rosebery: 'When I was a boy I used to think that to get into the Cabinet before I was 40 was for an Englishman who had to start at the level of the crowd, the highest height of achievement.'

Rosebery's Government was defeated in 1895. The Liberals remained in the wilderness until 1906 when the Conservatives could muster only 157 M.P.s. Asquith moved into 11 Downing Street as Chancellor of the Exchequer and then took up residence next door in 1908 on the death of Sir Henry Campbell-Bannerman. Henry Herbert Asquith had reached what a Conservative predecessor Benjamin Disraeli had described as 'the top of the greasy pole.'

Asquith and David Lloyd George laid the foundations of the Welfare State introduced by the post Second World War Labour Government. Their greatest achievement was the introduction of Old Age Pensions in 1909 when they faced hostility to their Budgets from the Conservative-dominated House of Lords, a problem overcome by a pact with George V who agreed, if necessary, to create 250 Liberal peers: a threat that succeeded.

In 1914 the Liberal Government faced militant challenges from the Suffragettes and Trade Unions and there were increasingly strident calls for Irish Home Rule. The outbreak of war offered Asquith temporary respite from a downward spiral but management of the war effort took its toll on him personally and the Liberal party. A Coalition government was formed in May 1915 which he headed for only 18 months before he was ousted and replaced by Lloyd George. After the War the Liberal Party was eclipsed by the Labour Party and never assumed overall power again.

Unsurprisingly Raymond Asquith and his siblings were raised in a rarified atmosphere; on many occasions the Asquiths' dinner table would be shared by the political *élite*. John Buchan, a fellow student of Asquith's, who would make his mark as a writer after the War, observed that Raymond had 'seen much of the distinguished people who to most of us were awful names, so he seemed all his time at Oxford to have one foot in the greater world.' Indeed Prime Minister Campbell-Bannerman was a witness at Raymond's marriage to Katharine Horner in 1907.

Katharine Frances Asquith (née Horner) and husband Raymond by Lady Ottoline Morrell National Portrait Gallery AX 140417

Raymond possessed, like his father, one of the finest minds of his generation, an intellectual colossus who shared his father's industrious nature despite self-deprecating comments in his letters to the contrary. There were occasional references in his termly reports from Winchester College of moments of indifference- it would appear that Raymond found life unchallenging but this did not prevent him from achieving a scholarship in 1896 to his father's *alma mater*, Balliol College, Oxford. He studied hard and was rewarded with a double first in Classics and Law and the University's Ireland, Derby, Craven and Eldon scholarships.

His intellectual prowess was marked by a Fellowship of All Souls College, Oxford. His academic success- he was regarded in Oxford as one of the best scholars of his generation, is all the more remarkable because of the plethora of his other interests which included rowing, tennis, rackets, fencing and boxing. At Winchester, in the special form of football played there, he was in 1896 'distinctly the best. He played a good game throughout.' Other than sport, he displayed a precocious talent for debating which was nurtured at Winchester where, defending the motion 'That this House regrets the decision of Lord Rosebery in resigning the leadership of the Liberal Party', Asquith's speech was considered by the editor of *The Wykehamist* as 'admirable, mellifluent sarcasm being tempered by shrewd common sense.' He argued that Rosebery's resignation was a sad loss and what was needed was not a 'provincial ironmonger. England must remember that it is possible to be strong without being brutal, refined without being weak.' Was he referring here to his father as a potential successor? His maiden speech in the Oxford Union was greeted with resounding cheers and in 1900 he was elected to the prestigious post of President despite his anti-Boer War sympathies.

By the end of his time at Oxford Raymond Asquith knew he had the world at his feet. The guests of honour at a Balliol College dinner were his father and Dr. Warre, the Headmaster of Eton College, father of his good friend Felix. When proposing their health, Raymond wittily described them as 'the fortunate fathers of two very distinguished sons.'

Raymond followed in his father's footsteps by becoming a barrister. Highlights of his career included being part of a legal team in the Hague in 1910 which represented the United Kingdom in a dispute between Canada and the United States over fishing rights off the coast of Newfoundland. He was also involved in the investigation into the sinking of the *Titanic* in 1912 and shortly before the War was appointed Junior Counsel to the Inland Revenue. His career had progressed well but hardly earth-shatteringly so. He was finding his field of work restrictive; he disliked its pomposity and convention and found the majority of his colleagues tedious.

Balliol, the Bar and then Politics: Raymond was shadowing his father. The seeds of an interest in a political career began to grow in 1912. He sought advice from his father about applying for the North West Norfolk constituency but it was, the Prime Minister warned, a large sprawling rural area that would require a lot of canvassing. He opted instead for the industrial Derby constituency where the sitting M.P. was planning to retire. Many felt that Raymond Asquith had the qualities required to be a successful politician- speech making was his *forte*, combined with clear and analytical thought and great self-confidence. The War, however, ensured that Raymond Asquith's political skills and credentials were never tested.

Raymond was a respected and revered member of a group of friends many of whom had been contemporaries at Balliol who described themselves as 'The Coterie'. A young, beautiful, star struck 'groupie' was Lady Diana Manners, the Duke of Rutland's daughter, who later wrote that Raymond was 'the King of the Coterie' and part of 'that "haloed" band who were to die in the war and leave us, our generation and England, woebegone and maimed.' They were the former *jeunesse dorée* of Edwardian England, intelligent and wealthy who were prepared gently to cock a snook at the prurience of the Victorian period. Nonetheless, as a group, they disliked war and all that it would entail but the overwhelming sense of duty was such that failure to volunteer was not an option and it was certainly not one for the eldest son of the British Prime Minister.

Asquith enlisted in December 1914. He received a commission with the 1/16 Queen's Westminster Rifles (London Regiment), a decision that did not meet with the approval of either his wife nor his father. They both harboured the hope that he would accept a safe Staff job but Raymond did not wish to have strings pulled on his behalf to remove him from the heart of the military action. His father had been at work behind the scenes as is evident from Raymond's letter to Sir John Cowans written from The Camp, Richmond Park, Roehampton on 7 August 1915: 'Thank you very much indeed for your most kind letter re. the offer of an appointment as an inspector of Quarter Master General's services. I fully appreciate the importance and desirability of this post but feel that I must refuse it, as I have definitely made up my mind to pursue another line. The arrangement for my exchange into the Grenadier Guards will I hope mature in the next ten days.'

Raymond Asquith in uniform
Balliol College Archives

Like most of the other subjects of this book, Raymond resented the endless and repetitive training and yearned to be across the Channel 'doing his bit'. On 27 May 1915 he grumbled that: 'Among the more dashing officers in this regiment, there is a growing spirit of disaffection. We are wasting time here on duties which make for weariness but not for efficiency.'

As he had predicted on 24 July he was transferred as a lieutenant to the 3/ Grenadier Guards where he received, he believed, more meaningful training. He finally sailed with the Guards to France and on 24 October he reported to Katharine that: 'We are comfortably housed in a French village the name of which I believe I am not allowed to say. But in any case I don't know it', he added dryly.

Three days later the Battalion was to be inspected by 'an important person', waspishly described by Asquith as 'a relative of the Kaiser's'. He commented with the cynicism of his youth that: 'Usually there is a hell of a din here of big guns, today absolute calm. Why? Because the King is at the Front and they don't want a damned noise when he is there.' On 29 October he protested that the day before, the Guards had marched six miles in drenching rain only to find that the King's visit had been postponed so they had to march back again. He learned later that the real reason for this was that, when King was inspecting other troops earlier in the day, his horse had reared and fallen on him 'doing him some injury, though I believe not a serious one' (see p.147) an event confirmed by the Coldstream Guards.

For such a brilliant man the War was often dull and unrewarding. He admitted to Katharine that he was 'too easily bored to be a soldier even in war time' and announced that 'I have determined to devote five minutes a day to serious reading and began this morning the *Odes* of Horace.' Raymond Asquith's grandson, the third Earl of Oxford and Asquith points out that he enjoyed being a soldier more than he was prepared to admit. He was evidently much loved by those under his command and was 'invigorated' by being with his men and officers of a similar rank. His letters to Katharine tended not to dwell on the aspects of soldiering he enjoyed.

The most laborious chore he had to undertake was reading and censoring his men's letters which were 'very long and very dull... But God knows, my own letters are hardly any better.' A definite case of false modesty as his letters, edited by his grandson John Jolliffe, in *Raymond Asquith Life and Letters*, are a spellbinding read: humorous, thoughtful, sensitive, critical and often passionate.

He experienced his first tour of duty in mud-filled trenches during a cold spell on 15 November 1915. He complained to Katharine about the stupidity of the authorities in failing to prepare men adequately for winter in the trenches. But there was probably less that could have been done to control the swarms of rats: 'This is no place for those who mind rats, as the little rascals are very numerous, well nourished and daring. They gnaw the corpses- then gallop over one's face when one lies down. Fortunately, I was always a lover of animals': inappropriate breakfast reading for his mother-in-law, Lady Horner, at her breakfast table in Mells, Somerset!

His letters abound with subtle humour and irony- when in the trenches he received a letter enclosing an income tax demand: 'It made me laugh heartily as I extricated myself from a puddle of frozen mud to receive a request for £193.2.6. which is more than I have earned during the whole of my career in the army.' At least on 22 November, on returning to his billet, he was able to forget the discomforts of the trenches and his tax demand with a 'bottle of the boy'- officers' description of Bollinger champagne.

Asquith found the War, like most, a 'loathsome ordeal' and in a letter to Diana Manners, he conceded that 'I take about the same interest in it as an ill-tempered tourist may take in an uncomfortable hotel.' But there were morale boosting perks available to the Prime Minister's son but not the average officer- for example meetings at the Front with Winston Churchill who had resigned from his post at the Admiralty on 12 November and by January 1916 was the commanding officer of the 6/ Royal Scots Fusiliers in the Ploegsteert area. Raymond had met him a year earlier on 9 October at a dinner in Downing Street when Asquith found his father, Sir Edward Grey and Churchill 'all rather gloomy' about the lack of military progress. 'Winston rode over and took tea with me. He seemed very well and in good spirits at having substituted the Cabinet for the trenches.' Raymond was able to pass on some sensitive information to Katharine- that in Churchill's opinion, it would not be long before conscription would be introduced. Churchill, for his part, recalled later that Asquith seemed 'to move through the cold, squalor and peril of the winter trenches as if he were above and immune from the common ills of the flesh...'

The Prime Minister was unhappy that his son had opted for front line duty. For his part Raymond was indignant that his father had been pressurising Sir Douglas Haig to move him into a safe Intelligence job behind the lines. He was caught on the horns of a dilemma, complaining to Katharine on 10 January 1916, how difficult it would be to 'refuse the bloody thing' but was concerned at how 'wretched and contemptible it would appear if he accepted it.' He predicted sardonically that he would probably side with the 'poodles' and thus 'die of a surfeit of lampreys instead of a high explosive shell.' He did take up the offer and found himself in the 'Secret Service' where he collated and edited reports from spies in France and Belgium; he insisted on a three month time limit. He was concerned, understandably, by the potential perception of his fellow officers. He confided in Diana Manners his belief that 'the Prime Minister in disregard of a perfectly explicit order from me to take no steps in that direction without my express permission, has tipped the wink to Haig.' He disliked leaving the camaraderie within his officer group and was fearful that no one would believe that the arrangement had been made without his knowledge.

He was at least able to employ his legal skills on 18 January 1916 when he acted as a 'prisoner's friend' in defence of Captain Sir Iain Colquhoun of the 1/ Scots Guards for allowing his men to fraternise with Germans on Christmas Day 1915 near Laventie after clear orders that a repetition of the armistices of 1914 was not to be repeated. The Court Martial decided that he should be 'reprimanded' but Field Marshal Haig overturned the sentence because of Sir Iain's 'distinguished conduct in the field'.

Raymond and Katharine were suffering from the strains experienced by all couples in a similar situation. 'Our moans go to and fro across the Channel like shuttlecocks across a net each applauding the other's master strokes of woe.' They had cause for celebration on 22 April when Katharine gave birth to their first son, Julian. Only his classically-educated father could have given him the idiosyncratic nickname of 'Trim' after Trimalchio, 'the greatest king' and host of lavish dinner parties in Petronius's *Satyricon*. Trim's christening was held during Raymond's leave at St. Paul's Cathedral on 6 June. Young 'Trim' was blissfully unaware that he was being upstaged by the sinking of *HMS Hampshire* by a German U-boat and the drowning of Lord Kitchener. The news of the war hero's death spread noisily and like wildfire around the shocked congregation.

Asquith had returned to front line action in May 1916 and was determined to set the record straight that he was not a shirker. The authorities again made use of his legal expertise; he was deputed to defend an officer accused of homosexuality, albeit unsuccessfully, as the defendant was cashiered (dismissed from service) and handed a year's prison sentence.

The 3/ Grenadier Guards were part of the preparations for a continuation of the advance on the Somme. Asquith was singularly unimpressed with one of the new tactics designed to overcome German trenches. His description of the 'creeping barrage' in his letter of 7 September to Katharine was withering in its criticism. It was a curtain of shellfire which 'moves on about 50 yards in front of the advancing infantry' which in practice sessions was represented by drummers. 'The spectacle of the whole four battalions moving in lines across the cornfields at a funereal pace headed by a line of rolling drums, produced the effect of some absurd religious ceremony conducted by a tribe of Maoris rather than a brigade of Guards in the attack.'

On the same day Raymond was surprised to receive a telegram: 'Lieut. Asquith will meet his father at cross roads K. 6d at 10.45 a.m.' The Prime Minister arrived an hour late. He was impressed by how well his son seemed to be coping. His Cabinet had been a battleground since August 1914, egos had been exploding on a regular basis but he was now experiencing real war at the sharp end. The British guns were blazing away and as they made their way to inspect a captured German dugout, a German shell 'came whizzing over our heads and fell a little way beyond.' Any sensible risk assessment would have pointed to the British Prime Minister being in severe danger… They swiftly went down to the safety of the lowest level of the typically well-constructed German trench. Raymond was struck by his father's coolness under fire; the Prime Minister was now only too aware of what dangers his son faced. Any difficulties between the two men were superseded by feelings of mutual respect. When Asquith senior was whisked away in his staff car, it was the last time he would see his son.

Raymond returned to his dugout where he wrote to Katharine about the meeting with his father. He loved the company of women (as did his father) and missed them dearly- he admitted to her that 'Yesterday, I saw a very handsome fly with a bottle green bodice and magenta skirt. This is the nearest I can get to a pretty woman.' Letters to his wife were sensitive and thoughtful and he had reminded her on 25 July that they should be celebrating nine years of marriage that 'seemed very short and wonderfully pleasant. You are sweeter and more lovely ever than you were then, and I adore you a million times more and I am not sorry, not a bit.'

The 3/ Grenadier Guards were part of a major offensive to take the small village of Lesboeufs which entailed

Premier's Eldest Son Killed In Action.

PEERS' HEIRS FIGURE WITH MILL-HAND V.C. IN THE GREAT OFFENSIVE CASUALTY LISTS.

Lieut. Raymond Asquith (x), who was the Premier's eldest son, with officers and men of the Queen's Westminsters, while training in England. He was a Guards officer in the Big Offensive.

Mr. Raymond Asquith photographed two months before the war.

Mrs. Raymond Asquith, with her little son Julian, the Premier's youngest grandson. He was born only last April.

Headline news- report of Raymond Asquith's death in the The Daily Sketch British Library Board (Daily Sketch)

capturing the strongly fortified Quadrilateral Redoubt. Raymond was feeling homesick but was determined to 'see out the fighting season.' He accepted his chances of survival were slim and prepared his loved ones accordingly on 14 September: 'Good bye darling, darling friend' he concluded his valedictory letter to Lady Diana Manners and to Katharine he wrote: 'Tomorrow we shall move forward again, probably into the line. Angel, I send you all my love. Remember me to Trim.' Raymond was not a deeply religious man but unusually, he went to a church and prayed before a lighted candle.

Next morning Lieutenant Asquith blew his whistle and led his men 'over the top'. He managed just a few steps before being hit in the chest by a hail of bullets. He was rescued by stretcher-bearers who gave him morphine to deaden the pain. To reassure his men, he lit a cigarette but died on his way to a Dressing Station. His body was first buried between Trônes Wood and Guillemont.

Only five out of 22 Guards' officers survived the attack. It had been hoped that the use of tanks for the first time would break enemy resistance but the 32 that were deployed were disappointingly ineffective. They were prone to break down and crucially, were unable to keep up with the infantry.

The Prime Minister received the news of Raymond's death two days after the Battle of Flers-Courcelette when he and his second wife Margot were holding a weekend party. Margot was informed by their secretary of Raymond's death and that Field Marshal Haig had expressed his deepest sympathy. She summoned the Prime Minister to see her: 'Henry opened the door and we stood facing each other. He saw my thin, wet face, and while he put his arm round me, I said: "Terrible, terrible news". At this he stopped me and said: "I know, I've known it… Raymond is dead." He put his hands over his face and we walked into an empty room and sat down in silence.'

Raymond's sister Violet could console herself that her brother had laid to rest any whispers of shirking front line action: 'God bless him! How he has vindicated himself before all those who thought him merely a scoffer- by the modest heroism with which he chose the simplest and most dangerous form of service- and having so much to keep for England gave it all to her with his life.'

'Raymond killed, my divine Raymond killed': Lady Diana Manners felt his death changed everything 'except the war that ground its murderous treadmill.'

Winston Churchill's front line meetings with Raymond led him to believe that the War never fazed him and 'when the Grenadiers strode into the crash and thunder of the Somme, he went to his fate cool, poised, resolute, matter of fact, debonair. And well we know that his father, then bearing the supreme burden of the State, would proudly have marched at his side.'

For Prime Minister Henry Herbert Asquith, the War was tragedy enough after the massive losses on the Somme but the death of his son was numbing and heart-rending. He poured his heart out in a letter to Sylvia Henley: 'I can honestly say that in my own life he was the thing of which I was truly proud and in him and his future I had invested all my stock of hope. This is all gone, and for the moment I feel bankrupt.' He confessed to Lady Ettie Desborough, who lost her sons Julian and Gerald (Billy): 'I am a broken man- but I try to go on day by day.'

A Lloyd George-orchestrated coup ended his waning leadership of the Coalition Government in November. He had failed to manage a warring cabinet; too much of his time was spent on healing rifts rather than focusing on the war effort.

His son's grave is one of the most visited on the Somme. The family chose the inscription:

SMALL TIME BUT IN THAT SMALL

MOST GREATLY LIVED

THIS STAR OF ENGLAND

a Shakespearean reference to the warrior King Henry V who also fought on French soil and died in his thirties.

Katharine Asquith received news from the Secretary of the War Office on 3 October 1916 presenting 'his compliments to Mrs. Raymond Asquith, and begs to inform her that a package of the kit of the late Lieutenant Raymond Asquith of the 3rd Battalion, Grenadier Guards has now been received and Messrs. Cox and Co's Shipping Agency have been instructed to forward it.' Katharine was not in a fit state to collect the package of her husband's effects-wrist watch, pocket compass, ID disc, whistle, cigarettes, cigars, a pipe and the pocket edition of Horace's *Odes*. Her mother, Lady Horner, did so, on her behalf. Asquith's widow received a gratuity of £140 and a pension of £100 per annum. Her three children each received a gratuity of £46.13.4 and a compassionate allowance of £24.

Raymond left everything in his will to Katharine. A daunting job would have been to sort out his huge collection of books: 'Many of my friends would like books or other things of mine for remembrance. She will know what to give and to whom.'

The death of the Prime Minister's son emphasised that no section of society was immune from the dark tentacles of the War. It symbolised the end of the Edwardian era. Raymond Asquith was merely one of thousands of the establishment and aristocratic *élite* who were slaughtered on the Western Front. Remarkably, their abiding sense of duty and devotion to their country was not subverted by their loathing of the War. No one hated it more than Raymond Asquith but no one was more acutely aware of his duty and obligation to his country.

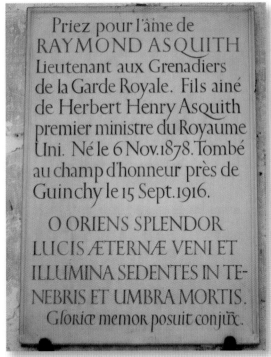

The Asquith plaque in Amiens Cathedral. The Latin inscription translates: 'O rising splendour of eternal light come and shine on those sitting in the darkness and shadow of death. His wife placed the memorial to his glory'
A Hamilton

RAYMOND ASQUITH:

Born:	6 November 1878, son of H.H. Asquith, Prime Minister 1908-16, (later Earl of Oxford and Asquith), husband of Katharine (née Horner) and father of Helen, Perdita and Julian ('Trim'), the future 2nd Earl of Oxford and Asquith
Education:	Winchester College and Balliol College, Oxford
Occupation:	Barrister and prospective Liberal M.P.
Unit/ Regiment:	1/16 Queen's Westminster Rifles (London Regiment) and 3/ Grenadier Guards
Rank:	Lieutenant
Died:	15 September 1916, Battle of the Somme
Age:	37
Buried:	Guillemont Road Cemetery I.B.3.
Inscription:	SMALL TIME BUT IN THAT SMALL MOST GREATLY LIVED THIS STAR OF ENGLAND

(from William Shakespeare's Henry V*)*

The cemetery was begun by fighting units (mainly of the Guards Division) and Field Ambulances after the Battle of Guillemont and was closed in March 1917 when it contained 121 burials. It was greatly increased after the Armistice when graves were brought in from the Somme battlefields immediately surrounding the village. It now contains 2,263 burials of which 523 are unidentified. It was designed by Sir Herbert Baker

Raymond Asquith's grave marker in the church of St. Andrew, Mells, Somerset
A. Hamilton

*Asquith's grave in Guillemont Road Cemetery-
one of the most visited in the Somme*
A. Hamilton

Other grave of interest:

Inscription: 2nd Lieutenant William Alexander Stanhope Forbes, 3/
Duke of Cornwall's Light Infantry, died on 3rd Sept 1916, aged 23. He
was the son of Stanhope Forbes R.A., founder of the Newlyn School of
Painting who composed the inscription for his son's headstone:

> HE SAW BEYOND THE FILTH
> OF BATTLE AND THOUGHT DEATH
> A FAIR PRICE TO PAY
> TO BELONG TO THE COMPANY
> OF THESE FELLOWS

The grave of William Stanhope Forbes J Kerr

*The entrance to Guillemont Road Cemetery,
designed by Sir Herbert Baker*
J Kerr

JAMES RICHARDSON V.C.

'The lad's whole soul was bound up in the glory of piping'

James (Jimmy) Richardson and his family decided to emigrate in 1913 from Belshill near Glasgow to Vancouver in Canada. His father David had been Police Inspector and Fire Chief for Rutherglen in South Lanarkshire and took up the post of Chief of Police in the town of Chilliwack. Born in 1895 Jimmy was only 17 years of age when he and his sister Alice (15) and brother David (13) sailed from Glasgow and arrived at Halifax Nova Scotia on 23 May 1913. In October their mother joined them in Chilliwack with the rest of the family, three daughters and a son.

It would appear that Jimmy did not follow his family to Chilliwack, opting to remain in Vancouver. He found a job as a driller but his main hobby away from work was his boyhood love of playing the bagpipes. He spent six months in the cadet corps of the 72/ Seaforth Highlanders (Canadian), which boasted a fine pipe band and on 1 July 1914, he confirmed his status as the best young piper in Canada when he won three first prizes in a bagpipe competition held in Victoria.

He had been a scout in Scotland and enjoyed adventure and the outdoor life. He was a positive and active young man; the courage and selflessness that he would show on the Western Front were in evidence early in 1914 when he dived into the cold waters of False Creek, Vancouver, in a vain attempt to rescue a small boy who had got into difficulties.

'Piper' James Richardson of the 16/ Canadian Expeditionary Force (Canadian Scottish)
Chilliwack Museum, Canada

When hostilities broke out in Europe it was natural that the bold and daring Jimmy Richardson answered the call to arms and on 23 September 1914, he enlisted with the 16/ Canadian Expeditionary Force (Canadian Scottish) into which the 72/ Seaforth Highlanders had been amalgamated. After four months of training, much of it in England on Salisbury Plain, the Battalion sailed for France and landed on 9 February 1915. The 16/ Canadian Expeditionary Force was in constant action in the Ypres Salient, particularly during the Battle of St. Julien from 24 April to 4 May 1915, when the Germans used chlorine gas.

Jimmy was keen to take on hazardous assignments and when near St. Julien three miles from Ypres, he volunteered to reconnoitre enemy lines. He stumbled across a farmhouse in a forest clearing but was confronted by a German officer and a detachment of men. He recalled in a letter to his father that he had two alternatives: 'Namely to shoot the nearest man I saw, which was the officer and make a dash for my pals or give myself up as a prisoner. I risked the former and aimed quick and true as I could at my man, who then rolled over like a log. Then you talk about running. There isn't a man who could've covered the ground quicker than I did, and nobody could be more thankful than I when I found myself amongst my own kith and kin. I told the sergeant major that the farmhouse was full of Germans and they would have to be cleared out if we intended to hold our position through the next day. Well, as the farmhouse was an ideal sniping post for the Huns, the matter was reported to the artillery, which needless to say, put the farmhouse out of business.'

Jimmy was at the forefront of Christmas and New Year celebrations in 1915- in a letter to his mother dated 27 December, he described the Battalion's festivities which definitely had a Scottish feel to them: 'To open the business I sung "One fine night in December" (perhaps you remember the song, at least Mary will). Then Harold Harkness sung "Cassidy" and Drummer Pomeroy gave a selection. Someone suggested a tune on the pipes and Ronald MacDonald struck up a lively one. Well this absolutely knocked the singing business out of action and everyone "hopped" to it and the dancing began. We had reels and schottishes galore also waltzing and patronella, (he probably meant 295

'Petronella', a well known Scottish dance) lancers, quadrilles etc. We finished up at about 2.30 a.m. and I can tell you I was tired, however we were up like larks in four hours time and got things squared up and we are looking forward to another dance at least, at the New Year.' It was all quiet at the Front over Christmas when not a shot was fired 'but both sides made up for lost time this morning with the guns. The weather is still rotten and the mud is getting deeper every day. We have wet feet all the time but of course we being out of the trenches get a chance to put on dry socks every morning. The men in the trenches are supplied with long rubber boots to the thighs so they are all right to a certain extent but we are not issued with them although the mud is a foot deep here.'

James Richardson at the Front
Times History of the War 1917

Jimmy then engages in a touching heart-to-heart with his mother about a Dutch lass he left behind in Vancouver: 'You mentioned in your letter about a girl called Betsy Folkers- it was she who sent me the silk handkerchief. I met her at Chapleau, Ontario, when we were on our way from Vancouver to Valcartier. The whole regiment was off at Chapleau for half an hour and had a march through the town. When we got back to the station we had another ten minutes to spare so we were told we could make any purchases we wished. I started off with a pal and we met this girl with her chum. This knocked the purchases on the head for we stood and spoke to them and they came to the station to see us off. I gave her my regimental address but it puzzles me to know how she got Mary's address. She must have written to the record office surely. She wrote to me and I to her although evidently she thought more of me. She sent me the handkerchief when I was at Salisbury… And after that she started writing love letters in the true sense. She seemingly thought I was going to "carry on" but I have two reasons for not so doing. In the first place she is a Hollander and for a second she is not good looking enough for this kid. "I want a girl just like the girl that married dear old dad." I am fighting for my country and I want one of my own country girls when the time comes which is not for a few years yet and until I see my way to support a wife etc. Well to carry on with the story "which I see now was nearly a romance" I stopped writing, (because as I already said she was writing too thick love stuff,) hence the reason for writing to Mary. She sent me a Christmas card and I had already sent her one to show that I hadn't forgotten her, however, I certainly am not going to keep it up. I don't mind writing her for friendship sake but I don't want to have her thinking wrong. I will enclose her photo which you must look after, it will be a good souvenir after the war.'

German regiments never relished encounters with Scottish opponents- dressed in kilts, uttering blood curdling war cries and inspired by wailing bagpipes, they were fearsome foes. The 16th Battalion, which consisted mainly of Scottish Seaforth Highlanders who had emigrated to Canada, moved into the Somme area. At 4.50 a.m. on 8 October 1916, they were preparing to 'go over the top' to attack the German held Regina Trench near Courcelette. It was dark and rain was falling. According to the description by Company Sergeant Major Mackie in the Battalion War Diary, after their side's barrage started, Mackie, Major Lynch, Captain Bell and Piper Richardson went out of the trench. 'After waiting for five minutes we bade goodbye to Captain Bell who was to take over the second line of the company, and Major Lynch gave the order to advance. The three of us walked in front of the leading line; Piper Richardson on the Major's left and I on his right. The going was easy as the ground was not cut up. About half way over I commenced to wonder why the piper wasn't playing and crossed over by the side of him to ask the reason. He said he had been told not to play until ordered to do so by the Major.'

They were met by intense German fire. Pre-attack bombardment to break up the German's barbed wire defences had failed so the progress of the Battalion was checked. They were marooned in front of the entanglements and were sitting ducks for enemy fire. Once their leader Major Lynch had been killed, the young piper felt he had a positive role to play and asked Company Sergeant Major William Mackie: 'Wull I give them wund?' He was given the all-clear and proceeded to play the *Reel of Tulloch* and many contemporaries believed that his playing did much to inspire over 100 soldiers to take the opposing trench against all the odds.

Private James Richardson never made it back to the safety of his own trenches. *The London Gazette* recorded on 18 October 1916 that Piper Richardson received the Victoria Cross 'for most conspicuous bravery and devotion to duty when prior to attack, he obtained permission from his commanding officer to play his company "over the top". As the company approached the objective, it was held up by very strong wire and came under intense fire, which caused heavy casualties and demoralised the formation for the moment. Realising the situation, Piper Richardson strode up and down outside the wire with such fury and determination that the obstacle was overcome and the position captured. Later, after participating in bombing operations, he was detailed to take back a wounded comrade and prisoners. After proceeding about 200 yards, Piper Richardson remembered that he had left his

pipes behind. Although strongly urged not to do so, he insisted on returning to recover his pipes. He has never been seen since, and death has been presumed accordingly owing to lapse of time.'

Jimmy Richardson's date of death was officially recorded as 9 October 1916. He was one of 8,000 soldiers of the Canadian Expeditionary Force to die at Courcelette. His remains were exhumed from a mass grave in 1920 and he was officially buried at Adanac Cemetery near Miraumont along with several hundred Canadians who were transferred from smaller cemeteries in the Somme- hence the cemetery's name, which is 'Canada' spelled backwards.

Memorials to pipers at Longueval, Somme (left) and to James Richardson in Chilliwack, Canada   J Kerr and Chilliwack Museum, Canada

Jimmy Richardson's commanding officer during the attack, Major Gavin Davis, wrote to his father offering sympathy and applauding his son's award of 'the greatest medal of them all. He was a delightful chap and in my company from when we left Vancouver. He never tired, however long the march was, and was always ready with a willing hand to do anything and give the boys a tune and always anxious to lead his company over the top. He was a great loss to the battalion and I am sure a greater loss to you. I was in the fight when Jimmy went back for his pipes but never returned. You have my deepest sympathy in his loss and best of congratulations on the great award.'

The Battalion's commanding officer, Lieutenant Colonel Cyrus Peck, a V.C. in 1918, described the piper's bravery as 'one of the great deeds of the war. The conditions were those of indescribable peril and terror. The lad's whole soul was bound up in the glory of piping.'

Many thought that Piper Jimmy Richardson's bagpipes had been unceremoniously swallowed up by the Somme mud and lost for ever until their amazing discovery in 2002 at Ardvreck Preparatory School at Crieff in Perthshire. A British Army chaplain, Major Edward Yeld Bate found a set of mud and blood-spattered bagpipes on the battlefield at Courcelette in 1917 and brought them back to Ardvreck where he taught for several years. He presented them to the school in 1931 on his retirement.

In 2002 they were identified as Richardson's because they were covered in the Lennox tartan which was worn by the newly created 16/ Canadian Expeditionary Force, although Richardson himself would have worn the original Seaforth Highlander tartan. His bagpipes were returned to Canada in 1916 and are now on display in the Canadian War Museum in Ottawa. Jimmy might, however, have considered Scotland as his bagpipes' true spiritual home…

During the Great War 628 soldiers were awarded the Victoria Cross of whom 71 were from Canadian regiments. Piper James Richardson deserves to be remembered as one of the most unusual winners of the British Empire's highest military decoration for valour.

JAMES RICHARDSON V.C.:

Born:	25 November 1895 at Belshill, North Lanarkshire, son of David and Mary Richardson
Education:	Belshill Academy and John Street School, Glasgow
Occupation:	Driller
Unit/ Regiment:	72/ Seaforth Highlanders (Canadian) then 16/ Canadian Expeditionary Force (Canadian Scottish)
Rank:	Private
Died:	9 October 1916, Battle of the Somme
Age:	20
Decoration:	V.C.
Buried:	Adanac Cemetery III.F.36.
Inscription:	GREATER LOVE HATH NO MAN THAN THIS

(King James Bible John 15:13)

The cemetery was designed by Sir Herbert Baker and created after 1918 when graves were collected from smaller cemeteries in the Courcelette area. Of over 3,000 burials, 1,700 are unidentified

James Richardson's grave in Adanac Cemetery   *J Kerr*

Adanac Cemetery *J Kerr*

Adanac Cemetery- Richardson's grave is third from the right- note the V.C. on the headstone *J Kerr*

299

THE SOMME
Day 5 Itinerary: Optional

Hangard Communal Cemetery Extension
A Hamilton

THE SOMME

Day 5 Itinerary: Optional

(See Map of the Somme p.204)

If you have caught the battlefields 'bug' and want to explore further after a second night in Arras or in Amiens, you could drive round 'off the beaten track' areas of the beautiful Somme valley. Visit Crouy-sur-Somme Cemetery, 17 kms north west of Amiens, where a talented young composer with a great future is buried. At Hangard Communal Cemetery lies one of five brothers killed in the Great War. About 20 kms to the east is Lihons, a French cemetery where an American poet and Francophile was laid to rest. As you make your way to Calais take a detour of 38 kms to stop off at Ronssoy Communal at the end of a small street opposite the Mairie (Town Hall) where you will find the grave of another promising musician and composer to die in the Somme.

Cemetery	Address/Post code/ Google map ref.	Name	Page
19 CROUY BRITISH	D95 80310 Crouy-Saint-Pierre, France 49.96188,2.08345	Cecil Coles	302
20 HANGARD COMMUNAL EXTENSION	D76 80110 Hangard, France 49.82415,2.51922	Arthur Souls	147
21 LIHONS FRENCH NATIONAL	D337 80320 Lihons, France 49.82782,2.748	Alan Seeger	305
22 RONSSOY COMMUNAL	1 Rue Marie Louise Frison, 80740 Ronssoy, France 49.98368,3.16114	Ernest Farrar	309

CECIL COLES

'...one of the great lost hopes of British music'

Cecil Coles was invited in July 1914 by Sir Henry Wood, founder of the Promenade Concerts, to conduct his own piece *Fra Giacome*, a monologue for voice and orchestra in the Queen's Hall, London. He could not have hoped for a better opportunity to showcase his talents. Based on macabre verses by Robert Williams Buchanan, it explores the dark nature of mankind that would soon manifest itself in the horror of the Great War that played its part in consigning Coles's work to dust-covered obscurity... until 2002.

Cecil Frederick Gottlieb Coles was born in Kirkcudbright in Scotland in 1888, the son of Margaret and Frederick, a landscape painter and archaeologist. The second oldest of five children, Cecil was deeply affected by the tragic death of his mother after she had given birth to her youngest child.

He was educated at George Watson's College in Edinburgh and when only 16 composed his first orchestral work, a *Concert Overture in E minor*. He studied music at Edinburgh University and was awarded a Cherubini Scholarship to study at the Royal College of Music in 1906. He was introduced to Morley College, an establishment founded for the education of working men and women, by a Miss Nancy Brooke, a devotee of his music, who taught wood carving and supervised the College's Orchestral Library.

The Director of Music at Morley College was the celebrated composer Gustav Holst with whom Coles formed a close friendship for the rest of his short life. They went on a walking holiday in the Swiss Alps in 1911 which prompted Holst to describe Coles in a letter home as an 'excellent, magnificent leader'. During his time at Morley, Coles composed *In the Cathedral* for String Orchestra for which he used his initials CFGC as a musical motif.

Like musician and composer F.S.Kelly, Coles trained in Germany; he attended the Stuttgart Conservatoire in 1908 and was appointed assistant conductor of the Stuttgart Royal Opera House, a post he held from 1911 to 1913. His *Comedy of Errors Overture* was first performed at the Cologne Conservatoire on 25 June 1913.

When in Stuttgart he struck up a friendship with the composer Richard Strauss whose influence can be heard in his work. He met his future wife Phoebe at the English Church of St. Katharine where he was the resident organist. Coles 'never joined in the ordinary hatred of Germany...' according to Holst and found the increasingly militaristic and jingoistic atmosphere in Germany so oppressive and depressing that he decided to relocate to London where he became Chorus Master of the touring Beecham Opera Company and a music teacher at Morley College.

Cecil Coles of the 1/9 London Regiment

By 1914 Cecil Coles was happily married with a young son Brooke, named after Nancy Brooke, who had kept house for him when in Stuttgart. Just as his career was about to take off, it was with a heavy heart, therefore, that he enlisted to fight against a country that had offered him great opportunities to further his musical career. He joined the 1/9 London Regiment, more commonly known as the Queen Victoria's Rifles, as a stretcher-bearer and for over three years rescued many beleaguered comrades in the most dangerous of locations.

Serjeant Coles formed a band that entertained the Battalion with concerts. Whereas George Butterworth turned his back on musical activity at the Front, Coles found the time and space to compose *Behind the Lines*, an orchestral piece in four movements which he signed off: 'February 4th 1918 in the Field.' The second and third movements, *The Wayside Shrine* and *Rumours*, unfortunately went missing, possibly destroyed by a shell. The first movement *Estaminet de Carrefour* evokes a pastoral tranquillity in villages and cafés behind the lines with a cheerful waltz that represents soldiers' escape from the horrors of trench warfare. The mournful *Cortège* epitomizes the overpowering and ever present aftermath of death. When at the Front, he also composed *Sorrowful Dance* which he dedicated to Phoebe 'My Dear Wife' and he had cause to celebrate the birth of his daughter on 14 March 1917, christened Phoebe Catherine but better known later as Penny Catherine.

Coles managed to dodge bullets and shells for three years. In late March and April of 1918, the Queen Victoria's Rifles were engaged in the operation to halt the German Spring Offensives. It was during an heroic attempt to bring in casualties that Cecil Coles was mortally wounded by a sniper and was reputed to have been humming Beethoven as he lay dying in a Casualty Clearing Station. He was buried in the cemetery at Crouy-sur-Somme; his inscription was composed by one of his comrades who described him as a 'genius' and it may be that the influence of Gustav Holst can be discerned in the tribute, as he had also described Coles as a 'genius'. Holst's moving *Ode to Death* for chorus and orchestra was dedicated to 'Coles and the Fallen'.

Cecil Coles's music was rarely if ever played for over 80 years after his death. His traumatised wife Phoebe had refused to mention her husband in conversation, so her children, Brooke and particularly Penny Catherine, knew little of his musical past. Phoebe gave the scores in her possession to George Watson's College.

It was not until her estranged brother told her on his death bed in 1993 about her father and the whereabouts of his musical manuscripts, that Penny Catherine Coles, the author of many children's novels, learnt of her father's past. She spent several years wrangling with the College to retrieve her father's mud-splattered manuscripts which she then donated to the National Library of Scotland.

In 2002, 84 years after Coles's death, concerts were given by the B.B.C. Scottish Symphony Orchestra conducted by Martyn Brabbins and acclaimed recordings made.

The Times considered that Coles's music 'has nobility, haunting beauty and a strange almost prophetic sense of tragedy,' and *The Daily Telegraph*'s review observed that Coles's orchestral skills were 'amply demonstrated by the lush, full bodied playing of the B.B.C. Scottish Symphony Orchestra.'

In an extraordinary twist to the story, Penny Catherine Coles who had been educated at St. Paul's School for Girls in London, discovered years after she left, that the Director of Music in her time there had been her father's great friend... Gustav Holst.

How might Cecil Coles have fared after the War? He was still searching for his own style- his music was derivative, influenced by a number of composers and the big orchestral pieces of the European Romantics- Wagner, Bruckner, Brahms and Strauss. There were also traces of the French impressionism of Debussy in his work and, of course, the influence of Holst can be heard. Holst did not gain recognition for his work until *The Planets* was given its first complete performance in 1920 when he was 46. Coles died at the age of 29.

Cecil Coles's music lives on, thanks to the CD recorded in 2002, which prompted *The Independent* to claim that 'Coles emerges as one of the great lost hopes of British music.'

Bandmaster Cecil Coles's grave in Crouy British Cemetery   *A Hamilton*

303

CECIL COLES:

Born:	7 October1888 at Kirkcudbright, son of Frederick and Margaret Coles; husband of Phoebe Coles of 11, Vancouver Road, Catford, London.
Education:	George Watson's College, Edinburgh
Occupation:	Musician and composer
Unit/ Regiment:	1/9 London Regiment (Queen Victoria's Rifles)
Rank:	Serjeant and Bandmaster
Died:	26 April 1918
Age:	29
Buried:	Crouy British Cemetery I.C.1.
Inscription:	HE WAS A GENIUS
	BEFORE ANYTHING ELSE
	AND A HERO
	OF THE FIRST WATER

The cemetery at Crouy-sur-Somme is about 16 kms north west of Amiens on the west side of the Somme and was used between April and August 1918 for burials for Casualty Clearing Stations No. 5 and No. 47. It was designed by Sir Reginald Blomfield

Crouy British Cemetery *A Hamilton*

ALAN SEEGER

'I have a Rendezvous with Death'

After graduating from Harvard University in 1910, Alan Seeger drifted into a bohemian lifestyle first in Greenwich Village, New York and from 1912 until the outbreak of war, in the Latin quarter of Paris. An intellectual who edited the Harvard monthly magazine in his final year, Seeger spent his time imbibing the culture and writing poetry that failed to impress the world of publishing. He studied fitfully at the Sorbonne and seeking inspiration for his writing, visited London in the summer of 1914 where he was a regular visitor to the British Museum Library. During his stay he met his father with whom he spent several happy days until it became clear that France was under serious threat from the invading German Army.

He felt duty bound to return post haste to his adopted country and rushed back to Paris on 25 July to offer his support for the defence of France from the German peril. He returned via Bruges, dropping off the manuscript of a collection of poems, *Juvenilia*, with a potential publisher.

Anti-German feeling was at fever pitch in the French capital. Seeger and 40 fellow Americans marched through Paris waving a large American flag. As Americans could not swear allegiance to France and because the United States had not as yet been drawn into the conflict, Seeger and compatriots joined the French Foreign Legion on 24 August 1914. He was passionate in his desire to fight for France, urged on by an indefatigable belief in the glory and nobility of death on the battlefield. He mused in May 1915: 'If it must be, let it come to in the heat of action. Why flinch? It is by far the noblest form in which death can come: it is in a sense almost a privilege.' Alan Seeger had no military experience, so undertook months of monotonous training at Toulouse and later at Rheims. He wrote to his mother about his happiness and excitement 'over the wonderful days ahead'.

Alan Seeger- the young student

Seeger fought in the Aisne area during early1915. In his poem *The Aisne* (1914-15) Seeger highlighted the bloody nature of the conflict: the destruction of buildings, the harshness of the winter conditions, the fellowship among the soldiers and the glory of fighting. It was a paradoxical situation for a man who had been a solitary, library-bound intellectual who was generally regarded as an arrogant and selfish loner. But here he was, eulogising the concept of war and enjoying the 'fellowship' of army life:

We first saw fire on the tragic slopes
Where the flood-tide of France's early gain
Big with wrecked promise and abandoned hopes,
Broke in a surf of blood along the Aisne.

There her heroes left us, we assumed,
What, dying, they reconquered, we preserved,
In the chill trenches, harried, shelled, entombed,
Winter came down on us, but no man swerved.

Alan Seeger- French Légionnaire

Winter came down on us. The low clouds, torn
In the stark branches of the riven pines,
Blurred the white rockets that from dusk till morn
Traced the wide curve of the close grappling lines…

For that high fellowship was ours then
With those who, championing another's good,
More than dull Peace or its poor votaries could,
Taught us the dignity of being men…

There where, firm links in unyielding chain,
Where fell the long-planned blow and fell in vain-
Hearts worthy of the honour and the trial,
Helped to hold the lines along the Aisne.

Alan Seeger was desperate for personal and collective glory. He was disappointed that for most of 1915, his battalion was in reserve and was irritated not to be involved in any action.

The opportunity arose in September when the French Legion forces were involved in the Battle of Champagne, an inconclusive action which nonetheless offered the young American the opportunity to pursue his objective of a Croix de Guerre for acts of bravery by going on patrols deep into enemy areas under the cover of darkness.

A bout of bronchitis removed him from the front line but he recovered in Biarritz and then Paris in time for the combined French and British 'Push' on the Somme in July 1916. He wrote animatedly on 28 June: 'We go up to the attack tomorrow. This will probably be the biggest thing yet. We are to have the honour of marching in the first wave.' As it happened, this was not the case; he was called up to the front line on 3 July and the French Foreign Legion troops went 'over the top' appropriately for Alan on 4 July- American Independence Day. The objective of the offensive was to capture the village of Belloy-en-Santerre. Running full tilt across No Man's Land, Alan Seeger was mown down by a battery of six machine-guns hidden in a shell crater. According to colleagues who survived, once grounded by a hail of bullets, he continued to cheer his colleagues on towards enemy lines. He had, therefore, achieved his aim of a glorious death.

He knew, like the majority of soldiers engaged in combat on the Western Front that his chances of survival were limited and in one of the best known of Great War poems he predicted his meeting with death:

I have a Rendezvous with Death

I have a Rendezvous with Death
At some disputed barricade,
When Spring comes back with rustling shade
And apple blossoms fill the air-
I have a Rendezvous with Death
When Spring brings back blue days and fair.

It may be he shall take my hand
And lead me into a dark land
And close my eyes and quench my breath-
It may be I shall pass him still.
I have a Rendezvous with Death
On some scarred slope of battered hill,
When Spring comes round again this year
And the first meadow flowers appear.

God knows 'twere better to be deep
Pillowed in silk and scented down,
Where love throbs out in blissful sleep,
Pulse nigh to pulse, and breath to breath,
Where hushed awakenings are dear…
But I've a Rendezvous with Death
At midnight in some flaming town,
When Spring trips north again this year,
And I to my pledged word am true,
I shall not fail that rendezvous.

Alan Seeger did not receive an instant burial but was buried in a mass grave at the French National Cemetery near Lihons. It was an unglamorous final resting place for a man who had considered himself honoured and privileged to fight for the defence of France and to whom a glorious death on the battlefield was so important.

Alan's parents paid for the new bell in the reconstructed church in the village of Belloy and there is a plaque in his memory on the wall of the Mairie.

His words from an *Ode in Memory of the American Volunteers Fallen for France* were etched into the Memorial in the Place des Etats-Unis in Paris which was dedicated on 4 July 1923 to the Americans who had lost their lives fighting for France:

The Memorial in Paris to Americans who lost their lives fighting for France
Dr. Alastair Robson

They did not pursue worldly rewards;
They wanted more than to live without regret,
Brothers pledged to the Honor implicit
In living one's own life
And dying one's own death. Hail brothers!
Goodbye to you, the exalted dead!
To you we owe two debts of gratitude forever:
The glory of having died for France
And the homage due to you in memories.'

The young American poet could rest content that *Poems* was published posthumously a year after his death. It probably would not have concerned him that reaction to his poetry was lukewarm and that an increasing disillusionment with the criminal inhumanity perpetrated in the War turned the reading public away from his lofty and idealistic journey to a glorious death.

Seeger's poetry may not have received the critical acclaim of, for example, Rupert Brooke's but at least his death was marked and honoured by the country he was prepared to sacrifice his life for and he could rest in peace in a corner of France, honoured by the award of the Croix de Guerre and the Médaille Militaire.

Alan Seeger and his poetry were not completely overlooked in the United States. The famous American folk singer and pacifist Pete Seeger, referred to his uncle Alan, whenever he introduced his audience to his song *The Torn Flag* by saying 'I had an uncle who wrote a poem with the lines: "I have a rendezvous with death / At midnight in some flaming town. . ." So I made some new verses.'

ALAN SEEGER:

Born:	22 June, 1888 in New York City, U.S.A., son of Charles Louis and Elsie Seeger
Education:	Hackley School and Harvard University, Massachusetts
Occupation:	Poet
Unit/ Regiment:	French Foreign Legion- 3rd Section, 1st Company, 'C' Battalion of 2nd Foreign Regiment
Rank:	Légionnaire
Died:	4 July 1916, Battle of the Somme
Age:	28
Decorations:	Croix de Guerre, Médaille Militaire
Buried:	Ossuaire No.1 (Mass grave) Lihons French National Cemetery, 30 kms east of Amiens

The cemetery was started in January 1915 and enlarged after the War. Over 6,500 French soldiers were buried there, about 1600 of them in four mass graves. There are six C.W.G.C. burials

Mass grave (ossuaire) at Lihons French National Cemetery   A Hamilton

ERNEST FARRAR

'...the tragic shadows of unfulfilled vicissitudes'

Ernest Farrar was a promising musician who, like F.S. Kelly and Cecil Coles, spent time in Germany honing his skills as a church organist.

He was born in Lewisham, London but his clergyman father moved to Mickleton, a parish in Leeds. Ernest attended Leeds Grammar School where his interest in playing the organ was fostered. In 1905 he won an Open Free scholarship to the Royal College of Music where he studied composition with Sir Charles Stanford and the organ with Sir Walter Parratt.

His scholarship had two terms to run when he was offered the post of organist in the English Church in Dresden for six months to cover an absence. He returned to take up the appointment as organist for a church in South Shields and moved to Christ Church, Harrogate in 1912.

According to his obituary in the magazine of the Royal College of Music, he joined the Army in August 1915, serving first as a private in the Grenadier Guards and later he received a commission in the 3/ Devonshire Regiment as a 2nd lieutenant on 27 February 1916.

He returned on leave in July 1918 and conducted the first performance of his *Heroic Elegy* composed in memory of his fallen comrades. Within days of his return to the trenches in September, he was killed at the age of 33 on 18 September at the Battle of Epehy south of Cambrai when the Devons attacked the Hindenburg Line. It was thought he was killed by machine-gun fire although no one saw him fall. He died 'as he had lived, modestly and unselfishly.' He was buried at the small Ronssoy Communal Cemetery with 37 other identified British casualties.

In his short life he composed five song, six orchestral, six choral, three chamber, six piano and five organ works, many of which were influenced by the pre-war pastoral 'folk' style of Ralph Vaughan Williams and George Butterworth. The most celebrated were *The Blessed Damozel*, *The Celtic Suite*, a song cycle *Vagabond Songs* and *English Pastoral Impressions* which were

2nd Lieutenant Ernest Farrar of the 3/ Devons

written in 1915. Farrar's final completed work was a set of *Organ Choral Preludes* which placed him, the Royal College of Music considered, among the most distinguished composers of the 'younger British School'. He left unfinished two movements of a String Quartet, *Celtic Impressions* and there was, according to his obituary, 'a pathetic, almost uncanny ring of prophecy about the first, *The Dominion of Dreams*, which was headed: "There are dreams beyond the thrust of the spear, and there are dreams and dreams; of what has been or what is to be, as well as the more idle fantasies of sleep. And this is perhaps of those whose gossamer is spun out of the invisible threads of sorrow; or it may be is woven out of the tragic shadows of unfulfilled vicissitudes."'

A concert in his memory was held at Harrogate on 17 September 1919 which included Farrar's *Variations in G* for pianoforte and orchestra on an old British sea shanty.

His teaching inspired the British composer Gerald Finzi who studied with him at Christ Church, Harrogate from 1915. Finzi was so affected by his teacher's death that he became a confirmed pacifist for the rest of his life.

Ernest Farrar's grave in Ronssoy Communal Cemetery   *A Hamilton*

ERNEST FARRAR:

Born:	7 July 1885 at Lewisham, son of Rev. and Mrs C.D. Farrar of Micklefield Vicarage, Leeds
Education:	Leeds Grammar School
Occupation:	Composer and organist
Unit/ Regiment:	Grenadier Guards and 3/ Devonshire
Rank:	2nd Lieutenant
Died:	18 September 1918
Age:	33
Buried:	Ronssoy Communal Cemetery B.27.
Inscription:	LORD ALL PITYING JESU BLEST
	GRANT HIM THINE ETERNAL REST

The cemetery, designed by A.J.S. Hutton, is 15 kms north west of St. Quentin and is located at the back of the communal cemetery. It was captured by the 7/ Royal West Kents on 18 September 1918. There are 40 graves, two of which are unidentified

Screw picket in the Somme, still in use 100 years on...
J Kerr

V

ABBREVIATIONS AND GLOSSARY

- A.D.C.   Aide-de-camp: a lieutenant or captain on a general's personal staff

- Archie   Anti-aircraft gun or gunfire, based on the words of a Music Hall song 'Archibald- certainly not!'

- A.S.C.   Army Service Corps: responsible for provision of ammunition, food and equipment, disparagingly known by the troops as 'Ally Sloper's Cavalry'. Ally Sloper was a lazy and scheming comic-book character

- Bar   The second award of a medal- i.e. V.C. and Bar means two V.C.s

- B.E.F.   British Expeditionary Force

    Ranks:

Field Marshal	Commander-in-Chief
General	i/c of an army of approximately 200,000
Lieutenant General	corps between 30,000 and 75,000
Major General	division of 20,000
Brigadier General	brigade of 4,000
Lieutenant Colonel	battalion of 1,000
Major	second i/c a battalion
Captain	company of 250
Lieutenant	platoon of 60
2nd lieutenant	platoon of 60
Other ranks	serjeants and corporals
No rank:	privates

    Units:

Army	consisting of three to five corps
Corps	two to five divisions
Division	three brigades
Brigade	four battalions
Battalion	four companies
Company	four platoons
Platoon	four sections of 15

- Blighty   from the Hindustani word 'belati' originally used by British troops posted to India to mean 'home', hence to 'catch a blighty one' was soldiers' slang for being wounded badly enough to be sent home for further treatment

- Brevet rank   was a reward for an officer's exceptional service. If there was a full complement of officers in his unit it would not be possible for him to be promoted so he could be given a brevet rank, i.e. one higher than his current rank but he would not be entitled to any extra pay

- C. in C.   Commander-in-Chief

- C.M.G.   Companion of the Order of St. Michael and St. George awarded at the monarch's pleasure since 1818

- C.O.   Commanding Officer of a battalion

- Fatigues   Chores, mostly heavy ones

- F.G.C.M.   Field General Court Martial

- German ranks: | Gefreiter | equivalent to lance corporal/ corporal |
Leutnant	2nd lieutenant
Oberleutnant	lieutenant
Unteroffizier	serjeant

- G.H.Q.   General Headquarters

- G.O.C.   General Officer Commanding a brigade, division, corps or army

- I.W.G.C.   Imperial War Graves Commission established by Royal Charter in 1917. It was renamed the Commonwealth War Graves Commission on 1 April 1960

- Jack Johnson   The name given to the burst of a 15 cm. German shell giving out a cloud of black smoke. Jack Johnson was a black American boxer who won the world heavyweight championship in 1908

- K.C.B.   Knight Commander of the Order of the Bath, it has been awarded 'at the Monarch's pleasure' since 1725

- M.C.C.   Marylebone Cricket Club founded in 1787

- Medals:
  - D.C.M.   Distinguished Conduct Medal awarded for 'gallantry in the field' to N.C.O.s and privates

  - D.S.C.   Distinguished Service Cross awarded to naval officers for 'gallantry during active operations against the enemy at sea'

  - D.S.O.   Distinguished Service Order awarded to officers for 'distinguished service during active operations against the enemy'

  - French: Médaille Militaire awarded to all ranks for 'valour in combat or long service'

    Légion d'Honneur was awarded for 'excellent civil or military conduct delivered upon official investigation'

  - M.C.   Military Cross awarded for the first time in December 1914 to commissioned officers for 'gallantry during active operations against the enemy'

  - M.M.   Military Medal awarded for 'acts of gallantry and devotion to duty under fire' to other ranks i.e. N.C.O.s and privates. Instituted in 1916 but backdated to 1914

  - T.D.   Territorial Decoration for 20 years of commissioned service

  - V.C.   The Victoria Cross was instituted in 1856 and was the highest award for 'most conspicuous bravery, or some daring or pre-eminent act of valour or self-sacrifice, or extreme devotion to duty in the presence of the enemy'

- M.G.   Machine-gun

- M.O.   Medical Officer

- N.C.O.   Non-Commissioned Officer e.g. corporals and serjeants

- O.C.   Officer Commanding a company or platoon

- O.R.   Other ranks: private soldiers or N.C.O.s

- O.T.C.   Officers' Training Corps established mostly in universities and Public Schools

- R.A.M.C.   Royal Army Medical Corps: it numbered over 110,000 personnel by 1918

- R.E.   Royal Engineers

- Redoubt   Defensive position fortified by machine-gun posts and dugouts e.g. Schwaben Redoubt

- R.F.A.   Royal Field Artillery

- R.F.C.   Royal Flying Corps which became the Royal Air Force on 1 April 1918

- R.S.M.   Regimental Serjeant Major

- Runner   Soldier who acted as a messenger

- Screw picket   A corkscrew-like metal bar screwed into the ground with three or four loops through which barbed wire was pulled to establish a defensive wall in No Man's Land. The French called it a 'queue de cochon' (pigtail)

- Serjeant   This was the spelling used by the British Army until November 1953. During the War, British and New Zealander soldiers of this rank were spelled 'serjeant'. Canadian units, from 1 to 7/Canadian Infantry were spelled with a 'j' but with a 'g' for the others. The Rifles Regiment in the British Army still spell it with a 'j'

- Soldiers' versions of place names:

Dickie Bus	Dickebusch
Passion Dale	Passchendaele
Plugstreet	Ploegsteert
Pop(s)	Poperinghe
White Sheet	Wytschaete
Wipers	Ypres

- Stand to   'Stand to your arms'- a time in the trenches when soldiers had to be on alert e.g. at dawn or dusk. When there was an attack, the sentry would shout 'Stand to'!

- Uhlan   German cavalryman armed with a lance

- V.A.D.   Voluntary Aid Detachment that provided Field Nursing Services. The nurses were affectionately known as 'Very Adorable Darlings'

- Zero Hour   Time given for the start of an attack

Trenches in Sanctuary Wood   *J Kerr*

Canadian Memorial on Vimy Ridge   *J Kerr*

German Cemetery near Wicres   *J Kerr*

VI

ACKNOWLEDGEMENTS AND BIBLIOGRAPHY

We should like to express our special thanks to the following without whose enthusiastic efforts and skills *Stolen Lives* would never have seen the light of day in its current format:

- Maurice and Liz Bott: Maurice for his meticulous proofreading and research and Liz for a number of German translations

- James Kerr for his outstanding photography (www.jameskerr.co.uk)

- Tom Morgan for painstakingly checking the penultimate draft, offering comments that were unfailingly apposite and for providing information and leads for a plethora of our questions (www.hellfirecorner.co.uk)

- Monica Ory for a most thorough final proofread

- George Sayell for producing four maps with great precision and two chapters of the book

- Ruth Smith for her excellent design and artwork for the book (www.damsoncreative.co.uk)

Below we have combined Acknowledgements and Bibliography/ Sources. We have tried to acknowledge those who have assisted and advised us and the authors and publications which we have referred to. We have been struck by the generosity of authors and owners of photographs and documents who have been most generous in allowing us to use their material. We have attempted to trace copyright holders with the occasional lack of success. If we have overlooked anyone, we offer our sincerest apologies and promise to include your name in the next edition.

GENERAL:
Terry Harrison for his help and knowledge on medals
Mark Sykes for ideas about subjects to include and other information

Banks, Arthur *A Military Atlas of the First World War* Leo Cooper 1998
Chasseaud, Peter *Rats Alley Trench Names of the Western Front 1914-1918* Spellmount 2006
Commonwealth War Graves Commission *Recipients of the Victoria Cross* 1997
Ellis, John and Cox, Michael *The World War I Databook* Aurum Press 1993
Harris, Clive and Whippy, Julian *The Greater Game Sporting Icons Who Fell in the Great War* Pen and Sword 2008
Haythornthwaite, Philip J. *The World War One Sourcebook* Brockhampton Press 1998
Hogg, Ian Vernon *Dictionary of World War I* Helicon 1994
Holmes, Richard *Tommy* Harper Perennial 2005
Keegan, John *The First World War* Hutchinson 1998
Lewis-Stempel, John *Six Weeks* Orion 2011
Macdonald, Lyn *Somme* Macmillan 1983
Pegler, Martin and Chappell, Mike *British Tommy 1914-1918* Osprey 1996
Pope, Stephen and Wheal, Elizabeth-Anne *Dictionary of the First World War* Pen and Sword 2003
Rawson, Andrew *British Army Handbook 1914-1918* Sutton Publishing 2006
Ruvigny, Marquis de *Roll of Honour 1914-1918*
Sheffield, Gary *Forgotten Victory* Headline Book Publishing 2001
Stevenson, David *The History of the First World War* Penguin 2004
Westlake, Ray *British Battalions in France and Belgium 1914* Leo Cooper 1997
Westlake, Ray *British Battalions on the Somme 1916* Leo Cooper 1994
www.1914-1918.net/ (The Long, Long Trail)
www.cwgc.org (Commonwealth War Graves Commission)

CEMETERIES and MEMORIALS: p. 13
James Fleming C.W.G.C. enquiries administrator

Corns, Cathryn and Hughes-Wilson, John *Blindfold and Alone* Cassell 2001
Davies, Frank and Maddocks, Graham *Bloody Red Tabs* Leo Cooper 1995
Kingsley Ward, G. and Gibson, Major Edwin *Courage Remembered* HMSO London 1995
National Archives WO93/ 49
Putkowski, Julian and Sykes, Julian *Shot at Dawn* Pen and Sword 1989
Stamp, Gavin *The Memorial to the Missing of the Somme* Profile Books 2007
Ware, Sir Fabian *The Immortal Heritage An Account of the Work and Policy of the Imperial War Graves Commission 1917-1937* Cambridge University Press 1937

THE BRITISH ARMY ON THE WESTERN FRONT 1914-1918: p. 19

Holmes, Richard *Tommy* Harper Perennial 2005
Pope, Stephen and Wheal, Elizabeth Anne *Dictionary of the First World War* Pen and Sword 2003
Simkins, Peter *The First World War (2) The Western Front 1914-1916* Osprey 2002
Simkins, Peter *The First World War (3) The Western Front 1917-1918* Osprey 2002

ASQUITH, Raymond: p. 287

Suzanne Foster, Archivist at Winchester College
The Earl of Oxford and Asquith for his most helpful comments on the text and for providing a fuller picture of his
    grandfather Raymond's attitude to the War and his relationship with his father, the Prime Minister, H.H. Asquith
Chris Urwin for his translation of the Latin inscription of the Asquith plaque in Amiens Cathedral

Buchan, John *Memory Hold-the-Door* Hodder and Stoughton 1942
Clifford, Colin *The Asquiths* John Murray 2002
Jolliffe, John *Raymond Asquith Life and Letters* Collins 1980
National Archives WO339/ 71879, WO95/ 1219 (Coldstream Guards)
The Wykehamist March, October and November 1896 and November 1916

BALL, Albert: p. 182

Simon Williams, Head of History Nottingham High School, for the transcript of his interview with Roy Henderson
    C.B.E., a fellow pupil of Albert Ball's

Bowyer, Chaz *Albert Ball V.C.* William Kimber and Co. 1977
Briscoe, Walter and Stannard, Russell H. *Captain Ball V.C.* Herbert Jenkins 1918
Leadbetter, F.W.B. *Albert Ball VC, young hero and tragic loss* Trent Association 2006
Pengelly, Colin *Albert Ball V.C.* Pen and Sword Aviation 2010
The Lenton Times Albert Ball V.C. 1981
Weekly Dispatch Sunday 20 May 1917 and Sunday 4 November 1917
Williams, J.K.. *Captain Albert Ball VC, DSO, MC* 2010
www.bbc.co.uk 8 May 2008 *Albert Ball- World War I Flying Ace*

BAND, Harry: p. 61

Iain Overton for permission to refer to his research: 'Nurse's Note Lends Credence to Story of Crucified Soldier'
    National Post: pp. B7 for the Channel 4 Documentary *The Crucified Soldier*

Hansard 12 and 19 May 1915
Letter by Ursula Chaloner July 1915 reproduced with the permission of University of Leeds Library
The Crucified Soldier WW1 Documentary Tiger Aspect Productions Ltd. in association with Channel 4 2002
The Times 9 and 16 May 1915

BATTENBERG, Prince Maurice of: p. 85

Major Ken Gray of the Royal Green Jackets (Rifles) Museum for extracts of the War Diary for 1/ Kings Royal Rifle
    Corps

Daily Sketch 29 October 1914
The King's Royal Rifle Corps Chronicle

BELL, Donald: p. 271

Green Howards Museum, Richmond, Yorkshire

Chapman, Roger *Two schoolfriends win the VC in the same battle*, an article for the Green Howards Museum
Gliddon, Gerald *VCs of the First World War The Somme* Gliddon Books 1991
Harris, Clive and Whippy, Julian *The Greater Game* Pen and Sword 2008
Joannou, Paul *United's V.C. Hero of the Somme* www.nufc.co.uk
Leake, Richard B. *Stand To!* No. 61 April 2001
The Harrogatorian 1914-21
The Westminsterian 2000

BENTLEY, Charles: p. 163

Moyra McLaren, School Resource Officer, McLaren High School, Callander, Scotland
Rona Morrison, Centre for Research Collections, Edinburgh University Library
Alan Tucker, historian of the Royal Warwickshire Regiment in the Great War

Hamilton, Andrew and Reed, Alan *Meet at Dawn, Unarmed* Dene House Publishing 2009
Sherriff, R.C. *Journey's End* Brentano 1929
The Bond of Sacrifice of British Officers who fell in the Great War

BLYTHE, Colin: p. 112
Ruvigny, Marquis de *Roll of Honour* 1914-1918
Scoble, Christopher *Colin Blythe* *Lament for a Legend* Sports Books 2005
Smart, John Blythe *The Real Colin Blythe* Blythe Smart Publications 2009
Wisden Cricketers' Almanack 1904 and 1917

BUTTERWORTH, George: p. 245
English Folk Dance and Song Society, Regent's Park Road, London
George Parris for detail about early 20th century English music
~
Barlow, Michael *Whom the Gods Love* *The Life and Music of George Butterworth* Toccata Press 1997
Butterworth, Sir Alexander *George Butterworth Memorial Volume* 1918
Copley, Ian *George Butterworth* *A Centennial Tribute* Thames Publishing 1985
Eton College Archives
National Archives WO339/ 12777
Osborne, Richard *Till I End My Song* *A Perspective from Eton* The Cygnet Press 2002

CHAVASSE, Noel: p. 54
The Chavasse family for permission to use Noel Chavasse's diaries and papers (Imperial War Museum)
Permission from Avril Williams to photograph the reconstructed Dressing Station at Auchonvillers (Somme)
~
Clayton, Ann *Chavasse Double VC* Pen and Sword 1997
Daily Sketch 15 September 1917 British Library
de la Billière, General Sir Peter *Supreme Courage* Abacus 2005
Gliddon, Gerald *VCs of the First World War* *The Somme* Gliddon Books 1991
Gummer, Selwyn *The Chavasse Twins* Hodder and Stoughton 1963
Snelling, Stephen *VCs of the First World War* *Passchendaele* *1917* Sutton Publishing 1998
The Bromsgrove, Droitwich and Redditch Weekly Messenger 18 August 1917 British Library

COLES, Cecil: p. 302
Blevins, Pamela and Lace, Ian *Reviews of Music from Behind the Lines* www.musicweb-international.com
Purser, John Sleeve notes to *Music from Behind the Lines* Hyperion CDA67293 BBC Scottish Symphony Orchestra

CROZIER, James: p. 235
Babington, Anthony *For the Sake of Example* Leo Cooper 1983
Corns, Cathryn and Hughes-Wilson, John *Blindfold and Alone* Cassell 2001
Crozier, F.P. *A Brass Hat in No Man's Land* Jonathan Cape 1930
Crozier, F.P. *The Men I Killed* Michael Joseph 1938
National Archives WO71/ 450
Orr, Philip Introduction to *A Brass Hat in No Man's Land* Gliddon Books 1991
Putkowski, Julian and Sykes, Julian *Shot at Dawn* Pen and Sword 1989
Walker, Stephen *Belfast Telegraph* 25 October 2007

DONALDSON, Geoffrey: p.137
Stephen Forge, Archivist of Oundle School
Hilary Hamilton, Geoffrey's cousin twice removed, for permission to use Geoffrey's diaries and letters
Richard Pearson, Archivist at King Edward VI Grammar School for Boys, Stratford-on-Avon
Alan Tucker, historian of the Royal Warwickshire Regiment in the Great War
~
Bradley, Hamish *Oundle School Memorials of the Great War*
Cleary, Helen *The Human Face of War* www.bbc.co.uk/history/worldwars/wwone/humanfaceofwar
Diary and letters of Geoffrey Donaldson IWM 69/25/1
National Archives WO374/ 20236
Pearson, Richard *The Boys of Shakespeare's School in the First World War* The History Press 2010

DOUDNEY, Rev. Charles: p. 31
Rachel Horne, wife of the late Jonathan Horne, son of Rev. Charles Doudney, for generous access to the family's
    collection of photographs and use of Jonathan Horne's biography of his grandfather: *The Best of Good Fellows* *The
    Diaries and Memoirs of the Rev. Charles Doudney (1871-1915)*
~
Horne, Jonathan *The Best of Good Fellows* *The Diaries and Memoirs of the Rev. Charles Doudney (1871-1915)*
    Jonathan Horne Publications 1995
Youngson, Revd. David T. *Greater Love* Printability Publishing 2008

EVANS, Ellis: p. 89

Alan Llwyd for permission to use material from *The Story of Hedd Wyn, the Poet of the Black Chair*
～

Dehandschutter, Lieven   *Hedd Wyn   A Welsh Tragedy in Flanders*   Vormingscentrum Lodewijk Dosfel (Gent)   1992
Holt, Tonie and Valmai   *Battlefield Guide to the Ypres Salient*   Leo Cooper   2000
Llwyd, Alan   *The Story of Hedd Wyn, the Poet of the Black Chair*   Barddas Publications   2009
www.flandersbattlefields.com/heddwyn

FARRAR, Ernest: p. 309

Robert Corp, Archivist at the Royal College of Music
～

R.C.M. Magazine Volume 15   15 January 1918

GUNZBURG, Baron Alexis de: p. 121

Frans De Leye for the tour of the church of St. Catherine's, Zillebeke and for permitting us access to his photographic
   collection
Penny Hatfield, Archivist at Eton College
Jerry Murland for information on the 'Aristocrats' Plot', Zillebeke
～

Murland, Jerry   *Aristocrats Go To War*   Pen and Sword   2010
Royal Horse Guards War Diary
Ruvigny, Marquis de   *Roll of Honour 1914-18*
The Bond of Sacrifice of British Officers who fell in the Great War

GUYNEMER, Georges: p. 101

Dignat, Alban   *La Dernière Mission de Georges Guynemer*   www.herodote.net
Guttman, Jon   *Georges Guynemer*   www.historynet.com (originally in Aviation History)
Jane's Fighting Aircraft of World War I   Random House Group   2001
Sherman, Stephen   *Georges Guynemer*   www.acepilots.com
www.greatwar.co.uk

HODGSON, William Noel: p. 279

Patricia Jakeway of MEL Publications for permission to use material from Jack Medomsley's *William Noel Hodgson,
   the Gentle Poet*
～

Freeman, Mary Ellen   *Poets and Pals of Picardy*   Leo Cooper   1999
Gardner, Brian (editor)   *Up the Line to Death The War Poets 1914-1918*   Methuen   1976
Haig, Catriona   *Hodgson, William Noel (1893-1916)*   Oxford Dictionary of National Biography   2004
Holt, Tonie and Valmai   *Poets of the Great War*   Leo Cooper   1996
Medomsley, Jack   *William Noel Hodgson The Gentle Poet*   Mel Publications (Durham)   1989
Powell, Anne   *A Deep Cry*   Palladour Books   1993
St. John Adcock, Arthur   *For Remembrance*   Hodder and Stoughton   1918

ILES, Horace: p. 240

Channel 4   *Britain's Boy Soldiers*
CWGC   *One Boy* (film)
Hamilton, Alan   *The Times*   1 July 2006
Van Emden, Richard   *Boy Soldiers of the Great War*   Headline   2005
www.leeds-pals.com

JACK the pet dog: p. 284

Daniel Pritchard, curator of the Staffordshire Regiment Museum, for permission to use the photograph of 'Prince'
～

Shaw Baker, Peter   *Animal War Heroes*   A. and C. Black   1933

JEEVES, Percy: p. 253

Phil Britt, Archivist at Warwickshire C.C.C. for newspaper articles and photographs
～

Cricket Weekly Record   A Chat with Percy Jeeves   15 November 1913
Halford, Brian   *Remember   Birmingham Mail*   30 October   2008
Letter of engagement sent to Percy Jeeves by Warwickshire C.C.C. 8 September 1911   Warwickshire C.C.C.
Ryder, Rowland   *How the cricketing Jeeves started a Wodehouse saga   The Birmingham Post*   1981
The Goole Times   Found- The Looks of Goole's own Jeeves   August 1913
Wisden   Cricketers' Almanack   1913-17

JEFFRIES, Clarence: p. 104

Carol Calderwood for sending information and photographs from Australia

Marcelle Powell, Community Engagement Officer, Callaghan College for contacting Bill Storer for the photograph of Clarence Jeffries

Peter J. Williams of the Abermain Heritage Preservation Society for useful information

~

Abermain War Memorial Abermain Heritage Preservation Society

Australian Dictionary of National Biography

Newcastle Morning Herald Abermain Honour Roll Monday 10 November 1919

KELLY, Frederick S.: p. 260

Lindsay Guest of the River and Rowing Museum, Henley-on-Thames, for assistance with photographs of F.S. Kelly and the 1908 Leander eight

National Library of Australia for permission to use extracts from F.S. Kelly's diary

Penny Hatfield, Archivist at Eton College

Thérèse Radic, Faculty of the Victorian College of the Arts and Melbourne Conservatorium of Music, for her advice and kindly granting permission to use material from her foreword to F.S. Kelly's diaries published by the National Library of Australia

KIPLING, John: p. 189

The poem *My Boy Jack* by Rudyard Kipling and his son's letters are reprinted by permission of United Agents on behalf of: The National Trust for Places of Historic Interest and Beauty

~

Brown, Jonathan *The Great War and its aftermath: The son who haunted Kipling* *The Independent* 29 August 2006

Holt, Tonie and Valmai *'My Boy Jack?'* *The Search for Kipling's Only Son* Leo Cooper 1996

Smith, David *'Wrong man' in Kipling son's grave* *The Observer* 4 November 2007

LEIGHTON, Roland: p. 218

Quotations from Vera Brittain's *Testament of Youth*, and her poem *Perhaps*, are included by kind permission of Mark Bostridge and T.J. Brittain-Catlin, Literary Executors for the Estate of Vera Brittain 1970.

David R. Leighton for generously allowing us to include his uncle Roland's poems- *Villanelle* and *Hédauville* and for advising us on the original punctuation used

McMaster University Ontario for permission to use photographs of Roland Leighton and Vera Brittain

Jerry Rudland, Archivist at Uppingham School for information and photographs

~

Bishop, Alan and Bostridge, Mark *Letters from a Lost Generation* Virago 2008

Brittain, Vera *Testament of Youth* Victor Gollancz 1933

Farr, Don *None That Go Return* *Leighton, Brittain and Friends, and the Lost Generation 1914-18* Helion 2010

Holt, Tonie and Valmai *Poets of the Great War* Leo Cooper 1996

Leighton, Marie *Boy of My Heart* Hodder and Stoughton 1916

National Archives WO374/ 41620

LODGE, Raymond: p. 116

Jane Kirby, Archivist at Bedales School

~

Lodge, Sir Oliver *Raymond or Life and Death* Methuen 1918

Spagnoly, Tony and Smith, Ted *Cameos of the Western Front* *Salient Points Four* Leo Cooper 1999

www.fst.org/lodge

www.r2mw.com/guide2mw/s/spiritualism-in-the-first-world-war

MACLAGAN, Gilchrist: p. 65

Lindsay Guest of the River and Rowing Museum, Henley-on-Thames, for assistance with photographs of Gilchrist Maclagan and the 1908 Leander eight

Penny Hatfield, Archivist at Eton College

Dr. Robert Treharne-Jones, Press and PR Officer for the Leander Club, Henley-on-Thames, for help with photographs in the Leander clubhouse and to the Leander Club for their use

~

Bairnsfather, Bruce *Bullets and Billets* Grant Richards 1916

Bairnsfather, Bruce *How I came back to Mac* *British Legion Journal* June 1935

Cleaver, Hylton *A History of Rowing* Herbert Jenkins 1957

Dodd, Christopher *The Story of Rowing* Hutchinson 1992

Fourth Olympiad 1908 London Official Report British Olympic Association 1909

Lehmann, R.C. *The Complete Oarsman* Methuen 1908

National Archives WO339/ 28972

The Eton College Chronicle 1894-1904 and 1915

MAUK, Paul: p. 243
Jünger, Ernst *Die Unvergessenen* Moser-Verlag (München) 1928
www.memoire.pas-de-calais.com Marie-Pierre Griffon

MILLER, James: p. 277
Museum of King's Own (Royal Lancaster Regiment)
~
Gliddon, Gerald *VCs of the First World War* *The Somme* Gliddon Books 1991
Middlebrook, Martin *First Day on the Somme* Military Book Society 1971

MILLINS, Frederick: p. 109
The author of this piece, George Sayell, wishes to thank:
Chris Baker, Great War consultant and 'Long, Long Trail' website www.1914-1918.net/
John Smith, Cheddington History Society
Pamela Stratton, family historian for invaluable help with genealogy
The story of the sewing machine was told to George by his late aunt Mary Maloney (née Humphrey).

MOBBS, Edgar: p. 69
Amy Rolph, World Museum of Rugby, Twickenham
~
Edwards, Jenny *Sportsman and Soldier* *A Personal Tribute* 1998
Harris, Clive and Whippy, Julian *The Greater Game* Pen and Sword 2008
Mortimer, Gavin *Fields of Glory* Andre Deutsch 2001
National Archives WO339/ 15240
Woodall, David *The Mobbs Own* Northants Regimental Association 1994
www.comeonyousaints.com
www.mkheritage.co.uk
www.therugbyhistorysociety.co.uk

MORRIS, Herbert: p. 50
Babington, Anthony *For the Sake of Example* Leo Cooper 1983
Corns, Catherine and Hughes-Wilson, John *Blindfold and Alone* Cassell 2001
National Archives WO95/495, WO71/ 594, WO93/49
Putkowski, Julian *Caribbean Volunteer* www.shotatdawn.info
Putkowski, Julian and Sykes, Julian *Shot at Dawn* Pen and Sword 1989

MUNRO, Hector ('Saki'): p. 256
Professor A.J. Langguth for his permission to quote from Saki *A Life of Hector Hugh Munro* Hamish Hamilton 1981

PARR, John and ELLISON, George p. 158 and 159
B.B.C. Timewatch *The Last Day of World War One* 2008
Holt, Tonie and Valmai *Battlefield Guide to the Western Front- North* Leo Cooper 2004
Horsfall, Jack and Cave, Nigel *Mons* Leo Cooper 2000
Persico, E. *Eleventh Month, Eleventh Day, Eleventh Hour: Armistice Day, 1918 World War I and its violent climax*
  Random House 2005

POULTON PALMER, Ronald: p. 141
Amy Rolph, World Museum of Rugby, Twickenham
~
Cooksey, John and McKechnie, Graham BBC Berkshire programme on Ronald Poulton Palmer 2008
Corsan, James *For Poulton and England* *The Life and Times of an Edwardian Hero* Matador 2009
Harris, Clive and Whippy, Julian *The Greater Game* *Sporting Icons Who Fell in the Great War* Pen and Sword 2008
Osborn E.B. *The New Elizabethans* 1919
Poulton, Edward Bagnall *The Life of Ronald Poulton* Sidgwick and Johnson 1919

PROWSE, Charles Bertie: p. 225
Davies, Frank and Maddocks, Graham *Bloody Red Tabs* Leo Cooper 1995
Powney, Dennis *The History of Bromham* Bromham Local History Society
Putkowski, Julian and Sykes, Julian *Shot at Dawn* Pen and Sword Books 1989
www.warstudies.bham.ac.uk University of Birmingham Centre for First World War Studies

RADFORD, Basil Hallam: p. 210
Sue Cole and Catherine Smith, Archivists at Charterhouse School
~
Cooper, Diana *Autobiography* Rupert Hart Davis 1958
Janis, Elsie *So far So Good* John Long 1933
Jolliffe, John *Raymond Asquith* *Life and Letters* Collins 1980

Kipling, Rudyard *The Irish Guards in the Great War* London 1923
National Archives WO339/ 58073 Kite Balloons Air 1/528/16/12/ 68
Osborn E.B. *The New Elizabethans* 1919
Payne, Dr. David *Observation Balloons on the Western Front* www.westernfrontassociation.com 22 May 2008
The Carthusian November 1916
Ziegler, Philip *Lady Diana Cooper* Hamish Hamilton 1980

REDMOND, William: p. 131
With thanks to Terence Denman for permission to refer to *A Lonely Grave The Life and Death of William Redmond*
〜
Denman, Terence *A Lonely Grave The Life and Death of William Redmond* Irish Academic Press 1995
Encyclopaedia Brittanica
Oxford Dictionary of National Biography
Richardson, Neil *A Coward if I Return, A Hero if I Fall* O'Brien Press 2010
Smith-Dampier, Miss *Introduction to Trench Pictures from France by Major William Redmond M.P.*
  Somme Association 2007

RICHARDSON, James: p. 295
Dictionary of Canadian Biography
Gliddon, Gerald *VCs of the First World War The Somme* Gliddon Books 1991
www.pipesofwar.com
www.thebloodisstrong.com

ROSENBERG, Isaac: p. 193
Bernard Wynick, nephew of Isaac Rosenberg and Joint Literary Executor, for generously allowing us to include Isaac
  Rosenberg's poems *Louse Hunting, Marching, Break of Day in the Trenches, Returning We Hear the Larks* and *Dead
  Man's Dump*
Jean Moorcroft Wilson for kind permission to use material from *Isaac Rosenberg, the Making of a Great War Poet*
  Weidenfeld and Nicolson 2008
〜
Akers, Geoff *Beating for Light The Story of Isaac Rosenberg* Juniper Books 2006
Cohen, Joseph *Journey to the Trenches* Robson Books 1976
Holt, Tonie and Valmai *Poets of the Great War* Leo Cooper 1996
Stallworthy, Jon *Anthem for Doomed Youth Twelve Soldier Poets of the First World War* Constable 2002
www.ox.ac.uk/wwlit/collections

SAYELL, Samuel: p. 39
The author of this piece, George Sayell, wishes to thank:
Chris Baker, Great War consultant and 'Long, Long Trail' website www.1914-1918.net/
Pamela Sratton, family historian
George Vickers, volunteer at St. Barnabas Church, Linslade for his help, and thanks to the Church for permission to
  take photographs
〜
Linslade Parish Magazine November 1917 (St. Barnabas Church, Linslade)
The Northamptonshire Gazette 17 August 1917
WO95/ 876 and WO95/ 2644 (Samuel Sayell)
WO95/ 3066 (Arthur)
WO95/ 2756 and 363 (Edward Thomas)
WO95/ 1966 (Ezra)
WO95/ 1325 (George)
WO95/ 2590 (James)
WO95/ 2644 (Milford)

SEEGER, Alan: p. 305
Gardner, Brian (editor) *Up the Line to Death The War Poets 1914-1918* Methuen 1976
Holt, Tonie and Valmai *Battlefield Guide to the Somme* Leo Cooper 2000
Holt, Tonie and Valmai *Poets of the Great War* Leo Cooper 1996

SINGH, Manta: p. 169
www.cwgc.org *Manta Singh and the Battle of Neuve Chapelle* and *Manta Singh and the English Hospitals*

SOULS, Alfred and brothers: p. 147
Brian Hall, grandson of Annie Souls, for information about the family
National Archives for use of 1911 National Census and Michael Walsh, author of *Brothers in War* (Ebury Press) for
  allowing us to refer to his work on the Souls brothers
〜
Cheltenham Chronicle and Gloucestershire Graphic Saturday 8 June 1918
Cobb, Paul *The Lost Brothers of Great Rissington* *Stand To!* Magazine No. 76 April 2006

Haig, Sir Douglas *War Diaries and Letters 1914-1918* (edited by Sheffield, Gary and Bourne, John) Weidenfeld and Nicholson 2006

Walsh, Michael *The Lost Souls SAGA magazine* November 2000

Windsor, Duke of *A King's Story The Memoirs of HRH the Duke of Windsor KG* Cassell 1951

www.bbc.co.uk/gloucestershirefocus/2002

www. cwgc.org

SPINDLER, Nellie: p. 44

Dahlia Harrison for providing information about nurses in the War

Sue Light of www.scarletfinders.co.uk for material about Nurse Minnie Wood

Tom Morgan for material on Kate Luard

Mavis Sellars of the West Riding Branch of the Western Front Association for providing details of Nellie's family

Vera Sheard for generously allowing us to use family material

Luard, Kate *Unknown Warriors* Chatto & Windus 1930

National Archives WO95/342, 345, 346, 562, 3990, WO399/ 6965, 7850, 9206

Pensions, Ministry of *Location of Hospitals and C.C.S., B.E.F., 1914-1919* published 1923

Powell, Anne *Women in the War Zone* The History Press 2009

Rawson, Andrew *British Army Handbook 1914-1918* Sutton Publishing 2006

www.awm.gov.au

www.cwgc.org.

www.scarletfinders.co.uk

www.throughtheselines.com.au

St. GEORGE, Avenel: p. 125

Frans De Leye for the tour of the church of St. Catherine's, Zillebeke and access to his photographic collection

Eton College Archives

Jerry Murland for information on the 'Aristocrats' Plot', Zillebeke

Melissa Murphy, Baker Library Historical Collections, Harvard Business School, Boston, U.S.A.

John Ulrich for research of Baker Library Historical Collections

Howard Avenel Bligh St. George Memorial Book Baker Library Historical Collections, Harvard Business School, Boston, U.S. 1920

Murland, Jerry *Aristocrats Go To War* Pen and Sword 2010

National Archives WO339/ 24826

Paine, Albert Bigelow *George Fisher Baker* Knickerbocker Press 1920

Royal Horse Guards War Diary

Ruvigny, Marquis de *Roll of Honour 1914-18*

The Bond of Sacrifice of British Officers who fell in the Great War

Upstone, Robert *Love and Beauty in an Age of Extremes* included in William Orpen *Politics Sex and Death* Philip Wilson IWM

STREETS, Will: p. 228

Victor Piuk for permission to use material from *A Dream within the Dark A Derbyshire Poet in the Trenches*

Freeman, Mary Ellen *Poets and Pals of Picardy* Leo Cooper 1999

Holt, Tonie and Valmai *Poets of the Great War* Leo Cooper 1996

Middlebrook, Martin *The First Day on the Somme* Military Book Society 1971

Piuk, Victor *A Dream within the Dark A Derbyshire Poet in the Trenches* Derbyshire County Council 2003

Powell, Anne *A Deep Cry* Palladour Books 1993

St. John Adcock, Arthur *For Remembrance* Hodder and Stoughton 1918

Westlake, Ray *British Battalions on the Somme 1916* Leo Cooper 1994

Wilkinson, Ronie *Pals on the Somme 1916* Pen and Sword Military 1994

SWEENEY, John: p. 278

Putkowski, Julian and Sykes, Julian *Shot at Dawn* Leo Cooper 2006

TAPP, William: p. 74

Stephanie Bennett, museum curator at The Royal Regiment of Fusiliers Museum (Royal Warwickshire), Warwick, for permission to quote from William Tapp's diary

Hamilton, Andrew and Reed, Alan *Meet at Dawn, Unarmed* Dene House Publishing 2009

TULL, Walter: p. 200

Pat Justad (née Finlayson), Walter Tull's niece, for generous permission to use photos from the Finlayson Collection and for Mairi Brackenridge for making contact for us

Vasili, Phil and Raw Press for permission to use material from *Walter Tull, 1888-1918, Officer, Footballer* Raw Press 2010

Channel 4 News   September 2007

Fennelly, John   *For Whom the Bell Tulls*   www. local.teachers.org.uk/templates/asset-relay.cfm?frmAssetFileID=8180

http://greatwarlondon.wordpress.com/2012/10/07/george-edward-kingsley-bemand-the-first-black-officer-in-the-british-army/

National Archives WO339/ 90293

VOSS, Werner: p. 95

Diggens, Barry   *September Evening*   Grub Street   2003

Imrie, Alex   *Pictorial History of the German Army Air Service*   Ian Allan   1971

Jane's Fighting Aircraft of World War I   Random House Group   2001

McCudden, James, V.C.   *Flying Fury*   Wren's Park Publishing   2000

www.blindkat.hegewisch.net/voss

www.greatwar.com

WEBBER, 'Harry': p. 275

Jane Davies, Curator, and Doug Farrington, Museum Researcher, Lancashire Infantry Museum, Preston, Lancashire

Amanda Ingram, Archivist at Pembroke College, Oxford

Beverley Matthews, Senior Librarian at Tonbridge School

Claire Whickman, historian of the Incogniti Cricket Club

Surrey Mirror and County Post   Friday 4 August 1916

Tonbridge and the Great War

Tonbridge School Register

WILDING, Anthony: p. 173

Bob Fuller for material and information

Len and Shelley Richardson for kind permission to use material from *Anthony Wilding   A Sporting Life*

Audrey Snell, Assistant Librarian of the All England Lawn Tennis Club, Wimbledon, for help in sourcing material

Forbes-Robertson, Diana   *My Aunt Maxine*   Viking Press   1964

National Archives   FO383/ 35 re. Otto Froitzheim's imprisonment

Richardson, Len and Shelley   *Anthony Wilding   A Sporting Life*   Canterbury University Press   2005

The Times History of the War   Vol. IV   1915

Trenlove, Alan   *The Story of the Davis Cup*   Stanley Paul   1985

Wallis Myers, A   *Captain Anthony Wilding*   Hodder and Stoughton   1916

Wilding, Anthony F.   *On the Court and Off*   Methuen   1912

Gordon Dump Cemetery   *A Hamilton*

VII

INDEX

There are main headings for:

- Aeroplanes
- Airpilots
- Architects of Cemeteries and Memorials
- Battles and Offensives
- Cemeteries and Memorials
- Hospitals
- Medals, Awards and Orders
- Newspapers, Memorial books, Periodicals and School Magazines
- Places in Belgium, France, U.K. and elsewhere
- Regiments and Units
- Schools and Colleges
- Soldiers mentioned in the text
- Training Camps
- Trench Names, Positions and Redoubts
- Universities and Colleges

Names highlighted are featured in the text and in the itineraries. A chapter is dedicated to those in capital letters

American squash tennis 125
Amiens Cathedral 293
Ancre, river and valley 17, 42, 214-15
Anglo-Belgian Treaty 1839 (Treaty of London) 19
Antwerp, fall of 19, 20

Architects of Cemeteries and Memorials:
Allward, Walter Seymour 16
Baker, Sir Herbert 13, 16, 107, 111, 168,
    172, 192, 239, 274, 293, 294, 298
Blomfield, Sir Reginald 13, 15, 16, 38, 41, 42, 52,
    60, 93, 115, 151, 199, 206, 217, 224, 234, 270, 304
Bradshaw, Harold Chalton 13, 16, 139, 140
Cowlishaw, W.H. 124, 136, 158, 225, 283
Goldsmith, G. 16
Henriques, E.C. 170
Holden, Charles 13, 151, 181
Holt, G.H. 16
Hutton, A.J.S. 310
Kenyon, Sir Frederic (I.W.G.C.'s architectural
    adviser) 13
Lutyens, Sir Edwin 13, 14, 15, 16, 17, 120, 151, 202,
    251, 277
Rees, V.O. 16
Rew, N.A. 242
Von Berg, W.C. 234
Winney, T. Herbert 171

'Aristocrats' Plot' 121-30
Armed Forces Military Act 52
Armistice/ Armistice Day (1918) 1, 25, 149, 158, 159,
    162, 293
Armoured Cars 178, 179, 180
Army Chaplains' Department 31
Army Service Corps (A.S.C.) 45
Asquith, H.H. (Prime Minister) 1, 3, 7, 22, 148, 263,
    266, 287, 291, 292
    Arthur 'Oc' 2, 7, 264, 265-9, 287
    Cyril 'Cys' 287
    Herbert 'Beb' 3, 263, 287
    Margot 266, 292
    Violet 2, 263-4, 266, 268, 292

**ASQUITH, Raymond 1, 3, 4, 5, 7, 22, 215, 216, 263,
266, 287-94**
    Julian 'Trim' 290-2
    Katharine (née Horner) 3, 287- 93

Athletes' Volunteer Force 31
Atrocities in Belgium 63, 229
Australian soldiers 16, 24, 105, 106, 266
Aviation Militaire 96, 98, 101

B
Baden-Powell, Lord Robert 215
Bairnsfather, Bruce and cartoons 7, 8, 25, 63, 67, 68,
    74, 75, 76, 77, 80, 138
Baker, George (American financier) 125, 127, 128
Balfour, A.J. (Prime Minister) 131, 132, 177, 256,
    257

**BALL V.C., Albert and family 96, 99, 102, 176,
182-8, 214**

Balmoral Castle 88

BAND, Harry 16, 20, 61-3

'Bantam' battalions 147-52, 196
Batmen, see Servants

**BATTENBERG K.C.V.O., Prince Maurice of
and family 1, 14, 20, 85-8, 263**
    Battenberg, Prince Leopold of 263

Battles and Offensives:
Aisne 226, 257
Amiens 24
Armentières 20
Arras 22, 24, 96, 187
Aubers Ridge 20, 169, 179, 181
Broodseinde 41
Cambrai 24
Champagne 306
Chemin des Dames 22
Epehy 309
Festubert 20
Flers-Courcelette 292
Fromelles 41, 138, 139
Gallipoli (Turkey) 152, 226, 264-7, 279
Guillemont 293
Hooge 34, 56, 118
Houplines 167
Jutland 226
La Bassée 20
Le Cateau 19, 166, 226
Loos 13, 20, 21, 71, 147, 190, 230, 280, 281
Lorette 243, 244
Marne 226, 257
Messines 22, 23, 39, 72, 92, 134-5, 148, 201
Méteren 166
Mons 19, 158, 160
Neuve Chapelle 20, 169
Pilkem Ridge 93
Poelkapelle 110
Somme 1, 5, 8, 17, 21, 22, 42, 57, 71, 80, 92, 95, 109
    114, 116, 118, 133, 137, 148, 151, 159, 171, 201-2,
    217, 226, 227, 229, 230, 231, 232, 233, 234, 242,
    244, 248-9, 251, 255, 258, 266, 267, 268, 269, 272
    273, 274, 276, 277, 281, 282, 283, 284, 285, 286,
    291-2, 296-7, 306
Suvla Bay (Turkey) 113, 279
Verdun 21, 95, 101
Vimy 22, 126
Ypres (1st) 16, 20, 61, 63, 88, 99, 121, 178
    (2nd) 7, 13, 16, 20, 56, 63, 67, 80, 159, 179, 226
    (3rd, Passchendaele) 16, 23, 24, 41, 45, 49, 58, 60
    72, 73, 89, 93, 100, 103, 105, 107, 110, 114, 134,
    148, 202

B.B.C. Radio 250
B.B.C. Scottish Symphony Orchestra 303
Beaverbrook, Lord 62
Beecham Opera Company 302
Beechey (five brothers killed) 140, 151-3
Belgian refugees 3, 31, 180
Belgian soldiers 19, 66, 126
Belgium 2, 3, 7, 11, 13, 16, 17, 19, 22, 25

BELL V.C., Donald 2, 5-6, 22, 251, 271-4
    Rhoda 272, 274

Bemand, George (one of first black British officers) 201

BENTLEY, Charles 4, 5, 10, 20, 163-8   **325**

Bunker at Hill 60, Belgium
J Kerr